MW01026959

CHINESE GRAMMATOLOGY

Chinese Grammatology

SCRIPT REVOLUTION AND CHINESE LITERARY
MODERNITY, 1916–1958

Yurou Zhong

Columbia University Press
New York

Columbia University Press wishes to express its appreciation for assistance given by the Wm. Theodore de Bary Fund and by the Department of East Asian Studies at the University of Toronto in the publication of this book.

Columbia University Press
Publishers Since 1893
New York   Chichester, West Sussex
cup.columbia.edu
Copyright © 2019 Columbia University Press
All rights reserved

Library of Congress Cataloging-in-Publication Data
Names: Zhong, Yurou, author.
Title: Chinese grammatology : script revolution and Chinese literary modernity, 1916–1958 / Yurou Zhong.
Description: New York : Columbia University Press, [2019] | Includes bibliographical references and index.
Identifiers: LCCN 2019011315 (print) | LCCN 2019018858 (ebook) | ISBN 9780231549899 (electronic) | ISBN 9780231192620 (cloth : alk. paper) | ISBN 9780231192637 (pbk. : alk. paper)
Subjects: LCSH: Chinese language—Reform—History—20th century. | Chinese language—Writing—History—20th century. | Chinese literature—20th century—History and criticism. | Politics and literature—China—History—20th century.
Classification: LCC PL1175 (ebook) | LCC PL1175 .Z47 2019 (print) | DDC 495.11/1—dc23
LC record available at https://lccn.loc.gov/2019011315

Columbia University Press books are printed on permanent and durable acid-free paper.
Printed in the United States of America

Cover image: Tang Lan's proposal, in *Gedi renshi jilai hanyu pinyin wenzi fang'an huibian* 1, no. 1 (1954)

Cover design: Milenda Nan Ok Lee

For my parents,
Rong Yueyu 戎躍魚 *and Zhong Gang* 鍾剛

CONTENTS

CONTENTS

ACKNOWLEDGMENTS

In writing this book, the intellectual debt I have incurred has become so enormous that writing a proper acknowledgment for it seems quite impossible.

The curious question of the script revolution first emerged when I was doing my undergraduate thesis and found that Hu Shi's *baihua* discourse made little sense to me. I thank my undergraduate mentors at Tsinghua University—Meng Yue, Ge Fei, Wang Zhongchen, and Wang Hui—for opening gates with their early inspiration and intellectual generosity, and for providing scholarly models and wise counsel throughout the years.

I could not have found a better place for continuing my probe of modern Chinese writing than Columbia University. I am grateful to my dissertation mentors, Lydia Liu, Shang Wei, Bao Weihong, David Lurie, and Rebecca Karl, for their exemplary scholarship and unstinting support. I thank Lydia for shaping my years at Columbia, for her conviction in my work before I was convinced of it myself, and for her uncompromising standards of research and writing. I am grateful to Li Tuo for his erudition, good humor, and vision. I also thank Bob Hymes, Haruo Shirane, and Tomi Suzuki for their timely advice. I am fortunate to count as my cohort Sayaka Chatani, Buyun Chen, Chen Kaijun, Anatoly Detwyler, Arunabh Ghosh, S. Kile, Su Jung Kim, Liza Lawrence, Lin Shing-ting, Andy Liu, Chelsea Schieder, Shiho Takai, Mi-Ryong Shim, Nate Shockey,

Brian Tsui, Yan Zi, Wu Lan, and Wu Minna. I thank in particular my library pals—Gal Gvili, Nan Ma Hartmann, Greg Patterson, Myra Sun, and the late Chang Yi-hsiang—for their friendship and camaraderie.

I am grateful to the Social Science Research Council, the Columbia University GSAS Travel Grant, and the Lane Cooper Foundation for funding the initial research and writing. Further research was supported by the University of Toronto Start-up Grant, Faculty Recruitment Award, and Connaught New Researcher Fund. The publication of the book is generously aided by a first-book subvention from the Department of East Asian Studies, University of Toronto.

I consider it a privilege to have joined the faculty of the University of Toronto. I am grateful to the Department of East Asian Studies not only for its strong institutional support that allowed me generous leave time and a manuscript workshop, but also for its example of scholarly excellence, down-to-earth collegiality, and progressivism. I am indebted to many Torontonian colleagues—in and outside of the department—who have spent time reading and commenting on my work: Bai Ruoyun, Antje Budde, Chen Li, Thom Dancer, Fan Xing, Linda Feng, Joshua Fogel, Tak Fujitani, Evie Gu, Joan Judge, Tom Keirstead, Thomas Lahusen, Tong Lam, Ikuko Komuro-Lee, Irina Mihalache, Johanna Liu, Graham Sanders, Atsuko Sakaki, the late Vincent Shen, Shen Chen, Wen-ching Sung, Chen-Pang Yeang, Lisa Yoneyama, Yvon Wang, and Yiching Wu. Particular thanks are due to Andre Schmid for being the first to say that my dissertation was salvageable; to Meng Yue for being my sounding board and never failing to ask the most fundamental questions; to Janet Poole for all the sage advice, including on why I should have a "green book"; and to J. Barton Scott for all those brainstorming sessions and for convincing me that I had found my title.

The research for the book would not have been possible but for the many able librarians at the C. V. Starr East Asian libraries at Columbia and Berkeley, the Bancroft Library, the Butler Library, the Cheng Yu Tung East Asian Library at the University of Toronto, the Chung-Chi Library at the Chinese University of Hong Kong, the Magdalene Old Library at the University of Cambridge, the Chinese National Library in Beijing, the Library of the State Language Commission, the Lu Xun Museum, the Qu Qiubai Museum, and the Tao Xingzhi Museum. I thank in particular Sasho Donovan, Lucy Gan, He Jianye, Richard Jandovitz, David Kessler,

Liana Lupas, Susan Snyder, Wang Chengzhi, and Zhang Rongxiang for teaching me much about research wizardry.

I have relied on the hospitality of many individuals while doing research. I am particularly grateful to Bei Dao, Richard Luckett, the late Rulan Chao Pian, Yan Guizhong, and Yu Rijin. I owe a special debt to Andrew Jones for supporting the project at the very beginning of my archival research at Berkeley, for his generous and unassuming input since, and for shaping my interest in sound studies. I am privileged to acknowledge that Li Ling and Li Shoukui gave me invaluable crash courses in paleography when I was deep in the woods of the socialist script reform. I am also grateful to Su Jinzhi for introducing me to the late Zhou Youguang.

Heartfelt thanks to Harald Fischer-Tiné, Rivi Handler-Spitz, Stefan Huebner, Ulug Kuzuoglu, Lin Shaoyang, Margaret Tillman, Brian Tsui, Sun Jinghao, Wen Guiliang, Chen-Pang Yeang, Xiong Ying, and Zhang Ling for organizing panels and conferences where I presented my work and received formative feedback. In addition, I thank all the commentators, teachers, colleagues, and friends who responded to conference papers and chapter drafts: Brett de Bary, David Branner, Janet Chan, Chen Xi, Tamara Chin, Cong Xiaoping, Arnika Fuhrmann, James Hevia, Michael Hill, Hirata Shoji, Calvin Hui, Marilyn Ivy, Cornelius Kubler, Jennifer Dorothy Lee, Eugenia Lean, Liang Zhan, Lin Yan, Robin McNeal, Meng Liansu, Murata Yujiro, Jacques Neefs, Mårten Saarela, Naoki Sakai, Q.S. Tong, Jing Tsu, Richard Jean So, David Wang, Wang Pin, Wen Shuang, Lorraine Wong, Wu Xiaodong, Zhao Jinghua, and Zhang Bojiang. I am also grateful to all the participants in the 2013–14 SIAS Summer Institute "Cultural Encounters" for energizing my initial rethinking of the dissertation as a book. Sincere thanks to Ted Huters, Thomas Lahusen, Andre Schmid, and Tang Xiaobing for braving the manuscript in its entirety when it was not worthy of their time and kindness.

I am deeply indebted to my editor, Christine Dunbar, as well as to Christian Winting and Leslie Kriesel for their unwavering support and professional wisdom in steering the book into publication. I cannot thank enough the three anonymous reviewers for their sympathetic and scintillating readings. In preparing the final draft, I have incorporated extensively their comments and suggestions. I hereby acknowledge their contributions, but any mistakes remain exclusively mine. I thank Anita O'Brien and Mike Ashby for their gentle and masterful hands at copyediting. I thank Vicki Low for producing an excellent and user-friendly index. I thank *Cross-Currents: East Asian History and Culture Review* for allowing me to reprint an earlier version of chapter 3, which appeared as " 'Sacred, the Laborers': Writing Chinese in the First World War," e-journal 22 (March): 135–59. I also owe a particular debt of gratitude to the various institutions and individuals in Sweden that helped me contact the Karlgren family, who graciously allowed the publication of Bernhard Karlgren's 1925 letter to Yuen Ren Chao.

I thank Wang Jing for being my joyful bedrock since we found each other again on the centennial anniversary of our alma mater. *Facta non verba*. Last but certainly not least, I owe my deepest debt to my parents, who love books and would love for their daughter to write one even if it means their own personal sacrifices. I dedicate this work to my father, Zhong Gang, and especially my mother, Rong Yueyu, without whom none of this would have been possible.

A NOTE ON ROMANIZATION

This book adopts the pinyin system for transliteration but makes exceptions for special transliterations used in the Chinese Romanization and Latinization movements, for instance Gwoyeu Romatzyh and Sin Wenz. For Chinese names, surnames come before given names, except for those historical figures who have personal and customary English names such as Yuen Ren Chao. Places and institutions are rendered in their official transliterations, for instance, Tsinghua University.

CHINESE GRAMMATOLOGY

INTRODUCTION

Voiceless China and Its Phonocentric Turn

Languages [*langues*] are made to be spoken, writing serves only as supplement to speech; if there are some languages that are only written, and that one cannot speak, proper only to the sciences, it would be of no use in civil life.

—ROUSSEAU, *ÉMILE*

One of the differences between civilized and barbaric peoples is that civilized peoples have a script through which they can communicate their thoughts and emotions to the masses while passing them down to the future. Though China has a script, it no longer has much to do with anyone. It is used to write unintelligible archaic prose, conveying obsolete archaic meanings. All of its voices belong to the past and hence amount to zero.

—LU XUN, "VOICELESS CHINA"

Chinese characters are a national treasure. This truism was reenacted by the Chinese hit television show *National Treasure* in its inaugural episode (2017). Introducing the Stone Drums of Qin—ten drum-shaped stones bearing ancient Chinese inscriptions dating roughly to the sixth century BCE, the TV show announced that "many say the Chinese have no religion, but our faith lies in our own script and history." Celebrated as the quintessential national treasure, the Chinese script not only embodied Chinese history and culture but also constituted a quasi-religious institution deifying the idea of a continuous and unified Chinese civilization, to which it elicited allegiance. As a captivated twenty-first-century audience came under the spell of the ancient Chinese script, it was almost inconceivable that, a mere century ago, the Chinese faith in that script wavered, crumbled, and imploded, launching a script revolution that aimed to eliminate Chinese characters and implement a Chinese alphabet. To the surprise of many, not only did the script revolution take place but also it lasted for almost half a century, reached an unprecedented scale, and became one of the biggest linguistic and grammatological experiments in human history.

This seismic revolution did not exit collective memory without leaving traces behind. The two most visible ones are the division between simplified and traditional characters and the auxiliary phonetic system called pinyin. Character simplification was an initial step taken to lower the threshold of character literacy, a reform measure adopted by both the Republic of China and the People's Republic of China (PRC).[1] Pinyin, on the other hand, was at once the reigning Romanization system anointed by the PRC, even escalating to a state ideology at one point, and the basic principle of the script revolution.[2] Literally meaning "to spell sound," pinyin was designed as a Chinese alphabet to replace characters before being made into an auxiliary system that phoneticizes characters. Although the script revolution came to a screeching halt at its zenith in 1958 when Premier Zhou Enlai announced its indefinite suspension,[3] its vestiges testify to the vitality of phonocentrism—the systematic privileging of speech over writing—at the heart of Chinese literary and cultural modernity.

This book takes seriously the series of puzzles triggered by the script revolution: Why did it happen? How did it unfold? In what ways did it impact modern Chinese writing, literature, and culture? How and why was it contained? I begin my inquiry with the dramatic discursive transition surrounding the Chinese script at the turn of the twentieth century, when a national treasure came to be regarded as a national liability. The erstwhile national treasure experienced a downfall from an ideal script with "cross-cultural legibility" and "representational legitimacy" in the eyes of such seventeenth-century Sinophiles as Francis Bacon, John Wilkins, and Gottfried Wilhelm Leibniz, to a "voiceless," lifeless, and worthless writing system, which both Chinese and international elites agreed was a roadblock to literacy, democracy, and science.[4] The condition of modernity seemed to necessitate the elimination of this national liability and recommended its replacement by the Roman-Latin alphabet. The zeitgeist was such that, to borrow words from the foremost modern Chinese writer Lu Xun, who built an unparalleled literary career all in characters, "Truly, we have heretofore two ways forward: either we cling to the old script and die; or we rid ourselves of it and live."[5] Despite Lu Xun's provocative call to arms, historical hindsight demonstrates that the truthful way forward was a third one, a modified Chinese script that grew out of the script revolution, together with a reenergized literary revolution that endeavored to enliven a "voiceless China."

In tracing what can be called the phonocentric turn of modern Chinese writing, this book develops along three trajectories. First, there is the script revolution itself—its provenance, transmutations, and containment—which sought to reinvent millennia-old Chinese writing. Second, the attempted sea change of the Chinese script conditioned the emergence and development of modern Chinese language and literature, giving rise to what may be understood as a double revolution of both script and literature. Third, as a representative of nonalphabetic writing systems undergoing script reforms, the Chinese script ended up reconfiguring the basis of grammatology (the science of writing) as well as its politics in the short twentieth century,[6] a question to which I return in the following. In short, the script revolution holds the key to understanding Chinese grammatological, literary, and cultural modernity on the one hand and, on the other, has enduring implications for the run-in between alphabetic and nonalphabetic writing systems and cultures. In this introduction, I present the two global moments that bookended the script revolution and illustrate what I call phonocentric antinomies—in other words, the negative and positive forces that animated the series of its transmutations and contributed to its final containment. Combing through precedents for phoneticization in Chinese literary tradition, I trace the discursive preparation for the phonocentric turn of a supposedly "voiceless China." Following Lu Xun's lead, I ponder how an antiphonocentric, grammatological critique could dialectically and surprisingly emerge from within the realm of phonocentrism, as Lu Xun's own writings on script and sound demonstrate. Taking "script revolution" as a basic question and a working method, I seek to understand the intertwining of script and literature, writing and politics in modern China as an example of the encounter between alphabetic and nonalphabetic writings and worlds.

TWO GLOBAL MOMENTS

I date the beginning of the modern Chinese script revolution—the first of the two global moments—to the momentous year of 1916. Marking the Chinese phonocentric turn, this year saw a young Yuen Ren Chao (or Zhao Yuanren 趙元任, 1892–1982)—the future father of modern Chinese linguistics—publish an English-language article titled "The Problem of the Chinese Language" that sought to sweep away all objections to alphabetizing

Chinese.[7] Two major alphabetization movements followed: first, the Chinese Romanization movement, spearheaded by a group of Chinese and international scholars and quickly endorsed by the Guomindang Nationalist government in the 1920s; second, the dissident Chinese Latinization movement, initiated in the Soviet Union and championed by the Chinese Communist Party in the 1930s, which placed a special premium on local speech and found renewed energy with the establishment of the People's Republic of China in 1949. Although the two movements clashed in their political ideologies, they shared a common disdain for the old Chinese script and a newfound faith in the notion of a Chinese alphabet. The script revolution attained an unprecedented level of political support and social mobilization under the socialist rule, before its abrupt ending at its peak and subsequent swift exit from collective memory.

Coincidentally, the same year bore witness to the posthumous publication of Ferdinand de Saussure's *Course in General Linguistics* (1916).[8] Although this monumental publication was, in many ways, as Saussure's biographer John E. Joseph puts it, "an accident of history," it was no accident that it became the declaration of independence of linguistics from philology and the birth certificate of structural linguistics.[9] Granted that Saussure was himself a philologist and was said not to have set out to sideline textual philology in the interest of advancing "synchronic linguistics," his *Course*—taken together with his entire career—was situated within and effectively accelerated the historical trend that saw the decline of German philology, formerly known as the queen of sciences; the ascendance of linguistics proudly defined as "the science of living languages"; and the eventual separation of linguistics from philology.[10] A more nuanced reading would point to Saussure's recognition of the intertwining of language and writing and his early warnings against the nationalistic—or worse, imperialistic—tendencies of phonocentrism.[11] The fact remained, however, that the *Course* was a much-anticipated founding document of the discipline of linguistics and Saussure a posthumous founding father.

Synchronizing the provenance of modern Chinese script revolution with the disciplinary independence of linguistics, the year 1916 seems like one of those golden moments of serendipity when history makes full sense. To be fair, such serendipity was long in the making with the rise of phonocentrism at the turn of the twentieth century. The retreat of the science of writing (grammatology), the insurgence of the science of languages (linguistics), and a wave of script revolutions around the globe did not coalesce without reason. The most immediate was none other than phonocentrism, which posited the inherent superiority of speech over a debased writing. If speech was a more authentic, less-mediated approximation of truth capable of invoking the metaphysical idea of absolute presence, then writing was understood to be no more than its transcription and thus determinately supplementary, always lacking, and as Plato dramatized it, "evil."[12]

This view of phonocentrism, deeply rooted in Western metaphysics and shared by thinkers from Plato to Hegel, from Rousseau to Saussure, systematically privileges speech over writing and works tirelessly to close the gap between the two. For logocentrism to endorse a particular form of writing meant writing must consistently work toward a full transcription of speech and a complete grasp of the real. As a result, phonetic writing seems an ideal candidate for its constant affirmation of speech over writing and its unique capacity to identify writing with speech. Moreover, inside phonetic writing systems, the Roman-Latin alphabet came to be understood as the most technologically advanced script for sound writing, an understanding established and enhanced by the foundation of comparative and historical linguistics, to which Saussure contributed his fair share.[13] As Walter Ong puts it, there have been "many scripts but only one alphabet."[14] If such singularity of "the alphabet" reads as an enthused endorsement of one particular signification system that visualizes speech in the written form, it is also an unequivocal statement of the hierarchy within the world's writing systems, catapulting the Roman-Latin alphabet to the top while downgrading other non–Roman-Latin writings altogether.[15] More significantly, the grammatological hierarchy carried with it civilizational connotations. When "the alphabet" becomes the synecdoche of the whole body of phonetic scripts and the acme of world civilization, its singularity marks how a Western ethnocentrism successfully imposes itself on the world as a global phenomenon.[16]

This phenomenon rose at the end of the European colonial conquests and the beginning of the rise of the American empire. It was armed by modern information technologies such as telegraphy, the telephone, and typewriter, all of which etched deep imprints all over the world.[17] From the late nineteenth century to the early twentieth century, various non–Roman-Latin alphabets were confronted with the challenge to become "the alphabet." The

Chinese submission to phonocentric rule coincided with script reforms in many parts of the world: of the Egyptian Arabic script, the Ottoman Turkish Arabic-Persian script, the Russian Cyrillic alphabet, the Vietnamese *chữ nôm*, and the Japanese kana system, to name a few.[18] The global force of script revolution changed, in one way or another, the faces of the variety of scripts that came into contact with the Roman-Latin alphabet. Some scripts submitted to the alphabetic model, modern Turkish and Vietnamese being two best-known cases. Some others survived the revolution but were invariably and subtly changed by the confrontation and negotiation with the established Roman-Latin alphabetic norm.

It is unlikely that Yuen Ren Chao was cognizant of the global trend of phonocentrism when penning the first theoretical treatise that paved the way for alphabetizing Chinese. It is equally unlikely that he and other script revolutionaries would regard the ensuing Romanization and Latinization movements as a capitulation to the colonizing power of phonocentric rule. However, this does not change the fact, as historian Ku-ming Kevin Chang convincingly demonstrates, that Chao was by training a product of the Anglo-French school of linguistics, which was a reaction to the German tradition of philology. His by-all-accounts illustrious career worked to advance the institutionalization of that school of linguistics in China.[19] It all began with his 1916 article. The inaugural moment of his lifelong vocation of modern Chinese linguistics was also square one of the script revolution ready to remove the old script and its philological tradition.

If the domination of phonocentrism defined this first global moment, it was not only because of the combination of the universalizing power of colonialism backed up by formidable technologies, nor was it merely a successful instantiation of Western ethnocentrism. Rather, the sheer force of the first global moment entailed what I have termed phonocentric antinomies. In the case of Chinese script revolution, the allegiance to phonocentrism reduced the Chinese script to an inadequate technology for transcribing speech sound, stripping it of any civilizational value and exacting indisputable violence against Chinese culture, philosophy, and epistemology in general. At the same time, such epistemic violence was registered as a necessary sacrifice because of its modernizing and revolutionizing tendencies, both technological and political. More than a bearer of national language and literature, the new alphabetic Chinese—with its perceived accessibility and superiority in speech transcription—symbolized to the underprivileged, marginalized, and repressed the possibility of speaking in their own voices and writing in a new alphabetic script and provided grammatological footing to the larger twentieth-century projects of democracy, liberation, and revolution. As the script revolution wore on, it was the antinomies of phonocentrism that permitted its various transmutations until it no longer resembled the original model of the Roman-Latin alphabet. The good faith that the progressive side of phonocentrism would inevitably outweigh its ethnocentric and identitarian violence gave room to the generative intertwining of the double revolution of script and literature.

It is by way of these phonocentric antinomies and from within the phonocentric regime that *Chinese Grammatology* makes sense of the containment of the script revolution. With unprecedented state sponsorship and an avowed determination to end the reign of characters for good, the socialist script reform was meant to be the definitive script revolution. Therefore, its sudden suspension in 1958, when Zhou Enlai delivered his speech "The Current Tasks of the Script Reform," came as a genuine surprise and dealt a heavy blow to international script revolutionaries, for the three tasks that Zhou enumerated were cautiously limited to the simplification of characters, the promotion of *putonghua* 普通話 (Mandarin), and the implementation of pinyin, conspicuously leaving out the institution of a Chinese alphabet.[20] How the climax of the script revolution ended up endorsing a simplified version of the characters that it vowed to eliminate has remained a puzzle for decades. While this book attempts to solve this puzzle in part 3, it suffices to note here that the final and surprising containment of the Chinese script revolution coincided with a second global moment, involving decolonization, anti-imperialism, and international solidarity in the immediate wake of World War II. The final years of the Chinese script revolution overlapped with the monumental Bandung Conference in 1955, which laid the groundwork for the Non-Aligned Movement. The Afro-Asian People's Solidarity Conference in Cairo soon followed in 1957, and in 1958 the Afro-Asian Writers' Conference was held in Tashkent, Uzbekistan, launching intellectual exchanges across the two camps of the Cold War for the next two decades.[21]

With its affirmation of political resistance to the colonial and imperial mode of world domination, this second global moment also announced the untenability of the phonocentric regime and its attempt to steamroll all non–Roman-Latin writings of the world. It encouraged "national form" as an antiethnocentric ethnocentrism—that is, as an ethnocentric antidote to Western ethnocentrism. While Chinese intellectuals started to experiment and invent a new literary "national form" during the Second Sino-Japanese War,[22] it was not until the last leg of the script revolution that a retheorization of a grammatological national form emerged inside the phonocentric domination. One particular approach that recalibrated the Chinese ideo-phonographs, what the Chinese paleographer Tang Lan called composite script, surfaced as a potential candidate for the national form of the Chinese alphabet. Recognizing the revolutionary pulsations of phonocentrism while resisting its epistemological violence, this at once millennia-old and freshly modern national form enabled a grammatological critique from within the phonocentric order.

In fact, the two bookends of the script revolution—1916 and 1958—neatly correlate the domination of phonocentrism and the emergence of Chinese grammatology. By reaching its apogee, phonocentrism summoned its negation. The greatest irony is perhaps that the containment of the script revolution was surprisingly worked out from within the phonocentric order, giving shape to a dialectic of phonocentrism in the true sense of the word. By delineating the provenance, transmutations, and containment of the script revolution, *Chinese Grammatology* tracks the process through which the dialectic of phonocentrism came into being.

It bears pointing out, despite its Western metaphysical lineage, that the attraction to speech in writing, and by extension the logic of speech over writing, was hardly alien to the Chinese literary tradition. For Chao and other script revolutionaries, Chinese writing did not lack phonetic studies. It was the lack of scientific methodology in what was, in fact, a millennia-old field of study in China that became their true grievance. Hence the very first step in the epistemological preparation for the implementation of pho-nocentrism developed in a scientifically minded evaluation of the Chinese tradition of phoneticization and an argument for its reform. By way of combing through these phoneticization precedents, script revolutionaries constructed a prehistory of phoneticization that held strong potential for a phonocentric turn, and this in turn mandated their own leadership in rein-venting Chinese writing.

FROM PHONETICIZATION TO PHONOCENTRISM

Altogether four earlier approaches to phoneticization predated the modern script revolution: first, a Chinese phonological method called cross spelling; second, a Sanskrit-inspired Chinese phonetic alphabet; third, a series of phoneticization schemes adopting the Roman-Latin alphabet developed by Jesuit and Protestant missionaries; fourth, the late-Qing wave of phoneticization, shorthand, and alphabetization. I should add that although philologists, monks, and missionaries brought an increasing awareness of phoneticization to the Chinese script over the millennia, participants of the four historical phoneticization movements rarely made the resolute case for the phonocentric takeover of Chinese characters by the Roman-Latin alphabet, and all phoneticization schemes that came out of those four movements were regarded, in varying degrees, as auxiliary programs to assist character learning. However, script revolutionaries—for instance, Chao, or Li Jinxi and Ni Haishu, who were leading historians for Romanization and Latinization movements, respectively—invariably invoked these precedents as a prequel to the phonocentric turn in the early twentieth century.[23]

The first scheme of phoneticization was known as the *fanqie* 反切 system. Usually translated as "cross spelling," it used two characters to approximate the pronunciation of a third character, using the consonant of the first character and the vowel of the second character as well as its ending when applicable. The phonetic use of characters was flexible, for it allowed one syllable to be "spelled" in unlimited ways so long as the combination of characters produced the intended phonetic attributes. This character-based phoneticization system was conceived in the late Han period (25–220), contemporaneous with the introduction of Buddhism into China. Some scholars argue that *fanqie* was invented to assist the translation of Buddhist sutras from Sanskrit into Chinese.[24] Beginning in the seventh century, the method was adopted by rhyme books to denote character pronunciations, the most prominent example being Lu Fayan's *Qieyun* 切韻 (601).[25]

Next came the various pronunciation spelling schemes produced in the Tang dynasty (618–907), which then saw further development in the Song (960–1279). A late Tang-dynasty Buddhist monk named Shou Wen 守溫

devised a thirty-letter spelling plan. Though Shou Wen's "letters" were still characters and his phoneticization rules complied with the *fanqie* system, he established a one-to-one correspondence between syllable and character, thus creating a set of characters-cum-letters.[26] Compared with the *fanqie* system, the commensurability created between character and letter in Shou Wen's scheme went one step further toward phoneticizing Chinese.

The third scheme was the missionaries' creation of phoneticized and alphabetic Chinese. Starting in the seventeenth century, Jesuit missionaries such as Matteo Ricci and Nicolas Trigault pioneered efforts to phoneticize Chinese in the Roman-Latin alphabet. Ricci's scheme, aided by fellow Jesuits Michele Ruggieri and Lazzaro Cattaneo, was recorded in his *The Miracle of Western Letters* (*Xizi qiji* 西字奇蹟) and contained twenty-six consonants and forty-four vowels. After Ricci's death, Trigault simplified his plan and devised a preliminary spelling scheme, downsizing it to twenty consonants and five vowels.[27] Though these plans inspired contemporaneous Chinese scholars such as Fang Yizhi 方以智 and Liu Xianting 劉獻廷 to speculate the potential benefit of alphabetizing Chinese, ultimately this spelling scheme served as no more than a learning aid for teaching characters to foreigners.[28] Following the Jesuits, Protestant missionaries created what I call the alphabetic dialect Bible—Chinese translations of the Bible in dialects transcribed in the Roman-Latin alphabet.[29] Since the publication of the first alphabetic Minnan dialect Bible in 1852, Protestant missionaries such as J. N. Talmage, W. A. Martin, John C. Gibson, Joshua Marshman, Robert Morrison, Walter Henry Medhurst, Karl Gützlaff, and Thomas Barclay, among others, created a vast body of Chinese Bible texts in both characters and the Roman-Latin alphabet, transcribing both Mandarin and dialects. These Bibles became popular readers, with a rough estimate of 137,870 copies being printed between 1891 and 1904 alone.[30] The alphabetic dialect Bible stood out, for not only was it the first instantiation of Chinese alphabetic texts to aid literacy but also it energized the literary imagination to use alphabetic and dialectal Chinese to compose new writing. More interestingly, by inspiring localized experiments in alphabetization—literally, "to spell sound" (*pinyin*)—the alphabetic dialect Bible unwittingly pointed to one inherent limit of the Chinese phonocentric turn—the incompatibility between dialect-based alphabetic literacy and the ambition to create a national literature.

The fourth and last attempt at phoneticizing Chinese in the prelude to the full explosion of the script revolution was the late-Qing Phonetic Script movement (*qieyin zi yundong* 切音字運動), which morphed into the National Alphabet movement (*zhuyin zimu yundong* 注音字母運動) in the first years of the Republic of China.[31] Though both movements bore foreign influences—missionary and Japanese—the turn-of-the-century script reform showcased the first Chinese attempt at alphabetizing Chinese without the explicit appeal to liquidate characters. The first Chinese scholar to propose phoneticization in the Roman-Latin alphabet was Lu Zhuangzhang 盧戇章, a Xiamen local who had access to the Chinese alphabetic Bibles, including the first one in the Minnan dialect. Lu created a series of Chinese phoneticization schemes using the Roman-Latin alphabet with a simplified orthography, including *A Primer at a Glance* (*Yimu liaoran chujie* 一目了然初階) (1892), *New Script at a Glance* (*Xinzi chujie* 新字初階) (1893), and *The Number-One Under Heaven Phoneticized New Script* (*Tianxia diyi qieyin xinzi* 天下第一切音新字) (1895).[32] These primers galvanized a stream of Chinese phoneticization plans, including Wu Zhihui's Bean-Sprout Alphabet (*douya zimu* 豆芽字母), Cai Xiyong's Phonetic Quick Script (*chuanyin kuaizi* 傳音快字), Li Jiesan's Quick Script for the Min Speech (*Minqiang kuaizi* 閩腔快字), Wang Bingyao's Phoneticized Script Notation (*pinyin zipu* 拼音字譜), and Shen Xue's Universal System (*shengshi yuanyin* 盛世元音) (his own English title), among others.[33] None of these early schemes, however, achieved wide circulation until the emergence of the Mandarin Alphabet (*guanhua zimu* 官話字母) created by Wang Zhao 王照 in 1900 and the Combined Tone Simple Script (*hesheng jianzi* 合聲簡字) of Lao Naixuan 勞乃宣 in 1905.[34]

Despite discontent with the Chinese script for its gap between speech and writing, it is important to acknowledge that none of these phonetic projects—regardless of whether they made use of shorthand systems, the Japanese kana, or the Roman-Latin alphabet—challenged the dominance of characters. Lu Zhuangzhang's rhetoric might have come closest to the implementation of the Roman-Latin alphabet in place of the old script but ended up arguing for the benefit of its capacity to aid character learning.[35] The legitimacy of the old Chinese script remained intact even when the newly founded Republic of China installed a National Alphabet 注音字母 at the end of the Conference on the Standardization of National Pronunciation in 1913. This National Alphabet, comprised of thirty-seven letters based on Zhang Taiyan's reconstructed symbols from the Chinese seal script, was taken to conclude the late imperial script reforms and their seemingly unending production of phoneticization schemes.[36] However, the National Alphabet turned out to be an overture, rather than the coda, of the Chinese script revolution.

The critical difference between these premodern phoneticizations and the twentieth-century phonocentric turn was by no means limited to the question of eliminating characters but extended to the reevaluation of character literacy and the cultural and epistemological valence of the whole body of texts that came with it. The increasing animosity toward characters was accompanied by a growing devaluation of their cultural and epistemological associations, ranging from rhyme studies and evidential research (*kaozheng* 考證) to classical learning and natural studies.[37] Lu Xun captured the epistemological trend with another succinct provocation: "I think that [youths today] should read fewer or no Chinese books."[38] A more patient reading of Lu Xun's Latinization writings, as the next section of this introduction demonstrates, showcases a far more nuanced position than a total negation of all writings Chinese. The crisis of the Chinese script did threaten, however, to implicate Chinese epistemology. It seemed, if only for a moment, that both were headed for the dustbin of history.

Evaluated against a phonocentric yardstick, the Chinese script was ridiculed as a technology of speech transcription, sound reproduction, and information exchange, criticized as dysfunctional at best and worthless at worst. As modern technologies amplified the need for phoneticizing writing, the mission of the script revolution became an alphabetization upgrade of an otherwise "voiceless" script. In aligning historical precedents of phoneticization as alphabetization prequels, script revolutionaries wove them together into a narrative where technologization and phoneticization seemed innate to Chinese writing, which was now fully prepared to make the phonocentric conversion.

Such preparation came to fruition and took to the international stage on May 31, 1926, when the *Diagram Showing the Evolution of Chinese over the Last Four Millenniums* 國語四千年來變化潮流圖 was presented at the Sesquicentennial International Exposition in Philadelphia, held in commemoration of the one hundred fiftieth anniversary of the founding of the United States.[39] Composed by the prominent philologist and the chief historian of the Romanization movement Li Jinxi 黎錦熙 (1890–1978), the diagram charted a sweeping genealogy of Chinese—both written and spoken—from the eighteenth century BCE to the twentieth century CE. It delineated the development of the script from "hieroglyphs" to the seal script and the free running hand, accounted for foreign influences on the Chinese language singling out Sanskrit Buddhist sutras and Western literature, paid special heed to the Chinese Romanization schemes created by Jesuits in the Ming dynasty, included all four aforementioned phoneticization precedents, and concluded that four thousand years of linguistic and grammatological "change" (*bianhua* 變化) would converge in the "evolution" (Li's own English translation) of a standard national language (*guoyu* 國語), culminating in "National Romanization."[40] Thus, a new national language known as Chinese made its international debut, celebrating at the same time the birth of a nation (the United States) and the birth of a national language (the Chinese *guoyu*).

Li's translingual practice—lumping together myriad Chinese scripts, languages, and phoneticization schemes under the English term "Chinese" and passing it off as a national language—did not go without notice. The diagram visualizes the process of putting together a teleological narrative of speech over writing in the case of the Chinese national language and national literature (*guoyu wenxue* 國語文學). The poignancy of the diagram arises not only from its showcasing the actual brushwork that went into the construction of a national language but also from the way it positioned the emergence of the national language within a larger world picture, what Martin Heidegger called *Weltbild*.[41] Insomuch as world pictures at the international exposition collectively enabled the representability of an orderly world, that very world order validated and activated the national status of each world picture—in this case, the Chinese national language.

Li's diagram therefore presented—and was presented as—the blueprint for the Chinese national language and literature. More important, the organization of an unruly Chinese literary tradition of four thousand years into a world picture effectively visualized the guiding principle of phonocentrism as a discernible evolutionary force. In arranging the linear chronology of the chart, Li gave shape and color to the trend of the "identification of the spoken and written language" (*yanwen yizhi* 言文一致) at the turn of the twentieth century, invoking the Meiji *genbun itchi* movement, whose title characters it shared.[42] Figured as a turquoise-colored river into which countless small streams converge, the force of phonocentric evolution forged ahead, leaving behind those incompatible philological and literary remnants to form two separate scholarly fields of "the history of writing" and "the history of literature." Eventually, the huge wave reaches and stops at its telos—a "national language" written in the "National Romanization"—as if phonocentrism would be the end of history.

FROM PHONOCENTRISM TO CHINESE GRAMMATOLOGY

The attraction of the phonocentric imagination is hardly limited to the abstract and artificial world picture that tends toward alphabetizing all national languages and scripts. Phonocentric antinomies entail the coexistence of abstraction, order, and even elegance of a world picture on the one hand and the concrete, clamorous, and necessarily plural anti-identitarian expressions on the other. Phonocentric violence therefore comes with phonocentric promises that assure all people the possibility to speak and to be heard in their own voices. *Chinese Grammatology* tells the story of the script revolutionaries' initial fascination with phonocentrism, including its antinomies, their gradual realization of its limits that prevent it from reaching its full potential, and the transmutations they accommodated themselves to in following through with the revolution they had started.[43] The biggest revelation of the script revolution is perhaps its containment, in the sense that it was the very pursuit of phonocentrism, together with its antinomies and by way of its transmutations, that made a Chinese grammatology—as a critique of phonocentrism—tenable.

Let us establish now that Jacques Derrida does not own the term "grammatology" (*grammatologie*). The term appeared as early as the 1820s and could mean either "treatise on grammar" or "typology" of writing.[44] The more commonly cited scholarly precedent in the field of modern linguistics is attributed to I. J. Gelb's *A Study of Writing* (1952), where Gelb defined it as "a full science of writing."[45] Derrida followed suit in his article "Writing Before the Letter" (L'écriture avant la lettre) (1965), published in the French journal *Critique* and which became the "matrix" of *Of Grammatology* (1967).[46] In comparison, "Chinese grammatology"—the concept, not the term—had already emerged by the end of the script revolution in 1958 and was arguably an earlier and more substantiated critique of the metaphysics of phonetic writing that grew organically from within the Chinese entanglement with phonocentrism. In coining the term "Chinese grammatology," however, I am indebted to Derrida for his groundbreaking treatment of grammatology as both a field of study and a methodology for engaging with metaphysics, through which the deconstruction of logocentrism became imaginable. Derrida treated logocentrism—"the metaphysics of phonetic writing"—as "the most original and powerful ethnocentrism," which imposed "itself upon the planet" in a three-step operation: a particular model of writing, the history of metaphysics, and the approach to science. Of all three steps, the question of phonetic writing sat at its very core.[47] In a different three-part operation, I define "Chinese grammatology" as a dialectical critique of phonocentrism that entails one model of the reinvented ideo-phonographic writing, one paradigm of progressive politics, and one argument to rejuvenate the old science of Chinese philology so that new inquiries become possible. The containment of the Chinese script revolution accomplished the same deconstructionist feat almost a decade earlier than Derrida and instantiated a more organic and dialectical answer to the problem of phonocentrism. This answer, although deeply rooted in the Chinese philological tradition (*wenzixue* 文字學), would have been inconceivable without the Chinese conversion to phonocentrism in the first place.

If the first global moment of 1916 witnessed phonocentric power, colonial expansion, and the rise of linguistics, then the second global moment of 1958 beckoned grammatological critique, anticolonial politics, and the return of the science of writing. In fact, Derrida's own intellectual growth was part and parcel of the second moment of decolonization and antiimperialism.[48] Therefore my ex post facto naming of "Chinese grammatology" is less an attempt to compete with Derrida or Gelb for the term than an effort to describe the Chinese encounter with phonocentrism in the same global flow that produced poststructuralism and to restore its due intellectual and epistemological weight. As a representative of the non–Roman-Latin alphabetic world, the Chinese script, albeit negotiated and reformed because of the script revolution, stands as a generative case of survival and regeneration.[49] To the surprise of many, including those most daring script revolutionaries, not only is there room for more than one alphabet but also it is possible to formulate an antiethnocentric, internationalist, and grammatological critique inside the phonocentric regime.

Lu Xun is a case in point. Of all script revolutionaries, the foremost modern Chinese writer embodied the tension between phonocentrism and

Chinese grammatology in perhaps the most dramatic fashion. As the best composer of writing in characters, Lu Xun was among the most radical and relentless script revolutionaries, even though he never tried his hand at composing alphabetic Chinese literature. His final years overlapped with the initial introduction and then flourishing of the Chinese Latinization movement. In a short span between 1934 and 1936, he drafted at least eight essays supporting Latinization in conjunction with the so-called massification movement that sought in the early 1930s to proletarianize arts and literature.[50] Calling the old script a case of terminal illness or tuberculosis and comparing character loyalists to people who "have lost their minds and been seized by madness,"[51] his attacks of the old script were uniquely colorful, consistent, and well documented.

In focusing on Lu Xun, I am less interested in dwelling on his radical support of alphabetization than probing his trajectory of thought on the question of phonocentrism. Despite his consistent, phonocentric-sounding arguments against the old script, within his own writings on script and sound stirred a complex grammatological critique that belabored the definition of *sheng* 聲, which could be translated as "voice," "speech sound," or "sound" in general. In the aforementioned essay "Voiceless China" (1927), where he adopted a Rousseauian civilizational reading of the world's writing systems and labeled the Chinese script as barbarian, he issued, toward the end of the essay, an invitation to the "youths" of China to fill their country with *sheng*, followed by a few quick remarks on what he had in mind for the desired sound/voice. To dispel the unfortunate silence that had long shrouded China, the true *sheng* should be both "modern" and "heartfelt." Lu Xun concluded with a plea, "Only true sound can move people of China and people of the world; only after [we have] true sound can we cohabit the world with people of the world."[52]

What is "true sound"? One might easily—and correctly—point to Lu Xun's support of the massification movement, together with his willing—albeit complicated—alignment with the League of Left-Wing Writers, and imagine the genuine *sheng* as a polyphonic chorus of the masses. While it is true that the revolutionary turn toward the end of Lu Xun's life is indisputable, his earlier writings drew a more nuanced distinction between different modes of *sheng*, though all were presented as signs of a progressive nature. In "Toward a Refutation of Malevolent Voices" (1908), one of his early essays published in the magazine *Henan*, he provided a more extensive, though incomplete, explication of true sound, or what he called the sound of the heart (*xinsheng* 心声).[53] Arguably one of the most abstruse texts in his oeuvre, "Malevolent Voices" was deliberately difficult in its archaic diction and references and unusually ambitious in its intellectual stance against some of the most well-established but nonetheless "malevolent" ideologies of the time. To annotate and closely read this piece of wonderfully strange literature will be, and already has been, the burden of other studies;[54] my purpose here is to listen closely to the sound of *sheng*, which leaves traces behind for an antiphonocentric critique central to Chinese grammatology.

"Malevolent Voices" opens with an almost poetic portrayal of what would in two decades become the "voiceless China," where "silence reigns" and "both heaven and earth are sealed off." It goes on to explain the nature of this particular "silence," which is actually rather loud, consisting of a "collective clamor" (*zhongxiao* 眾嚣, or *zhonghuan* 眾讙) either of "singing in one voice" or produced through "a mechanical imitation of others."[55] Within the regular triad of sound, noise, and silence, Lu Xun equates noise with silence and writes both off as the desolation and deprivation of true sound. In creating his own dyad of nonsound versus sound, he is careful to maintain a difference in naming. The nonsound could be "singing," "chorus," "language," or "solitary silence," but it is not once named *sheng*. To be called true sound, it needs to emanate from one's heart, hence "sound of the heart" (*xinsheng*). Lu Xun borrows the term from Han-dynasty scholar Yang Xiong's (53 BCE–18 CE) *Fa yan* 法言 (Words to live by), which signified "language."[56] Reanimating the old term, Lu Xun takes *xinsheng* to be capable of "deliverance from falsehood and chicanery" and equates it to one's "inner light" (*neiyao* 內曜), which breaks through darkness. He is quick to acknowledge that the full presence of heartfelt sound and inner brightness is no easy task and could be expected from no more than "one or two scholars" (*shi* 士). Serving as vanguards of true sound, they are to initiate the process igniting greater hope among more people: "Only when one speaks from the heart and becomes master of one's own soul can one begin to have an individual identity; only when each person possesses an individual identity will the public approach a total awakening."[57] What stands between the true sound of extraordinary scholars—not unlike the Nietzschean superman (*Übermensch*) that fascinates Lu Xun—and the collective but still individual self-enlightenment by inner light is precisely those "malevolent voices." He lists two major categories endorsed by what he mockingly called men of aspiration as golden rules "to survive the twentieth century": "The first suggests that one should think of oneself as a citizen of a particular nation, while the second conceives of the individual as a member of the world community" (8:28). He further breaks down the two seemingly opposing camps—nationalism versus cosmopolitanism—into three subcategories each: the former includes the "eradication of superstition," "worship of aggression," and "compulsory enforcement to fulfill one's obligations," while the latter entails the "unification of writing systems," "disavowal of one's nation," and "advocacy of identitarianism" (8:28). The rest of the essay goes on to explicate his objections to the first two subcategories of the first kind of malevolent voice, arguing for the preservation of the so-called superstitions and the sober realization of the danger of jingoism in the name of nationalism. In the first instance, Lu Xun sees in folk religion and superstitions the potential to channel the necessary creativity of metaphysical pursuits and facilitate healthy experiments in discovering one's interiority (8:28–33). In the second, he regards jingoism as the cheapest expression of nationalist sentiments and urges Chinese to learn from internationalist heroism performed by the Polish general Józef Bem and the British poet Lord Byron in aiding the independence movements of oppressed foreign nations such as Hungary and Greece, respectively (8:33–36). Ending the essay with "unfinished," Lu Xun leaves the third malevolent voice of nationalism and all three subcategories of cosmopolitanism unsounded.

One can only speculate what Lu Xun would have written about the rest of those "malevolent voices" had he finished the essay. One rule of thumb that he did provide was this: "Although the two aforementioned propositions may appear contradictory, they are by and large the same in their determination to disintegrate and destroy individuality" (8:28). To follow his own cue, his formulation and juxtaposition of the three malevolent cosmopolitan voices might well be read as a coherent argument against his own 1930s turn toward support for the script revolution.[58] In associating the unification of writing systems with the negation of one's own nation—and with it idiosyncratic national forms—he was practically describing the identitarian (*qiyi* 齊一) phonocentric violence and labeling it malevolent. However, his antiphonocentric position came only after his pledge to the "sound of the heart." Therefore, rather than flatly contradicting his own loyalty to *sheng*, his antiphonocentric critique functioned as an amend-ment seeking to strengthen the expression of the "sound of the heart." Taken together, his refutation of malevolent voices and his advocacy of the "modern," "heartfelt," and true sound provided vivid illustrations of both sides of the phonocentric antinomies. The allegiance to true sound man-dated the sublation (*Aufhebung*) of malevolent voices. The faith in pro-gressive phonocentrism—the creation, preservation, and amplification of the sound of the heart—was nothing short of the originary force that gave license to the transmutations of the script revolution, as well as Lu Xun's turn first toward Latinization, and then back to grammatology.

Two decades later and despite their phonocentric attack on the old script, Lu Xun's proalphabetization essays drove home the question of writing. Take "Outdoor Chats on Writing," for example. Representative of Lu Xun's Latinization series, it is a twelve-part essay serialized in *Shen bao* between August and September 1934 that he reported to be based on after-dinner chats about writing with his neighbors in Shanghai. The first four parts are devoted to the origin of writing, the fifth and sixth parts to the historical privilege associated with literacy. The seventh part turns to the necessity of breaking the monopoly over literacy by the few and to include those "illit-erate writers." The following two parts address the "how-to" question, with the eighth vouching for the Latinization movement and the ninth for mas-sification. The next two parts—the tenth and the eleventh—assuage pur-ported anxieties over massification and recommend the rightful place of intellectuals as a member of the people in the double revolution of script and literature. The essay ends with the twelfth part as a coda, proclaiming, "We have only one direction: forward!"[59]

Although apparently an unambiguous revolutionary call to arms under the banner of script revolution, when read against "Malevolent Voices" this essay can also be understood as Lu Xun's own grammatological postscript to his earlier moment of antiphonocentric critique. If "Malevolent Voices" showcases how a political-grammatological criticism could emerge within phonocentric fixation, then Lu Xun's Latinization essays—"Outdoor Chats on Writing" as a prime example—delineate the process through which the pursuit of phonocentrism morphs into the basic question of writing. Sum-marizing the message of his essay, Lu Xun writes, "In one sentence: give writ-ing [*wenzi* 文字] to everyone" (6:97). He continues to argue that among all potential alphabetization schemes, Latinization is the most cost-effective.

However, it will be recommendable only if it continues to serve as a conduit channeling the true sound and inner self of the underprivileged, illiterate people. Anything short of that would be "malevolent." Moreover, whether or not the heartfelt sound is expressed in a particular speech sound or transcribed in a certain script is secondary to the loyalty to the individual's self-enlightenment. Therefore, he remained vigilant to any attempt to shortchange the promise made to all people for the self-discovery, self-realization, and self-expression of their individual interiority, their individual "I." He called out those literacy reformers who preached that "one thousand characters" were more than enough for the people (6:95). He cautioned against Latinization's overzealous endorsement of dialect and overemphasis on its authenticity, which ran the risk of curtailing the growth of dialect literature (6:99). Last but not least, he pushed back against massification's resistance to the further Europeanization of Chinese grammar (6:79). If writing was both the medium and content of people's search for true sound, it must be in the hands of people and continue to grow as people approach their self-awakening. In the end, both the phonocentric fulfillment and its grammatological critique are attainable only through the commitment to giving writing to all people.

STRUCTURE OF THE BOOK

Inasmuch as this noble commitment confirms the positive side of the phonocentric antinomies while refuting the "malevolent voices," it also augurs the difficulties involved in its satisfactory fulfillment, inevitable transmutations, and curious containment. Indeed, the inauguration of phonocentrism in China would be followed by its various amendments in the attempt to honor its promises of progressiveness, whether successful or not, until its resolution surfaced in the form of Chinese grammatology. This book tells in three parts the story of this journey: the provenance, transmutations, and containment of the modern Chinese script revolution.

Chapter 1 investigates the beginning and the end of alphabetic universalism in China: the Chinese Romanization movement. In tracing its arch-theoretician Yuen Ren Chao's life and work, I approach the first leg of the script revolution as a product of international collaboration in allegiance to phonocentrism, evident in Chao's early correspondence with the Swedish linguist Bernhard Karlgren. At the same time, it was a challenge to the exclusive claim of Roman-Latin alphabetic universalism. If the 1928 National Language Romanization (Gwoyeu Romatzyh, or GR) credited to Chao marked the Chinese admission into the phonocentric realm, it also constituted the Chinese bid for alphabetic universalism. As Chao continued his search for visible speech, he endorsed Bell Labs' sound spectrograph as its consummate realization. While upholding the principle of phonocentrism, Chao inadvertently undermined the universality of any alphabet, whether Chinese or Roman-Latin. The provenance of the Chinese script revolution might have ensured a full phonocentric conversion, but it also unexpectedly marked both the beginning and the end of alphabetic universalism, leaving behind the haunting question of what writing really meant for the script and literary revolutionaries alike.

The second part of the book consists of three chapters discussing three transmutations. Chapter 2 begins with the investigation of the first transmutation of the script revolution, introducing the rival claimant to the phonocentric throne: the Chinese Latinization movement. Problematizing Romanization's endorsement of the national language, Latinization insisted on representing local speech. Combing through the genealogy of the Latinization movement, including the missionaries' dialect alphabetic Bible in the late-Qing era, the establishment of modern Chinese dialectology in the 1920s, and the Soviet Latinization effort in the 1930s, I examine how all three historical origins informed the encounter between the Chinese Latinization movement and modern Chinese realist writing. Reading the works of Latinization advocates Qu Qiubai and Xu Dishan, I develop the concept of "phonocentric antinomies," which probes the boundaries of phonocentric realist writing. As the Latinization movement laid bare the conflict between phonocentric promises and the project of national literature, it delineated the dynamic convergence of script revolution, the Proletkult (proletariat culture), and the so-called third literary revolution while exploring the possibilities for hearing the true voices of subalterns.

Chapter 3 asks the question, can subaltern workers write and locates the second and perhaps most enduring transmutation of the script revolution in the May Fourth *baihua* (plain speech) discourse. It opens by introducing the first modern Chinese literacy program, which emerged in the exchange between Chinese laborers and one YMCA volunteer, James Yen, later a leading figure of international rural education and mass education. By closely reading writings from the literacy program, I trace the process through which the colloquialized written language that emerged in the literacy program became retrospectively characterized as belonging to the May Fourth *baihua* discourse because of its aspirations toward pure orality. I further illustrate the limits of the phonocentric antinomies through an invaluable piece of political commentary penned by one of the Chinese laborers. Although both the laborer's choice of language and critical insights were appropriated and overtaken by his intellectual counterparts, his own writings bore witness to his and other laborers' contributions to the Allied war efforts, the subsequent Chinese May Fourth Movement, and critical reflections on World War I.

Chapter 4 investigates a third and final transmutation, which took the triangulated shape of war, literacy, and mass education at an unprecedented moment of Chinese national crisis. By examining writings of Chen Heqin, Tao Xingzhi, and Ye Shengtao, all Latinization supporters and advocates for the New Mass Education movement, this chapter delineates how script revolutionaries reconciled the contradiction between their nominal commitment to alphabetic writing and the reality of character-based colloquialized written language at the service of national salvation and mass liberation. I trace the recalibration of the Latinization movement, the redefinition of the double revolution of script and literature, and the reinvention of the figure of children in two major *Bildungsromane*, which taken together marked a leftist turn in modern Chinese literature with reverberating impacts for decades to come.

In the third and final part of the book, chapter 5 solves the puzzle that was the surprising resolution of the script revolution in 1958, at the height of the socialist script reform, and suggests alternative ways to imagine grammatology and its global politics. It starts by charting the scale and intensity of socialist script reform, which escalated into a state ideology. Tracing the life's work of two script reform dissidents, Chen Mengjia and Tang Lan, I explicate how the phonocentric ideology imploded from within. Coinciding with the global conjuncture of decolonization and anti-imperialism, the resolution of the Chinese script revolution in a generative reworking of Chinese grammatology raised crucial questions about the Western ethnocentrism embodied in alphabetic writing, the limits of phonocentrism, and the potential of grammatology, which was at once an anti-identitarian approach to writing systems of the world, a political arena of the short twentieth century, and a rejuvenated field of scientific inquiry for future generations.

The book ends with an epilogue describing my meeting shortly before his passing with Zhou Youguang, the last surviving member of the Committee for Chinese Script Reform (the state-sponsored organ in charge of revolutionizing writing in the PRC). The last custodian of the script revolution, Zhou's words and texts served as reminders of the movement's legacy. It is my hope that in commemorating one of the biggest linguistic and grammatological experiments in human history, *Chinese Grammatology* will pave the way toward a generative understanding of the fraught history and valuable politics, together with the debilitating limits and revolutionary promises, of the modern Chinese script revolution.

PART I

Provenance

Chapter One

THE BEGINNING AND THE END OF
ALPHABETIC UNIVERSALISM

First, we must consider the problem of phonocentrism as one which is not limited to the "West."

—KOJIN KARATANI, "NATIONALISM AND *ÉCRITURE*"

It was the summer of 1915, Hu Shi recalled years later in his *Autobiography at Forty*, that the Chinese literary revolution commenced. Celebrating its success as one of its leaders, Hu Shi credited a particular superintendent of Tsinghua College based in Washington, D.C., by the name of Zhong Wen'ao as an unexpected inspiration. In charge of mailing monthly stipend checks to overseas students enrolled at different American universities, Zhong kept slipping "little notes" inside the envelopes. A Christian who likely thought of his notes as tokens of social gospel, Zhong spread messages on a wide-ranging series of topics. For instance, "Do not take a wife until one reaches twenty-five years old"; "Plant more trees for they are beneficial"; and "Abolish Chinese characters and adopt an alphabet."[1] Shortly after writing back to censure Mr. Zhong for his ignorant radicalism, Hu Shi started brooding over the problem of the Chinese language and writing. He soon teamed up with Yuen Ren Chao—both studying at Cornell University at the time—to compose a four-part article, which was published by the *Chinese Students' Monthly* in 1916 under the title "The Problem of the Chinese Language."[2] While Hu Shi's one section focused on the teaching of Chinese, Chao devoted his three parts to the question of alphabetizing Chinese. Hu Shi never said it, but that was the beginning of the Chinese script revolution.

This chapter introduces the provenance of the script revolution as both a major grammatological and linguistic event that shaped the face and sound of the national Chinese language and a critical field in which phonocentrism played out first to buttress, then to undermine, and eventually to bankrupt the authority of alphabetic universalism. I define "alphabetic universalism" as two mutually enhancing convictions: first, the phonetic alphabet as the best technology to represent speech sound and second, the Roman-Latin alphabet as the most transparent and thus only bearer of phoneticization. I trace the beginning of alphabetic universalism in China to the publication of "The Problem of the Chinese Language"—specifically, the three parts composed by Yuen Ren Chao as a self-contained scholarly work—which unequivocally argued for the institution of a Chinese alphabet to replace characters and launched the Chinese Romanization movement in 1916. As the movement waded through the contention between two national languages, it embraced an increasingly technologizing view of sound and script, culminating in the birth of the Gwoyeu Romatzyh (國語羅馬字 National Language Romanization, or GR). GR marked, on the one hand, the Chinese submission to global phonocentric rule and, on the other, an attempt to nationalize the exclusive claim of Roman-Latin superiority. Loyal to the phonocentric enterprise, Chao followed his bid for alphabetic universalism with a search for scientifically advanced technology for sound reproduction and visual hearing. When the search introduced the sound spectrograph as a viable path toward visible speech, it became clear that no alphabet—Chinese or Roman-Latin—could match the spectrographic image for its unparalleled scientific quality. The pursuit of phonocentrism eventually and unwittingly brought about the bankruptcy of alphabetic universalism, leaving behind the haunting question of what writing really meant for all scripts—Roman-Latin or otherwise—in a world that might eventually become disenchanted with phonocentrism and start looking for alternative grammatological values.

ALPHABETIZING CHINESE

What does alphabetizing Chinese entail? This deceivingly simple question sits at the center of the script revolution. A common response pinpoints either pinyin or the "national phonetic alphabet" (*zhuyin fuhao* 注音符號), both auxiliary phoneticization systems for characters. Though the former adopts the Roman-Latin alphabet and the latter names itself as an alphabet, neither fulfills the task of eliminating characters, and both compromise the final realization of the script revolution. The straightforward question of what alphabetizing Chinese means is, in fact, a complicated problematic that defies an easy answer and defines the motive of the script revolution. The answers, necessarily plural and varying in their levels of radicalism, not only constituted the result of the revolution and charted its course— its provenance, transmutations, and containment—but also revealed the inner workings—ambition and anxiety—of the revolutionary cause.

Two propositions coexisted at the onset of the script revolution: first, the alphabetization of Chinese characters; second, the overhaul alphabetization of both script and language. Regardless of whether the alphabetization of Chinese should be so radical as to eliminate spoken Chinese and its many topolects, there was consensus that the time for the Chinese script had run out. Few self-respecting members of the Chinese elite objected to the abolishment of characters; most considered it a necessary cost of the advent of a new, legible Chinese nation-state.[3] Figures from opposing ends of the political spectrum—Cai Yuanpei, Hu Shi, and Wu Zhihui, on the one end, and Qu Qiubai, Lu Xun, and Mao Zedong, on the other—might have had different ideas about how to alphabetize Chinese, but they all shared the conviction that an alphabet was the future.[4] The first salvo was the 1920s Chinese Romanization movement, endorsed by the Guomindang (GMD, Nationalist Party), followed by the 1930s Chinese Latinization movement, led by the Chinese Communist Party. Though politically antagonistic, the two parties were united under the banner of phoneticization and alphabetization. This movement, unlike its pre–twentieth-century predecessors—the *fanqie* (cross spelling) system implemented no later than the Han dynasty, Tang-dynasty "letters" devised to translate Buddhist sutras, Ming-dynasty Romanization schemes created by Jesuit missionaries, and late-Qing phoneticization reforms—was the first attempt in millennia-long Chinese literary history to demolish the rule of the old Chinese script and implement a new alphabetic writing system strictly as a supplement to the spoken language.

If the first proposition established the main agenda of the script revolution, the second revealed the key motive of alphabetization, which was best captured in an article, "Questions Regarding the Future of the Chinese Script" (1918), by Qian Xuantong 錢玄同—a leading Chinese philologist and member of the Romanization coterie. Denouncing the Chinese script as "the worst kind of hieroglyph" that "does not represent speech sound" and wrote nothing but "Confucian doctrines and Daoist hearsay," Qian advocated not only "the abolishment of this kind of script" but also the replacement of the Chinese language with foreign languages. He mentioned both English and French, but the ideal candidate was Esperanto, for its supposedly "concise grammar, neat phonetics, and precise etymology" and the promise of becoming "a new language of ten thousand nations"—the Chinese translation of Esperanto (*wanguo xinyu* 萬國新語).[5] Such a proposition would have been easily dismissed as fanciful thinking or even brazen self-colonization had Qian been alone in his enthusiasm for Esperanto. On the contrary, sympathy for and interest in the language among Chinese intellectuals was expansive. Wu Zhihui penned similar arguments in the Paris-based journal *New Century* before Qian wrote his own article. Cai Yuanpei founded one of the first Esperanto schools in China. Lu Xun, regardless of the objections to Esperanto of his mentor, Zhang Taiyan, and his own earlier reservations as expressed in "Malevolent Voices," donated to the Esperanto Society in Shanghai and supported the Russian Esperantist and anarchist writer Vasili Eroshenko. Prominent writers like Hu Yuzhi, Zhou Zuoren, and Ba Jin achieved varying degrees of proficiency in Esperanto.[6] A proper interjection of a history of the Chinese chapter of the Esperanto movement is beyond the scope of this chapter, but the Chinese fascination with Esperanto is suggestive of the true mission of alphabetization.

It should be noted that when Ludwig Lazarus Zamenhof invented Esperanto in 1887, he did not intend for it to serve as the one and only "international language" replacing all national languages.[7] Such a move would have constituted linguistic and cultural imperialism and instantly disqualified Esperanto as a neutral, internationalistic, revolutionary, and universal language. Instead, Esperanto was envisioned as a second language for all, a path toward debabelization, and an opportunity to rise above—not at the cost of—national languages. Chinese Esperanto advocates were quick to latch on to the linguistic utopia promised by Esperanto. Qian's proposal to adopt the universal second language as the Chinese national language, at the same time outlandish and outrageous, was an honest, if not desperate, acknowledgment of the true motive that drove the script revolution. Granted that such a proposition begged the question of Chineseness once both the Chinese language and writing had been eliminated, it confessed to the

Chinese desire for linguistic commensurability, legibility, and even superiority, something that the country sorely lacked at the time of script revolution, and which was seemingly achievable by appropriating and transplanting Esperanto and its perceived universality. Alphabetization for alphabetization's sake was hardly reason enough to break away from the old Chinese script and language. The most ambitious and anxious answer to the question of alphabetization boiled down to the Chinese will for linguistic and grammatological universality.

Therefore the two answers to the alphabetization question marked the two tasks of alphabetization: first, to obtain the universal form of the Roman-Latin alphabet, and second, to nationalize it and substantiate the Chinese claim to universality. The former task conformed to both forms of alphabetic universalism by first acknowledging the universal claim of the phonetic alphabet in general and then complying with the Roman-Latin one specifically. In contrast, the latter task inevitably undermined the second form of alphabetic universalism by an attempt to nationalize the Roman-Latin alphabetic form. As the Chinese pursuit of alphabetic universalism became empowered by technological advancements that could write sound even better than the phonetic alphabet, the world of alphabetic universalism would tumble and topple, leaving intact the principle of phonocentrism.

Even though the Chinese chapter of the Esperanto movement stated, in the most radical fashion, the fundamental missions of the alphabetization movement, its implementation would cancel out any ground to nationalize universality. The first movement to undertake both tasks of alphabetization in any substantial way was the Chinese Romanization movement. Granted that this movement did not achieve full swing till the mid-1920s, its theoretical groundwork had been laid a decade earlier. Yuen Ren Chao's three-part English article under the full title "The Problem of the Chinese Language: Scientific Study of Chinese Philology" (1916) was, to date, the earliest and most scholarly writing on the subject of alphabetizing Chinese. Between April and June 1916, the journal *Chinese Students' Monthly*—published by Chinese overseas students in New England—serialized this founding document of the Romanization movement, which pledged allegiance to alphabetic universalism and at the same time hinted at the Chinese claim of universality.[8] The same year saw the posthumous publication of Ferdinand de Saussure's *Course in General Linguistics*, marking the independence of linguistics from philology—a disciplinary separation of speech from writing. Viewed separately, neither Chao's article nor Saussure's magnum opus was destined to appear in 1916. After all, talk of abolishing characters predated 1916, as testified by Zhong Wen'ao's radicalism that scandalized Hu Shi; and preparation to publish Saussure's work was well under way soon after his passing in 1913.[9] Nonetheless, the year 1916 offered nothing short of a historical insight framing modern China's encounter with phonocentrism as a representative from the non–Roman-Latin world. The serendipitous year of 1916 marked the beginning of the modern Chinese script revolution, when Chao—the future father of modern Chinese linguistics—inaugurated his academic career by arguing for the separation of phonetics from traditional Chinese philological learning, at the expense of Chinese characters.

Chao, then twenty-four years old, was to become one of the world's leading linguists of the twentieth century. As the foremost theorist of the Chinese Romanization movement, he was credited as the creator of a Chinese alphabet, Gwoyeu Romatzyh, the crown jewel of the movement. Trained in mathematics, physics, and philosophy, he shared interests and formed long-term friendships with Norbert Wiener, Ernest Lawrence, and Warren Weaver.[10] A modern Renaissance man, he was also a masterful translator of Lewis Carroll, a prolific composer, and a vanguard of cybernetics in China, as well as the only Chinese scholar invited to participate in the Macy Conferences.[11] His multifaceted talents made his linguistic turn a difficult decision. Musing about his true academic calling, he weighed his options in a diary entry in January 1916: "I thought that I am essentially a born linguist, mathematician, and musician."[12] Taking courses in all those subjects and particularly infatuated with a linguistics class taught by Charles H. Grandgent, Chao came to a revelation: "I might as well be a philologist as anything else."[13] Soon enough, this philologist was busy at work, paving the way for the Chinese Romanization movement.

The three-part article of 1916 was not the first piece of academic writing that Chao published, but it was the first piece that theorized the alphabetization of Chinese using the Roman-Latin alphabet.[14] Part 1 surveys the general problem of "the scientific study of Chinese philology"; part 2 singles out the subject of "Chinese Phonetics"; and the last part considers practical reforms, "with special reference to the alphabetization of Chinese."[15]

The first two parts advocate "scientific, or historical, research" and the last, "constructive reforms" (437).

In the first part, Chao charts four divisions under the general study of Chinese: "(1) Phonetics, (2) Grammar and idiom of the dialects, (3) Etymology, including the study of characters, and (4) Grammar and idiom of the literary language" (438). For Chao, "the problem of the Chinese language" lies not so much in the lack of the study of Chinese writing—after all, it is a millennia-old field that has produced classic studies such as *Explaining Graphs and Analyzing Characters* (*Shuowen jiezi* 說文解字), *Rime Storehouse of Esteemed Phrases* (*Peiwen yunfu* 佩文韻府), *Qieyun* (切韻), and *Kangxi Dictionary* (*Kangxi zidian* 康熙字典)—as in the historical neglect of Chinese phonetics. Before Chao devotes all of part 2 and later his entire career to tackle this issue, he confesses that his sense of the inadequacy of Chinese studies of phonetics comes from his initial encounter with the contemporary phonetics of Indo-European languages. The "extensiveness and thoroughness" in "the field of phonetics" done by "American, English, French, and German Scholars" puts in sharp relief the Chinese backwardness—both technical and theoretical—in recording and analyzing speech sound. Chao stipulates that methodological borrowing from the "scientific," "historical," and "empirical" field of the phonetics of Indo-European languages is imperative to remedy the problem of Chinese philological studies. In his words, it is necessary "to put the results of foreign works into Chinese" (438).

Part 2 surveys traditional "Chinese phonetics" and seeks ways to modernize it. In Chao's appraisal, though each offshoot of the philological tradition deserves due respect, none of them—from the classic *Qieyun* to the more recent *Kangxi Dictionary*—is adequate to perform the task of scientifically studying Chinese phonetics. Instead, they are themselves a constant source of inaccuracy and confusion for their outdated classifications, imprecise notation, and being simply "not analytical enough" (507). Chao instantiates his charge against traditional philological work by working through its underlying principle of *fanqie* 反切 (cross spelling), a phoneticization system that approximates the pronunciation of an unknown character by way of two other characters—the first indicating the initial sound and the second representing the rest of the syllable.[16] As ingenious and longstanding as the method might be, Chao objects that the analytical units of *fanqie* contain too many variables to guarantee the accuracy of the pronunciation: for one, the initials and the remaining syllables could contain unwanted elements, misleading the cross spelling; for another, all cross-spelling users rely on their own individual dialect for phoneticization, creating an infinite number of possibilities. Therefore, Chao stipulates, to always obtain the intended "beautiful correlation," "a real alphabet" is needed, where "each sign that we use shall represent one and only one sound," and "the denotation of signs should be independent of dialects" (504–5).

Chao thus launches the search for the "real alphabet." Quickly examining four earlier attempts at Chinese alphabets—(1) "the mandarin alphabet" (*guanhua zimu* 官話字母), (2) "Chinese shorthand" (*suji fa* 速記法), (3) "the system of the Committee on Unification of Pronunciation" (Duyin Tongyi Hui 讀音統一會), and (4) the system of Chang Ping-Ling (Zhang Binglin 章炳麟, i.e., Zhang Taiyan), all auxiliary phonetic systems developed at the turn of the twentieth century—Chao judges all four to be problematic, though he grants that the fourth is "more complete" than the others (506).[17] He swiftly turns to the West, where "three of the most important" systems capture his attention: the International System of Phonetic Transcription, Alexander Melville Bell's "visible speech," and Otto Jespersen's system of letter numerals and indexes in *Lehrbuch der Phonetik* (507). Although none of these could serve as the Chinese alphabet without considerable modification, Chao is convinced that alphabetic writing is the "logical form of writing adequate to a unified language" and is "in favor" of "the Roman letters" (582, 586).

In the final part, after drawing the blueprint for a reformed and unified Chinese language, Chao expresses confidence in devising a real Chinese alphabet that can write the Chinese speech sound. Pleading his case, he lists fourteen "Arguments for Alphabetization":

1. An alphabet is more adequate to our growing language.
2. It makes unification of dialects easier.
3. Pronunciation will be self-explanatory.
4. We have only one or two score signs to learn instead of several thousand signs.
5. Assimilation of foreign words is necessary to the growth of thought and language.
6. An important case of assimilation is that of technical terms.
7. Translation of proper names with an alphabet would be simpler. . . .

8. Foreign languages will be a little easier to learn if our own language is written with an alphabet.

9. The Chinese language will be a little easier for foreigners to learn if it is alphabetized.

10. Alphabetic Chinese is easier to print.

11. Alphabetic Chinese can be typewritten as fast as English.

12. Indexes, catalogues, dictionaries, directories, filing systems, etc., will be greatly helped by the use of an alphabet.

13. Telegraphs and secret codes can be more easily despatched [*sic*] with an alphabet.

14. I shall add the teaching of the blind and deaf as a 14th reason. (582–84)

Ranging from linguistic development (arguments 1, 2, 3), technological compatibility (6, 10, 11, 12, 13), and mass education and literacy programs (4, 14) to translingual and intercultural communication (5, 7, 8, 9), the case of the Roman-Latin alphabet versus Chinese is clearly ruled in favor of alphabetic universalism. The superiority of the Roman-Latin alphabet boils down to its technological prowess to write sound and its universal compatibility with other alphabetic writing and information technologies, such as telegraphy and the typewriter, two technologies highlighted by Chao. While the advantage of language pedagogy is a bonus, the real allure is the legibility in and compatibility with the modern world brought about by scientific and alphabetic Chinese.

As if these fourteen points were not enough to establish the case for alphabetization, Chao goes on to inundate readers with sixteen questions and answers (587–91). These preemptive responses to potential objections to alphabetization, which Chao rehashed and reduced to ten points in his article "A Study of the Romanized Chinese Writing" (1922),[18] cover the principle of linguistic evolution, the correct treatment of literary legacy, the distinction between sound and script, the economy of an alphabetic script, standardization of the Chinese language, and unification of the spoken and the written. Chao assures both camps for and against alphabetization, whom he calls "alphabetists" and "anti's," respectively, that alphabetizing Chinese is a worthy cause that "will not be plain sailing, nor quick work" (587). He is confident, however, that the alphabetization of Chinese has the potential not only to write standardized Chinese with "maximum agreement among the dialects" (573, 574) but also to make the Chinese alphabet (orthography) more "regular" than the "irregular" and "unphonetic" English (590). Implicitly, he sketches both tasks of alphabetizing Chinese: to appropriate the Roman-Latin alphabet for Chinese writing and to nationalize its claim to universality. If done correctly, this superior Chinese alphabet will secure the future of modern Chinese writing, language, and literature and, by extension, the legibility and universality of a new China in the modern world.

TWO NATIONAL LANGUAGES

The establishment of the case for alphabetizing Chinese, despite its varying approaches at the beginning of the script revolution, only to be followed by more varying approaches, orthographies, and political allegiances in the following decades, inaugurated the phonocentric takeover in imagining the relationship between language and writing. Under the phonocentric regime, writing would no longer serve as a repository for Chinese culture and episteme. Instead, it would be technologized to become, it was hoped, a transparent transcription of speech sound. Strictly a supplement to the Chinese language, the new Chinese alphabetic writing, once adopted, standardized, and perfected, as Chao went on to do, immediately highlighted the difficult and potentially divisive problem of which Chinese language to transcribe. For Romanization loyalists supported by the Nationalist government, the right answer was *guoyu* 國語 (the national language), or, as Chao put it, "a unified language."[19]

There were at least two national languages—or, two national pronunciations—in the early Republican era: the old national language codified in 1913 and the new one that emerged in the early 1920s and was consolidated in 1924.[20] As the Republican language reformers used the terms national language (*guoyu*) and national pronunciation (*guoyin*) interchangeably, they played up the already high premium on Chinese phonetics, raising the thorny question of whether and how it was possible to negotiate a standardized national language that maintained "maximum agreement among the dialects."

Such phonetic negotiations resulted in the first version of the national language, which was decreed by the Committee on Standardization of National Pronunciation in 1913 at the end of a six-month marathon conference on the issue.[21] Eighty participants from twenty-three provinces convened and contested over a number of dialects as candidates for the national language. The committee, after much travail, settled on an eclectic and artificial system that strove to scientifically accommodate the maximum amount of dialectal varieties and to achieve the paramount degree of unity for the new imagined community. It regulated the pronunciation of more than sixty-five hundred characters, kept some of the oldest consonants from the Wu dialect and the most ancient endings from Cantonese, and included the so-called fifth tone—that is, the checked tone (*rusheng* 入聲).[22] This 1913 version of the national language was not announced until 1918 and was made official only with the publication of the *New National Dictionary* (*Guoyin zidian* 國音字典) in 1919, which coincided with the name change of the committee to the Preparatory Committee for the Unification of the National Language, reflecting the shifting mission of the time. This committee soon added to its roster such familiar names as Cai Yuanpei, Wu Zhihui, Hu Shi, Zhou Zuoren, Lin Yutang, Qian Xuantong, and Yuen Ren Chao. Chao was put in charge of recording a series of phonographs titled *National Language Records* (1921) to promote the new national pronunciation-cum-language.[23] The unification of the national language seemed to be well under way. However, this national pronunciation, albeit phonetically respectful of dialectal differences and hence truly "unifying," was soon greeted with questions about its impracticality, which swiftly turned into a well-documented debate in 1920–1921 between the national pronunciation (*guoyin*) and Pekingese (*jingyin*), the latter eventually becoming the new national language and the basis of the present-day Mandarin.[24] Advocates of the old national pronunciation barely had time to revel in its official codification before they realized that they had to reckon with the new one.

Chao was one of them. Even with official backing and his own scholarly reasoning in favor of the old and more unifying national language, Chao felt the pressure from advocates for the rival Beijing dialect. In response, he took it on himself to make another set of phonograph records to promote the old national language for foreigners in China and then to create a proper Romanization scheme for the old national language. He reported both moves in a May 1922 letter to his fellow linguist, committee colleague, and Romanization historian Li Jinxi. Chao noted in the letter that he had been asked by the Commercial Press "to devise, aside from the sixteen-lesson phonograph of the national language, another set of Chinese phonographs for foreigners together with an English explanation." Not only had he agreed to the job but also he "thought why not try my hand at a practical scheme of Romanization," especially when he found out from W. B. Pettus, president of the College of Chinese Studies in Peking, that "at his college, they only teach Pekingese." Chao relayed to Li the two reasons that drove Pettus's pro-Pekingese decision: "For one he could find Pekingese teachers easily, for another the national language exists only on paper with no teachers to hire." He concluded, "I wrote to him earlier saying that if there were phonographs of the national language, this conundrum could be solved. Then we will have one more force working in favor of the national language."[25]

Both Chao's letter and his article "A Study of the Romanized Chinese Writing" featuring the Romanization system for the old national pronunciation appeared in the 1922 special issue of the *National Language Monthly* with an original English title, "Reformation of the Chinese Characters."[26] By making the old national language accessible via both phonographs and an orthography that adopted the Roman-Latin alphabet, Chao was hoping for an international and scientific coalition to defend the 1913 national pronunciation. However, the biggest obstacle to the advancement of the old national language was its artificiality, so difficult that even Chao—the voice and self-appointed guardian of national pronunciation—found it demanding. Still adamant about its unifying potential, Chao set out to bring the language that "exists on paper" to life but ended up confessing, perhaps unwittingly, to its artificiality, technicality, and impossibility, now highlighted by a human-machine dynamic that emerged during the recording of the *National Language Records*. In his "Second Green Letter," Chao described his recording experience at the Columbia Gramophone Company in New York:

I was born to speak Pekingese, learned some other dialects while young, and acquired a central New Yorkese after a prolonged stay in Ithaca. Here comes a sort of High Chinese, something like the standard Parisian of the Academy, or the High German of the German stage, something which nobody speaks but which I was expected to speak with such fluency as to stand the test of a machine, which caricatures whatever is only slightly characteristic. So I looked up every doubtful word in the New National Dictionary and red-inked the pronunciation on the MS [manuscript], tried different expressions and made tempo and dynamic marks."[27]

As Chao invited us to hear the official national language that "nobody speaks," he also lets us know how strenuous the endeavor is. To write the "High Chinese" in phonographic form—the literal meaning of "phonograph" being the writing of sound—demands the smooth operation of a human-machine continuum. Chao needs to generate the speech sound of the old national language error-free, in real time, and to the best of his ability in order to accommodate the machine. To deliver the most accurate enunciation that could be captured by the phonograph, Chao adjusted his body to the effects of the machine, making himself an extension of the etching hand of the phonograph while fine-tuning High Chinese as another piece of machinery. Therefore this human-machine relationship stems not from the rim of the phonographic speaker, nor from Chao's vocal cords, but from the intricate phonetics of High Chinese itself. The production of the High Chinese phonograph records heightens for Chao the technical nature of Chinese phonetics, part and parcel of the mechanical reproduction of the old national language.

This implicit revelation would come back to Chao by the time he entered the final leg of the Romanization movement's pursuit to write sound, to which I return subsequently. For now, it is safe to speculate that most listeners and students of the old national language, unlike Chao, would not have found such an experience of working the inner mechanics of the old national language "interesting."[28] In May 1924 Chao was commissioned to make a second set of records of the national language with the Columbia Gramophone Company, to be released by the Commercial Press, bearing the title *New Phonographs of the National Language* (figure 1.1).[29] It bears pointing out that although Chao's was the official recording, it was not the only one, for other literary luminaries, such as Lao She 老舍 and Qian Zhongshu 錢鍾書, also made recordings and supposedly adopted the new national pronunciation as well.[30] As Chao told his friends in his "Third Green Letter," "This time, I used a pure Pekinese pronunciation, instead of the National Pronunciation or Kuo Yin [*guoyin*], as—between you and me—I think the pure Pekinese of an educated native of Peking has a better chance of success in the future than the Kuo Yin pronunciation. However, my attitude towards this is not yet well defined enough for a public statement."[31]

However scientific, precise, and progressive the old national pronunciation and Chao's rendition of it might be, the idealist "unified language" was

FIGURE 1.1. *New Phonographs of the National Language* (1924). Photo courtesy of the Chinese University of Hong Kong.

far too difficult to navigate compared with its simpler Pekingese counterpart. Pitted against each other, the old and new national languages conformed strictly to the law of linguistic evolution formulated by Max Müller, which was quoted by Charles Darwin: "The better, the shorter, the easier forms are constantly gaining the upper hand."[32] By 1923 the "easier" Pekingese gained a Darwinian upper hand over the old national language. After a decade of backing the old national pronunciation and language, the Committee on Unification of the National Language agreed on the adoption of the new Pekingese pronunciation, though the official abolishment of the old national pronunciation did not take place until 1932.

Chao, the erstwhile loyal supporter of the old national language, had to acknowledge that advocating the artificial old national language was a losing battle. In no trivial manner, Chao's personal conversion from the old national pronunciation to the new captured the history of the two national languages, which was etched into two phonographs—the old *National Language Records* (1921) and the *New National Language Records* (1924)—and was recorded in the two Romanization schemes in correspondence to both the old and the new national languages: Chao's old Romanization scheme of 1923[33] and the new scheme completed in 1926, with input from the Society of a Few Men (Shuren Hui 數人會).[34] If the first form of sound writing (the phonographic) technologized the human body into the production loop of sound reproduction, then the second form (the alphabetic) instantiated the increasing technologization of writing with the fruition of the Chinese alphabet.

THE BIRTH OF GWOYEU ROMATZYH

The birth of the Chinese alphabet—Gwoyeu Romatzyh, literally, in its own system, the "National Language Romanization Script"—was no doubt the pinnacle of the Chinese Romanization movement. Designed to transcribe the new national pronunciation based on the Beijing dialect, it received official recognition in 1928, when the GMD government named it the Second Form of the National Alphabet.[35] Second only to the 1913 National Alphabet—*zhuyin fuhao*—the alphabet named in the 1928 decree was the first and hitherto strongest official endorsement of Romanization. The script revolution now had a national form and could hope for the second form to become the first. Commemorating this landmark in his diary, Chao used the new national alphabet: "G.R. yii yu jeou yueh 26 ry gong buh le. Hoo-ray!!!" (G.R. was officially announced on September 26. Hooray!!!).[36]

The triple exclamation marks registered his pride in the official recognition of GR's superiority and his confidence in GR's future. Writing at the height of the Chinese Romanization movement, Chao had bigger dreams for his brainchild than simply serving as a supplement to the new Chinese national language. Now that GR had stood out from the myriad Romanization schemes, which, according to Swedish Sinologist and linguist Bernhard Karlgren, were as numerous "as days in the year,"[37] it was reasonable to expect it to grow into a true universal alphabet—or, more accurately, universal orthography—that transcribed all national languages. Inasmuch as the official status of GR marked the fulfillment of the first task of alphabetization, successfully appropriating the Roman-Latin alphabet for Chinese writing, Chao moved on to the second task, which aimed to claim alphabetic universalism for the Chinese alphabet. This ambition, more often than not glossed over by GR's own complex orthography, to which GR's later obscurity was usually attributed, revealed the real stakes of the Chinese script revolution, which partook in the complete domination by phonocentrism with an increasingly strong impetus to technologize. These stakes not only helped frame the Romanization movement within the global moment of phonocentric conversion but also shed light on GR's lack of popularity soon after its glorious moment of official recognition. The stakes of GR were laid out from the beginning of its planning and were best captured by an important letter from Karlgren to Chao on February 24, 1925. A revealing guide to understanding the birth of GR, this letter showcased the Chinese endorsement of and then bid for alphabetic universalism, as well as the growing fixation on scientific sound writing, which was both a blessing and a curse for the Chinese alphabet (appendix 1.1).[38]

Bernhard Karlgren (1889–1978), a polymath, folklorist, and dialectologist of his native Sweden before his interests turned eastward, became and remains to this day one of the best-known Swedish Sinologists. A pioneer in historical linguistics, he was the first to reconstruct what he termed ancient and archaic Chinese, now categorized as Middle and Old Chinese. After teaching at the University of Gothenburg, he took up a twenty-year directorship at the Museum of Far Eastern Antiquities (Östasiatiska Museet).[39] He came into contact with Chao in 1924 in Gothenburg and maintained a lifelong collaborative relationship with him, which bore important fruits in the development of Chinese philology and phonetics. One particularly significant and often-cited collaborative project was Chao's translation into Chinese—invited by Karlgren and conducted with two other linguists, Fang-Kuei Li 李方桂 and Luo Changpei 羅常培—of Karlgren's doctoral dissertation, *Études sur la phonologie chinoise* (1915), which in no small part informed the dialect survey led by Chao and Academia Sinica.[40] However, Karlgren's collaboration and later competition with Chao over the birth of GR was just as meaningful, if not more complicated.

The timing of the letter was not insignificant. Although Chao, as the leader of the Romanization movement, had started his conversion to the new national language, he was at the time still hesitant to make his view "a public statement."[41] Within less than a year from the receipt of Karlgren's letter, Chao completed his transition to the new national language, formalized the GR scheme, and submitted it for official recognition. Even with the absence of Chao's prior letter to Karlgren, it is not difficult to read the latter's reply as a response to Chao's solicitation of suggestions and advice for the future of the Chinese Romanization movement, starting with the question of the national language.

Time-stamped to this transitional moment, Karlgren's letter adopts a friendly advisory tone in addressing "the matter in question" and gives thoughtful and concrete advice, which could be summarized in three main points. First, Karlgren draws the blueprint for the future of Chinese sound and script, casting his vote firmly for Pekingese in the contention between the old and new national languages—plainly stating that "Pekinese has to be 'High Chinese' "—and then giving detailed instructions for devising a proper Romanization system for it. Second, he introduces and promotes his own Romanization system used in his *Analytic Dictionary of Chinese and Sino-Japanese* (1923) as a candidate for a practical Chinese alphabet, which partially explains his later discontent with the GR system. Finally, he offers general encouragement and warnings for "leading young spirits" like Chao and urges him to act immediately in conducting practical reform, writing primers, and producing new literature. Otherwise, the "evolution" of the Chinese script would slip into "inferior" hands. Demonstrating judgment and foresight, Karlgren comes across as an authority on the issue of alphabetizing Chinese, often employing the imperative mode of speech, evoking nine times the modal verb "should," twice "do not," and expressions such as "can never" and "can only." Karlgren's letter was remarkable not so much because he was proven correct in all his prophecies for the movement, from the High Chinese of Pekingese to necessary measures to be taken for orthographic simplicity, primer production, and reform promotion, but rather as a letter extraordinaire in manifesting the inner workings—indoctrination, complicity, and competition—within a transitional alliance for the Romanization movement at a moment of global conversion to phonocentrism.

This transnational alliance grew from its overseas origin—Chao's 1916 English article—to a fraught Euro-American-Chinese partnership as exemplified by Karlgren and Chao. After settling scores on the old pronunciation vis-à-vis the new, ruling in favor of the latter, Karlgren advises, "As a control and support for this 'high Chinese' Pekinese you should make it a phonetically written language with a new and flourishing literature." Preaching to the choir, he continues, "There is one thing which more than anything else would help to bring new China in contact with and make it really useful to and appreciated by the rest of the intellectual world: a common script, making it easy and natural to read the new Chinese literature and reproduce it, print it as quotations in western works. This can only be done by writing New high Chinese with Roman letters."

It is important to note that the equivalence Karlgren draws between the "common script" and the "Roman letters" is a hypothetical one constructed by the long-standing tradition of "debabelization" in search of a universal structure that could unite all linguistic and grammatological differences. The history of the search for the common script construes, as linguists Roy Harris and Talbot Taylor demonstrate, a crash course on European linguistic thought. Early pioneers include but are not limited to the Jansenist school's *The Port-Royal Grammar* (1660), Gottfried Leibniz's calculus ratiocinator, Wilhelm von Humboldt's work on linguistic difference and human intellect, George Dalgarno's *Art of Signs* (*Ars signorum*, 1661), and John Wilkins's seminal piece *Essay Towards a Real Character and a Philosophical Language* (1668), which influenced Jeremy Bentham's idea of the Panopticon. In Chao's and Karlgren's lifetimes, the search extended to include many more language and writing reforms, such as the Esperanto movement, as well as Basic English (acronym for British American Scientific International and Commercial English), which was invented by C. K. Ogden and I. A. Richards, with Ogden taking direct inspiration from Bentham and penning a study on universal languages bearing the very title *Debabelization*.[42] It was not a coincidence that Chao's collaboration with

Basic English helped coin the term "Basic Chinese." Though the Chinese "Basic" did not entail the same acronym, both Basics adopted the same statistical method in determining a word limit—850 for English, 1,100 or 1,200 or so for Chinese—for general, if not universal, communication. Toward the end of Chao's life, Basic Chinese morphed into "General Chinese" (*tongyong hanzi* 通用漢字), a project he kept working on till the end of his life.[43]

Although the dream of debabelization did not limit itself to the Roman-Latin alphabet before Karlgren's letter or after, as Leibniz's calculus and its twentieth-century upgrade to binary code demonstrate, Karlgren's working premise that the "common script" equals "Roman letters" had become a ruling opinion. As Karlgren notes, the most useful move to enable China's membership into the international community was to print Chinese "as quotations in western works." Somewhere between patronization and camaraderie, Karlgren's suggestion is a clear manifestation of the consolidation of alphabetic universalism in both its forms: the superiority of alphabetic writing, on the one hand, and the uniqueness of the Roman-Latin alphabet on the other.

Now that the new Chinese writing transcribing "High Chinese Pekinese" was invited and willing to join the "common script," any suspicion of alphabetic colonialism was dissipated. The looming violence of the universal alphabet dominating over all other non–Roman-Latin scripts was thus translated into the consent of the latter, reaffirming the desirability of the commonwealth of the common script. Like many other non–Roman-Latin alphabets, Chinese writing willingly severed ties with the old script and converted to alphabetic universalism, in the hope of scriptal legibility and legitimacy in "the intellectual world," albeit with an entry position as "quotations." The story of the Chinese script revolution would be commonplace if the complicity of grammatological (self-)colonization had ended with Karlgren's advice and Chao's consent. Instead, the Chinese bid for alphabetic universalism had just begun.

Having welcomed his Romanization comrades to the transnational Roman-Latin-alphabetic alliance, Karlgren moves on to his second main point in the letter: "The writing system should be as simple as possible, with few diacritical marks (except the tones). It does not matter if it does not reproduce the pronunciation shades quite closely, if it is only logical and consistent." Specifically, Karlgren recommends to Chao his own *Analytic*

Dictionary of Chinese and Sino-Japanese, arguing that "my new dictionary is about as simple and in the same time as scientific as you can ever make a practical system." Karlgren's self-promotion, however brief, provides an important clue to his later dissatisfaction with and criticism of Chao's system. Only months before GR's official recognition, Karlgren, in a paper titled "The Romanization of Chinese" presented to a London audience, commented on GR: "I confess that I am not a great admirer of it."[44]

Chao never openly responded to Karlgren's criticism but also never spoke of seeking his advice on Romanization before the birth of GR and downplayed Karlgren's importance in the matter during later interviews.[45] What Karlgren had difficulty appreciating happened to be what Chao took most pride in: the representation of tones, or what Chao later called speech melody, using nothing but the "Roman letters" and eliminating altogether diacritical marks for tonal representation. Chao had already adopted this "tone-in-letter" approach in his earlier Romanization system of the old national language and had updated it in the new GR system to reflect the four-tone Beijing dialect. By embedding tones in the common script, GR differentiated itself from all other systems—Karlgren's included—and prepared the Chinese alphabet for its bid for both scientific universality and unique Chineseness. As shown in the official GR orthography, the tone-in-letter system involves a "Basic Form" for the first tone, adding an "r" to the second tone, doubling vowels for the third, and changing finals for the fourth, eliminating diacritics in marking tonal values.[46]

Although Karlgren instructed Chao in the 1925 letter to make the Romanization system "as simple as possible" and not to make it into "a clumsy and illogical missionary system," he also advised doing it "with few diacritical marks (except the tones)." Making an exception for tonal diacritics, his own Romanization system—as in the 1923 *Analytic Dictionary of Chinese and Sino-Japanese*, which he recommended to Chao, and in a 1928 modification called the C system—preserved tonal diacritics. Chao's innovations became Karlgren's grievances. By way of annotating the tonal rules of GR, Karlgren critiqued the tone-in-letter system:

As you notice, the 2nd tone is marked in certain syllables by an r which has to be mute, in other syllables by -i- and -u- being changed into -y-, -w-. The 3rd tone is marked by doubling the vowel, or by changing -i-, -u- into -e-, -o-. The 4th tone is marked by a final -h, or by doubling the final -n, or by changing the -ng into -nq. This is all very ingenious, but in my opinion it has the fault of deviating too far from phonetic truth to be practical.[47]

Karlgren and Chao obviously had different opinions in regard to the superiority of their preferred tonal systems. A fair adjudication of their differences would perhaps require an army of phoneticians, whose potentially highly technical argument would belie a more poignant point of contention: a competition for the title of the Chinese alphabet within the transnational alliance. If Karlgren was oblivious to Chao's ambition for the Chinese alphabet in the 1925 epistolary exchange, he was made aware of it by Chao's actual creation of one, of which he was "not a great admirer." The confidence in Karlgren's self-recommendation that his was the simplest and most practically "scientific" system was registered in the brevity of his statement, which was followed by detailed instructions on how to make primers, supposedly using his Romanization. Karlgren notes, "Do not make too many primers about the new language, but make primers on all subjects" and produce "good new Chinese literature."

Indeed, Chao soon produced one primer of the new alphabetic literature titled *The Last Five Minutes* (1929), in which he opted to use his own GR system. Taking the dispute over the technicality of tonal representation to the next level, the unsaid discontent between Chao and Karlgren spoke to GR's desire for alphabetic universalism. With the birth of GR, both tasks of Romanization were fulfilled: first, to transplant the Roman-Latin alphabet to Chinese writing; second, to nationalize it with a Chinese inflection. The tone-in-letter system was at once Chinese—spelling a uniquely tonal language—and universal, equipped with the orthographic potential to capture more acoustic components of all languages than existing orthographies using the Roman-Latin alphabet. As Chao complained in his 1916 inaugural essay, Indo-European languages, written in Roman letters, were inaccurate and "unphonetic" in their representation of vowels and consonants.[48] Moreover, he argued in his essay "Physical Elements of Speech" (1924) that a full representation of speech should reach beyond a simple combination of vowels and consonants to include other acoustic elements, such as duration, intensity, fundamental pitch, overtone, and noise.[49] GR, as Chao conceived it and believed it to be, in spite of Karlgren's unfavorable appraisal, was a superior system capable of more and better acoustic representation, starting with an embedded tonal portrayal. As long as Chinese Romanization could keep at its quest for accurate and scientific phoneticization, Chao was confident that in a century's time GR would establish its claim to alphabetic universalism firmly enough so that Chinese children, when starting to learn English, would wonder, "Why do the British use our Chinese script too?"[50]

This witty one-liner—Chao's signature style—epitomized the grand vision of both tasks of Romanization. While the Chinese Romanization movement marked the phonocentric turn in China—as testified by the formation and fortification of the Karlgren–Chao collaboration—it also flagged the potential ascendancy of the Chinese alphabet in claiming universality, as the Karlgren–Chao competition vividly illustrated. Inasmuch as Karlgren welcomed the transnational coalition in allegiance to alphabetic universalism—the general superiority of alphabetic writing under the phonocentric regime—he was not prepared to accept the Chinese bid for it. As Chao brought experimental phonetics together with its many acoustic elements to bear on the birth and growth of GR, it should be clear that the only way forward to advance the Chinese claim of alphabetic universalism was an increasingly scientific and technologizing approach to speech representation, which ironically brought an end to alphabetic universalism while safeguarding the rule of phonocentrism. As Karlgren remained hung up on the truthfulness of the tone-in-letter method, GR kept at its quest for the utmost level of scientific quality in speech representation, culminating in what Chao called the GR drama score.

A CHINESE HEIR TO ALPHABETIC UNIVERSALISM

Inasmuch as GR staked out the Chinese claim to spell all languages, the new national language being but one of many, the GR drama score took the scientific representation of speech sound to a whole new level. The GR drama score refers to Chao's primer *Gwoyeu Romatzyh deuyhuah shih shihpuu: Tzueyhow wuu-fen jong* 國語羅馬字對話戲戲譜: 最後五分鐘 (A conversational drama score in GR: The last five minutes) (1929; figure 1.2).[51] In a letter dated June 25, 1927, Chao explained the design for his debut primer to Karlgren, who had recommended that he start making GR primers: "I translated A. A. Milne's *Camberley Triangle*, a one-act comedy, into both the Gwoyeu Romatzyh and characters and have arranged to have it printed

GWOYEU ROMATZYH DUEYHUAH SHIH SHIHPUU

TZUEYHOW WUU-FEN JONG

Jaw Yuanrenn puu

Shanqhae Jonghwa Shujyu

Mingwo 18 Nian (1929)

國語羅馬字對話戲戲譜

最 後 五 分 鐘

趙 元 任 譜

上 海 中 華 書 局

民 國 十 八 年 (一 九 二 九)

FIGURE 1.2. Yuen Ren Chao, *Last Five Minutes* (1929).

with the two on opposite pages. As an overgrown appendix, I put in a study of the speech melody of Peking."[52] Chao was excited, for it would be not only a debut of one of the first GR primers but also "the first attempt to write a *bairhuah wen* as one actually *shuo huah*," which would take the Chinese Romanization movement to the next stage.[53]

A drama score (*shihpuu* 戲譜), as the name suggests, is a score of a conversational drama, not unlike an opera score. It combines the system of phonetics with that of musical notation, aiming for a precise representation of different aspects of a speech sound, including duration, fundamental pitch, and overtone. All acoustic elements are to be precisely laid out by the writer-cum-composer and closely followed by the actor-cum-singer. Ambitious and original, the GR drama score promised to revolutionize the paradigm of alphabetic sound writing, steering it toward a maximized amount of scientific quality and phonetic control. The inspiration of the drama score came to Chao after watching the Macdona Players' performance of George Bernard Shaw's *Pygmalion* in Paris.[54] Unhappy with Eliza Doolittle's poor command of Cockney—the working-class topolect spoken in London's East End—Chao, a phonetician himself, took on the role of Professor Higgins in rectifying Eliza's pronunciation for the desired phonemes, intonations, and delivery. He reasoned why a drama score should seek and exert phonetic control:

I think before long we shall adapt the notation of music and phonetics to the uses of the dramatic art. Time and pitch (including slides, which is more usual than fixed pitch in speech) must be indicated, if not throughout a play, at least here and there where they are of decisive significance. . . . If we do not excuse a singer for singing the wrong tune or out of time in an opera, where pitch and time when you come to think of it don't really matter, why shouldn't we hold a player strictly to a proper and therefore varied style of using pitch and time in a play, where pitch and time matter very much?[55]

Collapsing the boundary between speech and music, Chao proposes to combine the two, writing dialogues using both the International Phonetic Alphabet and a five-line musical staff, adding notations such as "*andante, crescendo, mf, pp*" (26, 28). Realizing that it would be excessive and expensive to print the entire play in the double-notation system, which, unlike

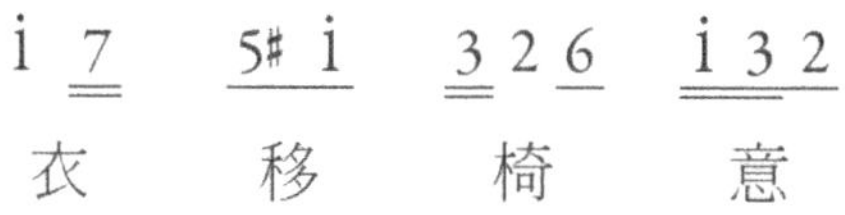

FIGURE 1.3. Example of "speech melody," four tones of *yi*, *Last Five Minutes*, 121.

an opera, rarely requires multiple characters to speak simultaneously, Chao opts to use the basic form of GR and supplement it with a numbered musical notation (also known as the *Ziffersystem*) for key words and phrases only (28, 30). Such is the so-called GR drama score. As an example, Chao illustrates how the four tones in Pekingese should be represented as "speech melody" under the musical notation system (figure 1.3, example of four tones of *yi*) (121).

George Bernard Shaw might not have excelled in playing Professor Higgins for *Pygmalion*, but Chao was not going to pass up the opportunity to discipline his "fair ladies" to perfection in *The Last Five Minutes*. Updating A. A. Milne's post–World War I story of a love triangle between a returned British veteran named Dennis Camberley, his wife, Kate Camberley, and a certain Mr. Cyril Norwood, Chao renames Dennis Camberley as Chern Danlii 陳丹里 (Chen Danli)—no longer a British veteran coming home from the Ottoman Empire but a Chinese student returning from the United States—Kate Camberley as Kaelin 愷林 (Kailin), and Cyril Norwood as Luu Jihliou 魯季流 (Lu Jiliu). Following Milne's plotline, Chen Danli returns home to discover the affair and decides that he and Lu will each spend "five minutes" with Kailin before she makes her final choice. In his "last five minutes" with his wife, Chen Danli dissuades her from eloping with Lu, wins her back, and solves the "Camberley triangle."[56]

The Last Five Minutes, though by now largely obscure, was a work of great expectations upon its making. One of the first GR primers and the first GR drama score, as Chao reports to Karlgren, it is at the same time a study of Pekingese speech melody, an experiment in new alphabetic Chinese literature, and an instantiation of impeccable phonetic mimesis, exemplified by the ingenious drama score. While *The Last Five Minutes* accomplishes all three missions, it also helps illuminate the incomprehension, unpopularity, and eventual oblivion of the GR drama score. Before showcasing examples of its phonetic prowess, I should point out that although a contributing, even determinant, factor in its eventual failure, the drama score's scientific rigor constituted the very ground of the Chinese claim to universality and signaled the final step of the phonocentric pursuit that eventually overwhelmed the faith in alphabetic universalism.

The following paragraph, as an example, illustrates the workings of the GR drama score. Here Norwood/Lu Jiliu grumbles rather unwisely during his last five minutes with Kate/Kailin about how he sees no point in this game of "the last five minutes." Milne's English original with his own italic emphases—as a limited means of authorial control—reads as follows:

Norwood (*impatiently*). What does he *want* with five minutes? What's the *good* of it to him? Just to take a pathetic farewell of you, and pretend that you've ruined his life, when all the time he's chuckling in his sleeve at having got rid of you so easily. *I* know these young fellows. Some Major's wife in India is what *he's* got his eye on. . . . Or else he'll try fooling around with the hands-up business. You don't want to be mixed up with any scandal of *that* sort. No, the best thing we can do—I'm speaking for *your* sake, Kate—is to slip off quietly, while we've got the chance. We can *write* and explain all that we want to explain.[57]

Translating Milne's prose with great fidelity, except adapting "some Major's wife" to "some overseas female students in America" to conform to Dennis Camberley's new identity as Chen Danli, Chao juxtaposes the "character drama score" with the "GR drama score."

To perfect the execution of pronunciation and intonation, Chao introduces the colon (:) both before and after his playwright's instruction to mark the direction and range of application, such as *bunayfarnde:* (不耐煩的) and *:shang jii tzhy kuay* (上幾字快), denoting, respectively, that the content after the colon should be delivered "impatiently" and the content before the colon should be spoken "faster." Chao also uses a raised dot (·) to mark the neutral tone, the en dash (–) to link two or three syllables as one word, and the em dash (—) for any interruption or change in tones. Moreover, as Chao's "Explanatory Notes" states, the GR drama score notations also apply to characters. While the special instructions in GR employ italics, the corresponding characters are underlined (54–56). For characters that are meant to be pronounced in one unit, Chao uses the special quotation mark 「」 to group the words and change the GR spelling accordingly. For instance, 「格兒」「格兒」 (the onomatopoeia of laughter) is grouped into one unit and spelled as "gelx," in contrast to its regular separated spelling of "ger err" "ger err."

These rules, however meticulous, are nothing compared with Chao's real innovation that turned the drama score into a genuine speech-music continuum. Although Chao chooses not to execute the double notation throughout the primer, the highlights of his invention are the moments where the GR drama score and GR music score come together. Aside from the two examples of "上/shanq (:232)," and "阿/a (:5#64)," Chao gives a full sentence to be sung as a musical phrase: "不過就是對你說一套很悲慘的離別詞 / Buguoh jiowsh duey nii shuo i-taw—heen beitsaan de libye-tsyr," which means "[Chen Danli] will do nothing more than giving you a sorrowful farewell speech." Shown in figures 1.4 and 1.5, this phrase is set to both the *Ziffersystem* and the five-line musical staff, with seven bars and the tempo of 1/4.[58] Granted that Chao allows two different keys for the character score and for the GR score, gesturing toward the playwright's autonomy in adjusting keys for any given sentence, it is established that the flow of all sentences can and should be treated as a musical phrase and will be reproduced accordingly from the score. Inasmuch as the uniqueness of tones in Chinese lends itself well to be represented in music, as Chao demonstrates with the character *yi*, the doubleness of the GR drama and music score manifests the universal applicability of treating speech as music.

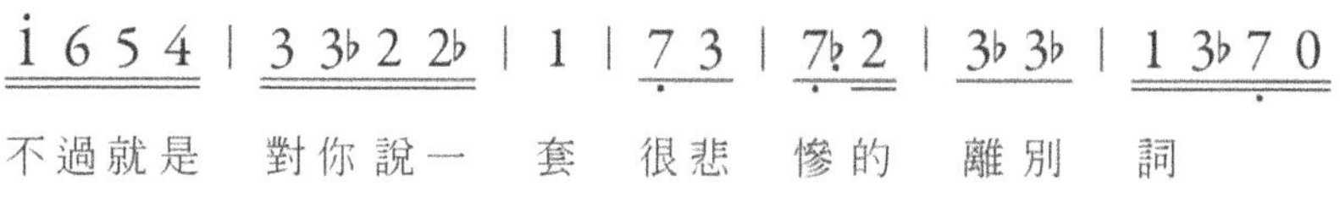

$$\underline{\dot{1}\ 6\ 5\ 4} \mid 3\ 3^{\flat}\ 2\ 2^{\flat} \mid 1 \mid \underline{7\ 3} \mid \underline{7^{\flat}\ 2} \mid \underline{3^{\flat}\ 3^{\flat}} \mid 1\ 3^{\flat}\ 7\ 0$$

不過就是　對你說一　套　很悲　慘的　離別　詞

FIGURE 1.4. *Ziffersystem* notation of "不過就是對你說一套很悲慘的離別詞," *Last Five Minutes*, 102.

FIGURE 1.5. Five-line music staff notation of "不過就是對你說一套很悲慘的離別詞" in GR drama score; *Last Five Minutes*, 103.

The result of the maximized control of time and pitch in phonetic representation is its indisputable accuracy and undeniable impracticality. The GR drama score, driven by its pursuit of scientific perfection, achieves the goal but turns itself into an unruly monster. GR's critics—Karlgren included—are right in pointing to its overly complex rules, rules that were impossible for nonexperts to master. Qu Qiubai, the chief theoretician of the later opposing Chinese Latinization movement, dubbed GR "gross," while Lu Xun compared it to "a plaything in a scholar's study," which had "no future."[59] However, GR's true ambition lay not in its appeal to practicality and popularity but in being the most scientific representation of all "physical elements of speech," as Chao's essay "Physical Elements of Speech" manifests. To fixate on GR's unpopular reception is to miss the Chinese claim to alphabetic universalism and international legibility, which are the real stakes of the GR drama score and the Chinese Romanization movement in general. More important, it lets go by a valuable opportunity to reflect on the very paradigm of phonocentric domination. If writing— alphabetic or nonalphabetic—is to be measured only in terms of its loyalty to and capacity for phonetic representation, then what is to become of it in the age of phonographs and other advanced technologies of sound reproduction? The perfection of writing as "supplementarity" of speech, as instantiated by the GR drama score, unwittingly disturbed the very ground where writing could take its meaningful place. In servitude to phonocentrism, writing—even alphabetic writing—pales in comparison with the more technologically advanced forms of visible speech. If the phonocentric fetish of the Roman-Latin alphabet was the driving force of GR's quest for scientificity in phoneticization, then it was the same force that exposed the limits of alphabetic writing and questioned the validity of alphabetic universalism.

VISIBLE SPEECH AND THE END OF
ALPHABETIC UNIVERSALISM

The new technology that was about to outweigh alphabetic writing was the sound spectrograph (figure 1.6, the machine). Hailed by Chao as "the revolutionary new development in experimental phonetics" in a 1947 letter,[60] this machine had its origin in a larger project of Bell Telephone Laboratories known as visible speech. Research on the sound spectrograph started

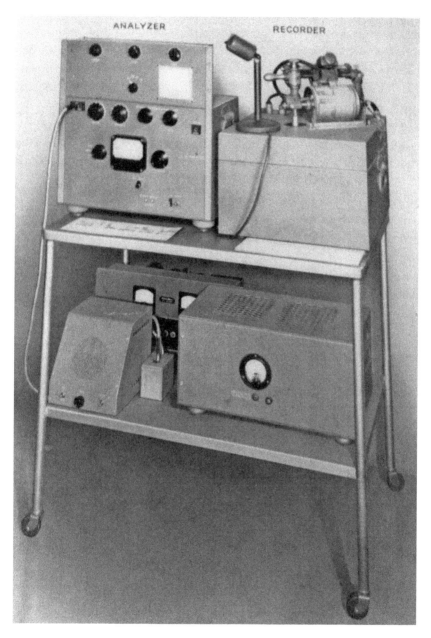

FIGURE 1.6. Sound spectrograph machine, Ralph K. Potter, George A. Kopp, and Harriet C. Green, *Visible Speech* (New York: Van Nostrand, 1947), 4–5.

in 1941, when "American participation in the war emphasized the military applications of, and needs for, a visual translation of sound."[61] "Military interests" delayed publication of relevant research until after the war. Bell Labs finally systematically introduced the project—its basic principles, lesson units, and applications—in a book bearing the same title, *Visible Speech* (1947), which defined the sound spectrograph as "a device for making visible records of the frequency, intensity, and time analysis of short samples of speech." The machine was designed to analyze "one band at a time, the simple oscillations of a complex wave," and record "the intensity variations in each band side by side in an orderly fashion upon a sheet of paper."[62] For any given spectrogram, the horizontal axis represented time, the vertical axis represented frequency, while the intensity of the sound wave at any given time and frequency was indicated by the darkness burned onto the paper. The result was a visual portrayal of all three fundamental acoustic elements—"frequency, intensity, and time"—of a given speech—that is, visible speech (figure 1.7).[63] As Oliver E. Buckley, then president of Bell Labs,

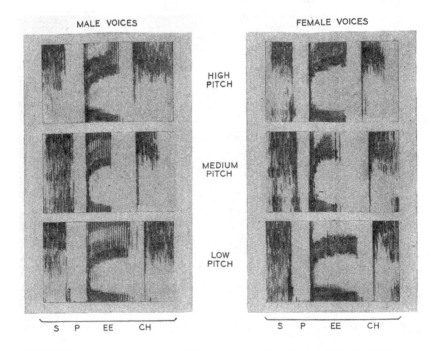

FIGURE 1.7. Spectrogram of speech by six different speakers with a wide range of voice qualities, Ralph K. Potter, George A. Kopp, and Harriet C. Green, *Visible Speech* (New York: Van Nostrand, 1947), 6.

put it in the book's foreword, "For the first time it has become possible to represent sound graphically so that pictures defining it fully can be printed in books."[64]

Not only was visible speech the future of human sound writing and visual hearing but also it had long been the dream in the search for the common script. Before the advent of the sound spectrograph, the Roman-Latin alphabet was largely taken to be the most advanced technology in rendering speech visible, underlining the basic reasoning of alphabetic universalism. In fact, *Visible Speech* described the visualization of speech as "an automatically written phonetic alphabet" (vii).[65] This identitarian observation was particularly fitting to the history of Bell Labs. Alexander Melville Bell, father of Alexander Graham Bell, the founder of Bell Labs, designed a version of visible speech of his own, a phoneticization system called universal alphabetics. Melville Bell published his work in his own *Visible Speech* in 1867, which was applauded as a major contribution to the fields of phonetics and the education of the deaf and greatly admired by Chao.[66] According to the self-reflexive prehistory documented in *Visible Speech*, the Bell father-and-son duo would often perform the "universal alphabetics" in public. With the son offstage and out of hearing range, the father would invite audience members, who had preferably traveled from afar, to speak in their own tongues, which were to be written in the father's system. Then the father would summon back the son, who would read aloud the visible speech, to be followed by the original speakers' reprising their words to show how "accurately imitated" the speech was and attest to the truthfulness of Bell's visible speech (3).

The attraction of visible speech was multifaceted. It had its origin in exploring visual hearing to enable communication for the deaf; developed sound writing to produce identifiable patterns; became incorporated into the American wartime research of speech visualization and analysis; and opened up new territories in medical research, musical notation, and animal speech.[67] Most important, it embodied and encouraged universal communicability, a dream shared by not only the Bells father and son but also Chao and Karlgren. It was, in fact, a concerted enterprise by all those who believed in and worked for a universal structure for human communication. As the 1947 book speculated, visible speech would evolve into "a form of writing" "that is universal, and in which the sounds of foreign language appear as they would be heard by the ear," and "spelling is automatically simplified" and "earned in the process of learning to speak" while also permitting "the use of voice writing as a substitution for handwriting" (421). Therefore Bell Labs' visible speech could be read and heard as part of the long-lasting search for the common script that fascinated the Port-Royal Grammarians, Leibniz, Humboldt, Zamenhof, C. K. Ogden, Karlgren, and Chao. The holy grail of visible speech seemed to have been obtained as different versions of the same dream coalesced and culminated in the newest, most scientific, state-of-the-art technology: the sound spectrograph.

Read in this light, Chao's unbridled excitement for the sound spectrograph was more than natural. As a phonetician, linguist, and, most of all, scientist who had a strong stake in the quest for the common script, Chao was no mere bystander but pursued an active role at the center of twentieth-century technological innovation of visible speech.[68] Between the beginning of research on the sound spectrograph in 1941 and the year of publication of *Visible Speech* (1947), Chao served as a consultant at Bell Labs. His contact with the company started as early as 1939, when he made inquiries about the possibility of conducting research there through Robert W. King, the assistant vice president and Chao's classmate at Cornell, asking if there would be "an opportunity to try out some time-pitch graph recording among other things" and if the labs were "stocked with books on linguistics."[69] Chao became a consultant with assistance from Hu Shi—the Chinese ambassador to the United States at the time—and held the position until 1947.[70]

While Chao proactively sought opportunities to collaborate with Bell Labs, the company also welcomed his input. In King's initial response to Chao, he expressed interest in Chao's "broad background in the study of phonetics and speech" and assured Chao that colleagues at Bell would be "enthusiastic about comparing notes with you."[71] In Oliver E. Buckley's letter of June 1944 confirming Bell Labs' decision to "retain" Chao as a consultant, he was invited to continue "working independently or jointly with employees of the Lab, in such studies of characteristics of speech."[72] Although Chao did not have full clearance, he closely observed permitted items of equipment, engaged with lab personnel such as Ralph Potter, who was directly responsible for the spectrograph project, and supposedly finished his work at the company with a report on visible speech.[73]

Given that Chao's initial interest in the company was its "time-pitch graph recording," it was fitting that his activities at Bell Labs revolved around visible speech, and fortuitous that his sojourn there overlapped with work on the sound spectrograph. In Chao's estimation, this was hitherto the most cutting-edge technological embodiment of the dream of visible speech, to the extent that all technologies before it belonged to the "pre-spectrograph" era.[74] In the absence of Chao's final report to Buckley, two outlines of his talks on the spectrograph—"The Visible Speech Spectrograph" and "The Sound Spectrograph"—allow a glimpse into Chao's initial observations of the new visible speech, which he later sorted through and incorporated into his *Language and Symbolic Systems* (1968).[75] The first talk, delivered on December 10, 1947, to what Chao called the U. C. Linguistics Group, focused mostly on the working mechanism of the speech spectrograph, while the second talk, given at University of California, Berkeley, on June 26, 1951, included a number of specific examples of spectrograms and their application in speech analysis. For Chao, the speech spectrograph was "revolutionizing," for it both corroborated and corrected the old theory and inspired new research in sound portrayal.

In Chao's analysis, the prespectrograph sound writing saw no regular one-to-one correspondence between sound and graph. In alphabetic sound writing, the same words spoken by different individuals were written the same. However, the same frequency generated by the flute and clarinet, or by a man and a child, certainly did not produce the same sound. The sound spectrograph improved the quality of phonetic analysis by supplementing the time-pitch visual hearing with three other forms: "position, velocity, and pressure."[76] As a result, spectrograms could not only scientifically represent any frequency-intensity-time correlation but also indicate idiosyncrasies in general sound patterns.[77] These spectrographic images of speech sound were so definitive that they were dubbed, in *Visible Speech*, the new ABCs.[78] It bears pointing out that the sound engineers had bigger plans for the spectrograms than sound writings sans alphabets, for they made available excellent data for sound analysis and manipulation. However, the quality of spectrographic sound writings was so discretely accurate that spectrograms were taken to constitute a new and superior alphabet. Take vowels and vowel-like sounds, for instance, which the sound spectrograph excelled in capturing. These spectrograms not only produced legible and unique sound patterns for each vowel and vowel-like sound, to the extent of providing "an unexpected confirmation of the traditional classification of vowel according to tongue height and front and back position"; they also furnished these sound patterns with individual accents. Granted that Chao did not suggest that spectrograms functioned like phonographs, capable of recording and reproducing all physical elements of sound, he was nonetheless enthusiastic about the speech spectrograph precisely for its ability to include more "frequency components" without reproducing noise.[79] In a way, the sound spectrograph was for Chao the ideal scientific instrument, analogous but superior to his own GR drama score. With its unprecedented amount of control in visual hearing, the sound spectrograph broke the confines of the phonetic alphabet, together with its inaccurate orthographies and cumbersome rules, such as what Chao had developed for the GR drama score.

There is little doubt that the sound spectrograph, as far as sound writing and visual hearing are concerned, is a superior technology compared with the Roman-Latin alphabet. The rhetoric claiming it as "the new ABCs" and "an automatically written phonetic alphabet" might have been enthusiastic, but it is hardly accurate and glosses over one crucial consequence of the quest for visible speech: the provincialization of alphabetic universalism. Compared with the color blocks of spectrographic visible speech, the Roman-Latin alphabetic visible speech is overly particular, scientifically insufficient, and far from universal. Though framed within the discourse of the phonetic alphabet, the sound spectrograph was "revolutionary" precisely because it went beyond the limits of alphabetic writing, challenged the superiority of the Roman-Latin alphabet, and contradicted the very assertion of alphabetic universalism.

Insofar as the sound spectrograph replaced the Roman-Latin alphabet as the best technology to transcribe speech sound, it upheld phonocentrism at the cost of alphabetic universalism. Ironically, the decline of "universal alphabetics" as the preferred technology of visual hearing served as an indisputable confirmation for phonocentrism. One obvious but overlooked fact, however, was that the universality of phonocentrism did not translate into the universality of communication. Far from it, phonocentrism and its chosen technologies operated within and worked to reinforce the specificities of languages. The seemingly neutral and universal spectrograms were first and foremost visual representations of particular speech sounds of particular languages. Trained readers of Bell Labs' *Visible Speech* might be able to read an English spectrogram, but they could not decipher a Japanese spectrogram without prior knowledge. The new visible speech turned out to be no more than a universally scientific written record of particularities, whose communicability was invariably subject to the vagaries of languages and cultures. In strict adherence to the tenet of phonocentrism, the sound spectrograph reinforced the supremacy of speech over writing—be it alphabetic, phonographic, or spectrographic writing of sound—and led to the end of alphabetic universalism.

What was remarkable about the Chinese Romanization movement, on top of marking the global moment of phonocentric domination and the Chinese submission to it, was that the provenance of the Chinese script revolution had already captured both the beginning and the end of alphabetic universalism, both of which were in conformity with the phonocentric doctrine. The beginning of alphabetic universalism informed the basic tasks of the alphabetization of Chinese and shaped the self-consciousness of Chinese writing in its yearning for universal form and its will to nationalize it for the creation of a national literature. The end of alphabetic universalism came into sight when definitive visible speech—the sound spectrograph—cast a long shadow over the limits of alphabetic writing and raised the necessary question of the true meaning of writing beyond the logic of supplementarity. Insofar as loyalty to phonocentrism clearly overruled any attachment to alphabetic universalism, the Chinese script revolution went on to explore other ways of privileging speech over writing. The transmutations of phonocentrism would start with the Chinese Latinization movement, its fascination with dialects, and its promise for a literary revolution.

APPENDIX 1.1

Bernhard Karlgren's letter to Yuen Ren Chao, February 24, 1925

Dear Mr. Chao,

I have hesitated for a long time to answer your last kind letter—because I was not sure what to advise in the matter in question. My philological experience insists on telling me that the evolution of a living language can never be led in a certain direction through a decision to speak in a certain way. You cannot make up, artificially, a language forming an average between a group of strongly divergent dialects and then make it to be freely spoken (you have made this experience yourself, as you told me). I believe the <u>one</u> way is to choose a <u>living</u> language as a norm and then make ever larger groups of people adopt it through the influence of those <u>who speak it naturally</u> as their mother tongue. There can be very little question as to which this language should be in China. That is decided, not by philology but by history. Just as Parisian must be the normative French, whatever its merits may be when historically viewed, in the same way Pekinese has to be "High Chinese," even if there are other dialects which have deviated less from the older stages of the language. This, however, does not mean that you should not eliminate extreme Peking *t'u hua*, particular vulgar phrases or the peculiar pronunciation of certain individual words (e.g. *kau-sung* for *kau-su*);[80] such normalization is the rule also regarding Parisian for instance.

As a control and support for this "high Chinese" Pekinese you should make it a <u>phonetically written language</u> with a new and flourishing literature. I fail to see the use of inventing new and complicated phonetic characters for this. There is one thing which more than anything else would help to bring new China in contact with and make it really useful to and appreciated by the rest of the intellectual world: a common <u>script</u>, making it easy and natural to read the new Chinese literature and <u>reproduce</u> it, print it as quotations in western works. This can only be done by writing New high Chinese with Roman letters. The Japanese are beginning to realize a similar truth for their part. You will finish by doing so for yourself. The <u>sooner</u> you do it, the less loss of work and valuable time. The writing system should be as simple as possible, with few diacritical marks (except the tones). It does not matter if it does not reproduce the pronunciation shades quite closely, if it is only logical and consistent. On one or two points it seems advisable to be conservative and write historically, with a view to the language as a whole, thus 經 *king* and 井 *tsing*, 行 *hing* and 星 *sing* according to etymology.

As a matter of fact I think that the system used in the Peking column of my new dictionary is about as simple and in the same time as scientific as you can ever make a practical system. There are very few peculiar signs, and all exist in every ordinary printing stock. X, r, ts etc.[81] are used since a hundred years in all western scientific literature and hence well known as to their phonetic value.

What the <u>kuo ë</u>[82] movement should do is to publish extensive texts (of high literary value) in this or some similar simple system and get them spread, read and loved. And what <u>you</u> should do next summer is to read these texts into the phonograph with <u>as exact Peking pronunciation</u> as you can make it. Interested people will compare your living record with your written representation, they will know what to read into the latter—and your New High Chinese is born! Above all: do not make too many primers <u>about</u> the new language, but make primers <u>on all subjects</u> (history, literature, geography etc.) written in the new language, and good new Chinese literature (fiction and thought) in it, and you will succeed.

I am afraid that my advice is not so tempting as it is sound. But one word of warning: if people <u>like you</u>, who can understand and appreciate the difference between a logical and scientific alphabetic writing and a clumsy and illogical missionary system, if <u>you</u> do not step forward in time and lead the movement in such a practical and reasonable direction but use up your force in utopian endeavors to carry through something still more desireable [sic] and historically elaborate—a new artificially made language—then evolution will go tis [sic] own way over your heads and carry through, with the force of necessity, something infinitely inferior still, e.g. a modern literature written in Wadee's system! Videant consules![83]

I will not say more than this because I believe that leading young spirits in every country have to work out the best course for their own country without being too much meddled with; I have written just enough to let you see what I would imagine be the best.

With many kind wishes,

Ever yours,
B. Karlgren.[84]

PART II

Transmutations

Chapter Two

PHONOCENTRIC ANTINOMIES

Whereof one cannot speak, thereof one must be silent.

—WITTGENSTEIN, *TRACTATUS* 7

The first transmutation of the Chinese script revolution took the shape of the Chinese Latinization movement and developed in conjunction with the literary revolution. Originating in the Soviet Union in the late 1920s and quickly endorsed by the Chinese Communist Party (CCP), the Chinese Latinization movement positioned itself as an opponent of the Guomindang (GMD)-backed Chinese Romanization movement. Relatively unknown to the Chinese audience until the early 1930s, the Latinization movement first became recognized by the Romanization camp through Yuen Ren Chao.[1] In 1934 Chao penned a blurb, "Regarding the Latinization of Chinese in the Soviet Union," in the *National Language Weekly*. Introducing a particular *Sin Wenz* 新文字 (New Script) primer brought back from Vladivostok, Chao reported that it was "a textbook used by the Russians to teach Chinese Romanization,"[2] gave an outline of its phonological and tonal plans, and ended with the official stamp of the Preparatory Committee for the Unification of the National Language, without proffering further judgment on the matter. To Chao and the rest of the committee, Sin Wenz was but one of many competing schemes of alphabetizing Chinese that would inevitably take a back seat as long as Gwoyeu Romatzyh (GR) was the state-sponsored Chinese alphabet.

To Chao's surprise, however, the Latinization movement would soon grow to be a formidable dissident movement. Its new script—Sin Wenz, in its own Latinization system—vouched for the definitive abolishment of Chinese characters and thus claimed its superiority over all schemes of Chinese alphabetization that came before it, GR included. Its polarizing rhetoric and revolutionary ethos soon won it vast popular support, leading to its ban by the Nationalist government between January 1936 and May 1938 and its adoption as a legal script by the CCP-controlled border region of Shaanxi, Gansu, and Ningxia Provinces in 1941.[3] Although united with the Romanization movement by their shared allegiance to alphabetizing Chinese under the phonocentric rule, the Latinization movement departed from its predecessor in every other possible way.

This chapter introduces the Chinese Latinization movement as the first transmutation of the script revolution, which was made possible by what I call phonocentric antinomies. Similar to Fredric Jameson's treatment of realism in *The Antinomies of Realism*, I approach phonocentrism "dialectically" and am interested in exploring how, within the phonocentric realm, "the negative and the positive are inextricably combined."[4] On the one hand, phonocentric violence threatened Chinese writing, culture, philosophy, and epistemology in general. On the other, multivalent negative phonocentrism cleaned the slate for the new Chinese alphabet, which symbolized to followers the possibility of speaking in their own voices and writing in a new alphabetic script. Inasmuch as positive phonocentrism provided the basic grammatological footing to the larger twentieth-century projects of democracy, liberation, and revolution, it also contributed to the transmutations of phonocentrism until they no longer resembled the original imagery of the Chinese alphabet. As Jameson puts it in the context of realism, "the stronger it gets, the weaker it gets; winner loses; its success is its failure."[5]

The axiomatic diagnosis of phonocentrism will gain clarity by the end of this chapter. I start by investigating the concrete differences between the Romanization and Latinization movements. Combing through the genealogy of the Chinese Latinization movement, I identify three of its historical precedents—the missionaries' dialect alphabetic Bible in the late-Qing period, the establishment of modern Chinese dialectology in the 1920s, and the Soviet Union's Latinization effort in the 1930s—and ponder how all three bear on the initial encounter between the script revolution and literary revolution.[6] Writing from the center of this intersection, Qu Qiubai and Xu Dishan—both Latinization advocates and prominent Chinese writers—demonstrated how the liberating promises of phonocentrism—now amplified by the Soviet Latinization movement and its commitment to the Proletkult (proletarian culture)—counteract and overwhelm the impending epistemological violence of a script overhaul, ushering in the so-called massification of literature and art. Xu Dishan's novella *Yu Guan* further showcased the dissolution of alphabetic universalism when its loyalty to dialect representation clashed with the basic task of weaving together a literary narrative in *baihua* (plain speech). By reading script revolution into literary revolution, I venture a new and preliminary understanding of Chinese literary and cultural modernity in the short twentieth century inflected through phonocentric antinomies. Riding the revolutionizing tide of modern Chinese writing, phonocentric antinomies mark both its liberatory promises and debilitating limits.

ROMANIZATION VERSUS LATINIZATION

In what was perhaps Chao's most comprehensive interview, conducted in English in 1977, he was careful not to mention his early introduction of the Latinization movement and not to comment on the well-publicized antagonism between GR and Sin Wenz.[7] When asked why the GMD "disapproved of" Sin Wenz, Chao invoked political rivalry between the Nationalists and Communists as well as GR's official status but refused to further substantiate the difference between the two alphabetization movements. When asked if he had discussions with any Sin Wenz proponents, such as Qu Qiubai, the chief theoretician of the Latinization movement, Chao informed the interviewers, "Not in detail, no; I never had long discussions with him."[8] Although no further information can be gleaned from either Chao's or Qu's writings to substantiate what transpired between the two, it is intriguing that these two leaders of Romanization and Latinization, respectively—both from a particular Qingguo Alley in Changzhou, Jiangsu Province—came together and conducted neither detailed nor long discussions with each other.[9]

Qu Qiubai 瞿秋白 (1899–1935) was one of the most talented and politically engaged literary figures of twentieth-century China. An expert and veteran translator of Russian literature, he was a pioneer of modern Chinese reportage and wrote two masterpieces—*A Journey to the Land of Hunger* and *A Personal History of the Red Capital*—about his travels in the Soviet Union in the early 1920s.[10] Politically active, he served as a member

of the Politburo of the CCP and twice as its chairman. Qu was also a founding member of the Department of Sociology at Shanghai University—the
first sociology department in China. While his multiple roles as politician,
writer, translator, educator, and even accomplished artist of seal engraving
were well documented, his participation in and leadership of the Chinese
Latinization movement was curiously lesser known. Qu, unlike Chao, who
seemed reluctant to voice his discontent with Sin Wenz, had no difficulty
in enumerating the failings of GR and articulated the real contention
between the two movements, starting with their opposing approaches to
orthographies—tonal expression in particular—and going on to the question of the national language vis-à-vis dialects and the significance of
national salvation, mass education, and literary revolution.

Qu's most elaborated explication of his objections to Romanization can
be found in an article dated July 24, 1931, "A GR Chinese Script or a Gross
Chinese Script." Although in agreement with GR's basic stance on the script
revolution, Qu takes serious issue with "the pitfalls of GR," starting with
the title of the article, which makes fun of the GR spelling of "roma" with
two possible pronunciations, *luoma* 羅馬 (Roman) and *rouma* 肉麻 (gross).[11]
Examining closely and quoting directly from the GR spelling rules listed
in Chao's *The Last Five Minutes*, Qu argues that, despite GR's self-appointed
status as the Chinese alphabet, it fails as a phoneticization system across
the board in its choices of consonants, vowels, and tonal expression.

Qu's objection to Chao's formulation of consonants is twofold. First,
Chao's portrayal of and distinction between compound consonants such
as *ts*, *tz*, *j*, *ch*, and *sh*, though rigorous, runs the risks of complying too much
with their pronunciation in English and turning the orthography into an
overly academic endeavor, unfit for a general audience. Second, Qu points
to GR's lack of consideration for the regional differences of dialects, high-
lighting his own project of Sin Wenz. As the "Second Form of the National
Alphabet," GR is designed to reflect Pekingese pronunciation and is closer
to northern dialects. Qu complains that the GR consonants, more often
than not, either fail to register the nuances and mutations of regional differences or impose dialectal idiosyncrasies of the north on other regions
of the country. He cites the example of retroflex sounds, explaining that
"regions of the Yangtze River—especially the provinces of Zhejiang and
Jiangsu, or even Fujian and Guangdong Provinces—have few or no retroflex
sounds" (220). Therefore, although it is important to mark the differences

of retroflex and nonretroflex consonants in northern dialects, it is equally important to accommodate partial and limited mastery of retroflex consonants for the benefit of southerners. Qu goes on to pick on two single vowels in GR, *e* and *u*, as well as diphthongs such as *au* and *ai*, arguing in general for a more systematic and simplified representation of speech sounds (223–25).[12]

Cautioning against unnecessary technicalities and arguing for simplicity and practicality, Qu then raises his key point of disagreement with GR—tonal expression. Affirming GR's value, especially the GR drama score and its use of "a music staff to mark tones," as "meticulous research," he contests that such pedantic practice "can neither be used to write everyday prose nor adopted by millions of people." He announces, "Therefore, we argue that expressions of tonal variations are not necessary" (226). Qu's proposition against tonal variation in spelling is in keeping with his stance on GR's use of consonants. Tonal relations in real speech do not lend themselves to accurate representations. Even GR's "tone-in-letter" method, albeit superior to the dogmatic diacritical marks, can at best approximate the four tones of Pekingese and could not fully capture how it sounds in real time and live conversations. The double notation of GR and the musical staff might have a chance at accuracy, but as Chao's *Last Five Minutes* demonstrates, both are too cumbersome to learn and promote. If tonal representation of Pekingese, which has one of the simplest tonal structures, is already a challenge, then it is even more unrealistic to expect satisfactory depictions of tonal variations in the majority of dialects across China, which invariably have more than four tones—seven or eight in Wu and Min dialects, nine in Cantonese, and up to ten in several Guangxi dialects. Taking seriously the vast variety of dialects and the pragmatics of speaking, Qu argues that "the orthography of the New Chinese Script should be simplified to the maximum degree" (226), while "the range of words to which we apply rules of tonal variation should be very limited and follow the general principle of 'if it can be avoided, then do not apply'" (233). In fact, between 1931 and 1932, different versions of the New Script increasingly simplified their representations of tonal variations. When the final *Draft of the New Chinese Script* came out in December 1932, all expressions of tonal variations and distinctions had been eliminated.

Qu does not fixate on minimizing tonal expression for the sake of argument. At the center of his reasoning and at the heart of Sin Wenz are two sides of the same coin—the Latinization movement's championing of dialect equality and its challenge to the hegemony of the national language. On both fronts, GR and Sin Wenz stand on opposite sides. Positioning Latinization as one of the more radical and progressive alphabetization movements, Qu asks the basic question, now that we are using an alphabetic script, which speech sound should be the standard for transcription? Unconvinced that GR's promotion of Pekingese as the new national language is the solution, for "in places where people from all over the country coexist, pure Pekingese is a rarity," and "if pure Pekingese spelling and pronunciation are forced upon people, the majority of them will probably feel gravely inconvenienced," Qu proffers an alternative: "We argue that it is better to adopt the pre-1925 national pronunciation for standardization" (228).

"The pre-1925 national pronunciation" referred to none other than the old national pronunciation, the artificial language that Chao unwillingly let go in the face of the strong argument for what Bernhard Karlgren called High Chinese Pekinese. It bears pointing out that GR, as an overly scholarly phoneticization system, could be used to transcribe any speech, which constituted the very basis of Chao's bid to alphabetic universalism. However, GR's official status and national recognition circumscribed its range of phonetic representation to the new national language of the Beijing dialect.[13] The irony was that as Chao and the Romanization movement moved away from their erstwhile position in support of the old and artificial national language, Qu and the Latinization movement returned to it and thus opened up new frontiers where linguistic equality, mass mobilization, and literary revolution awaited.

One of the new frontiers was Qu's attempt to rethink national language, by way of introducing the concept of the "common speech" (*putonghua* 普通話). This *putonghua*, which is not to be confused with present-day *putonghua*—the standardized national language of the People's Republic of China, based on Beijing and northern dialects—was, according to Qu, equivalent to "the pre-1925 national pronunciation" and had already been in use in major metropolises, where people from all over the country coexisted. This "hybrid Mandarin" (*lanqing guanhua* 藍青官話) was a welcome compromise among different linguistic groups, "has already become the de facto common speech," and will continue to evolve (228).[14] Constructing loose equivalences between the old national pronunciation, common speech, and hybrid Mandarin, Qu pits the common speech of *putonghua* against the hegemonic national language and envisions an ideal and new *putonghua* for all. This new common speech would no longer be a linguistic fairyland in which the old pronunciation reigned, only to be usurped by Pekingese; instead, it would be an egalitarian realm of linguistic heterogeneity and inclusiveness.

Latinization's commitment to linguistic heterogeneity was not nominal. For the first time in the Chinese script revolution, the argument was made for the legitimacy of using the same Roman-Latin alphabet to create different writing systems for various dialects. Qu writes, "We should accommodate the new alphabetic Chinese to ordinary readers. At the same time, any dialect, be it Beijing dialect, Guangzhou or Shanghai dialect, should be able to adopt the New Script or add adequate symbols in its transcription. If it is necessary, we can even design a special Guangzhou script and so forth" (674).

It seemed that dialects and their alphabetic inscriptions could finally coexist, not only among themselves but also alongside *putonghua*. Though Qu's own *Draft for the New Chinese Script* (1932) chose to transcribe the common speech of *putonghua*, which was based on the Beijing dialect but inclusive of southern dialects, numerous individuals and Latinization research societies localized Sin Wenz. During the fledgling period of Latinization between 1934 and 1937, more than ten dialects developed their own writing systems in accordance with the principles of Sin Wenz, covering big dialect groups such as the northern, Wu, Minnan, and Chaozhou, as well as Cantonese.[15] The chief historian of the Chinese Latinization movement, Ni Haishu, counted, though not exhaustively, eleven textbooks, eight books of bibliographies and references, nineteen introductory and theoretical books, and twenty-three primers within the short period of these three years, and at least thirty-six Sin Wenz periodicals—such as *Sin Wenz zhoukan* 新文字周刊 (New Script weekly), *Sin Wenz banjyekan* 新文字半月刊 (New Script bimonthly), and *Latinxua iangiu* 拉丁化研究 (Research of Latinization)—after the full outbreak of the Second Sino-Japanese War.[16] These journals, together with myriad Latinization publications, constituted a Sin Wenz archive, which has yet to be fully constructed and made sense of. It bears pointing out, however, that this body of Latinization literature consisted mainly of spelling schemes, teaching manuals, news reports, songs, correspondence, and transliteration-cum-translation of *baihua* literary writing, Lu Xun's short stories being some of the favorites among Sin

Wenz periodicals, as corroborated by Michael G. Hill's innovative study of a Sin Wenz version of Lu Xun's "Diary of a Madman"—the first modern Chinese short story.[17] Despite Hill's admirably executed rereading of the Sin Wenz translation as moving away from "the instrumentality of language" to focus on its "defamiliarized" formalistic attributes and experimental nature, the fact remains that the vast body of Sin Wenz literature was conceived less as literary creations than as literacy aids. This archive of Roman-Latin writings showcased the disconnection—rather than connection—between alphabetic Chinese and literary Chinese and has heretofore been taken as proof of the seemingly impossible convergence between the script revolution and literary revolution.

The unlikely convergence between the two revolutions—the main story of this chapter—became palpable when the script revolution underwent a popular, if not populist, makeover and evoked the power of the masses (*dazhong* 大眾). By rejecting the hegemony of "High Chinese" and reinforcing the right to phonetic representation for all dialects, the Latinization movement recognized those non-Pekingese-speaking, underprivileged, underrepresented people who presumably have no character literacy. Taken together, Latinization's minimalist style, simple orthography, and democratizing appeal created a narrative of emancipation and empowerment for all people and all local speech. Students of Sin Wenz sang "Songs of the New Script" in praise of the bond between the new Chinese alphabet and its people. As two examples of such songs—one in Shanghainese and the other in Cantonese—illustrate, the union between the masses and the new script disregarded people's age and rank but placed an emphasis on class.

"Song of the New Script" in Shanghai dialect

"Sin vensh gu"	「新文字歌」	"The Song of the New Script"
Sin vensh,	新文字，	The New Script,
Zen bhiedong,	真便當，	How convenient.
Hoqhuez shmu daq pin'in,	學會仔字母搭拼音，	Once you learn the alphabet and the spelling rules,
Koe s feq iao ngin siangbong,	看書勿要人相幫，	You can read books without asking others to assist.
Haeho tungtung siadeqceq,	閒話統統寫得出，	All conversations can be spelled and written,
Gung-nung huedeq zu venzong!	工農會得做文章！	Even workers and peasants learn to compose.[18]

The Cantonese version of "Song of the New Script"

"Sen menzi go"	『新文字歌』	"The Song of the New Script"
Sen menzi,	新文字，	The New Script,
Zen xae xou!	真係好！	How marvelous!
Mloen nei gei dai,	唔論你幾大，	No matter how grown-up you are,
Mloen nei gei lou,	唔論你幾老，	No matter how old you become,
Loenq-go yd,	兩個月，	In two months,
Bao nei xogdegdou . . .	包你學得到！ . . .	It is guaranteed that you will master it! . . .
Daiga jau zisig,	大家有知識，	Everybody has knowledge,
Daiga senqwad dou binxou!	大家生活都變好！	Everybody enjoys a better life![19]

The Latinization movement positioned itself as far as possible from a scholarly pursuit of alphabetic universalism or a literary experiment reinventing Chinese prose; instead, it was an alphabetization movement for "everybody," including and in particular "workers and peasants." The violence of phonocentrism seeking to eliminate characters was counteracted by its democratizing and revolutionizing impetus. This admirably inclusive phonocentrism prepared Latinization for its foray into adjunct movements of proletarian culture, mass education, and national salvation, as the following chapters show. Before the GMD's ban on Sin Wenz in 1936, Latinization's inclusive disposition was handsomely rewarded with unprecedented, nonpartisan, and high-profile support. One historic document attesting to the popularity and prestige enjoyed by the movement was a public letter issued by the Shanghai Chinese Latinization Research Society in December 1935 under the title "Our Opinion on the Promotion of the New Script (Sin Wenz)." It was cosigned by 688 leading Chinese writers, scholars, artists, and activists, including educators Cai Yuanpei and Li Gongpu, politicians Sun Ke and Liu Yazi, and writers Mao Dun, Guo Moruo, Ba Jin, Ye Shengtao, Tao Xingzhi, Xiao Hong, and Lu Xun. The letter recommended Sin Wenz—not GR—as the least-discriminating and "most economic" script for the task of "educating and organizing the people for the purpose of national salvation."[20]

Calling the Romanization movement and GR an enterprise suited for "the leisurely and the rich" and the indoctrination of a national language "an authoritarian rule of one particular dialect,"[21] the letter pinpointed the crucial differences between the two movements, on which Yuen Ren Chao was unwilling to elaborate. Aside from political antagonism between the GMD and the CCP, the Romanization and Latinization movements took opposite stances on the questions of tonal expression, common speech vis-à-vis national language, and the place of dialects. As the Romanization movement concerned itself with the Chinese claim to alphabetic universalism and the search for visible speech, Latinization prided itself on its commitment to linguistic and grammatological egalitarianism and its engagement with literary and political revolutions, all grounded in dialect representation, which had three historical precedents.

LATINIZATION PRECEDENTS

The first historical precedent of dialectal alphabetization flourished between the First Opium War and the early twentieth century. Inspired by seventeenth-century Jesuits' projects of Romanizing Chinese, Protestant missionaries—Joshua Marshman, Robert Morrison, Walter Henry Medhurst, Karl Gützlaff, and Thomas Barclay, to name a few—started to produce myriad Chinese Bibles translated in part or in full into either characters or the Roman-Latin alphabet. The character versions of the Chinese Bible were translated into classical Chinese (*wenli*), the literary or colloquial Mandarin (*guanhua*), or dialects.[22] Though the dialect translations of the Bible at the time was still in characters, they were sometimes used as phonetic symbols. Phoneticization continued to gather momentum, for if the Chinese people needed to hear "the Word of God in their mother-tongue," as the British Protestant missionary Marshall Broomhall put it, then "there must be translations into these dialects," and "the use of Romanized is necessary."[23] Missionaries' reports showed that, both for the purpose of proselytization and for anti-illiteracy initiatives, the Romanized dialect Bible functioned more effectively than the dialect Bible in characters, since the latter assumed basic character literacy and excluded illiterate people. As a result, versions of an alphabetic dialect Bible were developed in tandem with and as a crucial supplement to the character Bible. From the mid-nineteenth century to the early twentieth century, at least nineteen dialects were equipped with a corresponding alphabetic dialect Bible, including the northern dialect; several Wu dialects, such as Shanghai, Ningbo, and Hangzhou dialects; Cantonese; Hakka; and variations of the Fujian dialect, such as Fuzhou, Jianning, and Jianyang dialects; and the Amoy—commonly known as the Minnan—dialect.[24] The Minnan dialect, according to records of the American Bible Society, was not only the first for which was produced an alphabetic dialect Bible, as early as 1852, but also the dialect whose alphabetic Bible claimed the widest circulation. More important, this Bible and its literary reincarnation in Xu Dishan's novella *Yu Guan*, showcase both the promise and limit of dialect representation in modern Chinese writing.

The second source of dialectal representation can be traced to the origin of modern Chinese dialectology—the study of dialects. It departed from traditional scholarship on Chinese phonology and dialect studies done by Yang Xiong 扬雄, Hang Shijun 杭世駿, and Zhang Taiyan 章太炎, among others, and adopted a scientific approach to descriptive linguistics. The year 1924 was of particular importance, for while it marked the beginning of the official conversion to the new national pronunciation of Pekingese, it also witnessed the creation of the first dialect survey society—the Peking University Dialect Survey Society.[25] The state-sponsored Institute of History and Philology at Academia Sinica was founded in 1928 and went on to carry out six major dialect surveys: (1) the Guangdong and Guangxi dialects between 1929 and 1930; (2) the southern Shaanxi dialect in 1933; (3) the Anhui dialect in 1934; (4) the Jiangxi dialect in 1935; (5) the Hunan dialect in 1935; and (6) the Hubei dialect in 1936.[26] These surveys resulted in the first series of monographs on Chinese dialectology by Chinese scholars, including Yuen Ren Chao's *Studies of the Modern Wu Dialects* (1928), *The Dialect of Zhongxiang* (1939), *The Dialect of Zhongshan* (1948); Luo Changpei's *The Xiamen Sound System* (1931) and *The Sound System of Linchuan* (1941); Fang-Kuei Li's "Languages and Dialects of China" (1937); and a coauthored report titled *The Report of the Hubei Dialect Survey* (1948).[27]

Chinese dialectology was important because it situated the field within the development of historical and comparative linguistics on a global scale, which played a key role in asserting phonocentric dominance at the turn of the twentieth century. Further, it highlighted the question of temporality in reconstructing dialect kinship, which fed into the folkloric, anthropological, and colonial imagination of a linguistic other. More important, Chinese dialectology was crucial because it delineated the diverging trajectories of the Romanization and Latinization movements. For the Romanization movement, inasmuch as the codification of the new national language coincided with the birth of the first dialect survey society, the development of Chinese dialectology functioned as an indispensable supplement to the new national language. If dialectal differences could no longer seek accommodation in the national language, they could at least take refuge in dialect surveys, which simultaneously enabled a discourse of dialectal kinship, joined forces with folklore studies, and helped map out and paint portraits of linguistic and ethnic others in modern China. For the Latinization movement, the dialectal differences not only warranted representation (*Darstellung*); they demanded equality.

One central concern of dialectology is how synchronic linguistics and diachronic linguistics—per Saussure's definition—converge and construe a "historical science."[28] Inasmuch as dialect data can be read as amberlike records of the phonetic value of a given dialect at a particular static point, dialect variation across time and space enables inferences about historical change and can be used to test theories of dialectal kinship. The collection of synchronic linguistic data for diachronic linguistic studies constitutes the basic methodology shared by both historical and comparative linguistics, which is a two-step method: first, a phonetic description of the synchronic value of a chosen dialect or dialects; second, a diachronic comparison that sequences and deduces the dialectal kinship. In short, it is a method of description and comparison. As the American linguist Leonard Bloomfield observed, after its application to compare Sanskrit and European languages, this method led to the foundation of Indo-European linguistics, which established that "a number of languages of Europe and Asia are related" and that "these languages are divergent forms of an earlier uniform parent language."[29]

The first scholar to apply this two-step description-comparison method in the field of modern Chinese dialectology was Bernhard Karlgren. In his previously mentioned *Études sur la phonologie chinoise* (1915), translated into Chinese by Chao and Fang-Kuei Li, Karlgren professes that one of the top priorities of his pioneering reconstruction of Old and Middle Chinese was to show "how modern dialects were developed from 'Ancient Chinese.' "[30] To that end, Karlgren followed through with the two steps of description and comparison by first giving concrete phonetic value to more than thirty-one hundred characters as well as their respective rhyme categories using the Roman-Latin alphabet, and then conducting a systematic comparison of up to nineteen dialects, whose data were amassed during his own dialect survey in China between 1910 and 1912. *Études* thus constituted the first comprehensive investigation of Chinese dialects and philology, while producing, albeit controversially, a "necessary starting point" for the study of Old and Middle Chinese and their numerous dialectal descendants.

Karlgren incurred many criticisms, and *Études* went through many revisions.[31] Although the veracity of Karlgren's "Ancient Chinese" and his conflation of dialects when doing reconstruction were called into question, the fundamental method of description-comparison remained unchallenged and was enthusiastically adopted by Karlgren's critics and collaborators alike. For instance, Chao's own *Studies of the Modern Wu Dialects* could be construed as a response to Karlgren's *Études*. In a comparison between the two works, the linguist Mei Tsu-lin pointed out that dialect reconstruction should follow "regular procedures" that first reconstructed "the common Wu dialect, the common Cantonese, and the common Minnan dialect" before "reconstructing their common ancestor." Karlgren's hasty practice of conflating dialects from different dialect groups called for corrections, and Chao's book was one of the first steps, which "aimed at obtaining the firsthand material of the Wu dialects in order to reconstruct a common Wu dialect with a comparative method."[32]

The source of the contention was the specificity of dialect temporality. To wit, Karlgren's lack of discretion in distinguishing and maintaining the specific temporality that belonged to different dialects undermined his assertion of speech sound lineage. What Chao did in *Studies of the Modern Wu Dialects* was attempt to unpack the conflation, which narrowed the temporal gap between the individual dialects of disparate dialect zones and Middle Chinese via a study of modern Wu dialects. The reconstruction of the common Wu local speech served as a middle ground, upon which the linkage between Middle Chinese and individual dialects became more plausible. Similarly, the six aforementioned dialect surveys in Guangdong and Guangxi, Shaanxi, Anhui, Jiangxi, Hunan, and Hubei furthered the efforts of reconstructing models of common local speech at the level of dialect zones before recovering the ancestral and common language of Chinese.[33]

The mapping of dialect temporality was a form of "spatialization" of time, which undergirded the epistemological ground sanctioning the establishment of the "other" at the primitive end of history vis-à-vis the "self" in the superior modern present, as Johannes Fabian described in *Time and the Other*.[34] The dialect maps produced by the six dialect surveys carried out between 1929 and 1936 functioned, at least partially, as linguistic and anthropological projects of surveying, understanding, and containing the other.

The field of modern Chinese dialectology, on top of serving as a critical supplement to the newly established institution of national language, also provided the nascent nation-state with indispensable dialectal knowledge that simultaneously constructed and managed the linguistic others. As previous scholarship has demonstrated, a similar process took place around the same time in the field of Chinese folklore studies.[35] Both fields serviced the nation and enabled the discourse of "time and the other" by producing knowledge about the linguistic or ethnic others that belonged to a specific temporality, to be observed by an unmarked ethnographer, folklorist, and dialectologist. As the dialectologist gathered dialect data in the form of folk songs and folk stories, the folklorist needed an accurate linguistic description to record the collected materials usually executed in dialects. Their confluence was most fittingly marked when the journal *Folklore Weekly* published the manifesto of the Peking University Dialect Survey Society in 1924, which charted the new territories of dialectology as follows:

Aside from the study of word similarities or differences, the study of dialects should also include the migration of ethnicity and family, the linguistic nature of Miao and other minorities, the system of sound change from ancient times to present. Whenever we study a dialect, we must examine its background and history in order to understand its genealogy. Once we find a sound change, we must investigate its relationship with the sound of its neighboring dialects. In the case of languages of other ethnicities, for instance, Tibetan, Thai, etc., in spite of the absence of records regarding these languages in the classics, it does not hurt if we adopt the same comparative approach to understand their language systems before the Zhou and Qin dynasties. Therefore, dialect study in this day and age is inseparable from rhyme studies, colonial history, and the study of Indo-Chinese languages.[36]

At the center of this ambitious interdisciplinary field of modern Chinese dialectology was the comparative approach, which united synchronic and diachronic linguistics and opened up a nascent field to encompass all studies of and in relation to the "Indo-Chinese languages." This expansive category included, conspicuously, languages of other ethnicities, such as Tibetan, Thai, the Miao people, and other minority groups, the linguistic and ethnic others to which the society gave special attention.[37] The society's grand gesture to subsume all languages and dialects on the map of China under one umbrella of Indo-Chinese languages is in conformity with the disciplinary tradition of Indo-European linguistics and its way of making sense of languages, temporalities, and imagined communities. There is, however, another, more egalitarian—or at least more equalizing—approach that beckons a script revolution, to be followed by a literary revolution: the Latinization movement in the Soviet Union—the third and final precedent of the Chinese Latinization movement.

FROM SCRIPT REVOLUTION TO LITERARY REVOLUTION

Almost all accounts of the Soviet Latinization movement quote Lenin's declaration that "Latinization is the great revolution in the East."[38] Though it is debatable whether Lenin, who was reportedly already on his deathbed when singing the praises of Latinization, actually said the movement was a "great" one, what is indisputable is that the movement was a script revolution that led to a revolutionary movement of Proletkult (Пролеткýльт, "proletarian culture"). The Proletkult refers to a short-lived organization founded after the Bolsheviks took power in 1917, but the name is often used for the Proletarian Cultural Enlightenment (*kul'turno-prosvetitel'nye*) movements that marked the literary debates in the 1920s and early 1930s in the Soviet Union and influenced working-class culture around the world, including the development of the Chinese Latinization movement and the creation of Chinese revolutionary literature.[39]

The Soviet Latinization movement started in 1922 when an Azerbaijani political elite named Samed Agamali-Ogly initiated a campaign to Latinize the Turkic scripts. The Roman-Latin script was given equal status with Arabic in October 1923 and was made the only official script throughout Azerbaijan in 1924. A Turkological Congress in Baku followed in 1926, promoting the Roman-Latin alphabet outside Azerbaijan. By May 1930 thirty-six languages had adopted the new script. According to historian Terry Martin, in addition to the Turkic and North Caucasian peoples, three Mongolian nationalities took up the new script between 1929 and 1930: the Kalmyk, Buryat Mongols, and Mongols of the Soviet client state of Mongolia. These three peoples held their own miniature "pan-Mongol" summit in Moscow to unify their alphabets. Moreover, seven Iranian languages adopted the new alphabet, including the Mountain Jews of Dagestan and the Central Asian Bukharan Jews, both abandoning the Hebrew script. Though no concrete plan materialized, numerous Soviet Jewish organizations passed resolutions to Latinize Yiddish. The Assyrian and Armenian peoples also rejected the Cyrillic alphabet and the Armenian script in favor of the Roman-Latin script.[40] With the exception of the Georgian alphabet, almost all scripts in the Soviet Union—Russian Cyrillic included—experienced some form of shock therapy of Latinization.[41]

The Cyrillic alphabet, increasingly seen as the symbol of the "colonial, missionary russification policies of the Tsarist regime" and "a weapon of propaganda of Russian imperialism abroad," became the biggest stronghold blocking the complete victory of the Soviet Latinization movement.[42] Between November 1929 and January 1930, the script revolution of the Soviet Union reached its peak when the Russian Cyrillic alphabet took the hit. Under the tutelage of Anatoly Lunacharsky—the first Soviet people's commissar for education and a harbinger of the Proletkult, whom Qu Qiubai met with briefly during his first trip to the Soviet Union—three committees were formed within the Scientific Department of the Education Commissariat to reform the Russian writing system: one on orthography, another on spelling, and the third on the Latinization of the Russian alphabet.[43] Another special committee, overseeing the publication of reform materials and results, was established under the Council of Defense and Labor. The crusade against the Cyrillic alphabet came to a sudden halt on January 25, 1930, when the Politburo—the highest political organ in the Soviet Union— issued a terse resolution: "On Latinization: Order *glavnauka* to cease its work on the question of Latinizing the Russian alphabet."[44]

The Stalinization of the Soviet Union might have put a stop to the script revolution of the Cyrillic alphabet and raised questions about the pan-Turkish tendencies of Latinization activities in the western Soviet Union, but it did not stop the Latinization movement from flourishing in the East and spreading further east.[45] For instance, the Cyrillic used to inscribe the Mari language by the eastern Finns and the Chuvash language were Latinized; the same applied to Korean and Chinese.[46] According to John DeFrancis, as early as 1926 unsuccessful attempts had been made to Latinize the writing system of the Dungan people, who were Chinese Muslim emigrants. In late 1928 the Scientific Research Institute of China in Moscow formally took up the issue of alphabetizing Chinese.[47] Though somewhat confined to the eastern part of the Soviet Union, the Latinization movement fashioned itself as a liberation campaign of all small peoples from the old tsarist regime. The new Soviet Union was to underwrite their equal recognition, using one Roman-Latin alphabet, transcribing all local speech, and thus producing multiple writing systems. Such radical egalitarianism was a hallmark of the Soviet Latinization movement, and by extension the socialist revolution, and paved the way for its export to the rest of the world. By forging collaborative relationships with Soviet experts, the Chinese Latinization movement was ready to embrace its revolutionary ethos.

One of the most visible collaborations between Soviet Sinologists and Chinese scholars was carried out between Qu Qiubai and Vsevolod Sergeevich Kolokolov (V. S. Kolokolov). Qu addressed Kolokolov by his Chinese name, Guo Zhisheng 郭質生. Kolokolov was a Soviet linguist and Sinologist and became Qu's guide, interlocutor, and friend during Qu's first sojourn in the Soviet Union.[48] In October 1929 Qu, with the assistance of Kolokolov, published the first Chinese Latinization pamphlet, *The Chinese Latinized Alphabet* 中國拉丁化的字母, in Moscow, which was eventually published in revised form as *The Draft of the New Chinese Script* 新中國文草案 in December 1932.[49] In the preface of the first edition of *The Chinese Latinized Alphabet*, Qu credited Kolokolov's contribution to the project of Latinizing Chinese in Sin Wenz: "Wo bien zhé-ben siaocéz, dedao Kolokolof tonze di hydo banzhu, wo dueju ta feichań gansie" (In compiling this pamphlet, I have gained much help from Comrade Kolokolov. I thank him very much).[50] The relationship between Qu and Kolokolov resembled to some degree that between Bernhard Karlgren and Yuen Ren Chao, where a foreign expert and a Chinese scholar teamed up, but Qu's open recognition of Kolokolov suggested a stronger sense of camaraderie, with little hint of competition. Granted that the Romanization camp criticized the Sino-Soviet friendliness as a sign of Chinese submission to foreign interference,[51] Qu and Kolokolov took their Sino-Soviet collaboration as a concerted effort for—not a power struggle within—the collective enterprise of alphabetic universalism, which had come to be associated with a socialist, cultural, internationalist revolution. Soon after the First Conference on the Latinization of Chinese was held in Vladivostok in 1931, the proposed Latinization scheme based on Qu Qiubai's plan was adopted,[52] and it became compulsory to introduce the Chinese Latinized alphabet beginning in 1932 in all Chinese schools in the Soviet Union.[53] A year later the Chinese Latinization movement in the Soviet Union was finally exported to China. What was put in circulation, more than a Latinized script, was a new way of conceptualizing the linguistic and grammatological makeup of a new China and a new wave of the Chinese literary revolution. As the Latinization movement in the Soviet Union established the guiding principle of representing people in their own voices and giving all minority groups a script for their languages, it energized the making of proletarian culture and literature.

Between the composition of *The Chinese Latinized Alphabet* and *The Draft of the New Chinese Script*, Qu pondered the future of the Chinese writing system and Chinese literature. Immersed in the Soviet context and under the direct influence of Lunacharsky, Qu designed a future for Chinese languages, writing, and literature that increasingly resembled developments in the Soviet Union.[54] In a February 7, 1931, letter to Kolokolov, Qu wrote,

Now I am sending you a copy of *The Model Primer of Gwoyeu Romatzyh*. This primer is edited entirely in accordance with the National Romanization scheme adopted by the Nationalist government. It is much more complicated than our orthography and is utter Pekingese. . . . I think that we should still preserve and develop the common speech [*putonghua*] while creating new pinyin methods for dialects, thus making all of them "coexist." In the future when characters are completely eradicated, China will have to undergo a period of multilingualism, with multiple systems of writing. As for the four-tone notation, it is indeed a difficult issue, as exemplified by this primer. . . . What I ask of you is this: could you please mail me any pamphlet, monograph, or magazine on Latinization, as well as general books on linguistics, new or old literature, novels, and essays? I beg of you to take the trouble and help me with this matter. If you could mail them to me regularly, I shall be most grateful![55]

The telos of Latinization, as Qu acknowledges, is the coexistence of "multilingualism" and "multiple systems of writing" in China. Reaching out to Kolokolov for reading and research materials, Qu does not hesitate to admit that the realization of the telos of Latinization will be a Sino-Russian joint venture. Following the blueprint laid out by Soviet Latinization, either wittingly or not, the Chinese Latinization charter also envisions the unity of a single Chinese alphabet and a plurality of Chinese languages, writing systems, and peoples. By pitting "our orthography" of *putonghua* against the Nationalists' GR transcription of Pekingese, Qu commands Latinization's capacity enabling all dialects to "coexist," together with its prospects of bringing about a multilingual and multiscriptal China.

Within a few months, Qu would make explicit the connection between the new Chinese writing system and a new Chinese literary revolution in his article "War Outside the Gate of the Demons" (May 30, 1931). In this polemic, Qu defines three literary revolutions, the first two of which took place in the late imperial and May Fourth periods, respectively. Though avant-garde for their time, both have failed miserably, producing bad prose and "demonic speech." Qu is particularly vehement in his attack on the so-called new *baihua*—the proud production of the May Fourth and New Culture Movements—as an overly Europeanized language and hence a new *wenyan*—classical, literary, and presumably dead language—of the bourgeois elites. More than anything else, it deserves liquidation in order to usher in a new wave of literary revolution. Qu maintains that "the new Chinese script of the common speech [*putonghua*] should be customarily used by people all over China, reflecting the 'speech of humans' and should be multisyllabic, with word endings, and written in a Romanized alphabet. It is the task of the Third Literary Revolution that such a new Chinese script should be accomplished."[56]

Qu coined the term "Third Literary Revolution" to sever ties with linguistic and literary baggage from the "first" and "second" literary revolutions. That the term did not catch on mattered little to him, for, on the one hand, he soon coupled it with the more visible "massification" discussions and, on the other, made it abundantly clear that this New May Fourth Movement in the 1930s set itself apart from the two previous, failed attempts in one fundamental aspect: its alliance with the Latinization movement. Qu was confident that now that Latinization was on the horizon, any new and progressive literary revolution would need to associate itself with Sin Wenz. Inasmuch as Latinization would reinvent Chinese writing to transcribe a progressive *putonghua*—more suited to produce a new literary language for a new China—a successful Third Literary Revolution would help solidify the accomplishments of the script revolution. A reciprocal relationship binding the script and literary revolutions took shape.

Qu wasted no time in grafting his double revolution onto the massification (*dazhonghua* 大眾化) discussions, a definitive event that shaped the revolutionizing trajectory of 1930s culture and politics. Qu's participation in the discussions helped sharpen his already radical position and teased out the real politics in the creation of a true proletarian culture. Altogether, three rounds of massification discussions took place between 1930 and 1934. The first round coincided with the founding of the League of Left-Wing Writers in 1930, when the Chinese term *dazhong* 大眾—a returned Japanese kanji formulation—became hotly contested, for fear that this sweeping category would conflate the bourgeois hoi polloi with the real proletariat, thus depriving the working class of their chance at forging a culture of their own.[57] Two more rounds of discussions followed: the second in 1932, which was purportedly sparked by Qu's compositions; and the third in 1934, which, despite Qu's absence, was said to have derived the key term of *dazhongyu* 大眾語 (language of the masses) partly from Qu's previous contributions. Concrete topics that emerged from the discussions ranged from "who the masses are" to "should the masses write for themselves or have writers write for them," and from whether commercial literature and art could work for working-class culture—featuring an apology made by Lu Xun in defense of the comic strip—to how best to employ old-fashioned literary language and genres.[58] Granted that both the massification question and Latinization were powered by the same belief in the popular voice and everyone's right to representation and recognition, they remained two separate movements until Qu Qiubai's interventions. Between March and July 1932, Qu produced a cluster of articles—"The Question of Massification" (March 5), "Realistic Questions of Proletarian Mass Literature and Culture" (April 25), "Who Are 'We'?" (May 4), "Europeanized Literature and Art" (May 5), and "More on Mass Literature and Art, a Reply to Zhijing [Mao Dun]" (July 1932)—unequivocally binding the goal of creating a working-class culture with the means of the script revolution.[59]

Following his own thoughts on the May Fourth *baihua* being a "bastard" and finding the proposal to "massify proletarian literature and art" a preposterous oxymoron, Qu took a step beyond uniting the two revolutions of script and literature and toward revolutionizing the relationship between the intellectuals and their working-class counterpart in his exchange with Mao Dun.[60] A fellow traveler and supporter of both Latinization and massification, Mao Dun was of the view that intellectuals were better equipped to represent the working class than workers themselves, a view shared by the majority of more moderate leftist writers. Despite strong camaraderie between the two—after all, not long before this particular exchange, the two were busy discussing Mao Dun's soon-to-be-released epic novel *Midnight* (1933)—Qu remained unyielding in his opposition and asserted the proletarians' right to self-represent. He saw in the script revolution a real chance at finding the common language that afforded proletarians not only basic literacy but also literary and artistic self-representation. As a conclusion to his massification series, Qu stated in "More on Mass Literature and Art, a Reply to Zhijing" that "the goal of the new literary revolution is to create for the laboring masses' their own literary language."[61]

It should be clear by now that the commonly understood epochal "massification of literature and art" was directly linked to the Latinization movement, even if the link has not been taken seriously by scholars and was visible to no more than a handful of massification participants such as Qu Qiubai, Lu Xun, and the linguist Chen Wangdao. It is my intention to establish that the formidable motor directing the leftist turn of modern Chinese literature and culture beginning in the 1930s could locate its grammatological and linguistic engine in the Chinese Latinization movement; the admirably progressive transmutations of phonocentrism in turn provided theoretical footing to the most radical, if somewhat utopian, version of the Proletkult. For the first time in Chinese literary history, it became theoretically feasible and ideologically favorable to represent all dialect groups, literacy levels, and social strata and even let people, no matter their dialect groups, literacy levels, and social strata, represent themselves.

If Qu were to answer the classic postcolonial question of can the subaltern speak, the answer must have been a resounding yes with a Sin Wenz proposal for proletarians' self-representation. To be clear, in a perfect world where subalterns can speak and be heard, there would be no room for *Vertretung* but only *Darstellung*, and in fact *Selbstdarstellung* (self-representation), following Marx's distinction as relayed by Gayatri Spivak.[62] It is then a fair question to ask if Qu put his affirmative answer into action. The closest he ever came to a literary composition under his own Latinization guidelines was perhaps a Shanghainese-Pekingese double edition of a poem titled "The Japanese Sent Troops" (September 1931), written under a pseudonym and in characters.[63] Unfortunately, as a high-ranking CCP official, albeit sidelined by the time of the flurry of his massification articles, his literary and cultural work was suspended when he was ordered to go to the Jiangxi–Fujian Soviet in January 1934. Between the second round of massification discussions in 1932 and Qu's eventual capture and execution by the GMD in 1935, he was not able to either carry out further experiments himself or coach workers to produce Sin Wenz literature. If

Qu proclaimed the possibility of practicing phonocentric empowerment without exploring in depth its literary implementation—though to my knowledge no Sin Wenz advocate has successfully addressed the question, which would have amounted to the triumphant closure of the double revolution of script and literature—then it is Qu's friend Xu Dishan 許地山 (1894–1941) who found himself, perhaps unwittingly, in a formidable challenge of representing and empowering the subaltern under the Latinization and massification principles. In a novella about a subaltern woman, whose livelihood depends on her alphabetic Bible, Xu Dishan, a Latinization advocate and an accomplished novelist and scholar, tried his hand at answering the difficult question, can the real voice of the masses—both literally and figuratively—be represented?

THE LIMITS OF PHONOCENTRISM

Xu Dishan and Qu Qiubai were decadelong friends. Their first contact dated to 1920, when both started writing social commentaries for the journal *New Society* (*Xin shehui* 新社會), published by the Students Social Club (Shijin Hui 實進會) under the Beijing YMCA.[64] Although Qu chose a political path and Xu adhered to a scholarly and literary one, their friendship lasted beyond their *New Society* phase until Qu's capture by the GMD in 1935. Xu and others led an active campaign to rescue Qu, which ended in failure and Qu's martyrdom.

In his own right, Xu Dishan was an essential figure in the May Fourth and New Culture Movements and was among the twelve founding members of the first modern Chinese literary society—the Literary Research Society (Wenxue Yanjiu Hui 文學研究會)—in early 1921.[65] It is worth noting that the Literary Research Society was one of the more realist-oriented literary societies, in contrast to the more Romanticist-inclined groups such as the Creation Society and the Crescent Moon. Accordingly, Xu's oeuvre largely fit the parameters of realism, though some critics have suggested that his earlier work aligned more closely with Romanticism and classicism before his turn to more hard-core realism. As a native of Taiwan who grew up in Fujian and Guangdong Provinces and had extensive overseas experiences in Myanmar and India, Xu had a unique and lasting interest in southern China and South Asia, which proved to be his most distinctive trademark as a writer. In addition to his literary career, Xu was a teacher of

Sanskrit, a folklorist, translator, and educator, who created from scratch the Chinese department at Hong Kong University. A Christian himself, he was an accomplished scholar of several religions, including Manichaeism, Daoism, Buddhism, and Christianity. He also maintained a consistent research interest in material culture, such as Chinese costumes and ancient coins. Last but not least, as a cofounder of the Hong Kong New Script Learning Society 香港新文字學會 in 1938, Xu remained until his death in 1941 a steadfast advocate for the Chinese Latinization movement.

Between March and May 1939, Xu published his last novella, *Yu Guan* 玉官, which was serialized in the Hong Kong–based journal *Da feng* 大風.[66] It was a story of the life journey of a "Bible woman" called Yu Guan. Bible women were female converts who were trained by Protestant missionaries to become lay church workers in India, China, and other parts of the world. The basic duty of these "woman evangelists" was "going from house-to-house and reading the Bible to those who will listen," but they would also be trained to "lead meetings of Christian women, teach classes of inquirers, visit women in their homes, and sometimes in the country districts even take part in the preaching at markets and on village streets."[67] The Bible woman Yu Guan serves her community in a small county in southern Fujian, approximately where Xu Dishan himself grew up. The novella spans more than forty years, from the 1890s to the late 1930s, encompassing major historical events within that period, such as the First Sino-Japanese War, the Boxer Rebellion, the abolishment of the civil-service exam, the 1911 Revolution, World War I, and the rise of communism. An attempt to capture modern Chinese history mediated through and encapsulated in the life story of a Bible woman from Fujian, *Yu Guan* was arguably the most ambitious work Xu ever produced and marked a decided change of style. In an appraisal of Xu Dishan and his early works, C. T. Hsia asserts that Xu was "by temperament" "a writer of Romance," with his earlier fiction aligning closer to "popular Buddhist tales and medieval Christian legends."[68] According to Zheng Zhenduo, Xu's lifelong friend and a cofounder of the Literary Research Society, the shift in style took place around 1935, when Xu relocated from Yenching University in Beijing to Hong Kong. In Zheng's estimation, "Works that [Xu] produced in this period became sharper and more realist in terms of style and the choice of materials."[69]

To be clear, "this period" that Zheng refers to was the period of the Third Literary Revolution, the one that was fueled by and in turn fomented the

Chinese Latinization movement. Xu himself, in an article called "On 'Anti–New Romanticism' " written around this period, stated his objections:

The reason that the works of some young writers fall back into the paradigm of Romanticism should be attributed to the fact that their tools of expression—their language and their approach—still belong to the leisure class. . . . Therefore, to change one's style, one has to first make the language clear so that the meaning can be comprehended. Those who can make their language clear naturally understand the reality better and have the potential of opening a new path for the people.[70]

Xu's objection to the language of the leisure class echoes Qu Qiubai's critique of the May Fourth *baihua* as a new bourgeois *wenyan*, while the connection he makes between a clearer language and a better understanding of reality reflects the "goal of the new literary revolution," as Qu puts it. Although Xu himself did not explicitly mention the Third Literary Revolution, he did compose a series of articles and speeches discussing its two tenets—the new Chinese script and new Chinese literature—after his relocation to Hong Kong. Making reference to the issues of script and literary revolution, these articles were all written around the same time that Xu produced *Yu Guan*.[71] Whether intentionally or not, *Yu Guan*, the choice of the protagonist—a subaltern woman—and Xu's decision to include the issue of the script bear the historical imprint of massification and reflect the impact of the convergence of the script and literary revolutions.

The novella's eponymous heroine, Yu Guan, is an illiterate woman from southern Fujian who loses her husband in the First Sino-Japanese War. She struggles as a widow against poverty and molestation by her brother-in-law, who covets the family compound. Her sole hope is to follow the path of (neo-)Confucian widowhood, to bring up her son to become a scholar-official, who would in turn establish a chastity memorial arch for her. Under the influence of a friend, Xing Guan 杏官, a local Bible woman, Yu Guan discovers and learns to read the alphabetic Minnan Bible, converts to Christianity, and becomes a Bible woman herself. In a third-person narrative, Yu Guan encounters the Bible at Xing Guan's house:

There was not much furniture in Xing Guan's two-bedroom house, but everything in it was spick-and-span. In the living room there was a picture from *The Pilgrim's Progress* hanging in the middle of the wall, and on the desk there was a very thick

Bible of the Old and New Testaments with gilt edges and a black lambskin cover. Much of the gilt had already turned dark red, and the leather had also lost its sheen. Its dog-eared corners, as well as the slips of paper sticking out as markers, showed only too well that the owner of the book must consult it several times a day. . . . She secretly opened the Bible and sneaked a glance or two. It was a pity that it was all in a foreign alphabet, which made no sense to her. She thought to herself: Xing Guan speaks no foreign languages, so how could she read foreign books? She had to ask, and Xing Guan told her that this was "*baihua* script," which one could learn to read in three days, learn to write in seven, and use to express freely one's mind in ten. Xing Guan encouraged Yu Guan to give the new script a try. For days on end, Yu Guan chanted "A, B, C" as though they were a kind of incantation. It really worked! In seven days, she could read the thick book as fluently as running water.[72]

Though a combined alphabetic Minnan Bible of both the Old and New Testaments has not been found, two separate alphabetic Bibles in Minnan dialect surfaced during my archival research at the American Bible Society. Both the Old Testament (1902) and the New Testament (1916)—translated and transcribed as "Kū-Iok" and "Sin Iok," respectively, in Minnan dialect— were commissioned by the British and Foreign Bible Society (figures 2.1 and 2.2). Not unlike Xing Guan's Bible, the two Minnan Bibles were bound originally with "gilt edges and a black lambskin cover," while "much of the gilt had already turned dark red, and the leather had also lost its sheen." These and similar versions of the Minnan Bible granted women like Yu Guan true access to literacy, with indelible mediation through the power of religion.

By training illiterate female converts to aid their evangelical and social gospel missions, Protestant missionaries highlighted the issue of gendered illiteracy in less-developed regions, nineteenth-century China included. If a large part of the Chinese population at the time remained illiterate, an even bigger percentage of women were denied access to literacy in all forms. More often than not, reports, pamphlets, and fiction written by missionaries about female converts, as well as Bible women, began with the issue of gendered illiteracy.[73] The introduction to literacy adopting either characters or the Roman-Latin alphabet was, in most cases, the prerequisite for the indoctrination of Protestant gospel. Early missionary fictions about Bible women featured the teaching of the Latin alphabet.[74] For example, in *Leng Tso*—one of the first novels about a Chinese Bible woman—the protagonist Leng Tso begins her address to her audience by preaching how "the

FIGURE 2.1. Minnan Bibles: Old Testament (1902) at bottom, New Testament (1916) above. Photo courtesy of the American Bible Society Library and Archives, New York.

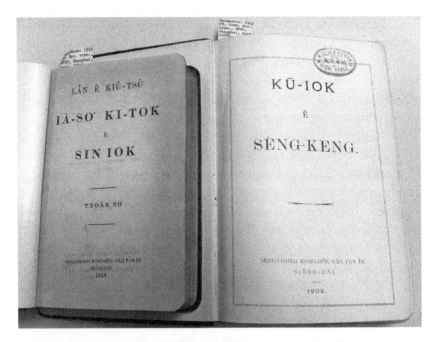

FIGURE 2.2. Sin Iok (New Testament) and Kū-Iok (Old Testament) in Minnan dialect. Photo courtesy of the American Bible Society Library and Archives, New York.

small characters" of the Roman-Latin alphabet can help you "read every book written with them." Challenging the patriarchal monopoly over literacy, she poses rhetorical questions to her audience of presumably illiterate women: "Because we were not taught to read, shall the girls of the present time be compelled to grow up in ignorance? Because mothers were not taught, shall girls never be allowed to learn to read the Bible?" The alphabetic Bible functions first and foremost as a new technology to have "girls read"—a symbol of a feminist will to literacy and enlightenment—before it serves to spread Protestant gospel, or to call into question neo-Confucianist teachings.[75] A thematized staple since one of the earliest novels involving Bible women, the alphabetic Bible takes on new valence in Xu Dishan's magnum opus as it is thrust into the new literary revolution.

The Minnan dialect Bible functions in *Yu Guan* neither merely as a token of feminist literacy nor as only a metonym for Yu Guan's newfound religion, with which she has a fraught relationship at best. More significant, the alphabetic Minnan Bible serves as a narrative device that plays a part in every twist of the plot. It is only after Yu Guan learns to read the Bible that she can afford to put her son through a Western education and leave the family compound for a residency in the church. She thus successfully dodges her brother-in-law, who in turn steals Xing Guan's eldest daughter, flees the county, and later returns as a Communist Party member working for the regional Soviet government. Yu Guan, now a Bible woman, takes the alphabetic Bible with her whenever she goes on field trips. She develops a romantic attachment to a peddler named Chen Lian 陳廉, whom she meets in a neighboring village. Yu Guan does not find out until much later that Chen is in fact Xing Guan's husband, who has had to run away from home for offenses committed against missionaries. Chen teaches Yu Guan that carrying only the alphabetic Minnan Bible is not enough and that she needs a copy of *The Book of Change* 易經 in addition to ward off the country ghosts. The Bible also proves useful when Yu Guan stops a group of Communist soldiers, who have taken over the county, from harassing local women, by preaching the gospel to them. Yu Guan then goes to Nanjing to live with her son—now a returned student from the United States and an official in the Nationalist government in Nanjing. He has remarried, after his first wife—Xing Guan's younger daughter—dies. His second wife happens to be Xing Guan's elder daughter, whom he meets while in the United States. Before long Yu Guan finds Nanjing disagreeable, experiences a religious epiphany, and decides to return to Fujian and starts serving her community with newfound piety. The narrative comes to a terse end when Yu Guan takes off to Southeast Asia (Nanyang 南洋) to find Chen Lian. Together with her Bible and *The Book of Change*, she fades into the southern seas, taking the story with her.[76]

If the alphabetic dialect Bible is present in every step of the plot development, so is Yu Guan's ambivalence toward Christianity. She becomes a Bible woman partially, if not mostly, for her own and her son's livelihood. She is unconvinced—and remains so till the very end of the story—of the "Christian ideal" and keeps her ritual of ancestral worship. Her syncretic and pragmatic view on religion allows room for *The Book of Change* and her romantic encounter with Chen Lian. Finally, the recognition she receives for her forty years of service is a commemorative bridge, resembling in shape the neo-Confucian chastity arch that she never gets. Critics of *Yu Guan* have been heretofore largely and rightfully attracted to the question of religion—the murky boundaries between Confucianism, ancestral worship, and Christianity, the troubled encounter of the East and West, invoking the seventeenth-century Chinese Rites Controversy all over again.[77] The question of religion, specifically Yu Guan's question for Christianity, remains an unresolved enigma, as hastily concluded as the narrative of the novella. Xu Dishan's narrator gives full volume to Yu Guan's inner thoughts doubting her faith:

She could not see the meaning of the "Christian ideal." What she wanted was still the "realistic." To have the respect and compliments of one's friends and relatives while living, and to enjoy posthumous fame after one passed, that should be what life was all about. Although she was treading the heavenly path, she was, in fact, looking for a worldly way that would take her to that end. She was not sure she was on the right track. She was afraid that her old age might be terribly lonely and miserable, since both her son and daughter-in-law were so cold to her, and she did not believe that one could live in this world all by oneself. Of the six blessings in this world—wealth, position, fortune, longevity, prosperity, and peace—one should try to procure at least one.[78]

Following this inner monologue, Yu Guan decides to quit her position and proposes to Chen Lian, who agrees to elope with her to Southeast Asia but unwittingly reveals his identity as Xing Guan's lost husband. Although she does not go through with her plan, Yu Guan remains uncommitted to her faith until her sudden embrace of a "truer" form of Christianity. In stark contrast to Yu Guan's conflicted faith that the narrator makes the reader privy to, her religious epiphany is announced by the narrator in one sentence: "She wanted to go back to the country to start a genuine missionary life."[79] Xu's imbalanced portrayal of Yu Guan's religious growth, arguably the central question of the novella, sits at odds with Xu's ambition and accomplishments, the richness of the story, as well as an otherwise poised narrative voice. This overlooked but jarring incongruity in treating the religion question, I suggest, embodies a narratological conundrum brought about by allegiance to phonocentrism, exposing its inherent limits.

For a novella born in the age of the Third Literary Revolution that champions localized and common speech over writing, this novella is strangely silent. The narrator, taking a third-person perspective, maintains throughout the novella a highly controlled narrative voice to the extent of eliminating nearly all conversations.[80] Lest the characters wrest control from the narrator and impinge on the plotline, the narrative voice maintains full control by using indirect speech, direct psychological depiction, and free indirect speech. For instance, the passage of Yu Guan's doubts on the Christian ideal just quoted shifts back and forth between direct psychological depiction and free indirect speech, but it does not slide into direct representation to let the Fujian woman speak for herself. The irony is that for a major piece of literature that aims to represent and empower a subaltern woman, Xu's narrator ends up depriving the protagonist of her own voice, the only known occurrence in Xu's entire oeuvre. Such treatment runs the risk of contradicting Xu's intention and his past practice, where other subaltern women, such as protagonists in "Chun Tao" and "The Merchant's Wife," have no trouble speaking in their own voices. It also throws in jeopardy Xu's own position on dialects in literature, which he laid out in an early 1921 essay, in which Xu argues that "it matters little for a piece of literary work when it comes to the questions such as in what dialect [方言] it is written or to what extent it involves what kind of dialect. As long as it conveys the author's meaning, it should be fine. Critics ought not to find it necessary to pick on slang and inelegant expressions but should note that sometimes truth comes from slang."[81] Given Xu's commitment to representing dialect in literature, Yu Guan's dialect, slang, and inelegant expressions, if any, should have no difficulty in making their way into Xu's narrative. However, what prevents the narrator from giving the heroine her true voice is precisely Xu's commitment and sensitivity to realist representation of local speech, now highlighted by the alphabetic Minnan Bible. The irredeemable conflict between phoneticization and literary narrative voice is most salient at the moment when the narrator takes readers through Yu Guan's misery in her son's house in Nanjing, right before she experiences her religious epiphany:

Since there was no genuine affection between the mother and daughter-in-law, An Ni [the daughter-in-law] and Yu Guan would sometimes sit face-to-face for a whole day without exchanging a word. An Ni always spoke in English to Jiande [Yu Guan's son], which was completely incomprehensible to Yu Guan. On the other hand, Yu Guan spoke to Jiande in their native speech, which was alien to An Ni. This [situation of noncommunication] naturally increased their mutual suspicion. . . . For the old lady living in an alienating city, even if she wanted to tell someone her grievances, there was nobody around to listen. When she went to church, her fellow church members could not understand her words; the minister couldn't give her any advice except to try to adapt to things and be more accepting. Yu Guan was so fed up that she stopped going to church.[82]

To Yu Guan, Nanjing is an alienating place, and that is not, as C. T. Hsia diagnoses, because Yu Guan is "a total stranger" to her son and daughter-in-law's "Westernized bourgeois ways."[83] Nor is it mainly because she does not get along with her second daughter-in-law, for she has trouble with the first one as well without experiencing a religious epiphany and relocating to the southern seas. Yu Guan's alienation stems from, as the narrator tells us, "her words," which could not be understood, either by her church members or by anyone outside the Minnan linguistic zone. Insofar as Yu Guan's literacy functions only in a specific Minnan environment—one of the most difficult topolects in China—she loses literacy and functionality as soon as she is uprooted. If Yu Guan's church members in Nanjing could not understand "her words," neither could the readers who do not have a working knowledge of the Minnan dialect. If Xu Dishan were to truthfully represent Yu Guan's speech, regardless of whether in alphabet or in characters, a good majority of his readers could not have comprehended it. The crux is thus the incompatibility between the spoken language of Minnan and a written language of *baihua*. As long as the narrative voice is written in *baihua*, the phoneticization of the Minnan dialect is decidedly ill-fated, though it is a fundamental reality to both Yu Guan and the dialect Bible. In order not to jeopardize the cohesive narrative of *Yu Guan*, which is meant to empower the Bible woman, Yu Guan herself has to be silenced, her speech translated into and mediated through *baihua*, turning into a form of *erlebte Rede* (experienced speech). The Bible woman, instead of gaining her own voice ends up forfeiting the right to speak directly. This fundamental incompatibility points to the nature of *baihua*, the foundation of modern Chinese literature, as a written language or a writing system rooted in the Chinese script. In the age of global phonocentrism, the expansive concept of *baihua*—encompassing the old *baihua*, the May Fourth new *baihua*, and the alphabetic dialect *baihua*—becomes the conceptual meeting point of the script and literary revolutions. However, even as *baihua* aspires to become fully radicalized during the Third Literary Revolution as a new literary language of the masses, written in an alphabetic script and transcribing all dialects, its remnants—in fact, essence—as a written language grounded in characters resists the full materialization of such a fantasy, as well as its revolutionary impulses.

As *Yu Guan* testifies, phonocentric antinomies—its utopian vision and sweeping violence, its democratizing gestures and involuntary self-restraint—not only bring together the two revolutions of script and literature but also take over phonocentrism itself. Yu Guan's muted voice speaks to how the revolutionary side of phonocentrism is at once the source of the generative power that gives the Bible woman hope as well as the thwarting constriction that deprives her of her voice. In sustaining the reign of phonocentrism, its loyal vanguards are tasked with finding permissible transmutations. In reconciling dialect phoneticization and the *baihua* narrative, the liberating tendency of phonocentrism needs outlets other than a dogmatic execution of alphabetic transcription of speech sound. One way taken up by left-leaning writers was to put the Chinese alphabet on hold while allowing the domination of speech over writing to morph into the creation and liberation of voices, more often than not figuratively, in revolutionary literature, socialist realism, and proletarian culture in general. The promise to give voice to all takes on a thematic spin in seeking representations—both *Vertretung* and *Darstellung*—of the silenced, marginalized, and underrepresented women, children, and working class, among others, while carefully walking the line between character literacy and phonocentric aspirations. As it achieves domination in both script and literary revolutions, phonocentrism no longer needs to take the particular Roman-Latin form but finds it useful to hold out for the eventual advent of the Chinese alphabet.

The processes of phonocentric transmutations also embody, on the elemental and concrete level of script, what Marston Anderson calls limits of realism. As Anderson masterfully diagnoses, the limits of realism in the modern Chinese novel stem in part from the gap between realism's perceived power for social change and its "true nature" gradually discovered by its Chinese converts as more of "an aesthetic withdrawal than an activist engagement in social issues."[84] Similarly, the limits of phonocentrism, or rather phonocentric realism, stem from the radical promise of voice for all and the gradual realization that as long as the conjunction of script and literary revolutions operates in a *baihua* mode, the honorable pursuit of the popular voice will be inevitably compromised. Writers committed to both revolutions will be ineluctably confronted with the tension and incompatibility between the two. Compelled to make a decision, writers need to strike a balance between the degree of transparent speech representation and the integrity of a narrative written in characters. In determining the level of phoneticization—in the extreme case of *Yu Guan*, none at all—Xu and others are, perhaps not self-reflexively, engaged in the negotiation of what is the representable real, while testing the narratological, linguistic, and political limits of the modern Chinese literary language.[85] To be caught between the two revolutions, their liberatory intentions and constricting productions, is to attempt a resolution of phonocentric antinomies, a reconciliation between phonocentrism and national literature, while striving for the maximum degree of linguistic and grammatological progressiveness. The next two chapters account for two more cases of negotiations and transmutations of the phonocentric dominance—first in a redefinition of *baihua* emerging from the Chinese labor corps in the first modern Chinese literacy program in World War I France, and second in the liquidation of the nature of *baihua* and the rediscovery of the image of children in World War II China. Granted that the three transmutations—Latinization and the Third Literary Revolution, the May Fourth *baihua* discourse, and the New Mass Education movement—are in fact three compromises of the purest form of phonocentrism, its domination continues.

Chapter Three

CAN SUBALTERN WORKERS WRITE?

Still today intelligent men confuse language and writing.

—SAUSSURE, *COURSE IN GENERAL LINGUISTICS*

In fact, the deader the written language—the farther it was from speech—the better: in principle everyone has access to a pure world of signs.

—BENEDICT ANDERSON, *IMAGINED COMMUNITIES*

On May 4, 1941—the twenty-second anniversary of the May Fourth Movement—Xu Dishan gave a talk on the meaning of the movement. As one of the three thousand students who gathered at Tian'anmen Square in protest against the Treaty of Versailles, Xu informed his audience that meaningful celebrations of that momentous Sunday should focus on inheriting the May Fourth legacy. One important aspect of it was the pursuit of "alphabetic Chinese." For Xu, not only was the "progress of the Chinese nation" dependent on "reforming the Chinese script," the reform should not stop with "the national alphabet" (*zhuyin fuhao*) and could succeed only with the implementation of "the Roman-Latin alphabet" (*pinyin zi*).[1]

Departing from the common understanding of the impact of the May Fourth Movement on modern Chinese language and literature, which focused on the establishment of *baihua* (plain speech),[2] Xu Dishan articulated its radical, fundamental, but forgotten mission—a phonocentric pursuit to be materialized in the concrete form of the Roman-Latin alphabet—without any mention of *baihua*. Adding this omission to Xu's speech, the second and perhaps more lasting transmutation of the Chinese script revolution surfaces: the May Fourth *baihua* discourse. This *baihua*, following a trend of what Theodore Huters calls the simplification of *wen*,[3] had three important attributes that differentiated it from previous genres of oral literature in the Chinese tradition: first, it was a colloquialized written language (*yutiwen* 語體文) with the promise of further colloquialization until full phoneticization, or the unification of speech and writing; second, it was a scientific language, not only compatible with modern epistemology and technologies but also scientifically—in fact, statistically—measured, constructed, and experimented on; and third, it built support mechanisms ranging from small-scale literacy programs to mass-education movements and state-sponsored curricula of national language and literature. The May Fourth *baihua* discourse presents a new linguistic, literary, and pedagogical reality on the one hand and, on the other, creates a new dichotomy between itself and *wenyan* (classical and literary language), which pugnaciously defined the contours of the traditional episteme and proactively sought Chinese literary and cultural modernity. Marked by phonocentric antinomies, the May Fourth *baihua*'s violent attack on the old language, literature, and philosophy was to be compensated by the promise of the modern, granted that *baihua*'s progressive connotations of equality, liberation, and self-expression were not without their limits. A resounding success, the May Fourth *baihua* almost completely effaced the script revolution as both its driving force and its endgame, if it were not for the occasional reminder from May Fourth veterans such as Xu Dishan.

The first test run of the May Fourth *baihua*—the advocacy of a colloquialized written language, the statistical method in determining its vocabulary, and its application in the first modern Chinese literacy program—took place in close affinity to the origin of the May Fourth Movement. Between 1916 and 1918 a rough estimate of between one hundred forty thousand and two hundred thousand Chinese laborers—most of them illiterate peasants from Shandong, Fujian, and Zhejiang Provinces—were recruited by the Allies and sent to Europe; the majority were stationed in France. The presence of these laborers in World War I was the precondition that enabled the Chinese Beiyang government's ill-fated participation in the postwar peace negotiations, which led to the May Fourth demonstrations. Between these Chinese laborers and one particular volunteer sent by the YMCA named James Yen 晏陽初 (Yan Yangchu, 1893–1990), the first modern Chinese literacy program emerged in World War I France.[4] This chapter examines the question of writing as a technology for wartime long-distance communication, a medium for experimenting on the staple of the modern Chinese language, and a forum where Chinese elites and laborers negotiated their subjectivities in a moment of postwar reflection. I start by surveying the program under which laborers came to be recruited by the Allies. I explore how writing was configured to support the Allied war efforts, and why it became central to the laborers' everyday experience in the war. By closely reading writings produced during the actual literacy program, I delineate the process through which the colloquialized written language penned by both the laborers and James Yen became incorporated retrospectively into the May Fourth *baihua* discourse for its appeal of pure orality. Finally, I ponder the limits of the positive phonocentrism, now resurfaced in the context of the May Fourth *baihua* and a particular version of the Chinese enlightenment. Inasmuch as the *baihua* discourse showcased the power of phonocentrism, it also reprised its limits when it simultaneously empowered and marginalized laborers by inviting them to speak and write and managing how they did so. Although laborers' voices—in both their choice of the written language and their critical stance on the war—were overtaken by those of their intellectual counterparts, one invaluable piece of a laborer's writing corroborated that the subaltern laborers, not unlike their intellectual counterparts, drove home the critique of the Great War and the Chinese enlightenment.

MAY FOURTH, WAR, AND LITERACY

It is not news that Chinese workers labored overseas. For centuries, Chinese coolies worked in Mexican silver mines, laid American railroads, and travailed in the South African gold rush.[5] But that Chinese laborers participated in World War I is a less-known story. As Cai Yuanpei, then president of Peking University, put it in a rallying speech commemorating the end of World War I, "Amongst us four hundred million Chinese, who else but the 150,000 laborers in France has engaged directly in the war?"[6] These laborers constituted, in fact, the Chinese bid for the return of the German leasehold territory in the Jiaodong Peninsula, then occupied by the Japanese. Were it not for the laborers, Chinese diplomat Wellington Koo would not have had the chance to make a plea in Paris for the return of the Chinese territory. The conference's decision to permit Japan's seizure of Qingdao, despite the laborers' presence and performance in the war as part of the Allied forces, was therefore interpreted as a betrayal, "a dagger at the heart of China,"[7] and ignited widespread fury across the country.

Despite the laborers' historic role in the May Fourth Movement and World War I and being hailed by Cai as "sacred, the laborers,"[8] generations of historians have largely left out their story. Canonical studies on May Fourth—such as Tse-Tsung Chow's *The May Fourth Movement* and Vera Schwarcz's *The Chinese Enlightenment*—affirm the causal relationship between the war and the movement but invariably overlook the laborers and their experience in the war.[9] The May Fourth Movement, one of the most important political, intellectual, and literary landmarks in modern Chinese history, is thus generally subsumed under a narrative of intellectual history. Fabio Lanza's exemplary study on the emergence of the student figure during the movement corroborates such a tendency.[10] Aside from the lack of primary materials from the laborers' sojourn in Europe, Paul Bailey speculates that the systematic oversight of these workers is partly owing to the interpretation of indentured labor in the war as but another episode in the Western exploitation of China; partly, too, the laborers' story has also been eclipsed by the contemporaneous, high-profile work-study program of the 1920s in France.[11] Be that as it may, even when historians do pay attention and homage to laborers in World War I, the workers have remained marginal to the May Fourth Movement and irrelevant to reflections on the war.[12] They either constituted "an important and significant aspect of China's twentieth-century labour history"[13] or shed "important new light on the history of emigration."[14] Xu Guoqi characterizes the significance of the laborers' presence and participation in the war as providing "a critical tool" to the Chinese diplomats at the Peace Conference arguing "for recognition, inclusion on the world stage, and internationalization."[15] Subsequently, the May Fourth Movement "grew from the many Chinese elite groups' disillusionment with the Western powers."[16] It seemed as though the "sacred laborers," once saluted, were ushered out of the narrative in both official and scholarly accounts of the movement. By focusing on the question of writing, I aim to write the workers back into the historical narrative that connects China, World War I, and May Fourth, for the substantial connections between the laborers' wartime experience and their contribution to May Fourth can be best located in the laborers' writing activities and the primary writings that emerged from their European sojourn.

The program that recruited the laborers was called Laborers as Soldiers, adopted in May 1916 as a compromise between an eager Beiyang government and the reluctant Allies. From the onset of the war, the Beiyang government had made repeated attempts to send troops and arms to the Allies in hopes of reinventing itself during the postwar peace negotiations. The Allies, however, adamantly refused a direct Chinese military presence, fearful of having to grant China postwar trophies as well as of causing complications with Japan, which was one of the allies under the Anglo-Japanese Treaty of Alliance (1902).[17] It was not until late 1915, when the French and British armies had to square with a growing labor shortage, that the scheme of Laborers as Soldiers was put back on the table.[18] Instead of sending troops, the Beiyang government would provide the manpower to release Allied troops from wartime labor such as digging trenches, working in munitions plants and arsenals, clearing camps and airfields, repairing roads, constructing railways, and transporting supplies.[19] To avoid German suspicion and Japanese objections, dummy companies were established under the Allies' supervision and put in charge of recruitment. These companies acted as representatives of the laborers and produced contracts binding them and the French and British governments. From the signing of the first contract in May 1916 to the end of the war in November 1918, one hundred forty thousand to two hundred thousand Chinese laborers were recruited and served the Allies.[20]

While firsthand accounts of the Laborers as Soldiers program are scarce, surviving historical records such as the labor contracts produced by these dummy companies offer a glimpse into the Chinese presence in the war, where the issue of "literacy"—specifically, reading and writing letters—comes to the fore. Perhaps in view of preceding labor abuses of the Chinese in Peru and the United States, these contracts appear to have been carefully negotiated to ensure a smooth and steady supply of Chinese manpower.[21] The parameters laid out in the contracts included, but were not limited to, transportation, work conditions, food quotas, health care, penalization, and payment methods.[22] The language adopted in the payment clause merits special attention. Take, for instance, the contract between the Huimin Company and the French government:

Article 4. The wage is one franc per day, which should be paid to the workers by the employer weekly or biweekly, according to the employer's payment policy. The treatment of the Chinese workers should be no different from that of the French workers. Aside from the daily wages, the employers must pay *another 30 francs* per worker every month to one of the appointed banks by the Huimin Company so that Huimin will deposit the money *in China* for the use of *the worker, his family, or any person designated by the worker.* The employer must give a proper receipt to the laborer for deposits or remittances.[23]

What stands out is the two-part structure built into the wage payment, which also applied to workers recruited by the British and prefigures the centrality of literacy for the Chinese labor corps.[24] The full commodification of labor in this case included both the actual labor performed in Europe and the laborers' displacement from home. The two-part wage distribution system accentuated the international nature of the circulation and exchange of labor, which necessitated frequent long-distance communications. Sound in theory, the payment system could continue to function only when the laborer received constant confirmation that his absence from home was compensated in timely fashion and payment continued to arrive on the other side of the world. Instead of relying solely on the employer to provide "a proper receipt" for remittances per the Huimin contract, the laborer sought a less-mediated and more reassuring method for confirmation: direct communication with his family. His limited means excluded expensive telecommunication technologies such as telegraphy and telephone. His employment by the Allies determined strict military supervision of his communications.[25] Affordable and permissible, epistolary communication became the channel through which the laborer and his family could confirm the monthly payment of the half wage. The structure of the two-part wage distribution added an economic reason for letter writing. The desire to write and be written to became not a mere emotional need but a financial necessity that was written into the very contract of the Laborers as Soldiers program.

To be sure, the laborers' fierce demand for letter writing was less a demonstration of their active agency in pursuing literacy than an organic response to the wage-distribution system, on the one hand, and the lack of alternative means for long-distance communication on the other. This historical contingency—the laborers' demand for literacy—might have functioned as the perfect catalyst for the emergence of the first modern Chinese literacy program, but that program would not have come to fruition were it not for the YMCA in the United States and its War Work Council. In the spirit of the Progressive Era (1890s–1920s) and under the guidelines of the Social Gospel Movement, the YMCA established more than sixty service stations for Chinese laborers across Europe.[26] To staff these stations, it also dispatched a group of volunteers, mostly overseas Chinese students in the United States and Britain. The stations provided a range of services, including sports programs, film screenings, and news translation. However, not long after the YMCA staff started working with the laborers, they realized that "the laborers' most needed service was letter writing," and the service stations came to function above everything else as surrogate writing centers.[27] The centrality of literacy thus reinstated itself in the form of lack. Soon after the YMCA identified illiteracy as the root cause of strained and disrupted epistolary communication between Europe and China, a particular volunteer took the lead in combating it. That it took a YMCA volunteer to bring about the first modern Chinese literacy program was hardly coincidental. The organization had become, since the Progressive Era, a major practitioner of the new philosophy of American philanthropy, which put an increasing premium on employing scientific methods to eliminate the root causes of social ills.[28] If illiteracy stood in the way of effective communication, sustainment of the labor corps, and the fulfillment of the YMCA's mission abroad, then it would be eradicated.

The volunteer in question was James Yen. A Yale graduate, Yen was to become one of the most influential educators in modern China and a leading figure of international mass education and rural reconstruction. Cofounder of the Chinese National Association of the Mass Education Movement and later the International Institute of Rural Reconstruction, Yen's reform programs proliferated around the globe to France, China, the United States, the Philippines, Cuba, Mexico, Colombia, and Ghana, the most famous perhaps being his 1930s Ting Hsien Experiment in Hebei Province in northern China.[29] A visible and popular figure across the Pacific, Yen was named in 1943 upon the quadricentennial anniversary of Copernicus's death one of the ten most outstanding "modern revolutionaries," alongside John Dewey, Henry Ford, Walt Disney, and Albert Einstein. In 1948 the U.S. Congress earmarked 10 percent of $275,000,000 in economic aid to China for rural reconstruction, a commission later nicknamed the "Jimmy Yen Provision."[30] As Yen himself recollected numerous times, his entire career owed its roots to his initial contact with the Chinese laborers in Boulogne, France. There he was to meet a kind of "new men" who would inspire him to find his lifelong vocation. As Yen put it, "Before heading off to France, my plan was to educate the Chinese laborers, but who would imagine that it was the laborers that educated me. Their intellect and enthusiasm led me to the discovery of a kind of 'new men,' whose importance might outweigh the archeologists' discovery of the Peking Man."[31]

Yen arrived in mid-June 1918 and immediately started his service in a Chinese labor camp of five thousand workers. The mass literacy program did not install itself in one fell swoop but groped its way through three stages. The first stage was a night class held in the labor camp canteen. After coping with surrogate letter writing and money remittance every day for a few months, sometimes at a rate of several hundred cases each night, Yen was more than ready to tackle the high demand for literacy among the laborers. Calling a meeting for all five thousand workers in the station, Yen announced that they would learn to write their own letters and cease to borrow literacy from the Y volunteers. The laborers roared with disbelief and laughter. Only a handful were bold enough to join Yen's class that night. Held in the labor corps canteen, these letter-writing classes started with Chinese and Arabic numerals and progressed to teaching the laborers how to write their own names and address their parents and family. Over a period of four months, more than forty laborers attended the embryonic literacy class; thirty-five "graduated" with basic literacy.[32]

As the canteen class thrived, the next step was teaching the "one thousand characters" (also called the foundation characters). Inspired by the classic *One Thousand Characters* (*Qian zi wen*), which had been used for basic literacy since the sixth century, Yen selected approximately a thousand of the most frequently used characters from "a Chinese dictionary, some newspaper articles sent from China, colloquial expressions of the laborers, and the most employed characters and phrases in their letters."[33] These one thousand characters were later largely corroborated by a group of statisticians headed by Chen Heqin—Yen's colleague and also a YMCA member—in the study "Determination of the Vocabulary of the Common People."[34] Strengthened with statistical precision, one of the oldest literacy primers in Chinese literary tradition reemerged as a modern approach in combating illiteracy. A new set of the one thousand characters was recognized as a scientific antidote to illiteracy, much in line with the YMCA's emphasis on employing scientific methods in addressing social ailments. The one thousand characters program soon proliferated beyond its pilot version in France and was launched as a national mass-education movement in China beginning in the 1920s.

Eventually, in January 1919, the YMCA created a newspaper titled the *YMCA Chinese Labor Workers' Weekly* (*Jidujiao qingnianhui zhufa huagong zhoubao*). Conceived for advanced students in the literacy class, the *Weekly* functioned as supplementary reading material, with a circulation of between five hundred and a thousand. Yen served as its chief editor until his YMCA post ended in 1920. The *Weekly*, though no more than four pages per issue, included an array of sections, such as "Commentaries," "China Stories," "News from Europe and America," "A Brief History of the Great War," and "Laborers' Updates." Not the first journal to envision laborers as potential readers, the *Weekly* was preceded by two other journals: the *Magazine of Chinese in Europe* and the *Chinese Laborers' Magazine*.[35] Otherwise similar to its predecessors in content and format, the *Weekly* distinguished itself on two fronts: first, it featured writing by the workers, and second, its publication at the time and discussions of it thereafter revealed important clues to the nature of the modern Chinese language.

ORALITY AND LITERACY

The publication of the *Weekly* was crucial not only because it was the capstone of the first modern Chinese literacy program before its influence spread from World War I France to Republican China. More important, the retrospective renaming of the written language used in the *Weekly* signaled an important discrepancy between the laborers' actual writing (a colloquialized written language) and the intellectuals' categorization of it (as *baihua*). While the writing practices of the laborers were taken over by intellectuals to conform to the linguistic legacy of the May Fourth Movement, the critical content penned by one of the laborers was kept buried in the discourse of a particular brand of the Chinese enlightenment.

There is scholarly consensus that the modern Chinese language is a new national language, a linguistic legacy shaped by and passed down from the May Fourth period, defined broadly to include both the New Culture and May Fourth Movements.[36] Historians and literary critics follow the reform intellectuals' own branding of it as plain speech and attribute its prevalence in modern China to those very intellectuals. Tse-Tsung Chow summarized the *baihua* legacy as a "literary revolution" that manifested "the new intellectuals' intention."[37] Vera Schwarcz saw it as a "collaboration" between two generations of intellectuals—the May Fourth students and their teachers.[38] Together, they created a *baihua* rhetoric, in essence a constructed binary between the more classical and literary language known as *wenyan* and the plain speech of *baihua*. This modern *baihua*, flaunting its phonetic—or, rather, phonocentric—nature, sets itself apart from its premodern counterpart. The premodern *baihua* literature accommodates an eclectic body of literature encompassing a wide spectrum of colloquialization and literariness, which included but was not limited to Tang-dynasty *baihua* poetry, Song-dynasty popular stories (*huaben* 話本), and *baihua* fictional works of the Ming and Qing dynasties. *Baihua* remained a literary and written language even in early twentieth-century newspapers such as the *Hangzhou Baihua Newspaper* and *Zhongguo Baihua Newspaper*, until leading intellectuals in the May Fourth and New Culture Movements envisioned pure orality for *baihua*, binding it to the principle of phonocentrism.[39] These spokespersons of the ideal *baihua* advocate the full realization of orality in writing, encourage the subjugation of writing under speech, and promise to lower the threshold of literacy for modern China. The pursuit of this ideal, though rooted in character literacy, indicates a future of the Chinese alphabet. However, even a cursory glance at May Fourth literary production indicates that the nominal, ideal *baihua* of plain speech—championed by May Fourth intellectuals—does not describe the actual written language that constituted the de facto new national language.[40] Instead of plain speech, the staple of modern Chinese language was a colloquialized written language, more in line with the eclectic premodern *baihua* than with the phonocentric modern *baihua*. This colloquialized written language, later renamed and claimed by the May Fourth new *baihua*, was practiced, rehearsed, and proven effective by the Chinese laborers in World War I France. While the collective choice made by the laborers and the YMCA men, as instantiated in the *Weekly*, proved to be a viable path toward linguistic and literary modernity, the name change, with its phonocentric inflection, preserved for cultural elites the possibility of further pursuing pure orality, to be embodied in a Chinese alphabet.

None other than James Yen performed the task of renaming the colloquialized written language. Writing a decade after the 1919 literacy classes, Yen summarized the model thousand-character literacy program in English as follows:

The system of teaching Chinese illiterates, which had its humble beginnings behind the firing lines of the battle-fields of France, consists of the following features: a) four readers written in Pei Hua (spoken language) based upon thirteen hundred "foundation characters" scientifically selected out of more than two hundred different kinds of literature and publications containing upward of 1,600,000 characters.[41]

Yen's conflation of "Pei Hua" (*baihua*) and script aside, it seems certain from his description that the language that emerged behind the firing lines was *baihua*-cum-speech, in strict accordance with the May Fourth rhetoric on the desired new national language. Although *baihua* never achieved the status of pure orality, its narrative as the new national language had been consolidated by 1929, which was when Yen ascribed his World War I literacy program to the tutelage of the May Fourth literary revolution. This invented genealogy would have been real had Yen actually used the term *baihua* to characterize the writing of the *Weekly* in the newspaper itself or had written *baihua* in it. Yet Yen never adopted the term in his own writings for the paper to capture the linguistic model at work, nor did he commit to writing the "spoken language" in it. Instead, he attempted three other, different characterizations—the "common language" (*putonghua*), "Mandarin" (*guanhua*), and "common Mandarin" (*putong guanhua*)—in the *Weekly*'s discussions of the desired style of writing for its prose competitions. Neither equivalent to the "spoken language" that Yen retrospectively evoked nor commensurate among themselves, these three categorizations fell under the umbrella of the colloquialized written language, with decreasing degrees of colloquialism.

In the second issue of the *Weekly*, Yen first proposed the "common language"—not to be conflated with Qu Qiubai's radical and dialect-friendly *putonghua*—when announcing a prose competition. Of all such competitions held by the *Weekly*, this was the only one whose results were announced, leading to the publication of a laborer's essay.[42] Yen detailed the requirements as follows:

To encourage brethren who can read and write, the YMCA has decided to award the first-prize winner of the prose competition 20 francs; the second place, 10 francs. The composition should be no more than 600 words and in *putonghua*. The deadline for submission is February 15. Late compositions will not be accepted. To avoid delay, please turn in your work to YMCA secretaries to be mailed to Paris. The topic of the composition is "The Pros and Cons of Chinese Laborers Being in France."[43]

The language in which Yen wrote and wanted the compositions to be written was named the "common language," be it spoken, written, or a combination of both. Although hardly the same, the common language did not stray far from the ideal of *baihua* as plain speech, since both indicated an aversion to and abstinence from the classical and literary language of *wenyan*. If Yen's use of the "common language" could still be read within the rubric of the constructed dichotomy between *baihua* and *wenyan*, the next characterization blurred the boundary.

In a general call for essays for the *Weekly*, Yen wrote in a distinct style and gave this style, which set the tone for future essay submissions, another name:

Knowing that our countrymen in France are all gentlemen serving the public and favoring righteousness, be they Y men in the Association or interpreters in the labor camps or workers in the factories or on the piers, [they] would not sit around and speculate on the success or failure of our journal. They must be willing to shoulder obligations and enable the advancement and development of our enterprise. Now that all has just commenced and is in dire need of help, our enterprise cannot thrive without all you gentlemen's assistance. We welcome all writings regardless of length, preferably in Mandarin [*guanhua*] and for the promotion of morality and intelligence.[44]

In the original Chinese, the call for essays reads as a mixture of *baihua*, which strives to register hints of the everyday spoken language (e.g., *de* 的), and *wenyan*, which frequently contains single characters (e.g., *zhi* 知, *mou* 謀, *zhi* 置, *kuang* 況), idioms (e.g., *jigonghaoyi* 急公好義), and four-character formulations (e.g., *xuzhuweiji* 需助為急). The latter three usages are all markers of literary composition and cannot pass for plain speech. Yen terms the mixed style Mandarin. The equivalence between "Mandarin" and "the common speech," though quietly implied, could hardly be maintained. On the one hand, Mandarin, defined strictly, meant the speech of officials, which changes diachronically and varies synchronically by region.[45] The necessary plurality of Mandarin thus confounds the assumed simplicity of the common speech. On the other hand, interpreted broadly, Mandarin can be taken to denote an administrative language generally used in government documents. Otherwise a fairly accurate description of the linguistic model in the *Weekly*, its explicit function as a written language contradicts the promise of the common language in alignment with the ideal of plain speech.

The last definition appears in the seventh issue of the *Weekly*, which ran a special section titled "The Laborers' Composition." After announcing the winners of the prose competition, Yen warns those who wrote in "literary language" and demands that all follow a "common Mandarin." He stipulates that future submissions will not be read if they do not abide by the linguistic model or if they exceed "the character limit of 600."[46] In adding "common" to "Mandarin," Yen's last definition unwittingly reveals the plurality of Mandarin speech and the conflation of written and spoken Mandarin. Although Yen pits "common Mandarin" against "literary language," his own admonition is penned in a style that is neither nonliterary nor anticlassical. The frequent use of single-character words like *ruo* 若 (if) and the habitual evocation of the idiom structure *shijubajiu* 十居八九 (eight or nine out of ten) cannot be glossed over by the attempt at colloquial auxiliaries that comes at the end (e.g., *lo* 咯). While Yen claimed in 1929 that the wartime literacy program followed the phonocentric ideal of *baihua*, his own writing in 1919 suggested otherwise.

Reminiscing almost six decades later, Yen finally clarified the linguistic model at work in the *Weekly*: "This paragraph of written prose is a kind of 'Mandarin' at that time. It is not *wenyan*. Nor does it measure up to 'my hand writing my mouth.' And the punctuation is only limited to the comma ',' and a full circle stop '.' "[47] Yen's confession is crucial, not only because it confirms the language adopted in the *Weekly* to be a linguistic amalgamation that was neither *baihua* nor *wenyan*; nor because the neither-nor style disproved the genealogy drawn between the World War I literacy program and the May Fourth *baihua* revolution. His confession ironically betrays the real linguistic and literary outcomes of May Fourth. What the intellectuals of that time ended up achieving was, in fact, the very linguistic amalgamation that defied the resolute dichotomy between *baihua* and *wenyan* as instantiated in the *Weekly* and the renaming of this eclectic language in accordance with the phonocentric principle. Yen's confession provided the definitive proof of the renaming. It was this renaming of *baihua* that united the May Fourth and New Culture Movements with the Chinese script revolution, two otherwise mutually exclusive forces working for the advancement of two different scripts and bodies of literature.

Yen was not alone in performing the act of renaming. The *baihua* discourse was so well established by the May Fourth generation that Yen merely gravitated toward it. An even more prominent example is Hu Shi, the best-known spokesman for *baihua* discourse. In an English speech titled "Chinese Renaissance" delivered at the University of Chicago in 1933, Hu recollected his definition of *baihua* in the late 1910s:

And the living language I proposed as the only possible medium of the future literature of China, was the *pei-hua* [*baihua*], the vulgar tongue of the vast majority of the population, the language which, in the last 500 years, had produced the numerous novels read and loved by the people, though despised by the men of letters. I wanted this much despised vulgar tongue of the people and the novels to be elevated to the position of the national language of China, to the position enjoyed by all the modern national languages in Europe.[48]

An advocate for both *baihua* and alphabetization,[49] Hu accommodates the two mutually exclusive propositions by his theorization of *baihua*. While the people's "vulgar tongue" is capable of being transcribed in the Roman-Latin alphabet, *baihua* is also already written in character form. He confesses that *baihua* "was already there, already standardized in its written form, in syntax, in diction, all by the few great novels which have gone to the heart and bosom of every man."[50] Suspending the alphabetic transcription of the vulgar tongue, Hu uses *baihua* as a hinge in hope of cohering literary composition into pure orality. Such a hinge, however, takes the concrete written form of "great novels"—for example, *The Journey to the West* and *The Dream of the Red Chamber*—to be learned and passed down as written manuals for writers, such as himself, who wished to learn the new *baihua*.[51] By appropriating the old *baihua* literature of the past "500 years" for the new *baihua* of pure orality, Hu Shi and his followers perform a subtle renaming and enter the colloquialized written language into the realm of phonocentrism. As *baihua* channels phonocentric imagination of pure orality without actually delivering the unification of speech and writing, it also constitutes an effective transmutation of the script revolution, which legitimizes its roots in characters and promises its growth into an alphabetic future. As the newly named *baihua* becomes the mainstay of modern Chinese, it comes to gloss over its own eclectic linguistic nature and its radical ties with the script revolution. What connects the May Fourth *baihua* discourse and the script revolution is not only their common pursuit of phonocentrism but also their shared limits. A rare piece of laborers' writing, presented below, exemplifies an affirmative answer to the question, can subaltern workers write and explicates the inherent limits to understanding and acknowledging the laborer's writing—the limits of the Chinese enlightenment.

A LABORER'S "CHINESE ENLIGHTENMENT"

James Yen was not the only one writing the colloquialized language. Although presumably an intellectuals' tour de force, this written language was not a monopoly of the intellectuals. A laborer named Fu Xingsan 傅省三, who won the aforementioned prose competition, penned his essay in the same style.[52] Perhaps the only extant work by a laborer, this piece of writing is reproduced in figure 3.1 and appendix 3.1 in its Chinese original and English translation, respectively.[53] Though rare and important, this laborer's reflections on war and equality and critique of one brand of the Chinese enlightenment have heretofore escaped critical attention. If the linguistic materiality of the World War I literacy program was misnamed to conform to the phonocentric impulse of the May Fourth *baihua* revolution, then the critical content of the laborer's writing has been eclipsed by the very brand of the Chinese enlightenment that it set out to critique.

Fu Xingsan writes in favor of the laborers' presence in France, first painting, in broad strokes, the geopolitical backdrop of the war. Attributing the outbreak of war to "the proud heart of the German kaiser" that "coveted taking over the whole world," Fu is quick to add, "the Allies were gravely offended." Pitting the proud kaiser against the offended Allies, he locates the cause of the war in a clash between European powers. Not unlike the enthusiastic Beiyang government, Fu expresses camaraderie with the Allies

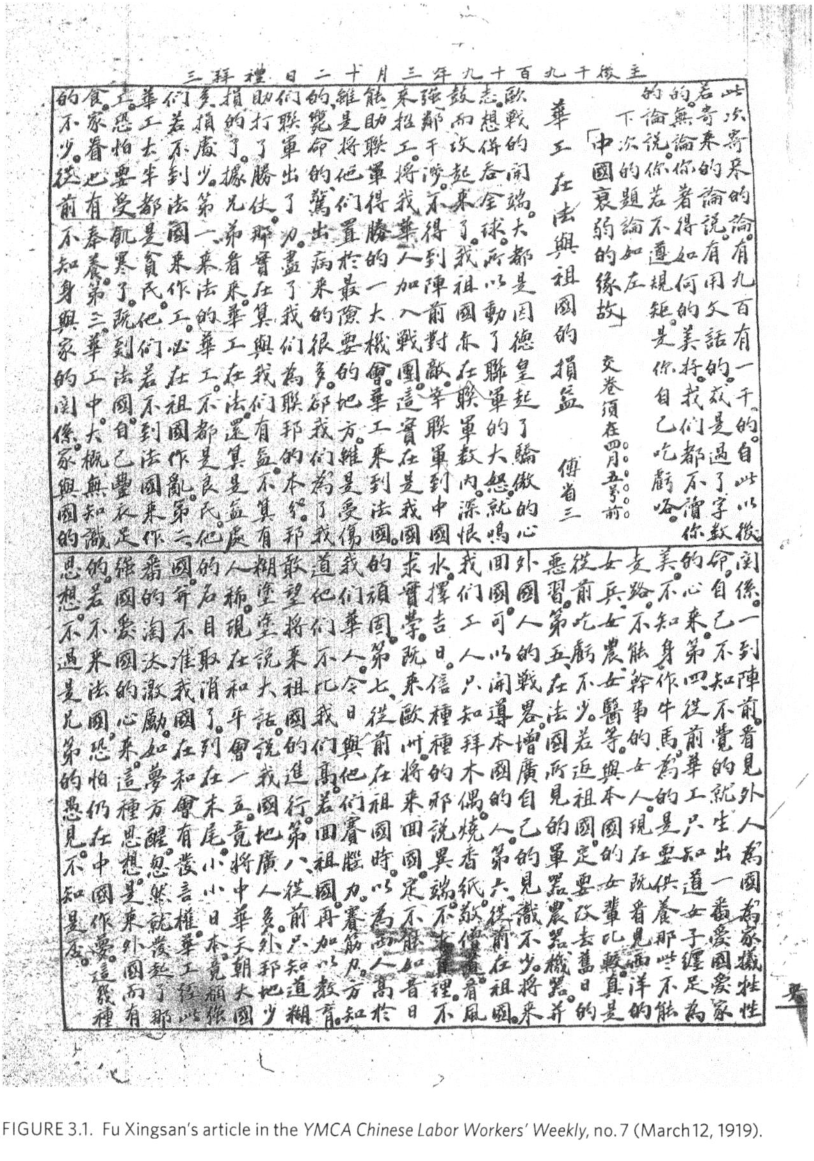

主後千九百十九年三月十二日禮拜三

此次寄來的論。有九百有一千的。自此以後若寄來的論說。有用文話的。就是過了字數的。無論你著得如何的美。將我們都不讀你的論說。你若不遵規矩。是你自己吃虧咯。

下次的題論如左

「中國衰弱的緣故」

交卷須在四月五號前。

華工在法與祖國的損益

傅省三

歐戰的開端。大都是因德皇起了驕傲的心志。想併吞全球。所以動了聯軍的大怒。就鳴鼓而攻起來了。我祖國亦在聯軍數內。深恨強鄰干涉。不得到陣前對敵。萃聯軍到中國來招工。將我華人加入戰團。這實在是我國能助聯軍得勝的一大機會。華工來到法國。雖是將他們置於最險要的地方。雖是受傷的、覺命的驚出病來的很多。卻我們為了我們聯軍出了力。盡了我們為聯邦的本分。邦助打了勝仗。那實在算與我們有益。不算有損的了。據兄弟看來。華工在法還算是益處多。損處少。第一。來法的華工。不都是良民。他們若不到法國來作工。必在祖國作亂。第二華工大半都是貧民。他們若不到法國來作工。恐怕要受飢寒了。既到法國自己豐衣足食。家眷也有奉養。第三華工中大概無知識的不少。從前不知身與家的關係。家與國的關係。一到陣前。看見外人為國為家犧牲性命。自己不知不覺的就生出一番愛國愛家的心來。第四。從前華工只知道女子纏足為美。不知身作牛馬為的是要供養那些不能走路。不能幹事的女人。現在既看見西洋的女兵女農女醫等。與本國的女輩比較真是從前吃虧不少。若返祖國定要改去舊日的惡習。第五、在法國所見的單器農器機器并外國人的戰略。增廣自己的見識不少。將來回國可以開導本國的人。第六、從前在祖國我們工人只知拜木偶燒香紙敬僧道看風水。擇吉日。信種種的邪說異端。不[illegible]理。不求實學。既來歐州將來回國定不能如昔日的頑固。第七、從前在祖國時。以為[illegible]人高於我們華人。今日與他們賽腦力。賽筋力。方知道他們不比我們高。若回祖國。再加以教育。敢望將來祖國的進行。第八、從前只知道糊糊塗塗說大話。說我國地廣人多。外邦地少人稀。現在和平會一五。竟將中華天朝大國的名目取消了。列在末尾。小小日本。竟顯強國。并不准我國在和會有發言權。華工經此番的淘汰激勵。如夢方醒。忽然就發熱了。那樣國愛國的心來。這種思想是東外國而有的。若不來法國。恐怕仍在中國作夢。這幾種思想。不過是兄弟的愚見。不知是否。

FIGURE 3.1. Fu Xingsan's article in the *YMCA Chinese Labor Workers' Weekly*, no. 7 (March 12, 1919).

but laments the limited membership. Nonetheless, he celebrates the Laborers as Soldiers program as "a golden opportunity for us to assist the Allies in winning the war."

Following an overall appraisal that "our cause has gained substantial advantage," Fu stipulates eight points explicating "the pros of laborers being in France." These points cover a wide spectrum of socioeconomic and political reasons—including a sophisticated gendered perspective—and offer an explanation of the Chinese rage in response to the Paris Peace Conference. The first three points are laid out as personal gains in terms of legal obedience, financial solvency, and access to literacy and knowledge. The next three touch on gender equality, industrialization, and religious practice. These first six points are organized around the issue of development, either on a personal-familial level or on a social scale. The last two points, however, take a different direction and escalate the argument into political commentary, echoing Fu's opening paragraph.

This shift in content is signaled and assisted by a concomitant shift in narratival perspective. In the first four sections on delinquency, poverty, ignorance, and gender discrimination, Fu employs a third-person narrative, addressing those who fall prey to these vices as "they" or "the Chinese laborers." Creating narrative distance, he is able to objectively describe the undesirable situation of the laborers if they had continued to stay in China and to argue that their displacement has benefited both themselves and society at large. From the fifth point on, a subtle shift takes place. In the absence of a formal subject, despite words like "self" and "one's own country," the section could be read from the point of view of either the first-person plural or a third-person narrative. Fu therefore could be either speaking in his own voice, appraising the prospects of transplanting European industrialization into China, or employing free indirect speech, casting the laborers as go-betweens for the cause of industrialization in China. The ambivalence extends to the sixth point, where Fu's wording of "we/our laborers" cannot be determined strictly as the first-person-plural perspective. Only in the seventh point does Fu clearly identify himself as the narrator speaking for a collective "we," before the text quickly slips back into the ambiguous "the Chinese laborers" and "our country" in the eighth point.

The seventh point—the one that Fu holds dearly enough to write in the unmistakable first-person plural—reads as a challenge to European superiority and a bid for racial equality. Fu, in a moderate tone, calls into question whether "the Westerners were superior to us fellow Chinese," as he and his fellow laborers had believed before they embarked on their European journey. His skepticism arises from daily contact with Europeans in "competing with them in intelligence and physical strength." The verb "to compete" denotes open comparison and defies a priori racial hierarchization. Fu's resistance to Western superiority was audaciously ahead of his time, considering that, a few months after his composition, the Paris Peace Conference rejected a treaty affirming racial equality. Fu's realization that his French colleagues and supervisors were "hardly any better" than the Chinese workers empowered him and his fellow laborers to dare aspire to self-reliance and self-determination, to "contribute to the development" of China upon their return.

It bears pointing out that Fu was not the only one who saw the laborers' abilities as competing with those of their European counterparts. Allied commanders who worked with the Chinese laborers also sang their praises. For instance, the British commander Douglas Haig observed, "Our experience with the Chinese labour in France has shown us that in all classes of routine work, both skilled and unskilled, Chinese men can labour as efficiently, if not more efficiently, than the best European workmen and with a persistence without rival. They are content with a far smaller wage, accustomed to less food, and expect fewer comforts."[54] The *Far Eastern Review* regarded the laborers' presence as possibly "one of the most important aspects of the Great European War."[55]

One crucial outcome of "the Great European War" was the possibility of a new world on the ruins of old empires, which promised all oppressed peoples their right to equality and self-determination. The *Far Eastern Review* might have been dramatic in its praise, but the importance assigned to the Chinese laborers—as one group of marginalized people with their own rights to equality and self-determination—was not too far-fetched. In the few months after the armistice and before the Treaty of Versailles, the ideals of racial equality and international justice, as well as the Wilsonian fourteen points, mobilized an array of anticolonial and anti-imperialist movements all over the world, the Chinese May Fourth Movement being but one. As Erez Manela argues, both the origin of "international anticolonial nationalism" and the rise of a new U.S. "diplomacy of liberal internationalism" may be traced to this particular time slice, which he calls the Wilsonian moment.[56]

Woodrow Wilson's rhetoric of equality among nations and self-determination may have galvanized the development of many anti-imperialist and independence movements in various parts of the world—the Korean March First Movement, the Egyptian Revolution of 1919, and the rising tide of the Indian independence movement, to name a few. However, to think that nationalists around the globe took their cue from the American president is mistaken. Manela argues that the driving force behind the Chinese protests against Versailles was "the mobilized Chinese nationalists around the world who had heard the call of self-determination and were determined that China, too, would have it." Though anti-imperial sentiments might have found solace in and support from the liberal rhetoric of equality and international justice, protests and uprisings broke out because of unfulfilled promises and eventual betrayal. The disillusionment of the Wilsonian moment—as much as the Wilsonian promise—contributed to the course of anticolonial and anti-imperial movements. Manela is right, however, in pointing out that the vision of equality and self-determination was certainly not Wilson's alone.[57] As Michael Adas demonstrates, the post–World War I reflection—a shared project among "thinkers from the Americas, Europe, Africa, and Asia"—had a prewar origin and constituted "the first genuinely global intellectual exchange."[58] In fact, the long list of thinkers who participated in the global interchange could well include several late-Qing Chinese intellectuals, such as Liang Qichao and Zhang Taiyan, as well as the Chinese laborer Fu Xingsan.

At the turn of the twentieth century, leading late-Qing intellectuals such as Zhang Taiyan had already started to grapple with the concept of equality as a central problematic of modernity.[59] The idea of equality also helped Chinese intellectuals cultivate a new global consciousness that began to recognize a colonial world order and see China's place in it among many other targets of imperial and colonial conquest, such as Poland, South Africa, and the Philippines.[60] As Rebecca Karl demonstrates, the late-Qing intellectuals' attempt to come to terms with the temporal and spatial order of the "capitalist linearity"—China being but one part of "the production of unevenness on a global scale"—construed the theoretical foundation for Chinese nationalism for decades to come.[61] To break with the colonial world order, one first had to comprehend it. To do that, journalistic writing—penned mostly in the colloquialized written language[62]—became the textual testing ground. The irony is that though retrospectively rebranded as the May Fourth *baihua* of pure orality, Fu's writing bore substantial resemblance, in both style and content, to late-Qing journalistic writing.[63] It is difficult to discern whether or how laborers like Fu Xingsan became influenced by contemporary journals and newspapers, but not unlike his intellectual counterpart, the Chinese laborer turned writing into a critical medium through which he attempted to unchain himself from the racial hierarchy he was recruited to serve and to partake in the discourse of equality and self-determination.

This discourse not only fostered anticolonial nationalism, as Manela, Adas, and Karl have convincingly argued, but also converged with the undercurrents of left-wing internationalism, to which the Chinese laborers contributed their fair share. A conservative estimate of more than thirty thousand Chinese laborers joined the Soviet Red Army and served in the Russian Revolution.[64] Among those who extended their stay beyond the end dates of their contracts,[65] at least ten made their way to the Spanish Civil War, Tchang Jaui Sau and Liou Kin Tien being the only known names.[66] Others took part in the World War II underground resistance. One, named Zhang Changsong, together with his French-Chinese son, worked for the antifascist underground organization.[67] The laborers' activism dovetailed with the left-wing ideology on the rise in both Europe and China. It was hardly coincidental that the massive May Fourth student demonstration was first conditioned by laborers' travails in World War I France and then assisted by workers' strikes in major cities across China. If May Fourth marked the beginning of the complete Westernization of China,[68] it also signaled a new political alliance between the working class and intellectuals, a powerful leitmotif that was to dominate the Chinese revolution for the entire twentieth century. From this moment on, the Chinese enlightenment—to borrow Vera Schwarcz's formulation—was inadvertently caught between a full Westernization playing out along with capitalist linearity and a socialist revolution seeking to remap the world order. That a representative of the laborers understood and registered the argument for equality on which the short twentieth century unfolded was more than fitting.[69]

Fu Xingsan's eighth and final point of commentary on the Paris Peace Conference pointed to the crucial crossroads that China faced in the postwar world. Writing in the first month of the conference, Fu seemed to be well informed about its proceedings. Within this period, the conference reduced the five seats of the Chinese delegation to two, though the first rounds of Sino-Japanese debate on the Shandong question ended in favor of China. Fu would not have foreseen the final disposal of Shandong at the time of composition and had reason to remain cautiously optimistic. However, he captured the sense of astonishment and betrayal by using the word "unexpectedly" twice in a few lines. The conference's definition of nations—China as a "little" one and Japan a "great" one—came as a wake-up call that suddenly "awakened" the laborers as if "from a dream." Invoking the tropes of "awakening" and "dream," already popular in the late imperial period and increasingly relevant in the early Republican era,[70] Fu went on to perform a critical act of "double awakening." His use of "dream"—it is unclear in the Chinese original whether it was meant to be singular or plural—warranted two possible interpretations: one, a dream of the Chinese "celestial dynasty," and the other a dream of European superiority. Swiftly, Fu took on both dreams. As he lamented the laborers' self-aggrandizement boasting of China as a great nation, he immediately criticized the Allies' belittlement of it. The laborers' path to awakening was thus necessarily conditioned by disillusionment with both notions of Chinese and European superiority. Rooted in the principles of equality and self-reliance, the act of "double awakening" defined the laborers' take on the Chinese enlightenment.

Fu was not alone in suggesting a "double awakening." Liang Qichao, who made the trip to Paris to observe the peace conference, shared similar sentiments in his *Reflections on the European Journey*. Witnessing firsthand the postwar destitution in Europe, Liang asked, "Who would have dared to say that the fiery European nations and their comfortable-living people would one day unexpectedly have no coal and rice?" Even though Liang, who claimed to be "used to leading a simple and clumsy life," found the situation "already arduous and embarrassing," he could only wonder, "How will the Europeans live?"[71] Now that both the Chinese and the Europeans shared a condition of "destitution," neither dream had much appeal. Using the same word, "unexpectedly," as Fu Xingsan, Liang was shocked into rethinking the superiority of European civilization and went on to raise the question of whether this civilization was complicit in the massive warmongering. The European dream—the perceived antidote to China's ailment—was called into question by the catastrophes of the war and the betrayal at Versailles. The disenchantment with both the Chinese and European dreams prefigured critical reflections on the war, for both laborer and leading intellectual.

Not unlike the writings produced by important thinkers around the world at the time, Fu's humble essay engaged with the most urgent discussions on equality and international justice and negotiated the postwar world order and the position of the marginalized within it. His writing was unusual not only because laborers' writings were scarce but also because critical engagement with war was rarely expressed in writing by subalterns and even less likely to be taken seriously by intellectuals. It would be naive to expect Fu's voice in the global postwar discourse to have gained much notice beyond its selection by James Yen and its appearance in the *Weekly*. In fact, it is doubtful that Yen picked up Fu's essay because of its critical pitch. In the statement announcing the result of the prose competition, although Yen refrained from directly commenting on Fu's arguments, he did take a moment to share his own thoughts on the issue.[72] After applauding all submissions, he contemplated that it was entirely "one's own action" that determined whether the pros could outweigh the cons. Yen focused on two aspects of laborers' actions: monetary matters and the treatment of the YMCA "teachers." On money, he cautioned the laborers against gambling lest they lose the opportunity to save up, "establish themselves, and benefit their families." Even worse, they would create for all Chinese "the reputation of a gambler in a foreign land." Yen paused and asked, "Is this pro or con?" He then moved on to some laborers' lack of appreciation of the YMCA programs. "The best part of the program," Yen stated, was that "university graduates from both China and the United States come and teach for free." Those who refused to seize "this unprecedented opportunity" lived as though "still in a dream." Yen reiterated the rhetorical question, "Is this pro or con?"

Employing the same trope of "dream," Yen's call to awakening did not, however, aim for the kind of "double awakening" that Fu had in mind.[73] The prose competition, as Yen's editorial message revealed, rather than a critical forum assessing the Chinese wartime experience was meant to function as a conduit for self-reflection and self-improvement. Although there was no reason why critical thinking could not go hand in hand with awareness of self-improvement—after all, Fu's "double awakening" has already demonstrated otherwise—Yen's vision of the laborers—disclosed by his editorial statement and echoed in his other writings[74]—excluded the former from the latter. Inasmuch as a gambling and illiterate laborer who refused to learn could hardly question racial inequality, a laborer who was capable of "double awakening" might not fit in Yen's enlightenment project. This liberal and reformist brand of enlightenment was neither the European Enlightenment, which pursued disenchantment from religious superstitions, nor the kind of Chinese enlightenment defined by Vera Schwarcz, which disavowed "the unquestioning obedience to patriarchal authority."[75] At its core, it was a civilizing mission that was predicated on the image of the uncivilized masses and their need for self-improvement and education under the guidance of the intellectuals. Yen wrote in *New Citizens for China*—the first of the three pamphlets written as part of a fund-raising effort—that "it is their [the intellectuals'] bounden duty to accept the challenge and seize the opportunity to educate China's illiterate millions for democracy. It was for this purpose that the Chinese Mass Education Movement has been organized, the slogan 'Eliminate illiteracy and make new citizens for China.' "[76]

Yen's concern for the illiterate laborers naturally contributed to his discontent with their refusal to be educated by teachers like himself. In contrast, his favorite story about the laborers—recorded in several speeches and articles—was the one in which a certain generous laborer wrote to him to donate 365 francs to the *Weekly* and to thank him, "Mr. Yen, big teacher," for teaching him "everything under the heavens."[77] In an interview with Pearl Buck, Yen confessed, "That is the kind of thing that touched me. I determined to use my life to enlarge his life. The word 'coolie' became for me a new word. I said, I will free him from his bitterness and help him to develop his strength."[78] The image of the underprivileged and grateful "coolie" became the cornerstone of the enlightenment project championed by Yen and his colleagues. It grew from literacy programs and mass education, integrated rural reconstruction and citizenship training, and eventually aimed to spread the gospel of Christian love.[79] By the same token, a different image of the Chinese laborer—enlightened and critical minded—was hardly appropriate for the civilizing mission. Therefore, although the *Weekly* solicited the laborers' writings, it could not have published many of their political commentaries, for such writings ran the risk of undermining the urgency of the literacy program, on the one hand, and undercutting the enlightenment agenda on the other. However, one winning essay from Fu Xingsan was enough to preserve the possibility of imagining the Chinese laborers differently. Granted that Yen framed Fu's work in the civilizing discourse, his silence over the critical dimension of Fu's essay confirmed that the laborer's voice was hard to tame. What was for Yen and his cohort a path toward a reformist and liberal brand of the Chinese enlightenment became for Fu and his fellow laborers a territory for critical thinking and writing, as well as a lasting medium for staking their claim to racial equality and international justice. The historical irony is manifold. For one, although the laborers demonstrated how a colloquialized written language could effectively check the phonocentric impulse for pure orality, their literacy program was retrospectively branded as the inaugural moment of the phonocentric reinvention of *baihua*. For another, although the positive side of the phonocentric antinomies reached out to empower the illiterate laborers, there were still limits to what they could and should write. Finally, although the story of the "sacred laborers" was written out of the collective memory of World War I, the laborers' writing stood as living testimony to the true postwar legacy that sought peace, equality, and justice, inspiring May Fourth and beyond.

APPENDIX 3.1

English Translation of Fu Xingsan, "The Pros and Cons
of the Laborers Being in France"

It was probably the proud heart of the German kaiser that gave rise to the outbreak of the Great War in Europe. As the kaiser coveted taking over the whole world, the Allies were gravely offended. They struck their drums and started the battles. My homeland China is also a member of the Allies. As much as China detested the intervention of a bullying neighbor, it could not join the Allies on the battlefront. Fortunately, the Allies came to recruit laborers and thus enabled China to participate in the war effort. This was indeed a golden opportunity for us to assist the Allies in winning the war.

Arriving in France, the Chinese laborers were installed in the most dangerous positions. Though many of them were hurt, dead, shaken up, and suffering illnesses, the laborers did contribute to the Allied troops and managed what we could for the final victory of the Allies. Far from being damaged, our cause has gained substantial advantage. Thus, in my mind, the pros of the laborers' presence in France outweigh the cons.

First, not all laborers who came to France are law-abiding citizens. If they had not come to France for work, they might have engaged in wrongdoing in China.

Second, the majority of the Chinese laborers are destitute. If they had not chosen to come to France, they might be suffering from cold and hunger. Now that they are here, not only are they themselves well fed and well clothed, so are their families in China.

Third, a good portion of the laborers might be poorly educated. They did not know heretofore the relationship between individuals and families, between families and countries. Now thrust into the forefront of the battlefield, they witness for themselves how others and foreigners sacrifice their lives for their own countries and families. Hence unwittingly their love for their families and a sense of patriotism are born.

Fourth, the workers used to think that foot-binding was a thing of beauty and did not know that they themselves needed to labor strenuously to provide for those bound-feet women who could neither walk nor work. They have now seen female soldiers, farmers, and doctors in the West who contrast sharply with these Chinese women and have therefore realized to what disadvantage they subjected themselves in the past. If they get to return home, the vicious habit of the old days will have to be reformed.

Fifth, the laborers opened up their horizons as they saw the weapons, farming devices, and various machinery used in France. At the same time, they were introduced to the military strategies employed by the foreigners. If they make their way home in the future, they will enlighten their countrymen.

Sixth, while in China, our laborers worshipped idols, burned incense, revered monks, conformed to the rules of feng shui, and picked so-called auspicious dates [for certain things]. They believed in all sorts of superstitions but did not explore the truth nor acquire true learning. Now that they have come to Europe, if they are one day homebound, they cannot be as stubborn-minded as before.

Seventh, while still in China, we thought that Westerners were superior to us fellow Chinese. Now that we are competing with them in intelligence and physical strength, we come to the realization that they are hardly any better than we are. Given the chance to go home and equip ourselves with adequate education, we dare to expect and contribute to the development of our motherland.

Finally, in the past all we knew was to boast that our country was vast in land and rich in population while slighting foreign nations as scant in territory and scarce in human resources. Now, as the Peace Conference was launched, China was unexpectedly denied its status as a great nation and a celestial dynasty and ranked at the bottom of countries. But a little country such as Japan was unexpectedly listed as a great nation. The peace conference went so far as to forbid China to speak at the conference. Confounded by such humiliation and instigation, the laborers awakened as if from a dream, and their patriotism for China and their will to strengthen it was suddenly aroused. This kind of thought would not have taken form had we not traveled to a foreign country. If we had not come to France, we might still be dreaming in China.

These few points are no more than my humble opinion. Whether they are true is subject to critique.

Chapter Four

REINVENTING CHILDREN

Save the children.

—LU XUN, "DIARY OF A MADMAN"

Children are the future giants of the nation.

—TAO XINGZHI

On August 21, 1923, James Yen arrived on the campus of what was then Tsinghua College in Beijing, where the Chinese National Association for the Advancement of Education (Zhonghua Jiaoyu Gaijinshe 中華教育改進社) was convening for its second annual meeting. One of the main items on the agenda for the year was the creation of a national association of mass education.[1] In a mere four years since his seminal literacy program in France and only three years since his departure from the United States, Yen had seen his mass-education campaigns proliferate in provinces such as Shandong, Hunan, and Zhejiang, created remarkable synergy between different groups of the Mass Education Movement, and called for, as Yen put it, "a central organization to give supervision and systematic promotion" for the movement.[2] The Tsinghua conference concluded with the founding of the Chinese National Association of the Mass Education Movement (Zhonghua Pingmin Jiaoyu Cujinhui 中華平民教育促進會)—the highest governing body overseeing all mass-education campaigns—and the election of Zhu Qihui (wife of then premier of the Republic, Xiong Xiling) as board president, Tao Xingzhi 陶行知 (1891–1946) as board secretary, and James Yen as general director. Yen and Tao—arguably two of the most iconic modern Chinese educators—thereby joined hands in educating and serving the masses. With strong leadership and the backing of the central government, the "Chinese mass education movement progresses strongly," as James Yen reported.[3]

By 1936, however, one could no longer speak of a unified, centralized, and singular Chinese mass-education movement. In an English essay titled "The New Mass Education Movement," dated March 15, 1936, Tao Xingzhi introduced his own, Shanghai-initiated movement, stressing that it "should not be confused with that type of education advocated by Mr. James Yen at Ting Hsien." The nominal difference between Yen's *pingmin jiaoyu* 平民教育—literally, "common people's education"—and Tao's *dazhong jiaoyu* 大眾教育, "education of the great masses," implied "fundamental differences in essentials." Tao did not find it necessary to be polite in stating, "Ting Hsien advocates mass education, but in practice it results in an education of the few, while the new mass education aims at a real education of the masses, by the masses and for the masses."[4] Aside from its devotion to the masses, three other commitments defined Tao's new mass education: it endorsed Sin Wenz, proposed life education, and taught national salvation.[5] Thus it set itself apart from Yen's old model, which subscribed to the *baihua* discourse, adhered to an enlightenment program, and retreated to the Chinese hinterland on the eve of the Second Sino-Japanese War.

Tao's public breakup with Yen was dramatic, considering that in 1923 it was Tao himself who had written to association board president Zhu Qihui defending Yen against objections to his appointment as general director, claiming that "there is no other more suited talent."[6] What had happened in the intervening years? This question is worth asking not because it is intriguing to find out why these old friends parted ways—many such friendships broke down at crucial historical junctures—but rather because answering it helps us understand the third and final transmutation of the script revolution. This chapter traces how the script revolution morphed into a movement that nominally advocated Latinization but in fact practiced character literacy, which was enabled by the support of the New Mass Education Movement at a time of unprecedented national crisis. The final transmutation of the script revolution took the triangulated shape of literacy, mass education, and war, which led to the production of major education literature in allegiance to national salvation and mass liberation and augured the reconfiguration of modern Chinese literary production for decades to come. I first delineate the scientific making of the colloquialized written language (*yutiwen* 語體文)—the technically more accurate term for the staple of modern Chinese writing—and ponder how that language, instead of exposing the mutual exclusivity between the script and literary revolutions, ended up serving as a linchpin connecting the two revolutions. By reading closely works produced by *yutiwen* writers, Sin Wenz sympathizers, and mass-education advocates Chen Heqin, Tao Xingzhi, and Ye Shengtao, I trace the recalibration of the Latinization movement, the redefinition of the literary revolution, and the reinvention of the figure of children, which, taken together, signaled a leftist turn in modern Chinese literature. I conclude with a tentative reflection on how the transmutations of the script revolution hold important clues to understanding the aspirations and frustrations of literary revolution.

ONE THOUSAND CHARACTERS, *YUTIWEN*, AND LATINIZATION

If James Yen was the initial creator of the "foundation characters system," it was Tao Xingzhi and Zhu Jingnong who executed the idea of grafting the one thousand foundation characters onto a four-reader curriculum for use in the Mass Education Movement. Tao summed up the applicability and efficacy of the *People's Thousand Character Lessons* to the movement in his English report titled "Education in China" (1924): "An average illiterate can complete the four readers in four months by spending one hour a day. At the end of four months, he will be able to read newspapers, books, and correspondence based on the vocabulary and to express himself by using the same. As these four readers cost altogether only twelve cents Mex., even the poorest can afford to buy."[7]

These affordable primers, populating "homes, stores, factories, schools, churches, monasteries, *yamens*, steamships, prisons, and army camps,"[8] turned all these locales into People's Reading Circles, People's Schools, and People's Question Stations.[9] According to Tao, the circulation of these primers reached two million between 1923 and 1924. Advocates of mass education were optimistic that "it will not be long before we see a compulsory popular education in operation in China with its tax on ignorance. Friends of popular education have the ambition to achieve the miracle of eliminating two hundred million of the illiterates in a generation."[10]

Aside from their ambition of eliminating illiteracy, the "friends of popular education" also envisioned "the making of a new literature."[11] The May

Fourth aspiration to produce accessible and living literature gained statistical precision in determining which thousand characters could provide the scriptal basis of a new literature. A quote from Lao She, speaking of his experience in writing his novel *Xiaopo's Birthday* (1929), demonstrated how the "people's thousand characters" had quickly become a respectable yardstick for measuring literary merit. On his sojourn in Singapore, Lao She worked as a Chinese teacher in a local middle school. Dismayed by the lack of time and means to write what would have been an epic on overseas Chinese in Southeast Asia or the South Sea (Nanyang),[12] he ended up writing about Chinese children in Southeast Asia. Speaking fondly of this piece, Lao She took most pride in its language, professing that writing *Xiaopo's Birthday* emboldened him to use "simplest," "almost childlike" language and enabled him to "understand the strength of *baihua*." Observing his own change of language, he made a discovery: "I did not calculate how many characters there were in *Xiaopo's Birthday*, but it gave me confidence that with the one thousand characters from the *People's Thousand Character Lessons*, I could produce very decent prose."[13]

Lao She's ease and confidence in the *People's Thousand Character Lessons* was no blind faith; rather, it went through empirical tests and received scientific and statistical support before being put into use for the national Mass Education Movement. A group of professional educators with statistical expertise researched and revised—but did not phoneticize—the initial list of a thousand characters, or, as James Yen called them, the foundation character system, before the characters made their way into the *People's Thousand Character Lessons*:

We identified the most frequently used characters, more or less relying on our experience in teaching the Chinese laborers in France and Belgium [during World War I]. . . . We were concerned that this method would not suffice, so we consulted with a wide range of experts. It so happened that my friend Mr. Chen Heqin, upon his return from overseas, had done intensive and rigorous research together with several of his colleagues at the Southeastern University on this very subject. They went to tremendous trouble and spent more than two years going over Chinese *baihua* literature, such as *The Water Margin* and *The Dream of the Red Chamber*, as well as books and newspapers in all fields. They categorized and checked all characters and noted the number of times each character was used. This amounted to a total of half a million characters' worth of literature, out of which they culled several thousand most frequently used characters.... The top one thousand characters, which were selected via Mr. Chen's scientific method and scored the highest in the frequency test among the several thousand, coincided almost 80 percent with the one thousand characters we chose based on experience. It was hence sufficient to say that the empirical and scientific methods could indeed complement each other.[14]

The scientific method proved in hindsight Yen's prescience in the first modern literacy program in World War I France. These one thousand characters, now armed with statistical precision, went on to lay the foundation for all primers of the People's Education series.[15] It is important to point out, however, that the database of "*baihua* literature" from which these characters were culled was a body of literature in colloquialized written language that did not concern itself with phonetic representability, not to mention its accuracy or superiority. Instead, the characters were chosen based on their frequency of usage. Aside from being an eclectic written language with phonocentric promise, the May Fourth *baihua* language also became a scientific language, capable of drawing the statistical parameters for a new, progressive, and teachable character literacy for all people. Though *baihua* caught on and became the accepted nomenclature to describe modern Chinese language and writing, there was, for a brief moment, research on and recognition of an alternative term with more technical precision.

That term was *yutiwen*—literally, "colloquialized written language." Granted that the concept of closing the gap between the spoken and the written was nothing new, and that this particular brand of colloquialized written language was rehearsed by James Yen and Chinese laborers in France with much success, a scientific study of it did not appear until 1928, when Chen Heqin 陳鶴琴 (1892–1982)—Yen's aforementioned friend "Mr. Chen"—published *The Applied Vocabulary of Yutiwen*. Although Chen's *yutiwen* project started as early as 1920, the book did not come out until 1928 owing to a fire that had destroyed part of its data.[16] Drawing on previous lexical scholarship, the book demonstrated the results of the first statistical research on character frequency in *yutiwen* conducted by Chinese scholars.[17] In the preface to the book, Tao Xingzhi acknowledged that the undertaking of *yutiwen* research provided, even before its publication, statistical backing for the first edition of the *People's Thousand Character Lessons* in 1923.[18]

Chen's *yutiwen* project, including its source of data, methodology, and final research output, was firmly grounded in characters with little or no concern for their phonetic values and representations. Harvesting a total of 554,478 characters (including repetition of some) from six categories of primary sources, Chen and his colleagues generated a list of 4,261 discrete characters.[19] Their guiding research questions were as follows:

How many characters are in common use in China? How many of them are used in classical Chinese prose? How many of them in *yutiwen*? And how many of them are being employed in both? Also, how many characters are most frequently used, how many less frequently used, and how many least frequently used? How many characters should primary school students learn? Which ones could be employed for the purpose of People's Education? These questions, so crucial for the popularization of education, could not be answered lightly without careful experiment and meticulous research.[20]

In short, it was all about characters. The source of data was a vast amount of *yutiwen* broken down to discrete units of half a million characters. The experimental method took these characters—half a million of them—and ran them through a statistical ranking in terms of frequency of usage. The research output was a list of 4,261 characters compiled in increasing order from the least frequently used—for instance, *lü* 僂 (hunchback), *ying* 罌 (long-necked jar), *qiang* 羌 (the Qiang people)—to the most frequently used, such as *yi* 一 (one), *bu* 不 (no), and *de* 的 (of).[21] Neither the objective of the experiment, the data pool, the statistical method, nor the final output mentioned "plain speech." In other words, the phonocentric take on the unification of the spoken and the written had no bearing on the linguistic reality of *yutiwen*—the staple of modern Chinese writing.

Chen Heqin, after finishing his study on *yutiwen*, rarely reprised the term himself. More than a mass-education enthusiast with statistical expertise, Chen showed extensive interest in biology, geology, and psychology during his undergraduate years at Tsinghua College and later at Johns Hopkins University. It was not until his graduate studies that he turned his focus to education, receiving his master's degree from Teachers College, Columbia University, in 1919.[22] Mentored by Paul Monroe, William Heard Kilpatrick, Edward Thorndike, and Robert Woodworth and influenced indirectly by John Dewey, Chen came to specialize in kindergarten education and was reputed to be the "father of Chinese early childhood education." A fellow YMCA member, Chen was acquainted with James Yen. Chen also became a colleague of Tao Xingzhi's as he assumed teaching positions at Nanjing Normal University and Southeastern University. That Chen, Yen, and Tao were all Chinese Christian educators who had studied in the United States did not prevent them from taking different approaches to education and politics.[23]

Chen's career as an academic and an educator took on new political urgency when he turned his attention to the Chinese Latinization movement at its height. In 1938 alone he wrote four articles in support of the campaign, including a historical overview of alphabetizing Chinese and three essays discussing Latinization's relationship to wartime refugees, children, and women.[24] He also produced, between 1937 and 1938, a two-volume Sin Wenz primer titled *People's Textbooks* (*Minzhong keben* 民眾課本), alongside sixteen supplementary readers in Sin Wenz, including a translation-cum-transliteration of Lu Xun's *The True Story of Ah Q*, a translation of Ouida's *Dog of Flanders*, and a story about the Qing-dynasty beggar-educator Wu Xun.[25] Serving on the board of the Committee of Chinese Script Reform, Chen continued to write about the new script of the Chinese people. His interest in and commitment to Latinization lasted beyond the surprising suspension of the script revolution in 1958.[26]

It was one thing for the May Fourth and New Culture enthusiasts to reconcile, either unknowingly or strategically, the two mutually exclusive projects of the script revolution and *yutiwen*, using the *baihua* discourse as a hinge;[27] it was quite another for the author of *The Applied Vocabulary of Yutiwen* to conduct statistical research on characters, which preserved and promoted character literacy, and then advocate for the creation of Sin Wenz in the Roman-Latin alphabet. In an article in English titled "Latinization of the Chinese Language" (1938; translated into Chinese in 1947), Chen willingly gave up the technically more accurate term and performed, not unlike Yen, the conceptual conflation of script and language, *yutiwen* and *baihua*.[28] The readers of Chen's 1938 article might well have thought that he was focusing on the Chinese language, as suggested by his subsections—"The Difficulty of Learning the Chinese Language," "Romanization of the Chinese Language," "Vernacular Language Movement," "Phonetic Signs Movement," "National Romanization or 'Kuo-yu' Romanization," and "Latinization of the Chinese Language." However, the 1947 Chinese translation uncovers the conceptual conflation of language and script, as the respective Chinese subsections, translated back into English, read as follows: "The Difficulty of Learning the Chinese Characters," "Romanizing the Chinese Script," "The *Baihua* Prose Movement," "The National Alphabet Movement," "GR," and "Latinizing the Chinese Script."[29] The incongruence between language and script was hardly a careless mistake that Chen was oblivious to or wanted to explain away. On the contrary, he provided in the English article a rationale for the necessity of this very conflation, a statistician's confession of how *baihua* took over the script revolution: "As the minds of the people were not ready to receive a reform so radical as the Romanized script, educators, philologists, and reformers began to agitate for the improvement of the Chinese written language. About a quarter of a century ago, Dr. Hu Shih, Tsai Yuen-pei, Mr. Y. T. Chien and others began to advocate the use of the vernacular language."[30]

Chen's honest account unwittingly revealed and confirmed how the *baihua* literary revolution was from the very beginning a compromise and transmutation of the script revolution. The concessions made by the script revolutionaries allowed room for the literary revolution, which, as the less "radical" cause, won support from the leading figures of the alphabetization movement. Chen's confession showcased how the script question could evolve into the conflation of language and script, as long as the conflation headed in the direction of phonocentric rule of speech over writing. Chen's omission of *yutiwen* also augured how the term *baihua* would prove to be more useful than that for the colloquialized written language, despite the latter's technical and scientific accuracy. *Baihua* was a better choice, for, on the one hand, it acknowledged the historical reality of modern Chinese writing as largely a written language within its own tradition and, on the other, it kept alive phonocentric hopes. Taking *yutiwen* under its wing, *baihua*'s appeal of pure orality sanctioned, albeit in a problematic way, the conceptual collapse between language and script. Holding the back door open for phonocentrism, the term *baihua* enabled the coexistence of script and literary revolutions while promising the future domination of speech over writing. In contrast to *baihua*'s adhesive and generative capacity, *yutiwen* was precise and divisive, its statistical rigor readily pointing to the mutual exclusivity between characters and the Roman-Latin alphabet. For Latinization to have a future in a mass education that taught character literacy, the script revolution was dependent on its transmutation into *baihua.* If Chen's statistical work with *yutiwen* served the cause of mass literacy, then his abstinence from using the term, despite his own study of it, facilitated the alphabetization—specifically, Latinization—of that very mass literacy. The reconciliation between Sin Wenz and *yutiwen* on the eve of the Second Sino-Japanese War ushered in the third and final transmutation of the phonocentric enterprise: the convergence of the Latinization movement, national salvation, and the New Mass Education Movement.

LATINIZATION, WAR, AND THE NEW MASS EDUCATION

Tao Xingzhi was perhaps the most vocal advocate of Sin Wenz among the 688 proponents who signed the public letter "Our Opinion on the Promotion of the New Script" in December 1935 and led the tidal waves bringing together script revolution, mass education, and national salvation at a time of unprecedented national crisis.[31] Tao, like Chen Heqin, had been trained at Columbia Teachers College and was praised by historian John King Fairbank as "the most creative disciple of John Dewey," one "who went beyond him in facing China's problems."[32] Upon returning to China, Tao devoted himself to mass education in both urban and rural areas. He developed his own theory of education and launched a number of schools in accordance with his education philosophy, the most famous being Xiaozhuang Experimental Rural Normal College in suburban Nanjing and Yucai Middle School in Chongqing.[33] He became one of the most important Chinese educators and appealed to both the Guomindang (GMD) and the Chinese Communist Party (CCP). Lauded by the CCP as the "People's Great Educator" and "a nonparty Bolshevik," Tao was also chosen by the GMD as the "People's Ambassador" to embark on a two-year journey between 1936 and 1938, visiting twenty-six countries and rallying international support for Chinese resistance against Japanese invasion. Although his bipartisan appeal made him one of the mediators between the two parties on the eve of the Civil War in 1945, it also caused him uneasiness with both parties. Tao was sometimes deemed to be either overly left leaning or insufficiently so.[34] As early as 1930 the GMD forced Xiaozhuang Normal College to shut down and Tao into a brief exile in Japan; as late as 1951 the CCP posthumously targeted his writings on the beggar-educator Wu Xun for severe criticism.[35] At the center of Tao's accomplishments and controversies were his commitment to mass education and his approach to literacy. Although

his stature as a great educator has heretofore eclipsed his role as a Latinization enthusiast, his writings on Sin Wenz, more so than his writings on education theory, provide a coherent understanding of the entanglement of
literacy, politics, and education—in other words, the triangular connections
between the Chinese Latinization movement, the Second Sino-Japanese
War, and the New Mass Education Movement.

After signing the public letter endorsing Sin Wenz, Tao penned within
a few months' time in 1936 a series of articles in relation to the Chinese Latinization movement.[36] These established and consolidated the three-way
relationship between Sin Wenz, national salvation, and the New Mass Education Movement. They also enabled a semantic transference of Sin Wenz,
through which the final transmutation of the script revolution took a determined leftist turn, merged with a new educational model, and fostered a
new image of children and those who were to teach them.

In "The Problem of Mass Education," Tao observes that Sin Wenz has
"an advantage in that it is easy to learn," which guarantees after a relatively
quick mastery—"intelligent people can learn it in a day; unintelligent people can learn it in a month"—that "students can also function as teachers
and teach their own students." As a result, "everyone can learn to read and
to reason. We will gather the strength to save the nation."[37] In the face of a
total war with Japan, any Chinese patriot would have warmly embraced the
union of script revolution and national salvation. Tao, however, had to
defend his choice of Sin Wenz as a means to achieve mass literacy, which
he did willingly and deliberately, turning it into a token of national resistance and solidarity. In a response to the objection to Sin Wenz by Romanization veteran Li Jinxi, who cited Latinization's "Soviet-Russian origin" and
maintained that it was the central government that had the means to implement the Chinese alphabet, and which was "no business" for individual
alphabetization enthusiasts, Tao begged to differ. Readily siding with Latinization, he called Sin Wenz "a crucial instrument for mass liberation for
all Chinese people" and stated, "To promote it requires the great power of
the entire nation. Now that we are part of the nation, we have the obliga-
tion to make it our own business!"[38]

Li Jinxi would not have forgotten that the endorsement of Gwoyeu
Romatzyh took "major political forces." What he opposed, as Tao observed,
was the major Soviet-Russian political forces associated with Sin Wenz. The
party politics between the CCP and the GMD was exacerbated as the threat

of a full Second Sino-Japanese War became increasingly real. The more significant difference between the two alphabetization advocates was that Li's "major political forces" were imagined as a top-down administrative chain of order, whereas Tao saw in Sin Wenz an opportunity to reshape the definition of both the "political" and its "force." If Sin Wenz envisioned a more efficient version of low-cost literacy than GR, then it also espoused a different kind of politics. Instead of counting on some form of external power to disseminate literacy, Sin Wenz committed itself to making Latinized literacy accessible, mobilizing an organic "political force" from the ground up and working toward national salvation and mass liberation.

Stressing the insoluble bonds between national salvation and mass liberation on various occasions,[39] Tao remarked that, based on the "circularity" of the two, "national salvation and mass liberation are one inseparable great revolution," which found its grammatological embodiment in Sin Wenz.[40] Having established the three-way relationship between literacy, politics, and education, Tao introduced nothing short of a semantic transference of Sin Wenz:

Sin Wenz! Sin Wenz! Sin Wenz is the people's script. It delivers the true voices of the masses and writes stories closest to their hearts. It is not difficult to read, write, or learn. A bayonet at the tip of a pen, it charges ahead and strikes once and again. It stabs at tonal distinctions and lances square characters. Sin Wenz teaches everyone to read, creates a culture of the masses, promotes the status of the people, and thus accomplishes the foremost mission of our time.[41]

Analogizing Sin Wenz to a bayonet, Tao instantly turns the Latinization movement into a symbolic call for military resistance. Sin Wenz, widely affordable and easily available like the bayonet, becomes a stand-in for the people's weapon of national defense, one safeguarding and strengthening the triangular bond connecting the script revolution, national salvation, and mass liberation. However, at the height of the Second Sino-Japanese War, it seemed more important to Latinization advocates like Tao Xingzhi and Chen Heqin to endorse the symbolic spirit of the new script than to commit themselves to writing in Latinized Chinese. In fact, Chen limited his Sin Wenz work to primers, and neither Tao nor Ye Shengtao composed Sin Wenz writing, despite their strong nominal support of Latinization. With national survival at stake, Sin Wenz experienced a semantic makeover from an anticharacter writing system to an antiaggression call to arms. Accordingly, its supporters accommodated themselves to writing in the old script a new *yutiwen*, in allegiance to national salvation and with promises of radical progressivism championed by the script revolution.

Tao took the symbol of Sin Wenz further to illustrate and facilitate a form of national alliance, which was later named the Second United Front.[42] The contention over script served as a fitting trope for the political tension between the CCP and the GMD—including the central government army and major warlords' forces—that needed to be done away with for the realization of the United Front. Tao pleaded, "Do not reject anyone who wants to join the battlefront. It is as though we are in a boat. When the waves are calm, it does not matter if you support Sin Wenz or if I want to preserve *guoyu* and characters. But when the boat runs into pirates, regardless if you support Sin Wenz or characters, you and I need to first of all form an alliance and fight off the pirates."[43]

The less-than-subtle metaphors were intended to argue for the urgency of a United Front. Tao maintained that party allegiance should take a second seat to national survival, and the tolerance of Sin Wenz symbolized the goodwill for a much-needed national alliance. As a Sin Wenz advocate and bipartisan intellectual, Tao gave several interviews and produced a series of writings between July and September 1936, urging cooperation between the GMD and the CCP.[44] The most influential was a coauthored treatise, "Several Basic Conditions and the Minimum Requirement for Uniting Against Humiliation."[45] Widely circulated as a pamphlet, this treatise made direct appeal to the different parties—the central government led by Chiang Kai-shek, the southwestern warlords, and the CCP—to cease domestic conflicts and unite against foreign aggression, which reverberated widely and was greeted promptly with a positive response from Mao Zedong.[46] The Xi'an Incident took place within a few months, and the Second United Front came to fruition on December 24, 1936.[47]

Tao became one of the faces representing the Second United Front, not only as one of its most steadfast believers and promoters but also as a chosen ambassador who appeared on its behalf in front of an international community. Tao's two-year journey from July 1936 to October 1938 took him to twenty-six countries, where he sought moral and financial support for the Chinese resistance against the Japanese from both international society and the overseas Chinese community. He presented at academic conferences, gave interviews and speeches, attended functions, and shook hands with international luminaries—Jawaharlal Nehru, Mahatma Gandhi, Lázaro Cárdenas, and Norman Bethune, to name a few—and commoners alike. He paid visits to Karl Marx's grave in London, Mexican farms, and Egyptian mosques.[48] While in the United States, Tao drafted for John Dewey a letter addressed to Gandhi, Romain Rolland, Albert Einstein, and Bertrand Russell, urging "all countries" to "organize voluntary boycott against Japanese goods" and to provide "every possible assistance to China for relief and self-defence."[49]

As Sin Wenz helped bring about the Second United Front, Tao's work with the latter also bore the imprint of Tao's theorization of a "New Mass Education Movement," thus completing the triangular bonds connecting the script revolution, national salvation, and mass education. This New Mass Education Movement adjusted the expectation of Sin Wenz, revamped Dewey's education philosophy, and signaled a changing focus from educator to educated. Tao remained a steadfast advocate of Sin Wenz, but now that it had become a trope in the service of the Second United Front and a symbol of national salvation, its symbolic value outweighed its technical execution. Albeit confident in Sin Wenz's future, Tao conceded that an indiscriminate treatment of all scripts—characters, National Alphabet, and Sin Wenz—worked best in the interests of the Second United Front.[50] This new development of the Latinization movement—the final transmutation of the script revolution—in the service of national defense gave new legitimacy to the contradictory coexistence of alphabetic Chinese and character literature. For Sin Wenz supporters, even the technical term *yutiwen*, which would have contradicted literary composition in characters, no longer posed a problem. As the final two sections of this chapter demonstrate, once the convergence of Latinization, national salvation, and mass education had taken place, the script revolution was finally equipped to incorporate *yutiwen* literature into its fold.

Besides redefining and expanding the scope of the Latinization movement, Tao's updated take on education theory also sought to retool Dewey's model of progressive education. The groundbreaking motto, "Education is life"—usually attributed to Dewey— effectively broke the boundary between school and society by paying special attention to the individual "experience."[51] Though Tao's earlier theory and practice fell in line with the

Dewey school of thought,[52] by late 1926 Tao had reversed "education is life" to "life is education," coupled it with "society is school," and established his new theory of "teaching, learning, and doing all in one," which later became the motto of his Xiaozhuang Normal College.[53] If these updated slogans were no more than necessary adjustments to Dewey's model in accordance with Chinese circumstances, having not much to do with the looming war, then Tao's formulation of and objections to the old mass-education movement were unequivocal in their political stance as a direct result of the war. With an increasing number of institutions, such as James Yen's Ting Hsien project, decamping from areas under Japanese threat, Tao outspokenly called for a New Mass Education Movement with a distinct class consciousness. In a pointed essay called "Education Fled Away" (1936), Tao criticized James Yen's old mass education as elitist and escapist, as Yen and his associates actively sought to relocate the Ting Hsien program, named after a rural northern county in Hebei, to the more secure southwestern provinces. Referring to the recent relocation of Tsinghua University to the safer hinterland, Tao chided that "higher education could run away with high-class Chinese," while "real common people have nowhere to turn" and "real mass education" ought to stay with them and become "genuine education that battles reality," thus contributing to "the liberation movement of the nation."[54] Tao welcomed the retreat of the elitist, mobile, high-class Chinese, so that the new mass education—"of the masses, by the masses, and for the masses"—could now take center stage. By rejecting the old mass-education movement and applauding the new, he broke away from liberal-education reform and further gravitated toward a class-conscious and revolutionary educational model. Two years prior to his public breakup with Yen, his children's play *At the Door of the Young Master* (1934) already manifested such tendencies. The one-act play brought to life a moment of awakening of a child beggar, a young vegetable vendor, and a newspaper boy as the three children discovered that together they could defeat the little bully—the "young master." An allegory of the future revolution, Tao's play augured the union of lower-class masses and their violent clash with the elitist few.[55]

Accompanying the rising class consciousness that revamped Dewey's education theory was the third and final attribute of the New Mass Education Movement, which saw a shift in focus from the educator to the educated and a recalibrated definition of children. After the shutdown of Xiaozhuang Normal College in 1930, Tao turned his attention from normal school to children's education, culminating in the foundation of Yucai Middle School for refugee children in 1939. It was in this period that the image of children underwent an interesting makeover, from the "little teacher" during the literacy campaign to the "little worker" during the national crisis.[56] In conjunction with his leftist turn away from the old mass education and toward the new, Tao also gave a class-conscious definition to the future generations of children. As early as 1932, he had commended children in the new age to become "little workers" who should engage in both physical and mental labor.[57] The theme of "little worker" intensified in a speech titled "Children Are the Future Giants of the Nation" (1938). Tao argued, "All children are masters of the future, army reserves to defeat enemies, and combatants during times of nation building. At present, the education that children ought to receive is an industrial one. For refugee children, local groups of industrial learning should be established."[58] Tao was explicit—even blunt—in stating China's dire need for industrial workers as it faced defeat in the industrialized warfare of World War II. His focus on children, although analogous to what Andrew F. Jones characterized as "the centrality of children in May Fourth nationalist discourse,"[59] shifted gears from children's education to national defense as the war-torn nation could no longer afford to view its children through the bourgeois concept of childhood but had to impose on them the responsibilities of "little teachers" and "little workers." Lu Xun's leitmotif of "saving the children" from both neo-Confucian suffocation and developmentalist commercialization took a second seat to the call of "saving the nation," which conditioned and precipitated the growth of a young working class. By preparing children with "industrial learning" and pronouncing them little workers, Tao fast-tracked them into "future giants of the nation" who would wrest leadership from the old elites that not so long ago had attempted their rescue. The changing conceptualization of children flagged a reconfiguration of modern Chinese literary production. Script and literary revolutionaries alike willingly composed and promoted *yutiwen* literature as long as it was in conformity with the ideals of Latinization and the New Mass Education Movement. As a result, education literature written in *yutiwen* saw the historical transformation from the May Fourth paradigm of enlightenment to the wartime discourse of national salvation and mass liberation, which was accompanied by a shift in focus from the liberal educator to the progressive educated, as well as a left turn of critical realism in search of a revolutionary subjectivity.

YUTIWEN AS MODERN CHINESE LITERATURE

Ye Shengtao 葉聖陶 (also known as Ye Shaojun 葉紹鈞, 1894–1988) was perhaps *the* writer of Chinese education literature.[60] Ye's long-lasting and prolific literary career—from his first publication in 1914 until his death in 1988—was praised by C. T. Hsia as having "best stood the test of time."[61] Ye started out writing short stories in emulation of Washington Irving and Oliver Goldsmith, first for the commercial magazine *Saturday*, of which he quickly grew weary since his true aspiration lay in critical realism.[62] Encouraged by Gu Jiegang 顧頡剛, a major Chinese historian and Ye's lifelong friend, Ye began to compose for the journal *New Tide*. His craftsmanship attracted Mao Dun and Zheng Zhenduo, who extended an invitation to Ye to become one of the twelve founding members of the Literary Research Society in January 1921.[63] He went on to create many firsts in modern Chinese literary history, producing the first collection of children's literature, *The Scarecrow* 稻草人, in 1922; the first bildungsroman in modern Chinese literary history, *Ni Huanzhi* 倪煥之, in 1928; and the first "novelistic writing manual" of *yutiwen*, *Wenxin* 文心 (The heart of writing), in 1934.[64]

Two themes dominated Ye's literary production—first, his preoccupation with children and education, and second, his tireless attention to language, which corresponded to his multiple roles as educator, editor, and publisher. A devoted educator, Ye taught primary and middle school for more than a decade starting in the 1910s and served as vice-minister of the People's Republic of China's Education Department after 1949. In his role as editor and publisher, he worked first at the Commercial Press and then at Kaiming Bookstore, both of which were dedicated to the promotion of what was in essence *yutiwen* and of many younger writers, such as Ba Jin and Ding Ling. Having his entire career revolve around writing during a period that redefined Chinese language and literature, Ye was hardly exempt from the historical struggle between Sin Wenz and *yutiwen*. In fact, the accomplished practitioner, promoter, and teacher of *yutiwen* was among the 688 activists who signed the 1935 public letter endorsing the new Chinese alphabet.[65] Ye's literary stature, devotion to language and writing, and investment in education thus showcased the intertwining of script revolution, literary revolution, and mass education at moments of national crisis. In the following pages I propose a reading of two major novels from Ye—*Ni Huanzhi* and *Wenxin*—through the lens of *yutiwen*. I raise a new set of questions: What did writers like Ye Shengtao who became Sin Wenz advocates write in their literary endeavors and why? How did their choice of literary language inform and interact with their chosen subject matter? If their adoption of *yutiwen* was the result of the negotiations between a literacy revolution, education reform, and war crises, then did the added dimension of *yutiwen* literature offer something new to the old structural interconnections between literacy, education, and war?

Ni Huanzhi, one of the first novels in modern Chinese literary history, was arguably Ye's most ambitious work. Before it, Ye had engaged mainly with short stories.[66] His attempt at novel writing was encouraged by his editor friends Li Shicen and Zhou Yutong, who commissioned the work for serial publication in the *Jiaoyu zazhi* 教育雜誌 (Journal of education) from January to November 1928.[67] It received instant critical attention. Qian Xingcun called it a "very powerful bildungsroman." Mao Dun commended it as "a weighty piece of work" of the post–May Fourth literary world. Xia Mianzun hailed it as "opening a new era."[68] This "powerful" piece of work, the first of its kind in modern Chinese literature, is written from the third-person perspective of its eponymous protagonist—a village primary-school teacher named Ni Huanzhi—and captures key episodes of modern Chinese history from the Revolution of 1911, to the May Fourth Movement, and eventually to the failure of the First GMD–CCP United Front in 1927. A thinly veiled autobiographical novel, it narrates in a linear chronology Ni's growth, maturation, and eventual demise as a progressive educator, believer in romantic love, and revolutionary youth.[69]

Ni Huanzhi starts out as an enthusiast of education reform despite considerable resistance to the progressive education measures that he tries to implement at his local school in a village near Shanghai. Shared education ideals bring together Ni and his love interest, Jin Peizhang 金佩璋. Disillusioned by married life and inspired by the May Fourth Movement, Ni leaves his village for Shanghai. He throws himself into radical politics in the city, refashioning himself as an "educator for revolution." He begins to design a rural normal college and gives speeches at street rallies. The May

Thirtieth Incident in 1925, during which Shanghai police opened fire on pro-testing workers and students, teaches Ni the brutality of revolution and the hollowness of his own "sermons." Lapsing into grave doubts about the legitimacy of his enlightenment project, he becomes increasingly dismayed at the prospects of the revolution and his own future in it. Ni is further sad-dened by the death of his Communist friend Wang Leshan. After the First United Front crumbles, Ni dies from typhoid, leaving behind his wife, son, and an unfinished blueprint of the rural normal college.

Previous scholarship on *Ni Huanzhi*, from the time of its composition to the present, largely concurs that the novel consists of two separate sub-novels: the first eighteen chapters constitute an education novel that takes place in a village, and the final twelve chapters make up a revolutionary novel set largely in the city of Shanghai. Some scholars focus on the novel as a literary treatment of the 1920s education reform, analyzing the work in relation to the mass-education movement and progressive education model, while taking the latter half as nothing more than the political back-ground.[70] Others pay little attention to the educational content and opt for a politicized reading of the novel, suggesting that it accurately captured the destined fall of "the petty-bourgeois intellectuals" in an age of revolution.[71] Though usually laudatory in their respective appraisals of the two parts individually, critics are more often than not discontented with the sense of disparity between them. C. T. Hsia rules that *Ni Huanzhi* "does not come off very well as a novel," before conceding that it is nonetheless "a notable achievement."[72] Marston Anderson, in a much more sympathetic reading, also points out that "the novel remains disconnected."[73] Critics might have been right in recognizing a level of formal incongruence between the two parts, which was created partially by the narrative clumsiness Ye's narrator seems to display. However, what the critics might have missed, I suggest, is *Ni Huanzhi*'s structural ingenuity that, on the one hand, provides a concrete linkage between the two subnovels and, on the other, comes very close to an important historical insight into the fall of the petty-bourgeois intellectu-als, the failure of the United Front, and the emerging tendencies of revolu-tionary literature. The key is the centrality of writing, more accurately *yuti-wen* writing. Among all Ni Huanzhi's life endeavors, from his professional career to his romantic relationship, from revolutionary zeal to final disillu-sionment, writing—its content, format, and mode of representation—stands at the center.

First, writing is part and parcel of Ni's pedagogical responsibility as a teacher. At the same time, it is the narrative frame through which the progressive educational program that Ni supports is presented. Ni chooses to teach *baihua*, as he tells his students. Writing thus becomes a daily activity that he engages in, and the kind of writing Ni prefers also becomes emblematic of the kind of educational model that he promotes. Chapter 1 of the novel unfolds on a boat trip from Ni's previous teaching position to his current one. On the boat, we are introduced to the protagonist and his future brother-in-law, Jin Shubo, who is sent by Ni's new principal, Jiang Bingru, to guide his way. Jiang is introduced as a hopeless idealist of education reform through Ni and Jin's conversation, which quickly zooms in on a piece of Jiang's writing. Having remarked that Ni shares the principal's quixotic mannerism, Jin informs him that Jiang "wrote an article on education" and that "the article is his dream."[74] Instantaneously energized by Jiang's ardor, Ni takes Jiang's precious article as a symbol of his own "new life" and cannot wait to read it upon his first meeting with the principal. "Huanzhi took the article and held it in hand. It was roughly two dozen sheets of blue-squared paper. Fine characters ran in neat columns. There were indeed many places of erasures, corrections, and insertions, but they all preserved the briskness and clarity of the original text."[75] As soon as this piece of writing is handed over to Ni and introduced into the narrative, it assumes considerable agency for almost a third of the novel. The article is circulated, invites ample discussion, but refuses direct quotations from it. A capable narrative device, it enables the introduction of the educational ideals and measures, which Jiang and Ni are excited to bring to the village school. A token of progressivism, it signifies pedagogical rigor and educational idealism while distinguishing Jiang and Ni from their conservative-minded colleagues.

The content of the article is in essence an argument for and a program of progressive education. In discussions of the article in ensuing chapters, we learn that "a school should be, instead of a special environment for students, a conducive environment for them to live in."[76] Therefore a school should not focus merely on book learning but ought to include its own "factory, farm, music hall, hospital, library, shops, and news press."[77] Clearly informed by the progressive education reform popular at the time, Ye's narrative is reminiscent of John Dewey's model of "education is life," to the extent of comparing Jiang Bingru's thought to Dewey's theory and gesturing toward Tao Xingzhi's "teaching, learning, and doing all in one."[78] However, as the fictive progressive educator, Ni finds to his dismay that Jiang's ideas turn out to be far more attractive in writing than in practice. Though summoned by the May Fourth and May Thirtieth Movements, Ni does not venture far beyond textual musings in his attempt at revolutionizing normal education. Jiang's article turns into Ni's drafts, first resisted by the village school and then tucked away in Ni's drawer. The fixation on writing is, on the one hand, as Mao Dun diagnoses, symptomatic of the petty-bourgeois intellectuals' "uselessness";[79] on the other, it tells of Ye's own limits in terms of narrative tactics, which Ye is quick to acknowledge: "I do not understood workers and peasants any more than I understand wealthy merchants and bureaucrats; the only group that I am familiar with is intellectuals and urban petty bourgeoisie."[80] External reality—whether education reform or radical politics—has to be inflected through writing before Ye's narrator can make use of it.[81] Writing, therefore, takes on a tertiary role in *Ni Huanzhi*, first as a theme, then as content employed by the narrator, and finally as a working narrative framework stitching together the two parts of the novel. The obsession with writing might have limited *Ni Huanzhi*'s representational possibility, but it reveals unwittingly the petty-bourgeois educator's essential dilemma in his struggle with enlightenment and revolution, which finds concrete embodiment in the problem of language.

The most expressive instantiation is the love letters exchanged between Ni Huanzhi and Jin Peizhang. A New Culture advocate, Ni believes in the efficacy of *baihua* prose, in which he composes his love letters. After confessing his love for Jin, Ni explains to her his choice of language: "This is my first time to try my hand at the *baihua* style to pen letters. Although it is nothing much to look at and could not be considered literature, it feels crisp and sharp. I feel that I am speaking to you face-to-face. This is proof that the literary reform can succeed. You won't laugh at my preference for the new and pursuit of the trendy?"[82] Ni's prose, rather than the plain speech of *baihua* that he dreams to pour out to Jin in person, is in fact *yutiwen*. Classical formulations such as *quejue* 確覺, *wuyi* 無異, and *xixinqushi* 喜新趨時 betray him, since they are of a literary—not at all colloquial—nature. Despite the colloquial marker *ba* 吧, what Ni claims to be a *baihua* style is at best a compromise between the literary and the colloquial, hence *yutiwen*. As a matter of fact, the narrative voice as well as dialogues between characters are all composed in *yutiwen*. The only exception is Jin Peizhang's writing. Jin, although in principle endorsing the New Culture spirit, decides that one has to write the decent classical and literary language of *wenyan* before one can be trusted with the plain "*baihua* style." In response to Ni's passion for *baihua*, Jin resorts to formal classical expression:

Baihua style indeed excels in composition. It benefits the conveyance of emotions and eliminates ambiguity and generalization. I fear only [were I to write in *baihua*] that my inadequate imitation will expose its uncomely nature. Therefore, I conceal my clumsiness and keep to *wenyan*. Will you please not mock my nostalgia and obduracy and laugh at my inability to follow your good example?[83]

My translation hardly captures the sense of formality of Jin's classical language, which is formulated mostly in four-character expressions such as *yiyu daqing* 宜於達情 and *xiaopinfuxiao* 效顰弗肖. Though conceding the superiority of the "*baihua* style," Jin insists on writing in *wenyan* and plays up the dichotomy between the two. Framing them as antithetical, her *wenyan* letter, like Ni's *baihua*-style letter, corroborates the polarizing discourse of *baihua* versus *wenyan*.

If letter writing bears witness to the budding romance between Ni and Jin, then it also registers the disillusionment of their relationship. Ye's narrator resorts once again to writing to give shape to an otherwise clichéd development of May Fourth romance stories, where the male intellectual grows disappointed in quotidian life and a vapid housewife who barely resembles his erstwhile lover. Ni departs for Shanghai, leaving Jin at home with their son and his mother. Upon receiving another *wenyan* letter from Jin, Ni feels as if he had eaten "some stale fruit." He cannot help but wonder what Jin would have been like had marriage and child-rearing not ruined her. In the ideal world, she would be the new woman with "bobbed hair, a close-fitting cotton gown," who would definitely prefer "the simple, straightforward *baihua* to something so tangled up in classical markers as 'ye.' "[84] The classical writing is thus feminized and stigmatized, while *baihua* gains authorial masculinity. An analysis of the relationship between writing and gender belongs to another study, but what pertains to our immediate interest is how Ni's own future is not exempt from the judgment of writing. If Jin's ruin is manifested through Ni's musings about her writing style, then his own demise is also prophesied by reflections on writing.

Ni Huanzhi has to die, but why? Ye Shengtao's contemporaneous critics such as Mao Dun and Qian Xingcun maintained that death was the fate of May Fourth petty-bourgeois intellectuals, for their enervated narcissism had no place in the age of the revolution. A more recent discussion of *Ni Huanzhi* by Marston Anderson backs up this historic ruling with a formal analysis of what he calls the moral impediments to realism, discernible throughout Ye's oeuvre. If the power of realism lies in its objective portrayal of reality, then that portrayal necessarily includes both the physical realities of the outside world and the "psychological and emotional realities" of the inner self, as well as an intricate balancing act between the two. As the narrator of *Ni Huanzhi* finds the two realities inherently incongruent, it becomes impossible to square "the questing bourgeois self" with the "inexorable march" of the revolution, which "grinds all sentimental idealism underfoot." In other words, Anderson observes, "realist fiction, formerly entrusted with the self's creation and expression, is in the end left only the task of enacting its deconstruction, a narrative suicide."[85] Unable to remedy the gap between Ni's personal subjectivity and the exigencies of his world, the narrative has to terminate the "bourgeois self" that it starts out to forge.

Historical and formalist insights aside, I suggest that there is a more concrete "narrative suicide" embedded in the question of writing, which is revealed by way of Ni's revelation over writing. Chapter 23 depicts how, in the wake of the May Thirtieth Movement, Ni finds himself often en route to the industrial quarters of Shanghai, where the strike first takes place. In admiration of the valiant workers in action, he enters a silent soliloquy, and the narrator, a direct psychologization:

Why aren't the peasants rising up during this present wave of unrest? They are too scattered. One must also blame the Chinese script, for all the while it remains so difficult to recognize and memorize that only those who have nothing else to do can master it. These poor peasants who toil all year round will have to resign themselves to never having a means of communicating news; without this instrument, they are naturally cut off from news of the outside world.[86]

The Chinese script is once again faulted. Ni now clearly sees the script for its role as a social medium, central to the mobilization of the peasants. However, the difficulty of the characters stands in the way of effective communication and mobilization. Ni offers no solution and lets the psychological musing in *yutiwen* continue to wander off and reflect on his "sermonlike speech" to the workers during the day. The narrator continues, "He [Huanzhi] could not help but doubt himself. . . . The immediate questions are, Do they [workers] really know so little? Are their minds really like a blank sheet of paper or a shapeless, uncut block of stone? Does he really know much more than they do? Is what he has been telling them actually of any use to them at all? . . . "[87] The chain of questions that Ni raises here is so fatal that his inability to address any of them leads to his own physical demise toward the end of the story.

To be fair, none of these questions is answerable, and all of them shoot right through the heart of the enlightenment project of May Fourth. They shake the theoretical, moral, and intellectual ground on which the power relations between the preaching intellectuals and the listening masses are imagined and practiced. These questions would not have been conceivable in the framework of the old mass-education movement led by James Yen but loom large in the mind of a frustrated liberal educator having an existential crisis of himself, the authority of the intellectuals, and the legitimacy of the enlightenment project. By articulating the unsolvable problem of the script, the narrative—despite its commitment to the intellectuals and educators—lands on a negation of them. If a *yutiwen* narrative dares not venture the elimination of the script of characters, then an alternative is the annihilation of the intellectuals and teachers of character literacy. Ni Huanzhi, with his sensitivity to writing, zest for the revolution, and class nature as a petty-bourgeois intellectual, unwittingly serves as the perfect victim of a structural narrative suicide. Though his demise is imminent, the narrator refrains from announcing his sentence on the spot, allowing a long section of self-reflection to wind down to an ellipsis. Following the ellipsis, readers see the gradual decline of the protagonist as he bids his old friends farewell, mourns the death of his new comrade, becomes tormented by his stalled progress with the rural normal college, is eventually inflicted by typhoid, and dies. The representative of the petty-bourgeois intellectual has to fade out before the new generation makes its entrance.

THE HEART OF LITERATURE

Wenxin 文心 (The heart of literature), coauthored by Ye Shengtao and Xia Mianzun between 1931 and 1934, was the final novel Ye Shengtao wrote before he shifted to education and teaching. Ye and Xia, who became in-laws while writing the book, were both editors for a journal published by Kaiming Bookstore titled *Zhongxuesheng* 中學生 (Middle school students). *Wenxin* was first serialized in this journal to teach teenagers in a fictional form "the total knowledge of the Chinese language."[88] Two older literary works framed the conceptualization of *Wenxin*. The first was a sixth-century work credited to Liu Xie 劉勰 titled *Wenxin diaolong* 文心雕龍 (The literary mind and the carving of dragons). The earliest systematic Chinese literary criticism, it was also the first book about "the total knowledge of the Chinese language," from which *Wenxin* got its title. The second source of origin, as observed by Charles Laughlin, was Edmondo De Amicis's novel *Cuore: Libro per i ragazzi* (The heart of a boy, 1887). Xia Mianzun had translated a Japanese version of it into Chinese in 1923, titled *Ai de jiaoyu* 愛的教育 (Education of love), which provided *Wenxin* with its narrative structure.[89]

Combining the theme of *Wenxin diaolong* and the student-centered structure of *Cuore*, *Wenxin* depicts life in a certain No. 1 Middle School in H city over the course of thirty-two chapters.[90] Anchored in the literary and linguistic education in the school on the eve of the full outbreak of the Second Sino-Japanese War, the narrative frames the school life as part of the social and political panorama of the time. Lodging a third-person perspective through the young protagonist, Zhou Lehua 周樂華, it takes readers through a tripartite educational process—school education, wartime education, and life education—in the period between the January 28 Incident in 1931 and the fall of Yuzhou to the Japanese in 1933. The story takes an unexpected turn as Zhou Lehua drops out of school and starts working at a local iron factory. The narrative winds to an end as Zhou grows into a factory leader and writes to his former classmates congratulating them on their upcoming graduation. A novel written in and about *yutiwen*, *Wenxin* is at the same time a teaching manual on how to write the future staple of modern Chinese literature and an *Erziehungsroman* (novel of education) on how a young student grows into a "little worker." A perfect instantiation of the union of literacy, education, and war, it brings together the pedagogy of *yutiwen*, the model of the New Mass Education Movement, and the urgency of national salvation and suggests one hopeful outcome of such a convergence by sketching the figure of a little worker who not only can read and write "books in characters" but also masters knowledge "without characters."[91]

Unlike other contemporary works in *yutiwen*—for instance, *Ni Huan-zhi*, where the term *yutiwen* is not invoked—*Wenxin* calls the colloquialized written language by its technical name. It opens with Zhou's and his classmate's difficulty in understanding two assigned essays in their *guowen* 國文 (national prose) class: one "*wenyan* prose" by the Qing literatus Yao Nai, the other "*baihua* prose" of Lu Xun's celebrated "Autumn Night." Sympathizing with Zhou and his friend's repeated "we don't understand," Zhou's father laments the lack of "suitable textbooks" that ought to have been "compiled especially" for middle school students but assures them that their new *guowen* teacher, Wang Yangshan, knows the right approach to teaching modern Chinese writing.[92] The right *guowen* for pedagogy—neither *wenyan* nor the May Fourth *baihua*—is none other than *yutiwen*. As the narrative and Mr. Wang's classes go on to dissect *yutiwen*'s literary origin, diction, syntax, grammar, composition, and even mistakes, both the reader and the students learn by heart the true name of the future staple of modern Chinese writing. Chapter 9 of the story depicts a class discussion of the popular column called Wenzhang bingyuan 文章病院 (Composition hospital) serialized in Ye and Xia's journal *Middle School Students*.[93] After closely reviewing three examples in the column—first, the dictionary *Ciyuan xubian* 辭源續編; second, an official declaration passed by a GMD conference; and third, a particular public letter issued by a group of middle school presidents in Jiangsu Province—and the column's detailed diagnosis, Zhou and his classmates present their findings of a litany of syntactical and semantic mistakes, ruling that, "those three pieces are all *wenyan* prose, while what we write is *yutiwen*."[94]

The insistence on calling *yutiwen* by its own name also demonstrates how an education of character literacy in line with national salvation and mass liberation had been readily perceived as compatible with the progressive ethos shared by both the script and the literary revolutions and had become instrumental to the wartime education prioritized by faculty and students alike. Students consult teachers on their own student magazine, *Anti-Japanese Resistance Weekly*, and often take inspiration from Ye and Xia's journal *Middle School Students*, which often features writings on the war.[95] They debate extensively on how to write a play with the central theme of resistance. They even compose a poster in protest of the GMD's lapse into classical prose education, objecting to such "feudal remnants" during a time of national humiliation and petitioning for the progressive *yutiwen*.[96] Although *Wenxin* emphasizes—even glorifies—the importance of *yutiwen* writing, the narrative is not incapable of self-reflexivity when it critiques pure book learning, poetry writing, and the self-referentiality of the intellectuals. After a whole chapter on a proresistance piece in *Middle School Students* and another essay drafted for their own *Weekly*, Mr. Wang's lament captures a sense of inadequacy and guilt: "We can only fight the enemies with our writing. How shamefaced we all are!"[97] In another discussion, of new-style poetry, Zhou's father cautions against his son's and his classmates' indulgence in the Jin-dynasty poet Tao Yuanming's pastoral poetry and introduces them to proletarian poetry from the Soviet Union.[98] That is why, when Zhou Lehua quits school to take a job at the local iron factory, he occupies a special place among students and teachers. At the farewell party held in his honor, both teachers and classmates, though sorry to see Zhou leave, celebrate his new role as a "little worker." They criticize mere book learning as "the expression of the selfishness of the upper and middle classes" and reassure Zhou that true learning "can take place wherever and whenever." The little-worker-to-be gives the concluding remarks, "I also want to read books that are not written in characters. I shall learn from and experience the library of society."[99] As though answering Tao Xingzhi's call for the little workers, Zhou quickly learns his trade in iron production, starts celebrating the May 1 International Workers' Day, and helps his fellow young workers at night school, contemplating the meaningful relationship between workers and machines. The narrative concludes in the coming together of school knowledge, factory experience, and life lessons as readers are led to anticipate, like Zhou's classmates, the little worker's speech at the commencement.[100]

Wenxin, read in this light, is a proposal for how to cope with the national crisis on the eve of the full outbreak of the Second Sino-Japanese War and a prophecy of the future of China. Endorsing in essence the new mass education, *Wenxin* recommends the reinvention of children into little workers, for not only are they needed for national defense but also they shoulder the responsibility to maintain future peace of China. As petty-bourgeois intellectuals such as Ni Huanzhi fade out from center stage, little workers like Zhou Lehua—who read and write *yutiwen*, who equip themselves with industrial know-how, and who are committed to national salvation—take charge. By weaving together the fictive narrative, the *yutiwen* textbook, and the popular journal *Middle School Students* edited by both authors of the novel, *Wenxin* is proactive in imagining, portraying, and establishing such a future. In a streamlined effort, the novel quotes frequently and directly from the journal, the journal serializes chapters from the novel, and both the novel and the journal pride themselves in providing much-needed textbook materials.[101] With unabashed self-referentiality, *Wenxin* creates a narrative complex where textbook, fiction, and popular journal congregate to enliven an otherwise abstract revolutionizing turn in literacy programs, mass education, and literary production.

Wenxin's somewhat mechanical narrative organized around each *yutiwen* lesson and its more-often-than-not didactic tone of a textbook compromised its literary merit. The fact remained, however, that this unusual novel instantiated the possibility of reconciling *yutiwen* composition with the script revolution at the historical juncture of national salvation, mass liberation, and proletarian culture. The convergence of the script and literary revolutions, brought about and hinging on *yutiwen*-cum-*baihua*, signaled the rising tide of the political revolution. Contemporaneous with the three "massification" discussions, *Wenxin* partook, perhaps not self-consciously, in the same discussions by offering a concrete literary example of what an ideal new mass education would look like and who the new masses were. Inasmuch as the new mass education was defined by the ethos of the script revolution and national salvation, the new masses to emerge from such an education would necessarily be *yutiwen* practitioners and Latinization sympathizers, who were willing and able to work toward national industrialization and defense at a time of military crisis. In the short period between *Ni Huanzhi* (1928) and *Wenxin* (1934), the transition was set in motion, from the dominance of the petty-bourgeois educator to the beckoning of a whole generation of revolutionized young student workers. In a longer period between the two world wars, the educator working for a liberal and reformist enlightenment project could no longer be sure of his project, either fleeing to the hinterland of China or perishing in his own studio. The workers would no longer submit *yutiwen* writings of critical thinking and not be taken seriously; instead, they were actively encouraged to think, speak, and write in their own voices, to produce a working-class culture that had been inconceivable a mere two decades before. The proletarianizing tendencies in literature and art continued to grow, culminating in Mao Zedong's "Talks at the Yan'an Conference on Literature and Art" (1942), which forcefully argued for a revolutionary and socialist realist recalibration of literature and art led by the working class and in the service of the majority "90 percent" of all people. Analogous to the democratizing side of the phonocentric antinomies described in chapter 2, the final transmutation of phonocentrism more explicitly set the tone for the entanglement of art and politics for decades to come.[102] A prophetic literary sketch, *Wenxin* captured the momentum that ushered in a new age of revolutionary literature and socialist realist literature in modern Chinese literary history and afforded its readers a glimpse of both the powerful impetus and potential limits of the Proletkult in the service of politics.

Hardly an insular Chinese case, the rise of a working-class culture—a corollary phenomenon of the development of capital—was repeated all over the world roughly around the same period as the Great Depression of the 1930s.[103] Soviet Russia took the lead in cultivating a proletarian culture as early as the Revolution of 1917, which reached a high point in the 1930s and saw the publication of works from major writers like Nikolay Ostrovsky, Aleksandr Fadeyev, Fyodor Gladkov, and Maxim Gorky, exerting direct and lasting influence on the development of revolutionary and socialist literature in China and elsewhere.[104] Both Japan and Korea witnessed institutionalized movements of proletarian literature—the Japanese Proletarian Arts Federation, the Union of Japanese Proletarian Cultural Organizations, and the Korean Artists' Proletarian Federation—cultivating young talents such as Takiji Kobayashi, Sunao Tokunaga, Im Hwa, and Kim Namch'ŏn.[105] European working-class writers who produced proletarian novels in the 1930s included the English novelist Walter Greenwood, the Welsh writer Jack Jones, and Henri Poulaille and Henri Barbusse from France, to name a few.[106] In the United States, the same year of *Wenxin*'s publication (1934) saw the eruption of general strikes, followed by the creation of the CIO (Committee for, later Congress of, Industrial Organizations), which won support from a constellation of artistic and literary talent such as Archibald MacLeish, Orson Welles, John Dos Passos, Langston Hughes, Duke Ellington, and Malcolm Cowley and forged what Michael Denning called a cultural front that reshaped American society.[107]

A comparative study of international proletarian writing is a task for other studies. Even an adequate take on Chinese proletarian literature and the development of socialist realism after the foundation of the PRC is beyond the scope of this book. I want to establish, however, that the originary pulsations of Chinese proletarian and revolutionary literature could be felt through the script revolution and its transmutations. Likewise, the seemingly impossible mission of the Chinese alphabetization movements channeled their phonocentric aspirations into the Old and New Mass Education Movements, converged via the "massification" question with literary and political revolutions, and finally took literary form in the Proletkult and socialist realism. The connections between the question of the script and the quest for the Proletkult run deeper, as the limits of phonocentrism—the constrictions of local speech, the blind spot of the reformist enlightenment, and the predictable growth and anticipated triumph of workers, peasants, and soldiers—provided crucial clues to understanding the restrictions of state-sponsored socialist realism in art and literature for years to come.[108] Although my present probe into the Proletkult is framed within and limited by the parameters of phonocentric antinomies, the entry point of the script revolution and its three transmutations open up a series of inquiries worthy of more scholarly attention in the future: Does the realization of the democratizing tendencies in phonocentrism necessarily take the form of the representation of topolects and the commitment to dialect literature? To what extent does phonetic representation (*Darstellung*) guarantee the subaltern—be it a Minnan-speaking Bible woman or a working-class writer composing proletarian novels—a real chance at speaking and writing? Last but not least, if the liberalizing and democratizing forces of phonocentrism unleash the tide of revolutionary literature and socialist realism, then does its radically egalitarian politics predetermine a class-conscious approach to literature and a fated—if not failing—aesthetics of simplification and typification?

As revolutionary literature, or the revolutionizing of literature, provided some literary closure to the script revolution, one question lingers: is this the end of the script revolution? Script revolutionaries had reason to believe that the phonocentric promises were alive and well, for they were the hinge that brought together alphabetization, *yutiwen*, mass education, and the Proletkult in the first place. Chapter 5 answers this question and ponders the implications of the surprising final containment of the theretofore most radical phase of the script revolution.

PART III

Containment

Chapter Five

TOWARD A CHINESE GRAMMATOLOGY

A writing that breaks with the phonè radically is perhaps the most rational and the most effective of scientific machines.

—DERRIDA, *OF GRAMMATOLOGY*

A record of speech is not writing. Writing is a kind of accumulation of history.

—TANG LAN

On January 10, 1958, Ye Shengtao—by then vice-minister of education of the People's Republic of China, director of the People's Education Press, and member of the Committee for Chinese Script Reform[1]—sat with other delegates at the plenary session of the Chinese People's Political Consultative Congress and listened to Premier Zhou Enlai's report on "The Current Tasks of the Script Reform." Two days later, Ye packed audiotapes of Zhou Enlai's speech and set off with Zhou Youguang—an economist turned script reformer who would become the longest-living member of the Committee for Chinese Script Reform—to southwestern China to promote the premier's directive on the reform.[2] With a direct lineage from the Chinese Latinization movement, the socialist script reform was anticipated—by party elites, domestic alphabetization enthusiasts, and foreign observers—to be the ultimate revolution that would finally end the reign of Chinese characters. Therefore it was an understatement to call Zhou Enlai's speech a surprise when he announced, "The current tasks of script reform are: simplify characters, promote *putonghua*, and issue and implement a pinyin plan."[3] The characters were there to stay, and the Chinese alphabet was shelved for an indefinite future.

With its unprecedented state sponsorship and affecting a population of six hundred million at the time, the socialist script reform was perhaps the biggest linguistic and grammatological experiment in human history. No research to date has explained its fundamental puzzle: how did the climax of the Chinese script revolution that vowed to terminate the rule of characters for good end up endorsing a simplified version of them and an auxiliary spelling system called pinyin? Mao Zedong's alleged conversation with Joseph Stalin—popularized by *New Yorker* staff writer Peter Hessler's best seller *Oracle Bones*[4]—during which Stalin was said to have encouraged Mao to develop a Chinese "national form" in writing, offers some insight, for the rise of the national form was a direct result of the global moment of decolonization, anti-imperialism, and international solidarity in the immediate aftermath of World War II. I suggest, however, that there is a less-anecdotal and more grammatologically grounded explanation to the puzzle.

This concluding chapter does not attempt to survey the socialist script reform in full. An adequate investigation of the creation of scripts for ethnic minorities, as well as different versions of simplified characters, is a burden for other monographs.[5] Instead, the chapter aims to solve the puzzle that is the surprising resolution to the half-century Chinese script revolution and to suggest meaningful ways of imagining grammatology. It starts by charting the scale and intensity of socialist script reform. As the philologist and dissident Chen Mengjia's fatal clash with the state policy of pinyin demonstrates, the commitment to the alphabetization of the script escalated from a state policy to a state ideology. This seemingly impenetrable pinyin ideology is, however, not entirely indestructible. Tracing the life's work of Chen's erstwhile teacher, the paleographer and archaeologist Tang Lan, I explore how the zest for the pinyin ideology lent itself to the redefinition of alphabetization within the Chinese grammatological tradition. Tang's proposition for the "new ideo-phonographs" as an alphabetized and simplified pinyin script first complied with and then imploded from within the pinyin ideology. More important, it raised crucial questions about the ethnocentrism of alphabetic writing, the limits of phonocentrism, and the potential of grammatology—at once a field of studies, a political arena, and an epistemological approach. As the half century of the Chinese script revolution concluded with a renegotiated concept of alphabetization, the new Chinese script registered a critical reflection over the metaphysics of phonetic writing and opened up a valuable realm of the intellectual activism that is grammatology.

SOCIALIST FERVOR

This supposedly final round of the Chinese script revolution took on new urgency as the new socialist state needed a script that underwrote scriptal egalitarianism, linguistic modernity, and international solidarity. The new script was to be both alphabetic and socialist. In the same manner that linguistic preparation predates the emergence of "imagined communities," the socialist script reform preceded the founding of the socialist state. In August 1949, two months before the founding of the PRC, preparation for an organization in charge of the script reform began. In October 1949, upon the founding of the PRC, the Association of Chinese Script Reform 中國文字改革協會 was launched with the support from top cadres, most noticeably Mao Zedong. The association was renamed twice shortly afterward, first as the Research Committee for Chinese Script Reform 中國文字改革研究委員會, in February 1952, and then as the Committee for Chinese Script Reform 中國文字改革委員會 (hereafter, "the committee") in October 1954, under the direct leadership of the State Council.[6] The first name change reflected the committee's self-designated scholarly rigor in "researching" a broadening range of tasks. The eclectic cluster of research projects grew from the alphabetization of the Chinese script, standardization of the Chinese language, and script reform for non-Han ethnic groups to include the national form of alphabetization and the survey and simplification of basic characters.[7] The second name change marked, as Director Wu Yuzhang put it in 1954, "a change in the nature of the committee," from "a research organ" to an institution of action that would "go to the people" and "take practical steps" in implementing the "policies" of the reform.[8] Despite competing tasks and a multiplicity of policies, which in retrospect provided crucial clues to the final containment of the script reform, it seemed as though all research on the socialist script reform had been concluded and final policies determined. Mao was frequently quoted as saying, "The Chinese script must reform. It shall follow the common direction of the phonetic alphabet (pinyin), shared by all scripts in the world."[9] It seemed that the Chinese alphabet was finally within reach.

Mao's instruction, though he himself never committed it to writing, was circulated widely as the mandate of the reform. The keyword that solicited unconditional agreement and aroused generative ambiguity was *pinyin*—literally, "to phoneticize." The pinyin script, by extension, signified a phoneticized script—that is, a phonetic alphabet. Building on this key word, the socialist script reform distinguished itself from its predecessors in two aspects: first, it implemented alphabetization (pinyin) as a state policy with firm institutional support; and second, it reworked the concept of pinyin to fit the program of social(ist) mobilization and to turn the state policy into a state ideology. Mao's call for pinyin, on the one hand, reaffirmed the legitimacy of phonocentrism in a new era and, on the other, opened up old possibilities previously foreclosed by the Romanization and Latinization movements. The road to pinyin, instead of the scriptal highway that many had imagined, became a forking path. Within the committee, debates on the Cyrillic alphabet versus the Roman-Latin alphabet resurfaced. The Cold War alliance between China and the Soviet Union brought about the Sino-Soviet Treaty of Friendship, Alliance, and Mutual Assistance 中蘇友好互助同盟條約 (1950), under which a Soviet advisers' program was put in place. Between 1950 and the beginning of the split between the PRC and the Soviet Union in 1960, thousands of engineers, mechanics, and teachers were sent to China, including an unknown number of linguists, headed by G. P. Serdyuchenko. Under the guidance of the "Soviet experts," the committee actively pursued the possibility of adopting a Cyrillic Chinese alphabet, not only for the Chinese language but also for languages spoken by groups of ethnic minorities.[10] Although the committee did not eventually recommend it, a Cyrillic pinyin script was a serious contender. Even Wu Yuzhang, who was a Latinization veteran and known to prefer the Roman-Latin alphabet, had to include one Cyrillic proposal in his "four proposals" developed between June 1954 and May 1955.[11]

It would be a mistake, however, to assume that the competition for the ultimate pinyin script was limited to Cyrillic versus Roman-Latin or was confined to the committee. Whether intentionally or not, the formulation of pinyin broke the monopoly of the Roman-Latin or the Cyrillic alphabets, served as a democratizing mechanism for script reform, and invited numerous others into the competition. Between 1950 and 1955 the committee received a total of 612 proposals from across China, publishing 264 of them with spelling schemes and sample sentences in a two-volume *Compilation of Pinyin Proposals from Around China*.[12] These Chinese alphabet hopefuls were developed from myriad choices: character-based national forms, the IPA (International Phonetic Alphabet), the Roman-Latin alphabet, Cyrillic, Korean Hangul, Japanese kana, the 1911 Chinese National Alphabet, various stenographic systems, irregular patterns, and even Arabic numbers. As noted by the volume's editors, proposals based on existing phonetic alphabets were labeled as "international," character-based proposals were grouped under the "character format," while all other choices came under "others." The fact that all these proposals—phonetic or numeric—fell into the category of a phonetic alphabet (pinyin) is worth pondering. Insofar as the graphemes of a given system were systematically assigned phonemic values, as shown in the *Compilation*, neither their shape nor their name mattered. Not unlike the conventional and "international" phonetic alphabets, both Arabic numbers and reformed Chinese characters could assume phonographic capacity in representing speech sound. This intrigue of character-cum-alphabet did not capture much attention at the height of the socialist fervor in quest of the Chinese pinyin script; rather, it was celebrated as the impending victory over the millennia-old script. As though echoing Mao, even the "character-format" alphabets were taken to indicate that the old script "must reform" and would have to "follow the common direction of the phonetic alphabet."

It seemed that this was truly the final chapter of the Chinese script revolution. Pinyin as a state policy meant that the socialist script reform would proceed with unprecedented official and institutional support; more important, it signified a new politics and eventually heralded an ideology of pinyin. First, it manifested a new political order. As the alphabetization cause received little support from the Republic of China after its relocation to Taiwan, the socialist script reform became the only active Chinese alphabetization movement. Now tied to the survival and success of the socialist state in an international community divided by the Cold War, the endorsement of the Chinese alphabet became synonymous with an affirmation of a socialist and revolutionary order. Second, pinyin as a state policy marked a new scale of politicization reaching for an unprecedented level of mass mobilization. The conceptual opening up of pinyin worked in favor of the democratization of the script reform. The 264 proposals published by the *Compilation* presented an incomplete paper trail whereby a highly specialized and intellectual script reform transformed itself into a mass movement. Third, pinyin as a state policy and a conduit for mass mobilization worked

itself into the most fundamental aspect of social engineering in the PRC—
the creation of socialist subjectivity. To investigate how state policies shaped
socialist subjectivity must be the subject of another study; it suffices to say
here that, for the purpose of understanding script, subject, and state, the
nationwide enthusiasm in searching for the new Chinese script bore witness to, literally, the rise of a new collective political consciousness. Some
of the most representative sample sentences in the *Compilation* read, "Long
live the People's Republic of China," "Resist the Americans, aid the Kore-
ans, and defend our motherland," and "Forcefully promote the revolutionary cultural movement for the people."[13] Pinyin was no longer a single state
policy as the support for it became associated with allegiance to the socialist state, commitment to Cold War military mobilization, and creation of
a proletarian culture. The pinyin script became a metonym for state policy
in general. The individual subscription to the pinyin cause accordingly constituted a proper response to the "interpellation" of the state and its dominating ideologies. If Louis Althusser was right in stipulating that "there is
no ideology except by the subject and for subjects," then there would be no
pinyin ideology without the category of the socialist subject and its "functioning."[14] To wit, the transformation from pinyin as state policy to pinyin as ideology took place when the socialist subject came into being by
responding to the call for alphabetization. The endorsement of pinyin as
ideology—an antinomy between its rigidity and ambiguity—affirmed the
functioning of the socialist new China.[15] The rejection of or even ambivalence about it risked being interpreted as questioning the very mechanism
that enabled the working of the script, subject, and state.

DISSIDENTS

The interpellation of the pinyin ideology was not without tension. Among
dissidents, the best known might be Chen Mengjia 陳夢家 (1911–1966), who
voiced the most thorough rejection of the socialist script reform and suf-
fered the most severe punishment.[16] At the height of the Hundred Flowers
Movement and on the eve of the Anti-Rightist Campaign of February to
May 1957, Chen openly and repeatedly criticized the committee, the first
batch of simplified characters it promoted,[17] and the Chinese alphabetization
movement in general. He was soon denounced as a "rightist," in collusion

with the "Luo Longji–Zhang Bojun Anti-Socialist and Anti-State Alliance."[18] After multiple suicide attempts, Chen ended his life at the beginning of the Cultural Revolution in 1966.[19]

It should not be surprising that Chen Mengjia—an expert in paleography, philology, and archaeology—would oppose the elimination of his object of study and his chosen lifelong vocation. In fact, he was not alone. Even within the Chinese Academy of Sciences (CAS), where he served between 1952 and his death in 1966, at least two colleagues who were affiliated with the committee—Li Rong 李榮 and Fu Maoji 傅懋勣—had reservations about the complete eradication of the Chinese script.[20] Moreover, Tang Lan, Chen's onetime teacher, critiqued the script reform in an even more radical and sustained manner. Only Chen, however, expressed disagreement in ways that could be construed as a complete rejection of the pinyin ideology, challenging the trinity of script, subject, and state.

Chen turned to the fields of oracle-bone inscriptions, archaeology, and paleography after his undergraduate degree in law and a brief yet much-celebrated career in new poetry.[21] Born into a well-educated Presbyterian family, he became the youngest poet of the Crescent Moon Society—a literary group that took its name from Rabindranath Tagore's eponymous collection and prided itself for freeing up modern Chinese new poetry while heeding poetic forms (gelü 格律).[22] He was recognized as one of the top four poets in the group, on a par with the scholar- painter Wen Yiduo, the philosophical aesthete Zhu Xiang, and the Romantic lyricist Xu Zhimo. Chen's work exemplified a combination of Xu Zhimo's lyrical sentimentalism and Wen Yiduo's commitment to form and struck a balance between "Chinese temperament" and Christian motifs.[23] One recurring trope—flying, flying from and to the sky—best illustrates how both sensibilities come together in Chen's repertory of references. Lofty imageries abound: there are "flying horses" greeting "the old man from the sky" and "little wind chimes" outside "an ancient temple" that would "fly up to the sky" once beckoned by the sun; there are "flying dragons, shouting: we want life" and Santa Claus flying down on Christmas with "hefty bags" and "flying white beard."[24] Between the publication of *Selected Poems of the Crescent Moon*, edited by Chen, and his own *Iron Horse Collection*, his interest shifted from composing "lyrical verses" influenced by "foreign literature" to seeking ways to "melt the virtues of old poetry into new poetry" and to give life to "new spring bamboos out of old soil."[25] Critics saw in him the Romanticist tradition of William Wordsworth and the lyrical mastery of Lord Tennyson and compared him to Wang Bo, one of the four greatest seventh-century Tang-dynasty poets.[26] Despite high praise and successful publication of his poetry anthologies, Chen decided that new poetry was "a minor technique eschewed by great men" and cursed his own survival from the battlefront of the anti-Japanese resistance as "shameful."[27] Recommended by Timothy Ting-fang Lew and encouraged by his future father-in-law, T. C. Chao (also known as Zhao Zichen), Chen pursued graduate work in archaeology and oracle-bone inscriptions at Yenching, turned his gaze toward the "old soil," and stopped publishing poetry.[28]

Chen assumed teaching positions at a number of institutions, such as Yenching, Tsinghua, and, briefly, the University of Chicago, before transferring to the Institute of Archaeology, CAS, in 1952. Criticisms of him started as early as his Tsinghua years during the Three-Anti Campaigns (1951–1952) and exploded in the Anti-Rightist Campaign (1957).[29] However, it was not until he opposed the script reform that his many other "faults"— his Christian ties, his connection with the Rockefeller Foundation and various bronze dealerships in the United States, and his costly collection of Ming-dynasty furniture—became serious targets for attack.[30] Through a series of articles and speeches composed and delivered over the course of a few months in 1957, Chen thoroughly negated both pinyin as state policy and pinyin as ideology and put his own status as a socialist subject in jeopardy.[31] To pinpoint his clash with the pinyin ideology at the center of accusations against him is not to normalize—nor to legitimize—the violence inflicted on victims of socialist state power such as Chen. Rather, his three-month crusade against the script reform holds the key to understanding that very violence, which also provides important clues to the workings of the ideological state apparatus known, in this case, as pinyin.

The first salvo was a short essay published by the *Guangming Daily* on February 4, 1957, titled "A Brief Note on Philology."[32] By way of reviewing the three-millennium history of philology, Chen calls for "a somewhat fair appraisal of Chinese characters."[33] Delineating the establishment of paleography, he argues for its indispensable disciplinary value to any scholarly work on Chinese literature, archaeology, and early history. He reasons that without adequate training in philology and especially paleography, archaeologists, historians, and literary scholars would not "be able to read their own source materials."[34] Chen makes no mention of the alphabetization movement but stipulates that the simplification of characters should proceed with great caution and true democracy, exemplified by the Han-dynasty philological conference held at the Weiyang Palace. Following up on the mention of democracy, Chen urges the committee, which "did not absorb enough ideas from philology experts," to "reconsider," for only scholarly expertise armed with popular consent from the people could lead to a solid plan of character simplification that would have a chance to stand the test of time. Last but not least, he cites a proposal from Tang Lan, his afore-mentioned teacher and colleague, whose suggestions, Chen argues, depart from the committee's call to alphabetize. Chen applauds Tang's philologically sound analyses, refuses to participate in what seemed like an organized group criticism of Tang, and establishes an alliance with him.[35]

The second and less-wayward objection was a transcript of Chen's speech delivered to the committee on March 22, with a postscript appended by Chen on May 1, which came out in the *Guangming Daily* on May 19, 1957, under the title "Regarding the Future of Chinese Characters."[36] Chen was hardly oblivious to the increasingly clear differences between him and the committee. He accepted the invitation in the spirit of open criticism, supposedly encouraged and fostered by the Hundred Flowers Movement. Finding the lack of any dissenting voice "strange,"[37] he assumed the role of representing the silent majority. He opened his speech by acknowledging that he would deliver some "remarks of disagreement" and "might not be polite." His criticism consisted of four parts: "What are characters and their merits?" "What are their faults?" "How to improve them?" and "Notes on philological research." His main argument is threefold: first, the merits of characters outweigh the faults; second, the so-called faults of the Chinese writing system are associated mainly with the "unscientific" pedagogies that teach characters;[38] and third, based on the previous two points, the future of Chinese characters should entail script "improvement" (*gaijin* 改進) instead of script reform (*gaige* 改革). As if his criticism of the committee were not biting enough, Chen writes in the postscript,

Personally, I disagree with the procedure through which the simplified characters were announced. They were devised incomprehensively, announced hastily, and did not invite critical feedback. They are, as a result, in some ways unscientific. They complied with neither the mass line nor the historical basis of characters. I therefore hope that we can consider retracting these simplified characters and start over. I also wonder if it is possible to establish a permanent institute of philology, which will conduct long-term research and "deal with" characters without preconceived notions.[39]

Granted that Chen does not once mention the committee, what he articulates is not merely impolite disagreement with its adopted "procedure." Much more seriously, he arms himself with the "mass line," demands a scientific makeover of the simplified characters,[40] and threatens to subvert the committee's legitimacy—both scholarly and political—in leading the script reform. Chen might have construed his own "remarks of disagreement" as one of the "Hundred Flowers" invited to bloom in early 1957, and probably thought others would too, but little did he know that the "preconceived notions" of the old script that he critiqued had by then turned into state-sponsored ideology, not to be reconsidered, and definitely not to be subverted.

If Chen's first essay laid the groundwork of the argument for a philology-based approach to the script reform, then his speech brought into sharper relief the difference between his proposed approach and the pinyin ideology, institutionally embodied by the committee. The most thorough negation of the script reform did not emerge, however, until Chen published his six-point entreaty titled "Be More Cautious About 'Reforming' Chinese Characters." Drafted on May 1, it hit the press on May 17, 1957. It synchronized, coincidentally, with the publication of Mao Zedong's "Things Are Changing," which signaled the drastic shift in policy from welcoming dissenting voices during the Hundred Flowers Movement to cracking down on disagreements in the Anti-Rightist Movement.[41] Chen opens the essay by recollecting the voices that he has heard defending characters and dissatisfaction with the committee's simplified characters. In fact, his entire six points revolve around the preservation of the characters and warning against wrong measures already taken or about to be taken by the committee. First, he reprises his objection to the approved simplified characters. Second, he reiterates his proposal for an alternative philological institute other than the committee that is less administrative in nature and more research oriented. Third, he admonishes certain typesetters from Shanghai for inventing new simplified characters. Then he stipulates his most fatal objection in the fourth point:

Before thorough research, do not announce the death penalty of the Chinese script. I personally do not agree with measures of adopting a foreign alphabet or the alphabetization of the national form to replace characters. As for the auxiliary alphabet denoting the pronunciation of characters, any form can work. Those who are for alphabetization, do not take it for granted that the majority of the country are all for that cause; this matter will need further discussions and should include those who oppose it.[42]

Chen's fifth point cites other examples voicing dissent, appealing to mutual trust and understanding between the committee and its critics.[43] Finally, he applauds the recent debate on both the simplified characters and the work done so far by the committee. Although he tries to soften the blow of his fourth point by invoking other dissenting voices and celebrating the debate that emerged during the Hundred Flowers Movement, his disagreement with character abolishment is a rare declaration in print that unequivocally disavows the core of the alphabetization movement in general and the state policy of pinyin in particular. By calling the measures taken by the committee hasty and accusing pinyin proponents—including top cadres and common script reformers—of being presumptuous, Chen effectively refuses to subject himself, as well as his philological expertise, to the leadership of the committee. Whether he realized that the committee took direct orders from the central government, whose power he had effectively challenged, as accusations against him would later point out, was unclear. His objection to alphabetization as a movement, state policy, and state ideology, however, constituted and was later interpreted as a de facto disavowal of the socialist script, subject, and state.

Chen's final appearance in print before he was banned from publication for three years was in the July 1957 issue of *Pinyin* magazine, which featured the transcript of a "Script Reform Symposium" held by the magazine at the National Club of the People's Political Consultative Conference.[44] The symposium met three times, on May 16, 20, and 27, and assembled a good number of members of the committee—Hu Yuzhi, Wei Que, Li Jinxi, Ni Haishu, and Zhou Youguang, as well as nonmembers such as Tang Lan and Chen himself.[45] The transcription registered Chen Mengjia's comments at the first and third meetings. These remarks did not deviate from his previous arguments, on top of which he accused the committee of practicing "bureaucratism" and engaged in a heated debate with Jiang Chaoxi, a physicist and pinyin loyalist, who challenged some of Chen's etymological findings. Hardly the only one critical of the simplified characters, Chen was, however, the lone participant asking the committee to "first discuss whether the Chinese script can be alphabetized before discussing what kind of alphabetization it should adopt."[46] Chen's antagonizing stance might have provoked much discussion, but the most revealing comments that problematized the very concept of alphabetization did not come from him.

REDEFINING ALPHABETIZATION

The most revelatory and problematical comments came from Chen's old teacher, Tang Lan 唐蘭 (1901–1979). Tang, the founding father of modern Chinese paleography, was born into an obscure merchant family in Jiaxing County, Zhejiang Province, in 1901. Growing up, he received an eclectic training in commerce, Chinese medicine, and literature,[47] until he developed serious interest in philology (*xiaoxue* 小學) at the age of eighteen. After three years of formal education at the Wuxi Academy of National Learning (now Suzhou University), Tang graduated at the top of his class in 1923. While holding various editorial positions and a lectureship, within ten years he grew to be a leading philologist, archaeologist, historian, and expert on bronze and oracle-bone inscriptions, on a par with the best in the respective fields.[48] Compared with his fellow scholars, Tang enjoyed a unique advantage from his hands-on experience at the Palace Museum, serving in various capacities, from a special committee member to the vice-director of the museum, between 1933 and his death in 1979. He headed excavations, deciphered inscriptions, and combined fieldwork with scholarly production. Throughout his long career revolving around Chinese characters, Tang never once consented to their unconditional and total abolishment. Instead, he managed to voice consistent disagreement with the total Romanization-Latinization of the Chinese script for two solid decades. His successful track record as what could be conceived of as another dissident of the socialist script reform raises the question of how he survived his own position while Chen did not. Granted that any attempt to answer that question does not mitigate the intellectual and physical violence that these dissidents have endured, a close reading of Tang's argument at the symposium might illuminate the nuance of his position, which suggests formerly unexplored possibilities to challenge and transform the pinyin apparatus from within.

According to the transcript in *Pinyin* magazine, Tang attended only the first of the three rounds of the symposium and was the first to speak. Tang opens by affirming that "the Chinese script should be reformed" and establishes firmly that he is of the same opinion as the committee's that Chinese characters "should follow the direction of alphabetization [*pinyin*]." He then categorizes three different approaches to reform of the Chinese script: first, minimum reform, which does not reach beyond the simplification of characters; second, a complete overhaul that strips characters of their title of "the ruling script" and launches a "new regime" claiming allegiance to a different script; and third, "to seek development from within characters." Tang confesses that he belongs to the third camp and argues for not only the possibility but also the superiority of "alphabetizing and phoneticizing part of the Chinese script." To start, the old script has always been and is capable of evolving and developing. Therefore there is no reason why a genuine national form of alphabetization cannot grow out of the changing script.[49] More important, the pros of the national form could only outweigh the cons. For one, the character-based national form would provide a level of cultural continuity that a Roman-Latin new script could not. For another, the alphabetization and phoneticization of the national form could find philological basis in the old script. What Tang invokes is, in fact, a game-changing retheorization of the Chinese script, though this is, in fact, not the first time that Tang articulated his theory of alphabetization from within. Here he condenses his reasoning into a quick example toward the end of his comments: "Chinese characters are not all ideographs [*yifu* 意符]. Some of the phonetic radicals are also phonographs [*shengfu* 聲符]," such as his own surname, Tang (唐).[50] Tang's proposal is simple: further develop the phonographic elements in the old script, seek a new alphabetic Chinese that is based on characters, and eventually create a genuine national form of alphabetization. He concludes by disclaiming any intention of promoting his own alphabetization proposals created before the symposium and reiterates the importance of finding the best form of alphabetization for the Chinese script.

Tang's comments were significant on multiple fronts. First, in a matter-of-fact manner, he redefined alphabetization. By supporting alphabetization as a principle that promotes the capacity of a given writing system in representing speech sound, he resisted, without articulating real words of objection, the accepted practice of both the Romanization and Latinization movements that equated pinyin with the Roman-Latin alphabet. By inserting the Chinese script—specifically, its phonetic radicals—into the concept of pinyin, he brought into question the monopoly of the Roman-Latin alphabet. The concept of pinyin transforms from an a priori Roman-Latin script to denote a desirable grammatological trend, which was projected to usher in a new Chinese and new China. Second, by invoking the ideophonographic nature of Chinese,[51] Tang refused to tie the old script to the ideographic totem pole and situated it in the spectrum of ideograph and phonograph.[52] This idea constituted not only the crux of Tang's argument at the symposium but also the analytical backbone of his theory regarding Chinese philology, paleography, and grammatology. If pinyin meant the phoneticization of writing, then the phonographic attributes of the old script should be recognized as fulfilling, to some degree, the pinyin function. Once scientific reform regulates and strengthens this function, Tang predicts, the entire body of characters will shift toward the phonographic end of the ideograph–phonograph spectrum. Therefore, he argued that instead of an immediate script revolution from without, Chinese characters ought to be allowed to undergo an alphabetization reform from within. Finally, by situating the Chinese script under the expanded conceptual umbrella of pinyin, Tang delivered the most unexpected surprise—the Chinese script has always already been phonetic—and gestured toward a radical reconsideration of grammatology.

It bears pointing out that Tang did not dwell on the phonetic or phoneticizable attributes of the Chinese script to rescue it from reform attempts, nor did he invoke the Derridean language of "always already," which would not be formulated until a decade later. Neither did he argue for the preservation of the Chinese script as an instantiation of "arche-writing" (archi-écriture) that embodies the originary intertwining of language and writing. Though the revelation that the Chinese script has always already been phonetic could well end the half-century struggle of the Chinese script reform, Tang had no intention of challenging the ironclad premise that characters must reform. On the contrary, he positioned himself as a script-reform sympathizer, if not enthusiast, who seemed to sincerely believe in the necessity and urgency of the script reform. Speaking as a paleographer, Tang's inaugural comments prompted a discussion of the committee's guidelines from the perspective of the nature of the Chinese script, attracting much attention from fellow participants in the symposium. For those who advocated for the national form, such as Xiao Zhang—a fellow philologist and guest of the committee—and Chen Mengjia, who mentioned Tang Lan's argument without endorsing Tang's previous pinyin proposal, Tang was a rare ally. For those who preferred the Roman-Latin form, such as Wei Que—the vice-director of the committee—and Jiang Chaoxi, Tang was an important expert who could assist the committee's push for pinyin. Although, not unlike Chen Mengjia, Tang articulated a dissenting voice that did not support the first batch of the simplified characters and endorsed a non–Roman-Latin approach to alphabetization, he was not accused of being a "rightist" seeking to sabotage the socialist script reform. No one seemed to realize that although Tang's dissenting arguments were phrased in a far milder manner compared with Chen's outright attack on the committee, Tang's theory was far more challenging to the phonocentric cause of pinyin envisioned by the committee and supported by the state. The committee's position was best summarized by Gao Mingkai—another symposium participant and committee member—when commenting on Tang Lan's remarks: "As long as we agree that the Chinese script should and could be reformed, whether it takes the 'Latinization' path or takes the national form is not a matter of principle but a technical problem." By safeguarding the "principle" of the script reform, Tang secured his position within the ideological state apparatus of pinyin, as well as his image upholding it. This does not mean, however, that Tang was exempt from criticism or, as Gao put it, "encircled attacks" by pinyin loyalists.[53]

The "attacks" lasted from January 1956 to March 1957 and were organized by the committee's institutional journal, *Zhongguo yuwen* 中國語文 (Chinese language and writing, hereafter *CLW*).[54] Its January 1956 issue featured Tang Lan's essay "On Marxism and the Basic Question of the Chinese Script Reform."[55] The *CLW* organized a roundtable of at least eighteen participants discussing Tang's work and published in the same issue a cluster of five reviews, including an opening criticism from committee vice-director Wei Que and a pointed critique penned by committee member and linguist Wang Li.[56] More criticisms ensued in the following issues, including a short essay from the Romanization veteran Li Jinxi.[57] They challenged Tang on his take on Marxist—more precisely, Stalinist—linguistic theory, questioned his proposal for the so-called composite script, and speculated that his attempt to alphabetize the Chinese script from within could well be an implicit disagreement with the committee, which would be taken advantage of by those who genuinely opposed the pinyin ideology.[58]A year later, in the March 1957 issue of *CLW*, Tang came back with an unyielding response, "Revisiting the Basic Question Regarding the Chinese Script Reform," turning the unidirectional group criticism into a public debate.[59] It is important to note that although Tang faced damning criticism, the strongest accusation leveled at him was that he was "a complete revisionist" who wanted to "stall indefinitely the script reform."[60] Unlike Chen Mengjia, Tang was never denounced as a reactionary "rightist" and survived the group criticism and public debate relatively unscathed.

Tang organizes his 1956 essay into seven sections and addresses three key questions: first, the relationship between the script reform and Marxism; second, the nature of the Chinese script; and third, practical reform. The first two sections—"Should Discussions of the Chinese Script Follow Marxist Theory" and "Can the Chinese Script Be Reformed by Way of Explosions?"—position Tang's discussion of the Chinese script reform strategically within the Marxist tradition. Adhering to the materialist and historical approach, he establishes that writing, like language, is not a superstructure. Without invoking the term "infrastructure," he states that writing is created by and should belong to all people and all classes in a society and is subject to change.[61] The change, however, does not take "the form of an explosion." Quoting Stalin that "history shows that languages possess great stability and a tremendous power of resistance to forcible assimilation," Tang explains that scripts operate similarly to languages and pinpoints the "stability and resistance" of the Chinese script as the reason why explosive alphabetization movements have yet to take root in Chinese soil. After tallying previous alphabetization attempts from the Jesuit Romanization schemes in the Ming dynasty to the late nineteenth-century alphabetic Bibles, from the 1920s Chinese Romanization movement to the 1930s Chinese Latinization movement,[62] Tang draws the conclusion that the Chinese alphabetization movement has failed for the simple reason that total alphabetization, discarding characters, contradicts the Marxist approach to linguistic and grammatological development, while Marxist thought mandates that the Chinese script reform allow the evolution of characters.[63]

Following the question of why the Chinese script has been so stable and resistant, Tang ventures an answer: "From a Marxist point of view, it is because of the structure of characters."[64] He dedicates the last half of the second through the fourth sections to explicating the historical development of the Chinese script and its nature. The concept he introduces is "composite script" (*zonghe wenzi* 綜合文字), "a combination of ideographs and phonographs."[65] Tang explains, "What is the basic structure of the Chinese script? It is characters, which represent syllables and take the form of the composite script, consisting mostly of ideo-phonographs [*xingsheng* 形聲]. There are two to three thousand basic characters [one thousand core characters]."[66] Though Tang offers no concrete examples, his own surname, 唐, provides a clear illustration. The character 唐 serves as a phonetic radical in the compound characters 糖, 塘, 瑭, and 膅 ("sugar," "pond," "jade," and "fat"), marking their shared phonetic value of "tang." The character 唐 is thus treated as a phonograph. Tang concedes that three millennia of character development have confounded the consistency of these phonetic radicals, but systematic research and reform measures would and could salvage these phonographs, which Tang calls elements (*yinsu* 因素), in order "for characters to develop into an alphabetic script." Ideo-phonographs such as 糖, 塘, 瑭, and 膅, in addition to their ideographic radicals' denoting meaning or indicating associations of meaning, are equipped to represent speech sound, thanks to their phonetic radical 唐. As Tang argues, these ideo-phonographs have been in Chinese writing "from the oldest times." Composed of both ideographs and phonographs, the whole body of the Chinese script is a highly composite script that resists generalization.[67]

If Tang is right that the Chinese script is a composite body of ideographs, ideo-phonographs, and phonographs—much to the surprise of most script revolutionaries—then there is little reason to replace these Chinese ideo-phonographs or phonographs with another phonograph—namely, the Roman-Latin alphabet. If the Chinese script is capable of developing ideo-phonographs marking the pronunciation of ideographs, then there is also no reason why the nonphonetic ideographs cannot be reformed into ideo-phonographs. Following this train of thought, Tang ponders practical reform measures in the final three sections. On the basis of the old script as a composite script, he proposes a more phonologically oriented new composite script to become the national form of pinyin. Compared with the committee's "Chinese alphabet" (*hanyu pinyin*), Tang argues that "the alphabetization of characters" (*hanzi pinyinhua*) not only does not cause an explosion in Chinese writing but also fits the program of the committee's other project, simplified characters—something that the Chinese alphabet fails to do. Tang writes, "The alphabetization of characters will take the form of simplification and can be implemented gradually." He estimates that it should not be too difficult to introduce "a thousand alphabetized simplified characters" "in a period of three to five years."[68] Eventually, Tang predicts, "the use of [unsimplified and unalphabetized] characters will decline, with the widening reach of alphabetized characters, to the extent that the Chinese script becomes fully alphabetized. This gradual transitioning of characters is entirely possible."[69]

Tang did not mean for that possibility to be only theoretical. At least twice he took on himself to transition old characters into alphabetized characters and tried his hand at designing Chinese pinyin. One version of his design appeared as the first proposal among the 264 published alphabets in the *Compilation of Pinyin Proposals from Around China* (1952).[70] Listed under the category of "character-format alphabet" (*hanzishi zimu* 漢字式字母), Tang's alphabet included fifty-one initials and fourteen finals, the majority of which were character simplifications and phonetic uses of characters, to be used in combination with a minimum of eight hundred characters.[71] An even earlier attempt had occurred in 1949, when Tang included in his scheme fifty-four initials and thirteen finals, with the same number of eight hundred basic characters.[72] While the basic characters served more often than not as ideographs, the free combination of the initials and finals would generate phonetic markers. Taken together, they would be the real composite script of alphabetized simplified characters. One example Tang provided was the idiom "to prosper like lush plants" (*xin xin xiang rong*; figure 5.1). Among the three characters in the phrase, Tang kept the basic character *xiang* but alphabetized both *xin* and *rong*. The two phonetic markers 菖 and 荣, spelled /x•in/ and /r•ong/, respectively, mark the phonetic value, minus the tones, of the two new ideo-phonographs.[73]

By the time of the public debate in 1956–1957, Tang no longer recommended his thousand alphabetized characters like *xin* and *rong* but stood by the principle that "alphabetization of characters" (*hanzi pinyinhua*) was

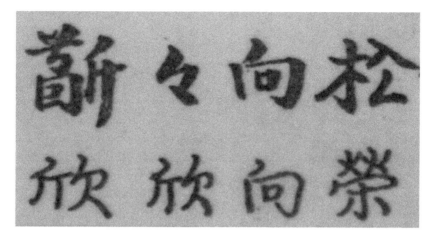

FIGURE 5.1. Tang Lan's new ideo-phonographs of *xīn xīn xiàng róng*, *Gedi renshi jilai hanyu pinyin wenzi fang'an huibian* (1954), 1:1.

as effective as and more philologically responsible than the "Chinese alpha-bet" (*hanyu pinyin*). He summed up the fundamental difference between himself and his critics with one question—also the title of section 4 of his 1956 article—"Alphabetization of characters or a Chinese alphabet?" This question, as well as Tang's consistent response to it, held the answer to how he survived the public debate, avoided further political persecution, and cracked open the pinyin ideology from within. Facing charges that his pro-posal was not alphabetic enough and that he himself was a "revisionist" who wished to preserve the old script, Tang conceded that it would take time for "those one thousand alphabetized characters" to "eventually help clear the path for complete alphabetization,"[74] but he riposted that "specu-lations can only be speculations" and "it is an established fact that I am advocating for the use of a pinyin script right this moment."[75] Tang's pin-yin script might be dubbed revisionist, but it is not counterrevolutionary. His critics, by arguing with him whether his program was alphabetic enough, confirmed the possibility of alphabetizing characters as a path—albeit unsatisfactory—toward pinyin. Tang remained a pinyin supporter and became the most vocal advocate for seeking an alternative and inter-nal solution to alphabetization. Speaking as the true paleographer that he was, Tang invoked, toward the end of his 1957 rebuttal, philological history as precedent and evidence for the impending evolution of the Chinese composite script:

There used to be only pictographs and ideographs. During the Yin and Shang dynasties, phonetic characters, i.e., ideo-phonographs, appeared, though they factored no more than 30 percent. By the Han dynasty, ideo-phonographs constituted almost 90 percent of all characters. In the old days, it took a genuinely long time—as long as a thousand years—for the natural development to occur, despite the fact that the phonetic characters were more progressive than ideographs. Now that alphabetic characters are even more progressive than the phonetic ones, in our own socialist time and under organized leadership, why cannot a progressive script evolve?[76]

Citing philological precedent, Tang situates his own program of alphabetizing characters in the *longue durée* of the Chinese scriptal evolution and thus establishes the historical legitimacy of the internal approach to alphabetization. By contrasting the erstwhile slow development of ideo-phonographs with the projected efficiency of the socialist script reform, he expresses confidence in implementing the alphabetization of characters while soliciting endorsement from atop. If only "organized leadership" such as the committee could recognize pinyin from within as a viable path toward the Chinese alphabet, then a pinyin script—in fact, at least two versions of it—would be readily accessible. Tang turns the tables: "It is not I who seeks to stall the script reform indefinitely. It is, in fact, some other comrades who do not allow people to gain quick access to a pinyin script."[77] Taunting rhetoric notwithstanding, Tang admits to his critics that his solution—a combination of both basic and alphabetized characters—is, at its present stage, both incomplete and composite. He cautions, however, that the objection to the composite script for its incomplete alphabetization is shortsighted, for once the "contradiction" between the thousand alphabetized characters and old characters is introduced, the Chinese script as a whole will evolve along the trajectory of the more progressive alphabetic, much like how the ideo-phonographic overwhelmed the ideographic and the pictographic in the first thousand years of the development of the Chinese script.[78] Connecting philological history to socialist script planning, Tang goes on to articulate the true superiority of the approach of pinyin from within. Insofar as all old characters "will eventually retire," a controlled phaseout of characters would avoid "irrevocable loss for the six hundred million Chinese people," ease the transition from partial to full alphabetic Chinese, and, most important, allow the organic growth of "a new script from within the old script."[79] Much to the surprise of Tang's critics and the committee, without challenging the authority of the pinyin ideology a new pinyin script could emerge from within the old Chinese script. Tang concludes, "To keep the basic form of characters now is to prepare for the future development of a new national Chinese script that is completely alphabetic."[80] By redefining pinyin to include alphabetized characters and opening up the possibility of cultivating a pinyin script from within, Tang gestures toward the final containment of the script reform—a compromise between the internal alphabetization of the characters (*hanzi pinyinhua*) and the external implementation of an auxiliary phonetic system known as *hanyu pinyin*.

It is perhaps naive to speculate to what extent Tang's arguments influenced the committee, if at all. It is, however, imperative to come to terms with the huge implications of Tang's redefined pinyin. For one, if pinyin is the telos of the Chinese script reform, then, as Tang shows, the telos is already embedded in its own elements. For another, the redefined pinyin, besides fulfilling the function of speech representation—just like the so-called international form—signifies something more than the Roman-Latin alphabet. This composite pinyin script harbors the potential for a new grammatology and, at the risk of sounding overly Derridean, a new metaphysics that exceeds the logic of supplement and awakens new possibilities of writing, meaning, and presence.

CHINESE GRAMMATOLOGY

It bears pointing out that Tang's redefinition of pinyin was not an expedient response to survive the pinyin apparatus. Far from it, Tang's conceptualization of and vision for Chinese writing had deep roots in paleography and his own work in the field, which could be traced throughout his career. Two prominent works in which Tang elucidates his take on how Chinese paleography could inform the script reform are *An Introduction to Paleography* (1934) and *A Study of Chinese Writing* (1949).[81] The former was widely acknowledged to have laid the "foundation of modern paleography," and the latter was understood to be Tang's effort at establishing a scientific study of Chinese writing—a Chinese grammatology.[82]

Taken together, these works show that Tang's analytical trajectory ran from an intervention in the theory of character formation and a critical recapitulation of Chinese philological history to a proposal for the "new ideo-phonograph" and, eventually, general ruminations on the meaning and potential of grammatology. Tang first proposed in *An Introduction to Paleography*—and maintained the argument thereafter—that the millennia-old six principles of character formation make better sense if condensed to three.[83] The original six principles—the bedrock of Chinese philological studies—were systematically explained by Xu Shen (55–149) in the first complete dictionary of Chinese characters, *Explaining Graphs and Analyzing Characters* (*Shuowen jiezi* 說文解字): simple indicative (*zhishi* 指事), pictograph (*xiangxing* 象形), ideo-phonograph (*xingsheng* 形聲), compound ideograph (*huiyi* 會意), related pairs (*zhuanzhu* 轉注), and loan characters (*jiajie* 假借). Tang argued that a simpler categorization of just three principles would not only provide a more complete coverage but also better clarify the historical development of characters: pictograph (*xiangxing* 象形), ideograph (*xiangyi* 象意), and ideo-phonograph (*xingsheng* 形聲).[84] Special emphasis was placed on the rise of the ideo-phonographs since "late antiquity." Citing Southern Song (1127–1279) philologist Zheng Qiao's *A Brief Account of the Six Principles* (*Liushu lüe* 六書略), by the twelfth century the number of phono-ideographs had become fifteen times that of the rest combined. Many ideo-phonographs were either "remodeled" or created based on pictographs and ideographs, while the number of pictographs kept dropping. Tang concludes that "the more characters there are, the bigger the proportion of the ideo-phonographs is."[85]

Insofar as the great majority of Chinese characters are ideo-phonographs, the problem of the Chinese script, as Tang sees it, is naturally that of this vast body of ideo-phonographs.[86] The source of confusion in determining the correct pronunciation of Chinese characters, Tang identifies, is the interchangeable use of phonographs (*shengfu*) and ideographs (*xingfu*), as well as the inconsistent use of the phonographs. One extreme example that Tang uses in *A Study of Chinese Writing* is the character 隹. When used as an ideograph, it means either a short-tailed bird or a hanging fruit and is pronounced /*zhuī*/. When used as a phonograph in combination with other ideographic radicals to form ideo-phonographs, it does not automatically guarantee the pronunciation /zhuī/. On the contrary, characters consisting of the phonograph 隹 have as many as thirty-four pronunciations: zhuī 椎 (vertebra), zhì 雉 (pheasant), wéi 唯 (only), tuī 推 (to push), cuī 崔 (lofty mountain), zhǔn 準 (accurate), jìn 進 (to advance), and duī 堆 (heap), to name a few.[87] Such phonetic unruliness—or "phonographic regression," as Tang puts it elsewhere[88]—introduced throughout the three millennia of Chinese writing, should and could be remedied by scientific reorganization, simplification, and alphabetization of the phonographs. If the old phonographs like 隹 no longer represent the phonetic value of ideo-phonographs that include it, then there is little reason to keep it. The old phonograph 隹, like many other outdated phonographs, could find accurate substitutes not only in Tang's 1949 and 1952 proposals for a character-format alphabet but already in his experiment of "new ideo-phonographs" (xin xingsheng zi 新形聲字) in his An Introduction to Paleography.[89] In this earlier and rudimentary proposal, Tang outlines ten technical principles for the creation of new ideo-phonographs[90] and articulates six advantages of this approach.[91] He concludes that these new ideo-phonographs—either updated from the old, outdated ones or created from scratch—will preserve the cultural legacy, be easy to learn, read, and print, and facilitate Chinese writing to best absorb foreign cultures and scientific knowledge. The new ideo-phonographs are not designed to satiate one's "selfish obsession with ancient culture." Far from it, the real purpose—"also the ultimate purpose of grammatology"—is "to research and determine the most reasonable script for the creation of a great new culture."[92]

It should be acknowledged that although Tang was forthcoming in his ambition to leave his mark on the scientific study of Chinese writing, he did not use the English term "grammatology" or the French grammatologie. Nor did he intend a conversation with I. J. Gelb or Jacques Derrida, whose Of Grammatology would not come out till 1967. However, Tang's original term wenzi xue 文字學 in this context could hardly be translated otherwise, for it constituted a disciplinary stance against linguistics with critical connotations. Insisting that the premise for a study of writing should distinguish writing from language, he proposed that all studies of and related to phonetics and semantics, including phonology 音韻 (yinyun) and philological exegetics 訓詁 (xungu), should be "sent back to the field of linguistics."[93] After the first global moment of the early twentieth century, which marked the divergence of linguistics and philology in favor of the phono-centric principle of speech over writing, Tang's insistence on further liqui-dating philology and ridding it of linguistic remnants was a rare reversal that put writing before speech. His study of writing is in its true sense a study of the science of writing. More substantially, the parallels between Tang and the poststructuralists run deeper. Not unlike Derrida's critique of the metaphysics of phonetic writing, Tang, in spite of his stance in favor of pinyin, ends up articulating a position of antiphonocentrism.

Derrida defines "logocentrism" as "the metaphysics of phonetic writing," which is "nothing but the most original and powerful ethnocentrism."[94] This ethnocentrism imposes itself on the world by assigning one model of phonetic writing, one history of metaphysics, and one concept of science as the only organizing order.[95] Among these three layers of ethnocentrism, Derrida locates the problem of phonetic writing at the core of the entire metaphysical machine in operation from Plato to Hegel, and from Rous-seau to Lévi-Strauss.[96] The Derridean feat of deconstruction is enabled by revealing how the domination of Western metaphysics rests on a particu-lar treatment of phonetic writing, which, on the one hand, valorizes the phoneticization of writing as the best techne to access full speech, self-presence, and the eventual *parousia*, and, on the other, predetermines the position of writing as supplementary, subordinate, always lacking, and inev-itably dangerous. This particular treatment—in essence a double proce-dure of first locating the truth, the scientific, and the unmediated voice always outside of writing and then regulating phonetic writing as the best, albeit inherently insufficient, access to it—configures the basic laws of the history of Western metaphysics and theology.[97] To be clear, Tang does not concern himself with a deconstructionist critique of Western metaphysics, nor does he explicitly invoke the term "ethnocentrism." Rather, his life's work on Chinese grammatology grew out of an organic rethinking of the national form, which predated the Derridean critique and came into frui-tion in the mid-1950s, coinciding with the second global moment of decol-onization and anti-imperialism.

Throughout Tang's work, he persistently asks two crucial questions: First, is phonetic writing—the Roman-Latin alphabet—an a priori and the only techne for phoneticization? Second, how can one imagine the relationship between speech and writing other than a predetermined separation, a per-petual binary of the originary and the supplement? On the question of alphabetic ethnocentrism, one of the most searching questions that Tang asks is a rhetorical one addressed to his critics during the 1956–1957 debate: if both the alphabetized characters that he has proposed and the Chinese alphabet advocated by the Roman-Latin loyalists could represent speech sound, then "why does it have to be the international form?"[98] The Roman-Latin loyalists' devotion to the international form raises as many questions as does their "uneasiness" with the national form. Pressing on as a non-member of the committee and hence an expert without official capacity, Tang asks, "Why are the experts unwilling to reconsider reasons from the other side, as well as faults of their own?"[99] Finding faults with the experts' unchecked faith in Roman-Latin alphabetic universalism, Tang compels them to provincialize what is seemingly universal. For one, even if the universal status of phonetic writing is in place, it does not automatically follow that the Roman-Latin alphabet is the true universal. For another, now that the new Chinese script strives for the universal status of phonetic writing, the national form ought to be a contender as valid as the international form. If the valorization of phonetic writing in principle masks the ethnocentrism of the Roman-Latin alphabet,[100] then Tang unveils its ethnocentric nature by comparing it with and preferring another ethnocentric script known as the national form, which makes no attempt at concealing its own ethnocentrism. Tang Lan's acknowledgment and embrace of ethnocentrism, quite counterintuitively, makes possible an antiethnocentric critical stance.

An equally relevant antiethnocentric critique is Tang's intervention in the study of Chinese philology through his retheorization of the nature of the Chinese script. The prevailing account of Chinese characters reinforces their inability to represent speech sound, curiously neglecting the largely coeval development of pictographs, ideographs, and ideo-phonographs, as well as the overwhelming proportion—90 percent—of the last category. It is almost as though the philological tradition of *Shuowen jiezi*, passed down from the second century CE, did not certify "ideo-phonograph" as one of the six principles of character formation. The history of such a curious downplay of the phonetic attributes of the Chinese script is long. As Bruce Rusk elucidates in a rich discussion of the Chinese and European scriptal encounter in the sixteenth and seventeenth centuries, the reasons are manifold. On the one hand, the Chinese use of characters tended to valorize the ideographic and even pictographic components over the ideo-phonographic portion of the script, for the former two were expected to either provide unmediated access to ancient sages or illuminate direct paths to new wisdom. For instance, the classic *Rites of Zhou* was used as a paleographic treasure trove by Wang Mang to legitimize his rule of the Xin dynasty (9–25), and etymology as a method fascinated Ming-dynasty scholars for it was believed to aid the "Learning of the Mind-and-Heart."[101] On the other hand, the European missionaries' characterization of the Chinese script as "a hieroglyphic *scripta franca* for East Asia" reinforced its seemingly voiceless characteristic.[102] Finally, the Chinese receptiveness to the European discourse—instantiated in writings of the Ming-dynasty literati such as Wang Shizhen 王世貞 (1526–1590) and Fang Yizhi 方以智 (1611–1671)—made the ideographic and monosyllabic myths as much an orientalizing fantasy as a Chinese self-identification. Tang, by condensing Xu Shen's six principles to three, highlights the phonetic attributes of the Chinese script from its early age, raises objections to a philological and grammatological tradition tainted by the ethnocentrism of both China and Europe, and flags the possibility of further phoneticization.

Insofar as Tang's coinage of the new ideo-phonograph and his theory of the three principles in character formation functioned as an important corrective to the study of the seemingly nonphonetic Chinese characters, it sounded as though he did not differ much from either his critics or those he criticized. Tang's emphasis on the phonetic nature and the potential of the composite script of Chinese lent itself well to be understood as a moderate reformist proposal in conformity to the phonocentric paradigm, which was precisely how Tang survived the pinyin ideology. However, what escaped Tang's contemporaneous critics and hitherto critical attention was his articulation of a radical position in stark opposition to phonocentrism. Harking back to his 1957 comment during the symposium organized by the committee, Tang stated, "I do not think that writing equals a recording of speech, nor a stenography or transcription. Some comrades take the creation of a script too lightly, thinking that the spelling of speech sound using a few signs will suffice. A record of speech is not writing. Writing is a kind of accumulation of history."[103]

As soon as Tang convinced his critics of the embeddedness of the phonetic elements in the Chinese old script, as well as the potential of the new ideo-phonographs in fully representing speech sound, he hastened to add that speech representation did not equal writing, that there was something more in writing that could not be contained by speech, and that this surplus in writing would add up to an "accumulation of history." What was remarkable about Tang's statement was not the fact that his attitude in favor of pinyin did not prevent him from forming an antiphonocentric critique, nor the realization that he might have worked his grammatological theory toward the advocacy of writing as something more than speech. Much more significantly, before Derrida articulated a critique of the metaphysics of phonetic writing as well as its proponents from Plato to Husserl, from Rousseau to Saussure, Tang's proposition invoked and substantiated a thorough inversion of the kind of grammatology that enabled Western ethnocentrism and shaped Chinese ethnocentrism throughout the script revolution.[104]

The inversion is nothing short of a complete reversal of the relationship between speech and writing. First, by negating writing as sheer speech representation, Tang effectively rejects the originary Platonic position that takes writing as the evil supplement that distorts speech, corrupts memory and community, and usurps the position of power. If Derrida demonstrates, through his belabored analyses of difference and trace, that there is no pure language and writing has always already inhabited speech,[105] then Tang takes a further step in turning writing from supplementarity to surplus. In the final analysis of the "originary supplement" toward the end of *Of Grammatology*, Derrida makes the distinction between the natural language "words" [*voix*, "vowels"] and the artificial "sound" [*sons*, "consonants"], distinguishable "by what permits writing—consonants and articulation." In other words, the flow of "natural language" as *voix* does not suffice for the birth of language; it has to be supplanted by the "consonants and articulation" of the *sons*. Hence this articulation—the originary supplement—is "the origin of language [*langage*]."[106] Taking what would be the Derridean lesson a step further, Tang reverses the perennial argument that writing fails to capture full and pure speech and argues that it is speech—vowels and consonants—that fails to register what writing has to offer. Going from supplementarity to surplus, Tang renders the logic of origin-supplement irrelevant.

It is important to note that Tang does not articulate and, to my knowledge, never articulated the real substance of the surplus of writing aside from assigning it to the overbearing concept of the "accumulation of history." However, the surplus of writing could be located in the very nature of the ideo-phonograph. By definition, in each ideo-phonographic character there is something extra in addition to the phonetic representation. As Tang indicates, the surplus in each character as a discrete unit of a writing system rolls over toward the accumulation of history. Here emerge the two sides of the same coin known as the ideo-phonograph: what for Tang is a valuable surplus is for the Roman-Latin enthusiast an ineffective, hence unwanted, supplement. It bears pointing out that although the side of supplementarity overwhelms the side of surplus within the discourse of phonocentrism, it did not do so without difficulties and intrigues. What has escaped critical attention—even that of Derrida—was Rousseau's uneasy treatment of ideo-phonographs, at the front and center of his theory on writing and civilizational hierarchy. Rousseau's three states of society— "savage/barbaric/civil"—correspond, respectively, to the three scripts— "pictography/ideo-phonography/analytical phonography."[107] Pictography is "the primitive way of writing," which does not represent sound but "objects themselves."[108] Although pure pictography boasts direct representation, the fact that it has no recourse to representing concepts and abstraction and lacks necessary predicates to make meaningful sentences relegates pictography to primitivism. The analytical phonography, however, "increases the power of representation for the worse," gestures toward "pure phonography," promises "pure presence," and is thus civilized.[109] The trick lies in "ideo-phonography" or "ideo-phonogram," two terms that Rousseau uses interchangeably. Rousseau's idea of ideo-phonography— formulated by Derrida—reads, "The ideo-phonogram presupposes a 'double convention': that which links the grapheme to its phonematic signified, and that which links this phonematic signified, as a signifier, to its signified sense, to its concept, if one wishes."[110] This "double convention" of the ideo-phonographs as "a mixture of signifier and signified" is intriguing, for, on the one hand, it locates in ideo-phonography "the birth of phoneticization," and, on the other, it dwells on "the pictographic residue of the ideo-phonogram that 'paints voices.' "[111] After identifying the thorny doubleness in ideo-phonographs, Rousseau hastens to renounce ideo-phonography as less than "pure representants,"[112] returns to a general discourse of writing as a devious corruption in the first place, and defends phonography's claim to full speech and self-presence.

What is curious is not that Rousseau could not lay out his discourse of civilizational hierarchy without first qualifying the double convention of the ideo-phonograph; nor that he downplays the inaugurating moment of phoneticization in ideo-phonography to focus on its doomed pictographic attempt to paint voice. After all, Rousseau's *Essay on the Origin of Languages*, as Derrida reads it in *Of Grammatology*, is such a perfect example of phonocentrism that Derrida's critique of it becomes the perfect example of antiphonocentrism. What is truly curious, rather, is how Derrida—Rousseau's critic—by way of explaining the way in which Rousseau disarms the threat of ideo-phonography allows the discourse of the "pictographic residue" to gloss over the equally valid "phonetic surplus" in ideo-phonography. While Derrida demonstrates how Rousseau's masterpiece, as a representative of eighteenth-century metaphysics, epitomizes the logocentric pursuit of self-presence and auto-affection, he misses an opportune moment—Rousseau's stumble over ideo-phonography—to deconstruct logocentrism from within. For Rousseau, pure pictography and pure phonography stand as "two poles" and "two ideas of reason"; in other words, "ideas of pure presence: in the first case, presence of the represented thing in its perfect imitation, and in the second, the self-presence of speech itself."[113] Therefore the ideo-phonography functions, in the full Derridean sense, as a "hinge" connecting both the pictograph and phonetic alphabet, opening itself up to both the pictographic auto-representation and the phonographic claim of full speech. It is precisely this double convention of "pictographic residue" and "phonetic surplus" in ideo-phonography that could have made it the ideal script to represent both the "phonic signifier" and "a thing named in its concept."[114] Thus one is presented with an ultimate Derridean question that Derrida does not ask: if it is indeed self-presence and auto-affection that Western metaphysical tradition desires from Plato to Rousseau, then is not ideo-phonography the superior script?

Whereas Tang Lan does not make this question explicit, he hints at an answer to it by affirming that there has to be something more to writing than speech and the accumulation of phonic signifiers. Thus the second level of the inversion follows, turning the millennia-old order of writing and language inside out: writing is no longer exterior, and language is no longer interior; rather, it is language that is relegated to exteriority, while writing becomes history itself. Plato inaugurates in *Phaedrus* the hostility toward writing by announcing, "The evil of writing comes from without." Similarly, Saussure has to first overcome "this strange external system that is writing" to proceed to his analysis of the internal structures of linguistics.[115] To be sure, phonetic and alphabetic writing as a record of language is tolerable only to the extent that it serves as the least-distorted exteriority that will always aim to capture the original, natural, and internal voice, albeit never in full. This self-serving structure of full speech—in other words, the epoch of logocentrism—is now cracked open, truncated, and taken over by another structure called history that is written in ideo-phonographs. As Tang Lan stipulates, "a record of speech is not writing." Speech representation, transcription, and recapitulation even as full speech do not enter the process of the "accumulation of history" known as writing. While writing constituted history proper, speech is kept outside of it. In his musings on the way out of logocentrism, Derrida uses "exteriority" in another light: "We wished to reach the point of a certain exteriority in relation to the totality of the epoch of logocentrism." One dares to say that the wish has come true in the resolution of the Chinese script revolution. Tang Lan's reconsideration of Chinese paleography and his recommendation of the new ideo-phonography substantiate such a starting point of exteriority, from which, as Derrida hopes, "a certain deconstruction of that totality could be broken through."[116]

If exteriority is to be reconsidered, so is interiority. The final level of inversion is to happen from within, where the potential lies to redirect the Chinese script revolution, on the one hand, and rejuvenate grammatology in general, on the other. In his associative reading of Nietzsche, Heidegger, and Hegel, Derrida contemplates deconstruction as a method that Nietzsche practices as a critique of metaphysics, which Hegel has already rehearsed: "The movements of deconstruction are not interested in [solliciter] structures from the outside. They are not possible and effective, they cannot take accurate aim, except by inhabiting those structures. Inhabiting them in a certain way, because one always inhabits, and all the more when one does not suspect it."[117] The Nietzschean breakthrough in and break away from the metaphysical tradition would not be possible without still utilizing it in a certain way.[118] Read in a Nietzschean light, Tang Lan's proposition of new ideo-phonographs constitutes a similar move of deconstruction: it operates "necessarily from within" and borrows "from the old structure all the strategic and economic resources of subversion" to the extent of being unable to "isolate their elements and atoms."[119] As Tang demonstrates, there are not one but two old structures to inhabit and deconstruct: first, a critique of the metaphysics of phonocentrism is not possible without first inhabiting the structure of the pinyin ideology; and second, a critique of the old Chinese script is effective only if the critic utilizes the many "elements and atoms" embedded in the old ideo-phonographs. This act of inhabiting old structures—at the same time destructive and productive—leads Tang to create, in his own words, "a new script from within the old script" that endorses phoneticization but resists phonocentrism. As Spivak puts it in her afterword of the new edition, such a move of "inhabiting" should be taken as the first step toward constructing and practicing an "intellectual activism that begins with *Grammatology*."[120] As it turns out, that intellectual activism *is* grammatology.

In the final analysis, the coda of the Chinese script revolution offers the biggest surprise. In rallying unprecedented political and popular support, phonocentrism became the ideology of pinyin. The irony is that, at its ideological acme phonocentrism culminates in its own negation. Not unlike the three transmutations driven by phonocentric antinomies—the Latinization movement in conjunction with the literary revolution, the May Fourth *baihua* discourse, and the New Mass Education Movement—where the stronger phonocentrism is, the weaker its implementation; the socialist script revolution, by reaching phonocentric climax, delivers its containment. In its attempt to override and occupy all national forms of writing, phonocentrism becomes inhabited by a two-step reworking of both the concept of pinyin and the national form of ideo-phonographs. In strict accordance with the definition of dialectics, phonocentrism gives rise to a Chinese grammatology. This grammatology, fully aware of its Chinese ethnocentrism, constitutes a critique of the Western ethnocentrism that predates Derrida's *Of Grammatology*. For Derrida and poststructuralists, the imposition of Western ethnocentrism is enabled by a three-part operation carried out by one model of phonetic writing, one history of metaphysics, and one concept of science as the only organizing order, with the Roman-Latin alphabetic writing as its underwritten golden rule.[121] In correlation, the Chinese grammatology becomes conceivable when a new three-step operation is in motion: one model of the reinvented ideo-phonographic writing, one paradigm of progressive politics, and one argument to rejuvenate an old science so that new inquiries are possible.

On the level of script, as Tang Lan's devotion to and work on paleography and script reform instantiates—also, as historical hindsight corroborates—the new Chinese script, alphabetized and simplified, would indeed rise from the old script. On February 1, 1956, the first batch of 230 simplified characters was decreed for all publications nationwide, to be followed by a less-successful second batch of 248 characters in 1977.[122] Insofar as the new Chinese script held the promise to improve phoneticization, the socialist state went on to "promote *putonghua* and issue and implement a pinyin plan."

Although Zhou Enlai's announcement of the state policy in 1958 had likely little to do with Tang, Tang's conceptualization of and experimentation with the new ideo-phonographs charted a veritable path for the containment of the script revolution. More important, besides the practical policy level, the ideo-phonographic writing represented a different grammatological imagination, where "phonetic surplus"—Rousseau's term—and "grammatological surplus"—playing on Rousseau's term—could coexist. This new Chinese grammatology is rooted in and might continue to grow from the old concept of *wen* 文, which means both "writing" and "pattern" (*wen* 紋) and reveals the Way as the most elemental and truthful principle that organizes the world. As Liu Xie's *The Literary Mind and the Carving of Dragons*—the sixth-century and first Chinese literary criticism that inspired the novel *Wenxin*—defines *wen*, it is nothing short of the "originary way" (*yuandao* 原道).[123] This Chinese grammatology—its recognition of its own ethnocentrism as a critical endorsement of antiethnocentrism—plays a part in making the argument for the nonidentitarian politics at a global moment of decolonialization, anti-imperialism, and international solidarity.

Last but not least, as the concluding statement to the closing chapter of the Chinese script revolution, the old discipline of the study of the Chinese script is called upon for a reenergized comeback. The beginning of the Chinese script revolution coincided with the rise of the discipline of linguistics—specifically, structural linguistics—when Saussure's posthumous *Course in General Linguistics* and Yuen Ren Chao's inaugurating "The Problem of the Chinese Language" appeared in the same year, 1916. The containment of phonocentrism in China seems to beckon a similar disciplinary response, which was succinctly captured by one of Tang's essay titles, "Grammatology Should Become an Independent Discipline."[124] Reiterating that "linguistics cannot replace grammatology," Tang makes the point that it is only within an independent and nonsupplementary study of an updated "twentieth-century grammatology" that a true science of writing can grow, which should include but is not limited to the study of the nature and characteristics of each system of writing, their historical development and patterns, interconnections between them, general rules of grammatological development, and specific attributes of writing as technology.

The final historical irony is that this rejuvenated grammatology would not have been possible without its antinomy called phonocentrism. The final hope is that this renewed grammatology could generate the kind of intellectual and epistemological activism that humanists strive for. The Chinese grammatology—enabled by the three interlocking steps—organically resists the ethnocentric model of speech over writing from within the phonocentric paradigm, vigorously opposes the reduction of national forms in favor of a nonidentitarian coexistence of world writing systems, and envisions nothing short of a reorganization of the world. In search of new meaning in a new world, Tang appealed to building "solidarity" among all grammatologists of "Egyptian, Sumerian, Indian, Greek, Latin, Arabic, or native American," among others. As though concluding the modern Chinese script revolution, Tang beckons, "All grammatologists of the world unite!"[125]

EPILOGUE

The Last Custodian

June 3, 2016, downtown Beijing, I finally met Zhou Youguang 周有光 (1906–2017). Then one hundred ten years old, Zhou had stopped receiving guests, and his nursing staff had turned down my several requests for an interview. Though his stunning productivity after his official retirement at the age of eight-five provided answers to most of my questions for him, I still wanted to meet with him, if only to pay tribute to the last surviving member of the Committee for Chinese Script Reform. Just when I was ready to accept that "the man forgotten by God," as Zhou jokingly called himself, should not be disturbed, Dr. Su Jinzhi—a linguist and professor at the Chinese Academy of Social Sciences and a senior researcher at the State Language Commission, as well as my reference to Zhou—led me through Zhou's door.[1]

Zhou's home was simple, almost austere, on the third floor of the commission's residential compound, the same building where many of his colleagues from the committee, like Wang Jun and Yin Binyong, had lived. For a supercentenarian, who was feeble from a recent hospital stay, Zhou was incredibly lucid and articulate. Propped up against pillows in his bed and in his soft Changzhou accent, he warmly received us. His hearing aid was being repaired, so I did the "brush talk" and Zhou did the actual talking. The irony that my interview with the last custodian of the script revolution had to resort to characters was hardly lost on any of us. My first question was, "Why is Qingguo Alley, Changzhou, such a special place?" Zhou read the big characters that I jotted down in my notebook and let out a hearty laugh. The same Qingguo Alley, a neighborhood from the sixteenth century, gave birth to three Chinese script revolutionaries within just a few years: Yuen Ren Chao, Qu Qiubai, and Zhou himself, representing, respectively, the Romanization, Latinization, and socialist legs of the script revolution. It seemed unlikely that this could be chalked up to just coincidence, but Zhou had no theory, remarking, "Yuen Ren Chao was extraordinary." Pausing for a while, he added, "If it is the entire city of Changzhou, then there is also Wu Zhihui." Wu (1865–1953) was one of the "four elders" of the Guomindang, an Esperanto activist, and chairman of the six-month-long Conference on the Standardization of National Pronunciation in 1913, which endorsed the "National Alphabet" (*zhuyin fuhao*). If Changzhou produced the most radical and visible script revolutionaries, it was also a center for late-Qing New Text Confucianist studies known as the Changzhou school—a philological approach that paid special attention to oral transmission of classics—which included figures such as Zhuang Cunyu (1719–1788) and Liu Fenglu (1776–1829).[2]

Zhou was not born a linguist. An economics major first at St. John's University and then at Guanghua University in Shanghai, he worked for mass-education programs in Hangzhou and Wuxi, then sought postgraduate studies in Japan, and ultimately became a successful banker.[3] Zhou had always been interested in linguistics and dabbled in alphabetization before his legendary career change in 1955. He had played with stenography as early as the 1920s and supported both Romanization and Latinization, though leaning more toward the latter.[4] Zhou has always been patriotic and left leaning, from his early decision to give up a prestigious St. John's diploma to support the May Thirtieth Movement to his association with underground Communist activities in Hangzhou; and from his return to China from the United States in 1949 to his involvement with Sin Wenz.

A piece he wrote as a pastime had caught the attention of the Chinese Script Reform Committee. It was a comparative study of various schemes of dialect Sin Wenz and a proposition arguing for some level of phonological standardization before nationwide promotion, which came out in his collected volume *Research on the Chinese Pinyin Script*.[5] Zhou became a member of the committee and was invited to attend the first National Script Reform Conference in Beijing in 1955. Zhou's conference trip to Beijing was supposed to take no more than a month. However, he was informed at the end of the conference that he would receive a new position with the committee, and that special instructions from Zhou Enlai regarding his transfer were on their way to Shanghai.

There were two groups at the committee—the character-simplification group and the pinyin group—and Zhou joined the latter. The pinyin group designed the final draft that was officially endorsed by the PRC (People's Republic of China) in 1958.[6] Zhou never embraced the title "father of pinyin," bestowed on him by the media, but gladly took credit for pinyin's international recognition by the International Organization for Standardization (ISO) in 1982, a quasi-diplomatic feat with huge cultural implications.[7]

I then asked Zhou about the future of Chinese characters. He did not hesitate: "They will have to progress." He defined "progress" in terms of "linguistic and grammatological technology" (*yuwen jishu*). Speaking as a true pinyin loyalist, Zhou maintained that the Roman-Latin alphabet was by far the most technologically advanced and integrated script, and the pinyin system that he had helped implement had opened up the old Chinese script to the alphabetic technological future. He reminded me that "characters became a problem again in the 1980s," precisely because of the difficulty with character-input systems on computers. "It's always the technology," he concluded.

This answer did not stray from Zhou's regular and persistent stance. His and the committee's project was "the modernization of Chinese language and writing."[8] Under the basic premise that the Chinese script was a technology, characters could live on as long as they maintained technological compatibility with the information age. Therefore, among the three tasks of the socialist script reform—to simplify characters, to promote *putonghua*, and to issue a pinyin plan—the pinyin plan was the centerpiece. Its Roman-Latin alphabetic form provided the technological infrastructure for the delivery of the other two tasks and would eventually take over the continuing Chinese script reform in the final realization of "a pinyin script." As Zhou put it in the conclusion of his *Brief Discussions on Chinese Script Reform*, "Although we have only just begun the construction of a Chinese pinyin script, the victorious and final goal is clearly in sight."[9]

It was with this telos in sight that Zhou supported the simplification of characters—at least the PRC's first batch and the 1935 attempt by the Republic of China, arguing that character unification across the Taiwan Strait could proceed from these two lists—and proposed the convergence of *yutiwen* 語體文 (colloquialized written language) and *wentiyu* 文體語 (literary colloquial language) as the future of *putonghua*.[10] From his first foray into pinyin to his outpouring of writings after he turned one hundred, Zhou's message never changed: the script revolution will prevail.

As we went down the list of more detailed questions, such as Zhou's notes on Yuen Ren Chao's lecture in Ann Arbor, the Romanization veteran Li Jinxi's role on the committee, the committee's exchange with North Korea and Japan, and the alphabetization work done with the minority groups, Zhou graciously instructed me that the committee's archive at the Ministry of Education would be a better bet than his fading memory. Soon his nurse informed us that it was his nap time. I made a bold final request for Zhou to sign my copy of his memoir, *Lost Years Like Water* (2015). Zhou was happy to see his four-hundred-page tome, saying that he was thankful for all the time he had had to commit everything he wanted to say in writing. His nurse told us that he had not held a pen since that January and that I was in luck. Laboriously, Zhou took my pen and slowly stitched his name onto the title page. We all watched him intently; after all, it was rare to see a supercentenarian sign a book. When he pondered what else to write next to his name, the nurse took the pen out of his hand and instructed him to rest. Zhou smilingly complied, clasping his hands together. As Dr. Su and I took our leave, Zhou said his parting words to me: "Come back home. There is much work to be done for the Chinese language and writing [*yuwen*]."

On January 14, 2017, when Zhou's passing on the day after his one hundred eleventh birthday made international news, I reached for the autographed memoir on my shelf. The last custodian had passed, but his writings live on, together with both the promises and limits of the Chinese script revolution. There *is* much work to do, for both language and writing.

NOTES

INTRODUCTION

1. The simplification of characters is as old as the characters themselves. Before the twentieth-century simplification efforts, two historical periods—the Song dynasty (960–1279) and Yuan dynasty (1271–1368)—saw significant development of simplified characters. The ROC (Republic of China) published the *List of the First Batch of Simplified Characters* in 1934; the PRC (People's Republic of China) released its first batch in 1956. In Yuen Ren Chao's estimation, 80 percent of present-day PRC simplified characters have historical origins; see Yuen Ren Chao, "Yuen Ren Chao, Chinese Linguist, Phonologist, Composer and Author," in *Zhao Yuanren quanji* 趙元任全集 (The complete works of Zhao Yuanren) (Beijing: Commercial Press, 2007), 16:245. Luo Jialun continued to argue for the necessity of simplification after the ROC relocated to Taiwan. See Luo Jialun 羅家倫, *Jiantizi yundong* 簡體字運動 (The movement for simplified characters) (Taipei: Zhongyang wenwu gongying-she, 1954), 1.
2. There have been numerous schemes of phoneticizing Chinese. The present pinyin in the PRC is largely "the successor to Latinxua." See Chao, *Zhao Yuanren quanji*, 16:120.
3. Zhou Enlai 周恩来, "Dangqian wenzi gaige de renwu" (The current tasks of the script reform), in *Dangdai zhongguo de wenzi gaige* 當代中國的文字改革 (The script reform of contemporary China), ed. Wang Jun 王均 (Beijing: Dangdai zhong-guo chubanshe, 1995), 556–69.
4. See David Porter, *Ideographia: The Chinese Cipher in the Early Modern Europe* (Stanford, Calif.: Stanford University Press, 2001), 18, 37. For two more rich studies on the literary, technological, and artistic play on the idea of ideograph, see Christopher Bush, *Ideographic Modernism: China, Writing, Media* (Oxford: Oxford University Press, 2010); Andrea Bachner, *Beyond Sinology: Chinese Writing and*

the Scripts of Culture (New York: Columbia University Press, 2014). Another concern for the legibility of "ideographia" compared with alphabetic writing was the question of grammar. See Lydia H. Liu, *The Clash of Empires: The Invention of China in Modern World Making* (Cambridge, Mass.: Harvard University Press, 2004), chap. 6; Lin Shaoyang 林少陽, "'Wusi' xinxue zhi xiuci xue: Yuyan sixiang zhi xiandai shanbian" 「五四」新學之修辭學：語言思想之現代嬗變 (Rhetoric as "May Fourth" new learning: Transmutations of modern linguistic thought), *Zhongguo xiandai wenxue* 中國現代文學 (Modern Chinese literature), no. 34 (2018): 33–64.

5. Lu Xun 魯迅, "Wusheng de zhongguo" 無聲的中國 (Voiceless China) (1927), in *Lu Xun quanji* 魯迅全集 (The complete works of Lu Xun) (Beijing: Renmin wenxue chubanshe, 2005), 4:15. Unless otherwise noted, all translations are mine.

6. Eric Hobsbawm defines the "short twentieth century" as the period from 1914 to the end of the Soviet era; *The Age of Extremes: A History of the World, 1914–1991* (New York: Vintage Books, 1996), ix–xii. Wang Hui further narrows the Chinese twentieth century to 1911 to 1976; *China's Twentieth Century: Revolution, Retreat and the Road to Equality*, trans. Saul Thomas (New York: Verso, 2016).

7. Yuen Ren Chao, "The Problem of the Chinese Language: Scientific Study of Chinese Philology," *Chinese Students' Monthly* 11, no. 6 (1916): 437–43; no. 7 (1916): 500–509; no. 8 (1916): 572–93.

8. Ferdinand de Saussure, *Cours de linguistique générale* (Lausanne: Payot, 1916).

9. John E. Joseph, *Saussure* (Oxford: Oxford University Press, 2012), 634, gives a detailed account of the publication of *Course*, which was subject to the assembly and organization of Saussure's lecture notes, the appointment of Saussure's literary executor, and the timing of the World War I.

10. Sheldon Pollock, introduction to *World Philology*, ed. Sheldon Pollock, Benjamin A. Elman, and Ku-ming Kevin Chang (Cambridge, Mass.: Harvard University Press, 2015), 2, 22; Ku-ming Kevin Chang, "Philology or Linguistics? Transcontinental Responses," in Pollock, Elman, and Chang, *World Philology*, 311–31. Saussure's decision to leave Paris and return to Geneva had to do with his penchant for doing historical linguistic analysis over textual philology, costing him a chair position in Sanskrit and comparative grammar at the Sorbonne. See Joseph, *Saussure*, 349–58.

11. See the first principle of the "Nature of the Linguistic Sign," in *Course in General Linguistics*, by Ferdinand de Saussure, trans. Wade Baskin, ed. Perry Meisel and Haun Saussy (New York: Columbia University Press, 2011), 65; Kojin Karatani, "Nationalism and *Écriture*," *Surfaces* 5, no. 201.1 (1995): 12.

12. Plato states in *Phaedrus*, "The evil of writing comes from the outside," quoted in Jacques Derrida, *Of Grammatology*, trans. Gayatri Chakravorty Spivak (Baltimore: Johns Hopkins University Press, 2016), 37. Rousseau takes the evil of writing even further to argue for implications of political evil; Derrida, *Of Grammatology*, 182.

13. John E. Joseph's biography of Saussure highlights his "encounter with Sanskrit" as one important beginning of comparativism and structural linguistics, also citing Sanskrit learning—particularly Pāṇini's work—to be an indispensable methodological inspiration for leading twentieth-century linguists like Leonard Bloomfield and Noam Chomsky; see Joseph, *Saussure*, 82–98. Bloomfield also remarks, "Modern linguistics more than any other phase of our cultural life, is a heritage

from India." See Leonard Bloomfield, *An Introduction to the Study of Language* (New York: Holt, 1914), 310.

14. Walter Ong, *Orality and Literacy: The Technologizing of the Word* (London: Routledge, 1991), 84.

15. Ong, *Orality and Literacy*, 88, explains the uniqueness of the alphabet as follows: "The most remarkable fact about the alphabet no doubt is that it was invented only once." Florian Coulmas has a useful reminder that the phonetic writing system is always language specific and historically constructed; *The Writing Systems of the World* (Oxford: Blackwell, 1989), 33–34.

16. Derrida pinpoints logocentrism as ethnocentrism and dissects Rousseau's formulation of three states of society, three languages, three scripts—savage/barbaric/civil; hunter/shepherd/ploughman; pictography/ideo-phonography/analytical phonography—in the section "The History and System of Scripts" in *Of Grammatology*, 3, 305–21.

17. For East Asian case studies, see Thomas Mullaney, *The Chinese Typewriter: A History* (Cambridge, Mass.: MIT Press, 2017); Kerim Yasar, *Electrified Voices: How the Telephone, Phonograph, and Radio Shaped Modern Japan, 1868–1945* (New York: Columbia University Press, 2018); and Youming Zhou, *Historicizing Online Politics: Telegraphy, the Internet, and Political Participation in China* (Stanford, Calif.: Stanford University Press, 2005).

18. Timothy Mitchell offers a brilliant account of writing in Egypt in *Colonizing Egypt* (Berkeley: University of California Press, 1991), chap. 5. Nergis Ertürk breaks new ground in elucidating the relationship between Turkish script revolution and the making of Turkish literature and comparative literature in Turkey in *Grammatology and Literary Modernity in Turkey* (Oxford: Oxford University Press, 2011). Terry Martin surveys the script, language, and culture reforms in the Soviet Union in *The Affirmative Action Empire: Nations and Nationalism in the Soviet Union, 1923–1939* (Ithaca, N.Y.: Cornell University Press, 2001). John DeFrancis gives a history of modern Vietnamese script and language policies in *Colonialism and Language Policy in Vietnam* (The Hague: Mouton, 1977). John Phan studies premodern Vietnamese writing in "Lacquered Words: The Evolution of Vietnamese under Sinitic Influences from the 1st Century BCE through the 17th Century" (PhD diss., Cornell University, 2013). For Japan, see Kojin Karatani, *Origins of Modern Japanese Literature*, trans. Brett de Bary et al. (Durham, N.C.: Duke University Press, 1993); Komori Yōichi 小森陽一, *Nihongo no kindai* 日本語の近代 (Tokyo: Iwanami Shoten, 2000); Lee Yeounsuk, *The Ideology of Kokugo: Nationalizing Language in Modern Japan*, trans. Maki Hirano Hubbard (Honolulu: University of Hawai'i Press, 2010); and David Lurie, *Realms of Literacy: Early Japan and the History of Writing* (Cambridge, Mass.: Harvard University Press, 2011).

19. Chang gives a brilliant read on the discrepancy between the institute's English and Chinese names—Institute of History and Philology (Lishi Yuyan Yanjiusuo 歷史語言研究所). While the official English name is History and Philology, the literal translation of the Chinese name reads "History and Languages." The difference in naming reflects not only a difference of personal preference between Chao and Fu Sinian—a Germany-trained historian, philologist, and founding director of the institute—but also "the divorce of linguistics from philology"; see Chang, "Philology or Linguistics?," 312, 317, 322.

20. Zhou Enlai, "Dangqian wenzi gaige de renwu." The English term "Mandarin" is used to translate both *putonghua* and *guanhua* 官話 and is generally understood to refer to a singular, standardized official language such as the one endorsed by Zhou Enlai. However, the historical usage of *guanhua* denotes multiple and changing official speech in different regions (chap. 3, n. 45), while the concept of *putonghua* also connotes a radically nonuniform speech that is different from the Chinese national language as we know it today (chap. 2, n. 14).

21. For a recent study on Bandung, see Seng Tan and Amitav Acharya, eds., *Bandung Revisited: The Legacy of the 1955 Asian-African Conference for International Order* (Singapore: National University of Singapore Press, 2008). Wang Zhongchen offers crucial insights into the Chinese writers' experience during the Asian-Afro Writers' Conference in *Zuowei shijiande wenxue yu lishi xushu* 作為事件的文學與歷史敘述 (Literature and historical narrative as events) (Taipei: Renjian chubanshe, 2016), 193–215.

22. See chap. 5, n. 49.

23. Li Jinxi 黎錦熙, *Guoyu si qian nian lai bianhua chaoliu tu* 國語四千年來變化潮流圖 (Diagram showing the evolution of Chinese over the past four millenniums) (Beiping: Wenhua xue she, 1929); Ni Haishu 倪海曙, *Hanyu pinyin de gushi* 漢語拼音的故事 (The story of Chinese pinyin) (Shanghai: Shaonian ertong chubanshe, 1958); Chao, "Problem of the Chinese Language."

24. See, for example, Zhao Yintang 趙蔭棠, *Dengyun yuanliu* 等韻源流 (The origins of *Dengyun*) (Beijing: Commercial Press, 2011).

25. Lu Fayan 陸法言, *Qieyun* 切韻 (Rhyme phoneticization) (Nanjing: Jiangsu guangling guji keyinshe, 1987).

26. Zhao Yintang, *Dengyun yuanliu*, app. 2, "Shou Wen yunxue canjuan houji" 守溫韻學殘卷後記 (Postscript of Shou Wen's incomplete phonological volume).

27. Ricci's work was lost. His spelling plan was recovered from his essays on Romanization, reproduced in *Chengshi moyuan* 程氏墨苑 (Cheng's garden of ink). Ni Haishu has replicated an example of Romanization from one of Ricci's essays, and Trigault's plan in its entirety can be found in Ni Haishu 倪海曙, *Zhongguo pinyin wenzi yundongshi jianbian* 中國拼音文字運動史簡編 (A concise chronology of the Chinese alphabetization movement) (Shanghai: Shidai shubao chubanshe, 1948), 5–6, 8. For a detailed account of the Jesuits' work on Chinese phonology, see Luo Changpei 羅常培, "Yesuhuishi zai yinyunxue shang de gongxian" 耶穌會士在音韻學上的貢獻 (The Jesuits' contributions in philology), *Bulletin of the Institute of History and Philology, Academia Sinica* 1, no. 3 (1930): 267–338.

28. Ni Haishu, *Zhongguo pinyin wenzi yundongshi jianbian*, 7–9.

29. I discuss my preservation of the term "dialect" in chapter 2, n. 6.

30. Ni Haishu, *Zhongguo pinyin wenzi yundongshi jianbian*, 18.

31. For more on the turn-of-the-century script reform, see Ni Haishu, *Zhongguo pinyin wenzi yundongshi jianbian*, 32–91; John DeFrancis, *Nationalism and Language Reform in China* (Princeton, N.J.: Princeton University Press, 1950), 31–54; Jing Tsu, *Sound and Script in Chinese Diaspora* (Cambridge, Mass.: Harvard University Press, 2010), 18–47; Elizabeth Kaske, *The Politics of Language in Chinese Education, 1895–1919* (Leiden: Brill, 2008), 27–54; W. K. Cheng, "Enlightenment and Unity: Language Reformism in Late Qing China," *Modern Asian Studies* 2 (2001): 469–93;

and Victor H. Mair, "Advocates of Script Reform," in *Sources of Chinese Tradition*, ed. Wm. Theodore de Bary and Richard Lufrano (New York: Columbia University Press, 2000), 2:302–7; Gina Anne Tam, *Dialect and Nationalism in China, c. 1860–1960* (Cambridge: Cambridge University Press, forthcoming), chap. 2.

32. Ni Haishu, *Zhongguo pinyin wenzi yundongshi jianbian*, 32.

33. Ni Haishu, *Zhongguo pinyin wenzi yundongshi jianbian*, 32–53, 59–62, carefully lists and classifies major and minor schemes of Chinese phoneticization. Among the earliest phoneticization proposals, Shen Xue's *Universal System* (1896) was arguably best known, with a preface by Liang Qichao, praising it to have contributed to the "unification of the written and the spoken"; see Ni Haishu 倪海曙, *Qingmo hanyu pinyin wenzi yundong biannianshi* 清末漢語拼音文字運動編年史 (Chronology of the late-Qing Chinese alphabetization movement) (Shanghai: Shanghai renmin chubanshe, 1959), 48.

34. Wang's scheme was designed for the northern dialects, while Lao's worked for the southern, Wu dialects. Lao was a late-Qing scholar-official specializing in law and phonology who also served as president of Peking University. Wang, on the other hand, was exiled by the Qing court for his participation in the 1898 reform. A phoneticization enthusiast, Wang devised, during his two-year exile in Japan, a "Mandarin alphabet" based on the Japanese kana system and returned to China with the new script under the guise of a Buddhist monk by way of Taiwan. For biographical accounts of Wang and Lao, see Ni Haishu, *Zhongguo pinyin wenzi yundongshi*, 42–52. Li Jinxi offers a gripping account of Wang's adventure in *Guoyu yundong shigang* 國語運動史綱 (The historical *Grundrisse* of the national language movement) (1935; repr., Beijing: Commercial Press, 2011), 100.

35. Lu Zhuangzhang 盧戇章, *Yimu liaoran chujie* 一目了然初階 (A primer at a glance) (1892; repr., Beijing: Wenzi gaige chubanshe, 1956), 5–6.

36. Zhang Taiyan originally devised thirty-six consonants and twenty-two vowels; see Zhang Taiyan 章太炎, "Bo zhongguo yong wanguo xinyu shuo" 駁中國用萬國新語說 (A rebuttal to the discourse of using Esperanto in China), in *Zhang Taiyan quanji* 章太炎全集 (The complete works of Zhang Taiyan) (Shanghai: Shanghai renmin chubanshe, 1985), 4:337–53. Wang Feng offers an insightful explanation of how the conference reached its consensus on the National Alphabet, in *Shiyun tuiyi yu wenzhang xingti—zhongguo jindai wenxue lunji* 世運推移與文章興替—中國近代文學論集 (Shifting times and changing writing: Anthology of modern Chinese literature) (Beijing: Beijing daxue chubanshe, 2015), 188–209; specifically on the conference, 207–8.

37. Late imperial China saw the devaluation of orthodox classical philosophy (*daoxue*), as well as of Chinese natural studies (*gezhi*, "investigating things and extending knowledge") and *bowu* (broad learning). The former became challenged by the rigor of evidential research (*kaozheng*), and the latter by the encounter with Western science. These major intellectual transitions from philosophy to philology, from Chinese natural studies to science, are captured brilliantly in Benjamin A. Elman, *From Philosophy to Philology: Intellectual and Social Aspects of Change in Late Imperial China*, 2nd ed. (Los Angeles: University of California Press, 2001); Benjamin A. Elman, *On Their Own Terms: Science in China, 1550–1900* (Cambridge, Mass.: Harvard University Press, 2005).

38. Lu Xun's "Qingnian bidu shu" 青年必讀書 (Must-reads for youth) was published in 1925 as a response to the newspaper *Jingbao*'s survey soliciting book recommendations for youth. Lu Xun's provocation caused instant controversies, which became a topic often revisited in his later essays well until 1933. See *Lu Xun quanji*, 3:12–13. His rhetorical abandonment of Chinese books does not cancel out prior and meaningful endeavors in preserving and reinventing Chinese episteme but bears witness to a kind of violence that rendered such practice obsolete. For an example of the Commercial Press's efforts in negotiating epistemological violence and "semiotic modernity," see Yue Meng, *Shanghai and the Edges of Empires* (Minneapolis: University of Minnesota Press, 2006), chap. 2.

39. The English title of the diagram is the original translation. The Sesquicentennial International Exposition also commemorated the fiftieth anniversary of the Centennial Exhibition, held in Philadelphia in 1876. For foreign participation in the exhibition, including China's, see E. L. Austin and Odell Hauser, *The Sesqui-Centennial International Exposition* (New York: Arno Press, 1976), 81–103.

40. Li Jinxi, *Guoyu si qian nian lai bianhua chaoliu tu*. This piece was solicited by the Chinese National Association for the Advancement of Education (Zhonghua Jiaoyu Gaijinshe 中華教育改進社), which was founded in 1921 in Beijing and played a key role in the Mass Education Movement in the 1920s and 1930s. Its publication was aided by Li's friends and colleagues Yuen Ren Chao, Liu Bannong, and Qian Xuantong. All phrases in quotation marks regarding the diagram are Li's original English wording.

41. Martin Heidegger, "The Age of the World Picture," in *The Question Concerning Technology and Other Essays*, trans. William Lovitt (New York: Harper Torchbooks, 1977).

42. *Genbun itchi* and *yanwen yizhi* use the same characters, 言文一致. One of the first Chinese intellectuals to adopt the term in the Chinese context was Huang Zunxian; see *Riben guozhi* 日本國志 (A record of Japan) (Shanghai: Shanghai guji chubanshe, 2001).

43. My treatment of phonocentrism is inspired by Marston Anderson's brilliant take on realism. As Anderson puts it, "Their [Chinese writers'] gradual discovery of the true nature of realism and their eventual relinquishment of the mode is the story of this book" (*The Limits of Realism: Chinese Fiction in the Revolutionary Period* [Berkeley: University of California Press, 1990], 25).

44. Two examples illustrating the two early meanings of grammatology are Gabriel Surenne, *French Grammatology; or, A Course of French* (1824), and George Dalgarno, *The Works of George Dalgarno of Aberdeen* (1834), respectively.

45. I. J. Gelb, *A Study of Writing* (Chicago: University of Chicago Press, 1952), 23, 249.

46. Benoît Peeters, *Derrida: A Biography*, trans. Andrew Brown (Cambridge: Polity Press, 2013), 159.

47. Derrida, *Of Grammatology*, 3. In addition, logocentrism is also "the epoch of full speech" in pursuit of a theological "presence." For Derrida on logocentrism, being, and presence, see 43, 19–28.

48. I thank J. Barton Scott for the timely reminder that Derrida was also a colonial figure. For Derrida's relationship to the French language as an Algerian Jew (*pied-noir*), see Jacques Derrida, *Monolingualism of the Other; or, The Prosthesis of Origin*, trans. Patrick Mensah (Stanford, Calif.: Stanford University Press, 1998).

49. Sheldon Pollock compares the preservation of historical languages to the preservation of global biological diversity; introduction to *World Philology*, 4.
50. An incomplete tally counts the following pieces: Lu Xun 魯迅, "Da Cao Juren xiansheng xin" 答曹聚仁先生信 (An answer to Mr. Cao Juren's letter) (August 2, 1934), "Menwai wentan" 門外文談 (Outdoor chats on writing) (August 16, 1934), "Hanzi he ladinghua" 漢字和拉丁化 (Chinese characters and Latinization) (August 23, 1934), "Zhongguo yuwen de xinsheng" 中國語文的新生 (The rebirth of Chinese language and writing) (September 24, 1934), "Guanyu xin wenzi" 關於新文字 (About Sin Wenz) (September 10, 1935), "Cong 'biezi' shuo kaiqu" 從"別字"說開去 (From "variant character forms" to other things) (March 21, 1935), "Lun xin wenzi" 論新文字 (On Sin Wenz) (December 23, 1935), and "Lun xianzai women de wenxue yundong" 論現在我們的文學運動 (On our present literary movement) (June 10, 1936), in *Lu Xun quanji*, 6:78–81, 86–114, 5:584–87, 6:118–20, 165–66, 289–94, 457–59, 612–14, respectively. All essay dates are dates of composition, except "About Sin Wenz," for which I noted the date of publication since the date of composition, December 9, did not include the year.
51. *Lu Xun quanji*, 6:289, 119; 5:586.
52. *Lu Xun quanji*, 4:15.
53. I thank Wang Hui for urging me to rethink the significance of this essay. Altogether, Lu Xun published five long pieces in *Henan* between 1907 and 1908: "Ren zhi lishi" 人之歷史 (Human history) (published in no. 1), "Moluo shilishuo" 摩羅詩力說 (On the power of Mara poetry) (nos. 2 and 3), "Kexue lishi jiaopian" 科學歷史教篇 (Lessons from the history of science) (no. 5), "Wenhua pianzhi lun" 文化偏至論 (On the imbalanced development of culture) (no. 7), and "Po e sheng lun" 破惡聲論 (Toward a refutation of malevolent voices) (no. 8), in *Lu Xun quanji*, 1:8–24, 65–120, 25–44, 45–64; 8:25–40; as well as one translation, "Pei tuan fei shilun" 裴象飛詩論 (On Sándor Petőfi's poetry) (no. 7), its preface in *Lu Xun quanji*, 10:457–58. For an admirable English translation, see Lu Xun, "Toward a Refutation of Malevolent Voices," trans. Jon Eugene von Kowallis, *boundary 2* 38, no. 2 (2011): 39–62. My translation references Kowallis's but is in most cases modified.
54. Wang Hui gives a masterful reading of Lu Xun's essay in "The Voices of Good and Evil: What Is Enlightenment? Rereading Lu Xun's 'Toward a Refutation of Malevolent Voices,'" trans. Ted Huters and Zong Yangyang, *boundary 2* 38, no. 2 (2011): 67–124; Ji Jianqing 季劍青 adds important insights on Lu Xun's choice of language in view of his earlier translation work, in "'Sheng' zhi tanqiu: Lu Xun baihua xiezuo de qiyuan" 聲之探求：魯迅白話寫作的起源 (In search of "sheng": The origin of Lu Xun's *baihua* writing), *Wenxue pinglun* 文學評論 (Literary review), no. 3 (2018): 104–14.
55. Lu Xun, "Po e sheng lun," in *Lu Xun quanji*, 8:25–28.
56. Lu Xun, "Moluo shilishuo," in *Lu Xun quanji*, 1:103n4. For an excellent reading on the connections between *xinsheng*, Byronic Romanticism, vitalism, and Lu Xun's poetic-political vision, see Pu Wang, "Poetics, Politics, and *Ursprung/Yuan*: On Lu Xun's Conception of 'Mara Poetry,'" *Modern Chinese Literature and Culture* 23, no. 2 (Fall 2011): 34–63.
57. The Chinese original reads as follows: "蓋惟聲發自心，朕歸於我，而人始自有己；人各有己，而群之大覺近矣。" *Lu Xun quanji*, 8:26. Hereafter, I cite this essay and Lu Xun's other work parenthetically by volume and page number.

58. It bears pointing out that, on the question of writing systems, Lu Xun was largely following his mentor, Zhang Taiyan, in his objection to Esperanto as a universal language and writing system, which did not necessarily extend itself to an opposition to the alphabetization of Chinese.

59. Lu Xun, "Menwai wentan" in *Lu Xun quanji* 6:105.

1. THE BEGINNING AND THE END OF
ALPHABETIC UNIVERSALISM

1. Tsinghua did not become a university until 1925. Zhong's original Chinese reads as follows: "廢除漢字，取用字母." See Hu Shi 胡適, "Bishang Liangshan" 逼上梁山 (Forced onto Mount Liang) (1933), in *Sishi zishu* 四十自述 (Autobiography at forty), in *Hu Shi wenji* 胡適文集 (The collected works of Hu Shi) (Beijing: Beijing daxue chubanshe, 1998), 1:140.

2. Of the four parts of the article, Chao wrote parts 1, 2, and 4, and Hu Shi contributed part 3; Yuen Ren Chao, "The Problem of the Chinese Language: Scientific Study of Chinese Philology," *Chinese Students' Monthly* 11, no. 6 (1916): 437–43; no. 7 (1916): 500–509; no. 8 (1916): 572–93.

3. Exceptions included Zhang Taiyan, Dai Jitao, and Chen Mengjia. Script revolutionaries experienced little or no pushback in most literary genres except classical poetry. For a fascinating history of classical-style poetry writing in the early twentieth century, see Shengqing Wu, *Modern Archaics: Continuity and Innovation in the Chinese Lyric Tradition, 1900–1937* (Cambridge, Mass.: Harvard University Asia Center Press, 2013). For an illuminating explication of Dai Jitao's conservative revolutionary vision and agenda that included an opposition to the script and language reform, see Brian Tsui, *China's Conservative Revolution: The Quest for a New Order, 1927–1949* (New York: Cambridge University Press, 2017), chap. 2.

4. The special issue on the script revolution was *Guoyu yuekan* 國語月刊 (National language monthly) 1, no. 7 (1922). Altogether, 688 public figures signed the 1935 open letter, "Women duiyu tuixing xinwenzi de yijian" 我們對於推行新文字的意見 (Our opinion on the promotion of Sin Wenz); Wo Dan 渥丹, *Zhungguo wenz latinxua wenxian* 中国文字拉丁化文献 (Documents on the Latinization of the Chinese script) (Shanghai: Latinxua chubanshe, 1940), 153–57.

5. Qian Xuantong 錢玄同, "Zhongguo jinhou zhi wenzi wenti" 中國今後之文字問題 (Questions regarding the future of the Chinese script), *Xin qingnian* 新青年 (New youth) 4, no. 4 (April 15, 1918): 350–56; also in *Qian Xuantong wenji* 錢玄同文集 (The collected works of Qian Xuantong), 6 vols. (Beijing: Renmin daxue chubanshe, 1999), 1:162–70.

6. The Zhou brothers' collaboration with Eroshenko in translating Esperanto literature is well documented. See the diary entry of February 24, 1922, in Zhou Zuoren 周作人, *Zhou Zuoren riji* 周作人日记 (Zhou Zuoren's diary) (Zhengzhou: Daxiang chubanshe, 1996), 2:228; Lu Xun, preface to the *Collection of Eroshenko's Fairy Tales* (Shanghai: Commercial Press, 1922); Meng Qingshu 孟慶澍, *Wuzhengfu zhuyi yu wusi xin wenhua* 無政府主義與五四新文化 (Anarchism and May Fourth new culture) (Kaifeng: Henan daxue chubanshe, 2006), chap. 2; Gerald Chan, "China and the Esperanto Movement," *Australian Journal of Chinese Affairs*, no. 15

(January 1986): 1–18; and Andrew F. Jones, *Developmental Fairy Tales: Evolutionary Thinking and Modern Chinese Culture* (Cambridge, Mass.: Harvard University Press, 2011), 150–53, 235.

7. Although the name Esperanto does not convey explicitly its aspiration to become a universal language (*espero* in Esperanto denotes "hope"), its Chinese-character translation (*wanguo xinyu* 萬國新語)—the one that Qian adopts—names it "the new language of ten thousand nations." See Qian, *Qian Xuantong wenji*, 1:167. For more on Esperanto, see L. L. Zamenhof, "What Is Esperanto?," *North American Review* 184, no. 606 (January 1907): 15–21; Peter G. Forster, *The Esperanto Movement* (New York: Mouton, 1982); Esther Shor, *Bridge of Words: Esperanto and the Dream of a Universal Language* (New York: Metropolitan Books, 2016).

8. In Hu Shi's account, the Chinese overseas student group in New England founded their own Institute of Arts and Sciences and chose "the problem of the Chinese language" as the topic for the year 1915 and published his and Chao's work in the following year. See Hu, *Hu Shi wenji*, 1:141.

9. For more on the publication of *Course in General Linguistics*, see John E. Joseph, *Saussure* (Oxford: Oxford University Press, 2012), 632–35.

10. Chao did his undergraduate studies in mathematics and physics at Cornell University and switched to philosophy for his doctoral studies at Harvard University. He is said to have held the record for highest overall grade-point average at Cornell even many years after he graduated; see Zhao Xinna 趙新那, *Zhao Yuanren nianpu* 趙元任年譜 (A chronicle of Yuen Ren Chao) (Beijing: Commercial Press, 2001), 75.

11. Chen-Pang Yeang gives an illuminating account of how Chao's linguistics work informed his unique approach to cybernetics; see "From Modernizing the Chinese Language to Information Science: Chao Yuen Ren's Route to Cybernetics," *Isis* 108, no. 3 (September 2017): 553–80. For more on Chao's work in cybernetics and during the Macy conferences, see Lydia H. Liu, *The Freudian Robot: Digital Media and the Future of the Unconscious* (Chicago: University of Chicago Press, 2010), chap. 3. On the Macy conferences, see N. Katherine Hayles, *How We Became Posthuman: Virtual Bodies in Cybernetics, Literature, and Informatics* (Chicago: University of Chicago Press, 1999).

12. See Zhao Xinna, *Zhao Yuanren nianpu*, 82. For a self-portrayal of his intellectual upbringing, see Yuen Ren Chao 趙元任, *Zhao Yuanren quanji* 趙元任全集 (The complete works of Yuen Ren Chao) (Beijing: Commercial Press, 2007), 16:59–74.

13. Zhao Xinna, *Zhao Yuanren nianpu*, 82. Chao took his first phonetics class with Hermann Davidsen, who translated Otto Jespersen's *Textbook on Phonetics* from Danish to German, and an introductory linguistics class with Charles H. Grandgent, the author of *An Outline of the Phonology and Morphology of Old Provençal* (Boston: Heath, 1905). Grandgent had studied with Paul Meyer, a French comparative philologist and colleague of Ferdinand de Saussure's at the École Pratique des Hautes Études, a headquarters of nineteenth-century philological and historical sciences. For an important discussion of the division between the German philological tradition and Anglo-French linguistics, see Ku-ming Kevin Chang, "Philology or Linguistics? Transcontinental Responses," in *World Philology*, ed. Sheldon Pollock, Benjamin A. Elman, and Ku-ming Kevin Chang (Cambridge, Mass.: Harvard University Press, 2015), 311–31.

14. Before this article Chao had published other essays, mainly in Chinese in the magazine *Kexue* 科學 (Science), which he cofounded in 1915. This was the first journal to discuss the use of punctuation in Chinese writing. See Hu Shi 胡適, "Lun judou ji wenzi fuhao" 論句讀及文字符號 (On punctuation and writing symbols), *Kexue* 2, no. 1 (January 1916): 9–34.

15. Chao's original English formulation is in Chao, "Problem of the Chinese Language," 438; the relevant page numbers are hereafter provided parenthetically in the main text.

16. Chao uses the following example: 老 lau² = 淪 (lun-un) + 島 (tau²-t) 反 = l + au² = lau². To subtract is to cut (*qie*); to cross or reverse spell is to *fan*; "Problem of the Chinese Language," 505, 509.

17. The Committee on Unification of Pronunciation (Chao's original English) is also referred to as the Committee on Standardization of National Pronunciation, which revised Zhang Binglin's system and established it as the National Alphabet (*zhuyin zimu* 注音字母). For a survey of the history of Chinese shorthand systems developed in tandem with Japanese and English methods, see Li Jinxi 黎錦熙, *Guoyu yundong shigang* 國語運動史綱 (The historical *Grundrisse* of the national language movement) (1935; repr., Beijing: Commercial Press, 2011), 98–99.

18. Yuen Ren Chao 趙元任, "Guoyu luomazi de yanjiu" 國語羅馬字的研究 (A study of Romanized Chinese writing), *Guoyu yuekan* 1, no. 7 (1922): 87–117.

19. Chinese *guoyu* shares the characters of the Japanese *kokugo* and takes inspiration from the Meiji language and writing reforms. For an archaeology of the origin of the Japanese concept of the national language, see Lee Yeounsuk, *The Ideology of Kokugo: Nationalizing Language in Modern Japan*, trans. Maki Hirano Hubbard (Honolulu: University of Hawai`i Press, 2010), 54–61. Around the time Chao penned his essay in 1916, Li Jinxi and others started to petition to change the subject heading of Chinese language and writing pedagogy from *guowen* (national prose) to *guoyu* (national language). Official recognition was granted in January 1920 when a decree from the Education Ministry of the Beiyang government mandated that all national schools abandon the subject title *guowen* and adopt *guoyu*. See Li Jinxi, *Guoyu yundong shigang*, 133, 161. The phonocentric overhaul privileging speech over writing was thus official, soon to be followed by various transmutations.

20. The year 1924 witnessed the official decision to adopt "the beautiful Beijing dialect" as national pronunciation and also inaugurated modern Chinese dialectology with the founding of the Peking University Dialect Survey Society. It was also the beginning of an eight-year period of relative cultural and political conservatism that forced the Chinese alphabetization and national language movement to go on the defense. See Li Jinxi, *Guoyu yundong shigang*, 173–79, 203.

21. The Committee on Standardization of National Pronunciation (1912–1916) was later replaced by the Committee on the Research of the National Language (Guoyu Yanjiu Hui 國語研究會, 1916–1923), which morphed into the Preparatory Committee for the Unification of the National Language (Guoyu Tongyi Choubei Hui 國語統一籌備會, 1919–1923). Chao was not one of its original members but joined in 1920. See Zhao Xinna, *Zhao Yuanren nianpu*, 101; Chao, *Zhao Yuanren quanji*, 16:110. The Conference on the Standardization of National Pronunciation lasted from December 1912 to May 1913, agreeing finally upon an artificial national pronunciation and the thirty-nine-letter National Alphabet (*zhuyin fuhao*). For the

proceedings of conference as well as a history of the three organs related to *guoyu*, see Li Jinxi, *Guoyu yundong shigang*, 121–39. David Moser offers a vivid account of the drama and colorful language used by the conference participants in *A Billion Voices: China's Search for a Common Language* (Sydney: Penguin Books Australia, 2016), 18–28.

22. Li Jinxi, *Guoyu yundong shigang*, 124, 150.

23. This series of phonographs is called *Guoyu liushengji pian* 國語留聲機片. Before Chao, language-reform activist Wang Pu had unsuccessfully attempted an earlier version. In Chao's "First Green Letter," he talks about Wang Pu's Pekingese pronunciation being not "correct" for the old national pronunciation: "The original speaker is a Peking native. His pronunciation falls short of being perfect in retaining some Peking localisms which have been eliminated in the standard, especially his using (inverted e) of Peking in place of the full (o) of correct mandarin" ("First Green Letter" [January 1921], in *Zhao Yuanren quanji*, 16:315). "Green letters" refers to a series of correspondence either written or printed on green paper that Chao sent out to his friends all over the world. During Chao's lifetime, he sent five in total and left a sixth letter unfinished. These letters, humorous in tone, usually include his life updates, new intellectual interests, and at times lengthy discussions of academic issues.

24. The debate climaxed when the journal *Xuedeng* 學燈 (Lantern of learning) published a series of polemical exchanges between the group in support of Pekingese, such as Zhang Shiyi 張士一 (an alumnus of Teachers College, Columbia University, and an educator of English in China), and the group loyal to the old national pronunciation, which included Li Jinxi and Chao. Li gave an overall account of the debate in Li Jinxi, *Guoyu yundong shigang*, 152–59. For details, see Zhu Lingong 朱麟公, ed., *Guoyu wenti taolun ji* 國語問題討論集 (An anthology of discussions on the national language) (Shanghai: Zhongguo shuju, 1921).

25. Yuen Ren Chao 趙元任, "Taolun guoyin zimu de liang fengxin" 討論國音字母的兩封信 (Two letters discussing the national alphabet), in *Zhao Yuanren yuyanxue lunwenji* 趙元任語言學論文集 (Collection of Yuen Ren Chao's linguistic essays) (Beijing: Commercial Press, 2002), 21. For both Chao's and Li's letters, see *Guoyu yuekan* 1, no. 7 (1922): 165–76.

26. For both Chao's and Li's letters, see *Guoyu yuekan* 1, no. 7 (1922): 165–76. Chao's 1922 article "Guoyu luomazi de yanjiu" reads like a reprisal of his 1916 article, opening with ten objections to Romanizing Chinese script followed by a point-by-point rebuttal. It then lays out the general spelling rules of the Romanization system, with twenty-five principles in using the new system. He finishes by offering ten points of uncertainties and nine measures to promote his Romanization system.

27. Yuen Ren Chao, "Second Green Letter," in *Zhao Yuanren quanji*, 16:328.

28. Chao, "Second Green Letter" (April 15, 1923), in *Zhao Yuanren quanji*, 16:328.

29. "Yuen Ren Chao, Chinese Linguist, Phonologist, Composer and Author," in *Zhao Yuanren quanji*, 16:109.

30. Both Lao She and Qian Zhongshu recorded with the School of Oriental Studies, University of London. Listen to Qian Zhongshu's *Linguaphone Language Courses* (date unclear), available at the Rulan Chao Pian Music Collection, Chung Chi College Elisabeth Luce Moore Library, Chinese University of Hong Kong. I have not

been able to track down Lao She's *Yanyu sheng pian* 言語聲片 (Linguaphone Oriental language courses, Chinese). Qian used a Pekingese-based standardized speech, while Lao She was a Beijing local and known for his Pekingese-inflected literary language.

31. Yuen Ren Chao, "Third Green Letter" (February 29, 1925), in *Zhao Yuanren quanji*, 16:368. The real date of the letter was likely March 1, 1925, for Chao's note on the date reads "February 29, if it weren't 1925."

32. Charles Darwin, *The Descent of Man, and Selection in Relation to Sex* (1871; repr., Cambridge: Cambridge University Press, 2009), 1:60.

33. For a succinct summary of the Romanization system that spells the old pronunciation, see Yuen Ren Chao 趙元任, "Xin wenzi yundong di taolun" 新文字運動底討論 (A discussion of the new script movement), *Guoyu yuekan* 2, no. 1 (1924): 1–17.

34. Chao explains the Society of a Few Men as follows: "Among members of that committee [the Committee on Unification of the National Language], a few of them formed a little group called Society of a Few Men . . . based on the preface of Lu Fa-yen's book, 601 A.D. Ch'ieh Yün [*Qie yun*] the primary source for ancient Chinese of 601 A.D., because in the preface they said, 'We few men decide and it is decided,' so we called ourselves the Society of a Few Men; some of them would rather have called it Society of a Handful of Men"; see *Zhao Yuanren quanji*, 16:110. For the 1926 edition of GR, see *Gwoyeu Romatzyh, Chinese National Association for the Advancement of Education Bulletin* 4, no. 4 (1926).

35. The first form of the national alphabet was *zhuyin fuhao*. This order was decreed by Cai Yuanpei, then president of the University Council 大學院 (Daxueyuan), on September 26, 1928. For the complete official announcement of the endorsement of GR, see Zhao Xinna, *Zhao Yuanren nianpu*, 154.

36. Diary entry of October 5, 1928 (parenthetical translation is mine).

37. Bernhard Karlgren, *The Romanization of Chinese: A Paper Read Before the China Society on January 19, 1928* (London: China Society, 1928), 1.

38. Correspondence from Karlgren to Chao, February 24, 1925, Yuen Ren Chao papers, BANC MSS 83/30 c, carton 5: Karlgren, Bancroft Library, University of California, Berkeley. Chao's letter to Karlgren soliciting Karlgren's response in this particular letter was not found in the archive.

39. Karlgren was a student of Johan August Lundell's while studying Russian at Uppsala University, where he returned to teach in 1915 after his sojourn abroad, first in Russia (1909–1910), then China (1910–1912), and finally France (1912–1915), where he met Paul Pelliot and Henri Maspero. See N. G. D. Malmqvist, *Bernhard Karlgren: Portrait of a Scholar* (Bethlehem, Penn.: Lehigh University Press, 2011).

40. Malmqvist points out that Karlgren's dissertation was one year earlier than Saussure's *Cours de linguistique générale* (1916); Malmqvist, *Bernhard Karlgren*, 154, 165, 174. Although the Chinese translation did not come out until 1940, Chao encountered Karlgren's dissertation in 1921, when the geologist Ding Wenjiang 丁文江 gave him a copy. At Karlgren's personal invitation, first in 1924 and then in 1928, Chao undertook the translation and editing work; see Zhao Xinna, *Zhao Yuanren nianpu*, 111, 151. Chao visited Karlgren in 1924 on his way back from the United States to Beijing to assume a post at Tsinghua University, where Chao became the youngest of the four so-called Great Mentors in the newly founded Institute of National Learning. The other three were the late-Qing reformist and

thinker Liang Qichao, literary scholar and poet Wang Guowei, and archaeologist Li Ji.

41. Chao's "Third Green Letter" (February 29, 1925), in *Zhao Yuanren quanji*, 16:368.
42. Roy Harris and Talbot Taylor, eds., *Landmarks in Linguistic Thought I: The Western Tradition from Socrates to Saussure* (New York: Routledge, 1997), xiv–xviii. See also Wilhelm von Humboldt, *Über die Verschiedenheit des menschlichen Sprachbaues und ihren Einfluss auf die geistige Entwickelung des Menschengeschlechts* (Berlin: Druckerei der Königlichen Akademie der Wissenschaften, 1836); C. K. Ogden, *Debabelization: With a Survey of Contemporary Opinion on the Problem of a Universal Language* (London: K. Paul, Trench, Trubner, 1931); and Roy Harris, *Language, Saussure and Wittgenstein: How to Play Games with Words* (New York: Routledge, 1990).
43. Aside from Basic English, Chao cites two other sources of inspiration for his coinage of "Basic Chinese": first, James Yen's literacy program designed for Chinese laborers in World War I France; second, the dramatist Hong Shen's concept of "basic characters." See Yuen Ren Chao, *Mandarin Primer: An Intensive Course in Spoken Chinese* (Cambridge, Mass.: Harvard University Press; London: Oxford University Press, 1964), 15. Li Jinxi also mentions the connection between Basic Chinese and Basic English in "Hanzi chuli banfa he xinwenzi de qiaoliang" 漢字處理辦法和新文字的橋樑 (Sorting Chinese characters and bridging the new script), in *1949 nian zhongguo wenzi gaige lunwenji* 一九四九年中國文字改革論文集 (Papers on Chinese language reform in 1949), ed. Du Zijing 杜子勁 (Beijing: Dazhong shudian, 1950), 69.
44. Karlgren named three types of Romanization: (1) A system as "a philological system, strictly phonetic, for scientific study"; (2) B system as "a sinological system, for dictionaries, text-books, treatises on Chinese history, etc."; and (3) C system as "a popular system to be used by the Chinese themselves in creating a new colloquial literature and for use in newspapers, etc."; Karlgren, *The Romanization of Chinese*, 2, 18.
45. When asked if Karlgren's comments on GR were damaging, Chao responded, "I don't think it had much effect because Karlgren's contacts with Chinese were mostly with the technical personnel in phonology"; see Chao, *Zhao Yuanren quanji*, 16:124.
46. See Yuen Ren Chao 趙元任, *Tzueyhow wuu-fen jong* 最後五分鐘 (The last five minutes) (Shanghai: Zhonghua shuju, 1929), 41; for the official announcement of GR and an incomplete glossary of character pronunciations, see 42–52; for Chao's "special spelling" and "performance instructions," see 53–58.
47. Karlgren goes on to observe seven "fatal points"; see Karlgren, *The Romanization of Chinese*, 19.
48. Chao, "Problem of the Chinese Language," 507, 590.
49. This is one of Chao's earlier forays into experimental phonetics. See Yuen Ren Chao 趙元任, "Yuyin de wuli chengsu" 語音的物理成素 (Physical elements of speech), *Kexue* 9, no. 5 (1924): 523–35.
50. Chao, "Guoyu luomazi de yanjiu," 117.
51. Before its publication, the play was staged at Tsinghua University on April 30, 1927, to celebrate the sixteenth anniversary of the university. See Chao, *Tzueyhow wuu-fen jong*, 32. Chao spent a considerable amount of time in drama translation and

production during his teaching years at Tsinghua. For a list of works he translated and adapted, see Zhao Xinna, *Zhao Yuanren nianpu*, 174–83.

52. Correspondence from Chao to Karlgren, June 25, 1927, Yuen Ren Chao papers, carton 5: Karlgren.

53. The GR word *bairhuah wen* is *baihua wen* (the prose of plain speech) in the pinyin system, while *shuo huah* is the GR version of *shuo hua* (to speak). The first published GR primer was in fact not Chao's but Li Jinxi's *Guoyu mofan duben shouce* 國語模範讀本首冊 (First volume of the model reader of the national language) (Shanghai: Zhonghua shuju, 1928). See Chao, *Tzueyhow wuu-fen jong*, 12. Chao later made another primer in GR, a translation of Lewis Carroll's *Through the Looking-Glass*. The title was written in GR as *Tzoou daw jingtz lii*. The manuscript was to be published in Shanghai in 1938 but was burned during the Second Sino-Japanese War and only republished in San Francisco in 1968, as volume 2 of *Sayable Chinese* (Ithaca, N.Y.: Spoken Language Services, 1974).

54. For Chao's experience in sitting through all twelve Macdona plays, see Chao, *Tzueyhow wuu-fen jong*, 23. Chao (131) lists several references that might have influenced his formulation of the GR drama score, such as Liu Fu, *Étude expérimentale sur les tons du chinois* (1925); D. Jones, *Intonation Curves: A Collection of Phonetic Texts* (1909); D. Jones, *An Outline of English Phonetics* ([1918] 1922), 135–68; H. E. Palmer, *English Intonation* (1922); H. Klinghardt and M. de Fourmestraux, *Französische Intonationsübungen* (1911); M. L. Barker, *French Intonation Exercises* (1923), and M. L. Barker, *A Handbook of German Intonation for University Students* (1925).

55. The actress portraying Eliza was not the only one who gave Chao grievance. He lists a series of offenses committed by the Macdona actors in his "Third Green Letter," as quoted in *Tzueyhow wuu-fen jong*, 23, 25. Hereafter I cite *Tzueyhow wuu-fen jong* parenthetically in the main text.

56. It is curious that Chao should choose to erase the Turkish background of the play as well as the emphasis on World War I. Connections between the Chinese and Turkish script revolutions are worthy of further study. For one, exponents of the Chinese script revolution hailed the success of the anti-Arab Persian script movement in Turkey. For another, the new Turkish script was made official in 1928, the same year that GR was announced as the Second Form of the National Alphabet.

57. A. A. Milne, *The Camberley Triangle*, in *Second Plays* (London: Chatto and Windus, 1928), 157. For Chao's translation of the same paragraph, see Chao, *Tzueyhow wuu-fen jong*, 102.

58. Under the five-line staff system, the notation is more accurate, with the bass clef and allegro specifying the pitch and tempo. Also a note on keys, if we take Chao's key in the *Ziffersystem* as C major, then that in the staff is G major.

59. Lu Xun 魯迅, "Lun xin wenzi" 論新文字 (On Sin Wenz) (December 23, 1935), and "Guanyu xin wenzi" 關於新文字 (About Sin Wenz) (September 10, 1935), in Lu Xun 魯迅, *Lu Xun quanji* 魯迅全集 (The complete works of Lu Xun), 18 vols. (Beijing: Renmin wenxue chubanshe, 2005), 6:458 and 165, respectively.

60. The letter was from Chao to Fu Sinian 傅斯年—his close friend, cofounder of Academia Sinica, and director of the Institute of History and Philology—urging Academia Sinica to purchase a set of the sound spectrographs as soon as possible; see

correspondence from Chao to Fu, October 9, 1947, Yuen Ren Chao papers, carton 3: Fu Sinian.

61. Ralph K. Potter, George A. Kopp, and Harriet C. Green, *Visible Speech* (New York: Van Nostrand, 1947), 4–5.

62. Potter, Kopp, and Green, *Visible Speech*, 4, 11.

63. Yuen Ren Chao, *Language and Symbolic Systems* (Cambridge: Cambridge University Press, 1968), 161–67.

64. Potter, Kopp, and Green, *Visible Speech*, xv. It is worth pointing out, however, that there had been earlier attempts at visual hearing in England, the Soviet Union, and Germany. See Thomas Y. Levin, "'Tones from out of Nowhere': Rudolph Pfenninger and the Archaeology of Synthetic Sound," *Grey Room*, no. 12 (Summer 2003): 32–79.

65. Hereafter, I cite *Visible Speech* (1947) parenthetically. There had been other technologies that attempted visual hearing and automatic writing. See Lisa Gitelman, *Scripts, Grooves, and Writing Machines: Representing Technology in the Edison Era* (Stanford, Calif.: Stanford University Press, 1999), chap. 5; Jonathan Sterne, *The Audible Past: Cultural Origins of Sound Reproduction* (Durham, N.C.: Duke University Press, 2003); and Haun Saussy, *The Ethnography of Rhythm: Orality and Its Technologies* (New York: Fordham University Press, 2016), chap. 3.

66. Alexander Melville Bell, *Visible Speech: The Science of Universal Alphabetics* (London: Simpkin, Marshall, 1867), ix; Chao, "Problem of the Chinese Language," 506–7.

67. Potter, Kopp, and Green, *Visible Speech*, 410–22. I thank Chen-Pang Yeang for helping me understand how the sound spectrograph further developed in the digital age to enhance voice telecommunications by way of transducing, digitizing, over- or undersampling, compressing or decompressing, and spectral decomposing voices.

68. Chao was much more invested in descriptive linguistics than in Saussurian structural linguistics. See Mei Tsu-lin 梅祖麟, "Bijiao fangfa zai zhongguo, 1926–1998" 比較方法在中國, 1926–1998 (The comparative method in China, 1926–1998), *Yuyan yanjiu* 語言研究 (Studies in language and linguistics) 23, no. 1 (March 2003), 16–27.

69. Correspondence from Chao to King, April 7, 1940, Yuen Ren Chao papers, carton 5: Robert W. and Dorothy King.

70. Chao did not become an American citizen until 1954. Because of his nationality, Bell Labs did not allow him full access to the labs, even with Hu Shi's reference letter written on his behalf. See reference letter by Hu Shi, March 22, 1940, Yuen Ren Chao papers, carton 4: Hu Shi. Hu Shi's letter reads as follows: "Sirs: It gives me pleasure to introduce to you Dr. Yuen-Ren Chao who has for the last ten years been the Chief of the Division of Linguistics at the Institute of History and Linguistics in the Academia Sinica. Dr. Chao is now Visiting Professor at the Graduate Department of Linguistics at Yale University. It is his great desire to be permitted to see the special experiments in artificial speaking in your Laboratories. Dr. Chao and I are schoolmates of Dr. Robert W. King of your Laboratory. Any courtesy that you can show Dr. Chao will be gratefully appreciated. Sincerely yours, Hu Shih."

71. Correspondence from King to Chao, May 14, 1940, Yuen Ren Chao papers, carton 5: Robert W. and Dorothy King.

72. Zhao Xinna, *Zhao Yuanren nianpu*, 272.

73. I was unable to locate Chao's actual report on visible speech, but it is indicated in his letter to Buckley that his report on visible speech would be delayed; see correspondence from Chao to Buckley, June 8, 1947, Yuen Ren Chao papers. Although more research needs to be done in regard to the specifics of Chao's activities at Bell Labs, it is plausible that one side project of Chao's called Legible Speech, funded by the Rockefeller Foundation, might have grown out of his time at Bell Labs.

74. Yuen Ren Chao, "The Sound Spectrograph" (June 26, 1951), Yuen Ren Chao papers.

75. Chao, "The Sound Spectrograph" and "The Visible Speech Spectrograph" (December 10, 1947), Yuen Ren Chao papers; see also Chao, *Language and Symbolic Systems*.

76. Chao, *Language and Symbolic Systems*, 161.

77. There are six sound patterns, which influence one another and become legible by focusing on the second bar—defined as "the hub"—of the three resonance bars that are frequently present in sound patterns. See Potter, Kopp, and Green, *Visible Speech*, 33–39.

78. Potter, Kopp, and Green, *Visible Speech*, 53–56.

79. Chao, *Language and Symbolic Systems*, 164, 169.

80. Explanations of Karlgren's letter in the notes are all mine. The term *t'u hua* in the present pinyin scheme is spelled *tu hua* (土話) and refers to strongly local and idiomatic expressions. *Kau-su* is *gaosu* (告訴), while *kau-sung* is a transcription of the Pekingese pronunciation of the word.

81. The "X, r, ts" is in pencil and not entirely legible and represents my guess.

82. "Kuo ë movement" refers to the *guoyu*, or national language, movement.

83. "Wadee's system" likely refers to the Wade-Giles Romanization system of the Beijing dialect devised in the mid-nineteenth century. "Videant consules" is Latin for "Let the consuls see to it."

84. Correspondence from Karlgren to Chao, February 24, 1925, Yuen Ren Chao papers, carton 5: Karlgren; underlining in original (letter extract courtesy of Bernhard Karlgren's family).

2. PHONOCENTRIC ANTINOMIES

1. Jiao Feng, Emi Siao (Xiao San), and Lu Xun also participated in the early introduction of Latinization in China. See Ni Haishu 倪海曙, *"Latinxua Sin Wenz yndong" de shi-mo he biannian jishi* 拉丁化新文字運動的始末和編年紀事 (The beginning and end of the Chinese Latinization movement and its chronology) (Shanghai: Zhishi chubanshe, 1987), 5–8. The "Latinization" of the book title and its publication information are in the original form. I preserve the original spelling of the primary sources from the Latinization movement, if available. Otherwise I use pinyin.

2. This blurb, published in the "Correspondence" section in *Guoyu zhoukan*, was originally written by Chao in Gwoyeu *Romatzyh* and later translated by the journal editor; Yuen Ren Chao 趙元任, "Guanyu su'e de ladinghua zhongguoyu" 關於蘇俄的拉丁化中國語, *Guoyu zhoukan* 國語週刊 (National language weekly) 6, no. 139 (May 26, 1934): 20.

3. The Nationalist government lifted the ban on the Latinization movement in May 1938 after the CCP and the GMD had reached a consensus on the Second United Front against the Japanese invasion. Latinization was permissible only on the condition that it remain a "pure academic pursuit" or "an instrument of social mobilization" and should not "impede or distract the anti-Japanese forces." See Ni Haishu, *"Latinxua Sin Wenz yndong,"* 15, 18. The CCP's support of Sin Wenz went as high up as Zhu De and Mao Zedong. Zhu De recommended promoting "the Sin Wenz that everyone uses to the rest of the country," while Mao ordered, "Effectively implement [Sin Wenz] as widely as possible." See *Sin Wenzi bao*, no. 1 (1941), cited in Li Mian 李绵, "Shaan gan ning bianqu yici henyou yiyi de wenzi gaige shiyan—huainian Wu Yuzhang tongzhi" 陝甘寧邊區一次很有意義的文字改革試驗—懷念吳玉章同志 (One meaningful experiment of the script reform in the Shaanxi-Gansu-Ningxia region—in commemoration of comrade Wu Yuzhang), *Shaanxi shida xuebao (zhexue shehui kexue ban)* 陝西師大學報 (哲學社會科學版) (Journal of Shaanxi Normal University, philosophy and social sciences edition), no. 2 (1980): 41.

4. Fredric Jameson, *The Antinomies of Realism* (New York: Verso, 2013), 6.

5. Jameson, *The Antinomies of Realism*, 6.

6. I reserve the term "dialect" to translate *fangyan* 方言 as the term was used historically. I should note, however, that the Chinese term could be taken to mean "language," "dialect," and "patois" (spoken dialect) all at once. According to Einar Haugen, while "language" denotes linguistic standardization and "dialect" its local variation, further distinctions within "dialect" should be made. In Greek, *dialektos* were understood as written variants of Greek, which were "based on spoken dialects of the regions whose names they bore." Later, in the French tradition, *patois* was used to mark the distinction between written dialects and spoken dialects without written forms. See Einar Haugen, "Dialect, Language, Nation," *American Anthropologist* 68, no. 4 (August 1966): 922–35.

7. The interview was conducted by Rosemary Levenson and Laurence Schneider. All quotes from the interview are in their English original. See Yuen Ren Chao 趙元任, *Zhao Yuanren quanji* 趙元任全集 (The complete works of Yuen Ren Chao) (Beijing: Commercial Press, 2007), 16:120.

8. Chao, *Zhao Yuanren quanji*, 16:120.

9. Qingguo Alley 青果巷 is one of the oldest neighborhoods in Changzhou, Jiangsu. Its long list of luminaries dates back to the sixteenth century. Aside from Chao and Qu, the last surviving member of the Committee of the Chinese Script Reform, Zhou Youguang (1906–2017), was also from the alley.

10. Qu Qiubai 瞿秋白, *Exiang jicheng* 餓鄉紀程, and *Chidu xinshi* 赤都心史, in *Qu Qiubai wenji wenxue bian* 瞿秋白文集文學編 (The literary compilation of the Qu Qiubai collection) (Beijing: Renmin wenxue chubanshe, 1985–1989), 1:3–110, 113–252, respectively. Both works were written during Qu's first extensive stay in the Soviet Union (December 1920–December 1922). Qu traveled to Russia again in April 1928 and returned to China in July 1930. See Zhou Yongxiang 周永祥, *Qu Qiubai nianpu* 瞿秋白年譜 (Chronicle of Qu Qiubai) (Guangzhou: Guangdong renmin chubanshe, 1983).

11. Qu Qiubai 瞿秋白, "Luomazi de zhongguowen haishi roumazi de zhongguowen" 羅馬字的中國文還是肉麻字的中國文, in *Qu Qiubai wenji wenxue bian*,

3:221. Citations of this article are hereafter given as parenthetical page numbers in the main text.

12. For the compound consonants, GR defines *j* as *zh*. As for diphthongs, according to Qu, the distinction between *au* and *ao* should be eliminated, reserving only *ao*, while the *ai* and *ae* sounds should also be combined into one spelling, *ae*.

13. Li Jinxi and Qian Xuantong recognized the irony and attempted to expand GR's repertoire of speech representation by using GR to transcribe dialect (*fangyan*), calling it F.R.; Li Jinxi 黎錦熙, *Guoyu yundong shigang* 國語運動史綱 (The historical *Grundrisse* of the national language movement) (1935; repr., Beijing: Commercial Press, 2011), 290–92.

14. Qu's definition of "hybrid Mandarin" is not to be equated with James Yen's use of "Mandarin." Qu's use stresses the colloquial nature of the speech, while Yen's gestures toward a literary language.

15. Ni Haishu divides the development of the Chinese Latinization movement into four stages: 1934–1937, 1937–1945, 1945–1949, and 1949–1955; *"Latinxua Sin Wenz yndong,"* 9–37. Though Sin Wenz was used to denote all Latinization schemes regardless of whether they transcribed the northern dialect or the Minnan dialect, some new scripts used their own dialect instead of the standard Sin Wenz—for instance, "Sin Vensh" in Wu dialect and "Sen Menzi" in Cantonese.

16. Ni's list of Sin Wenz publications can be found in *Zhongguo pinyin wenzi yundongshi jianbian* 中國拼音文字運動史簡編 (A concise chronology of the Chinese alphabetization movement) (Shanghai: Shidai shubao chubanshe, 1948), app. 1, 177–81, 187–90. The three journals listed here—the first two based in Shanghai and the third in Wuhan—are not included in Ni's tally but are from my own collection, all of which adopt a double-scriptal system allowing the coexistence of characters and Sin Wenz.

17. Michael G. Hill, "New Script and a New 'Madman's Diary,'" *Modern Chinese Literature and Culture* 27, no. 1 (Spring 2015): 79, 97.

18. Ni Haishu 倪海曙, *Zhungguo pinjin wenz gailun* 中國拼音文字概論 (An introduction to the Chinese alphabetic script) (Shanghai: Shidai chubanshe, 1948), 83. The Sin Wenz and character lyrics are as in the original; the English translation is mine.

19. Ni Haishu, *Zhungguo pinjin wenz gailun*, 95–96.

20. "Women duiyu tuixing xinwenzi de yijian" 我們對於推行新文字的意見 (Our opinion on the promotion of Sin Wenz), in Wo Dan 渥丹, *Zhungguo wenz latinxua wenxian* 中国文字拉丁化文献 (Documents on the Latinization of the Chinese script) (Shanghai: Latinxua chubanshe, 1940), 153–57. It bears pointing out that Cai Yuanpei also supported the Romanization movement. A selection of signatures follows the public letter (157). For a list of the signatures, see *Tao Xingzhi quanji* 陶行知全集 (The complete works of Tao Xingzhi), 8 vols. (Changsha: Hunan jiaoyu chubanshe, 1984–1985), 3:50–55.

21. Wo Dan, *Zhungguo wenz latinxua wenxian*, 153.

22. Major versions of the Bible in characters include Joshua Marshman and Joannes Lassar, trans., *Yesu jiushi shitu ruohan suoshu fuyin* 耶穌救世使徒若翰所書福音 (The Gospel of the Apostle John, translated into Chinese) (Serampore, Ind.: Mission Press, 1813); Joshua Marshman and Joannes Lassar, trans., *Shengjing* 聖經 (The Holy Bible) (Serampore: Mission Press, 1822); *Xinyue quanshu* 新約全書 (The New Testament, Delegates' version) and *Jiuyue quanshu* 舊約全書 (The Old Testament)

(1854); E. C. Bridgman and M. S. Culbertson, trans., *Xinyue quanshu* 新約全書 (The New Testament) (Shanghai: American Bible Society, 1863); W. Medhurst, K. F. A. Gützlaff, and E. C. Bridgman, trans., *Jiushizhu Yesu xin yizhaoshu* 救世主耶穌新遺詔書 (The New Testament) (Singapore: Jianxia shuyuan, 1839); *Union Version of the Easy Wenli Testament, Easy Wenli Translation, Tentative Edition* (Shanghai: British and Foreign Bible Society, 1902); *Union Version of the New Testament, Matthew–Romans, High Wen-li Translation, Tentative Edition* (Shanghai: American Bible Society, British and Foreign Bible Society, National Bible Society of Scotland, 1905). For a more comprehensive bibliography of the Bible in Chinese, see Jost Oliver Zetzsche, *The Bible in China: The History of the* Union Version, *or The Culmination of Protestant Missionary Bible Translation in China* (Nettetal, Ger.: Steyler, 1999), 400–403.

23. Marshall Broomhall, *The Bible in China* (London: China Inland Mission, 1934), 99.

24. Broomhall, *The Bible in China*. I thank Dr. Liana Lupas at the American Bible Society for sharing with me her inventory of dialects, for which corresponding versions of Romanized dialect Bibles were produced. These dialects included but were not limited to Dingzhou (1919), Fuzhou (1881, 1886, 1889, 1892), Hainan (1891, 1893, 1899, 1902, 1914), Hakka (1860, 1865, 1866, 1887, 1910, 1924, 1958, 1993), Hangzhou (1879, by George Evans Moule), Jianning (1896, 1912), Jianyang (1898, 1900), Jinhua (1866), Nanjing (1869), Ningbo (1852, 1865, 1870, 1871, 1880, 1885, 1887, 1895, 1898, 1923), Shandong (1892), Shanghai (1853, 1860, 1861, 1864, 1870, 1886, 1895), Shantou (1877, 1888), Shaowu (1892), Suzhou (1891, 1921), Taizhou (1880, 1897, 1914), Wenzhou (1892, 1894, 1902), Wujingfu (1910, 1924), Xinghua (1892, 1896, 1934), and Zhili (1925).

25. "Beida yanjiusuo guoxue men fangyan diaocha hui xuanyanshu" 北大研究所國學門方言調查會宣言書 (Manifesto of the Dialect Survey Society in the School of National Learning of Peking University), *Geyao zhoukan* 歌謠週刊 (Folklore weekly), no. 47 (March 16, 1924): 1–3.

26. Yuen Ren Chao 趙元任, *Xiandai wuyu de yanjiu* 現代吳語的研究 (Studies of the modern Wu dialects) (1928; repr., Beijing: Commercial Press, 2011); *Zhongxiang fangyan ji* 鐘祥方言記 (Records of the Zhongxiang dialect of Zhongxiang) (Beijing: Commercial Press, 1939); *Zhongshan fangyan* 中山方言 (The dialect of Zhongshan) (1948; repr., Beijing: Kexue chubanshe, 1956); Luo Changpei 羅常培, *Xiamen yinxi* 廈門音系 (The Xiamen sound system) (1930; repr., Beijing: Kexue chubanshe, 1956); *Linchuan yinxi* 臨川音系 (The Linchuan sound system) (1941; repr., Beijing: Kexue chubanshe, 1958); Fang-Kuei Li 李方桂, "Languages and Dialects of China," *Chinese Year Book*, 1936–1937, 121–28; repr., *Journal of Chinese Linguistics* 1, no. 1 (1973): 1–13; Yuen Ren Chao et al., *Hubei fangyan diaocha baogao* 湖北方言調查報告 (The report of the Hubei dialect survey) (Taipei: Commercial Press, 1948). See Zhai Shiyu 翟時雨, *Hanyu fangyan yu fangyan diaocha* 漢語方言與方言調查 (Chinese dialects and dialect surveys) (Chongqing: Xinan shifan daxue chubanshe, 1986), 14–15.

27. For dialect maps and dialect geography, see S. Robert Ramsey, *The Languages of China* (Princeton, N.J.: Princeton University Press, 1987), 15–16, 87–142; Yuan Jiahua 袁家驊, *Hanyu fangyan gaiyao* 漢語方言概要 (An introduction to the Chinese dialects) (Beijing: Wenzi gaige chubanshe, 1960).

28. Saussure also calls synchronic linguistics static linguistics and diachronic linguistics evolutionary linguistics and has a chapter on "Static and Evolutionary Linguistics." See Ferdinand de Saussure, *Course in General Linguistics*, trans. Wade Baskin, ed. Perry Meisel and Haun Saussy (New York: Columbia University Press, 2011), 79–100, 212–4.

29. Leonard Bloomfield, *An Introduction to the Study of Language* (New York: Holt, 1914), 310.

30. Bernhard Karlgren, *Études sur la phonologie chinoise* (Leiden: Brill, 1915–1926), 19–20.

31. Fang-Kuei Li, Jerry Norman, and Edwin Pulleyblank, among others, criticized and revised Karlgren's reconstruction in *Études*; see Ramsey, *The Languages of China*, 131–32.

32. Mei Tsu-lin 梅祖麟, "Bijiao fangfa zai zhongguo, 1926–1998" 比較方法在中國, 1926–1998 (The comparative method in China, 1926–1998), *Yuyan yanjiu* 語言研究 (Studies in language and linguistics) 23, no. 1 (March 2003): 18.

33. It is generally established that the Wu dialects are the oldest, followed by the Hunan dialects, Cantonese, Minnan dialect, and Hakka and Jiangxi dialects. For a survey of Chinese dialect genealogy in relation to population migration, see Zhou Zhenhe 周振鶴 and You Rujie 游汝杰, *Fangyan yu zhongguo wenhua* 方言與中國文化 (Dialects and Chinese culture) (Shanghai: Shanghai renmin chubanshe, 2006), 15–49; Lin Tao 林燾 and Geng Zhensheng 耿振生, *Yinyunxue gaiyao* 音韵学概要 (An outline of phonology) (Beijing: Commercial Press, 2004).

34. Johannes Fabian, *Time and the Other: How Anthropology Makes Its Object* (New York: Columbia University Press, 2002), 120.

35. Hung Chang-tai gives a comprehensive account of the modern Chinese folklore literature movement in *Going to the People: Chinese Intellectuals and Folk Literature, 1918–1937* (Cambridge, Mass.: Harvard University Press, 1985). Lydia H. Liu offers a critical examination of the transnational origin and the politics of colonial mimicry in the making of Chinese folklorics in "Translingual Folklore and Folklorics in China," in *A Companion to Folklore*, ed. Regina F. Bendix and Galit Hasan-Rokem, 190–210 (Malden, Mass.: Wiley-Blackwell, 2012).

36. "Beida yanjiusuo guoxue men fangyan diaocha," 1.

37. The manifesto includes seven specific tasks of the society:

1. Make dialect maps—this is the foundation of a linguistic survey.
2. Determine word pronunciation in the dialects and establish the use of letters for phonetic description.
3. Investigate colonial history—one important development in the field of linguistics is its understanding of the intimate relationship between dialects and local history.
4. Examine languages of the Miao people and other minority groups—this is especially encouraged by our society.
5. Use dialectal materials to produce in retrospect the ancient pronunciation.
6. The sort of vocabulary investigation carried out by Yang Xiong—dialectal difference in terms of pronunciation, grammar, and diction.
7. The study of dialectal grammar. ("Beida yanjiusuo guoxue men fangyan diaocha," 1–3)

38. According to Agamali-Ogly, Lenin said, "Da, eto velikaia revoliutsiia na Vostoke!" *Stenograficheskii otchet 2 plenuma VTsK NTA* (Baku, 1929): 2–3, as cited in Terry Martin, *The Affirmative Action Empire: Nations and Nationalism in the Soviet Union, 1923–1939* (Ithaca, N.Y.: Cornell University Press, 2001), 187.

39. For a brief history of the proletarian culture movement in the early Soviet Union, see Mark D. Steinberg, *Proletarian Imagination: Self, Modernity, and the Sacred in Russia, 1910–1925* (Ithaca, N.Y.: Cornell University Press, 2002), 50–56. After the dissolution of all existing proletarian organizations of literature and other arts in April 1932, "cultural enlightenment" became "socialist realism," the canonical method of writing in the Soviet Union. For the fraught creation of "socialist realism," see A. Kemp-Welch, *Stalin and the Literary Intelligentsia, 1928–39* (New York: Palgrave Macmillan, 1991), 142–60. I thank Thomas Lahusen for helping me understand the complexity of the Proletkult.

40. For historical accounts of the Soviet Latinization movement in its early stages, see Martin, *The Affirmative Action Empire*, 198–99; Lenore A. Grenoble, *Language Policy in the Soviet Union* (Dordrecht: Kluwer Academic, 2003), 35–57; Michael G. Smith, *Language and Power in the Creation of the USSR, 1917–1953* (Berlin: Mouton de Gruyter, 1998), 121–42.

41. The Georgian exception could be partially explained by the official endorsement of Nikolai Marr's "Japhetic theory," which dominated the Soviet Union between the 1920s and the 1950s, until Stalin himself denounced Marr in *Pravda*. The Japhetic theory stipulated Georgian—Marr's and Stalin's mother tongue—as a common ancestor for the Caucasian and Semitic languages. In line with paleontology and Marxist theory of materialism and class struggle, this Marrist belief in and drive at a universal language eased the anxiety of Latinization supporters fearing that multiple writing systems might encroach upon the unity of the Soviet; see Grenoble, *Language Policy*, 55–57; Smith, *Language and Power*, 81–102; Lawrence L. Thomas, *The Linguistic Theories of N. Ja. Marr*, University of California Publications in Linguistics, vol. 14 (Berkeley: University of California Press, 1957), 85–116.

42. Martin, *The Affirmative Action Empire*, 200.

43. For an introduction to Lunacharsky's writing, see Sheila Fitzpatrick, *The Commissariat of Enlightenment: Soviet Organization of Education and the Arts under Lunacharsky, October 1917–1921* (Cambridge: Cambridge University Press, 1970); Ken Kalfus, *The Commissariat of Enlightenment* (New York: Ecco, 2003); Timothy Edward O'Conner, *The Politics of Soviet Culture: Anatolii Lunacharskii* (Ann Arbor, Mich.: UMI Research Press, 1983). For Qu's meeting with Lunacharsky, see *Qu Qiubai wenji wenxue bian*, 1:124–26. Lunacharsky himself wrote several articles in support of Latinizing the Cyrillic alphabet; see Martin, *The Affirmative Action Empire*, 196.

44. Glavnauka refers to the Central Administration for Scientific, Scholarly-Artistic, and Museum Institutions, an administrative body that existed from 1922 to September 1933 as part of the Narkompros; see Martin, *The Affirmative Action Empire*, 198. The Politburo's sudden order was not unlike the GMD's ban of Sin Wenz in 1936 and the CCP's suspension of alphabetization in 1958.

45. Latinization activities targeting Ukrainian and Belorussian could be interpreted as Russophobia and even treason. Linguists who participated in the 1926–1927

conferences on writing reforms in Belorussia and Ukraine underwent trials and purges in the cultural revolution. See Martin, *The Affirmative Action Empire*, 204–6; George Y. Shevelov, *The Ukrainian Language in the First Half of the Twentieth Century (1900–1941): Its State and Status* (Cambridge, Mass.: Harvard Ukrainian Research Institute, 1989), 131–40. For an overview of the Stalinization of the Soviet Union, see Norman LaPorte, Kevin Morgan, and Matthew Worley, eds., *Bolshevism, Stalinism and the Comintern: Perspectives on Stalinization, 1917–53* (Houndmills, Basingstoke, Hampshire, U.K.: Palgrave Macmillan, 2008).

46. Between 1930 and 1932, the All-Union Central Committee of the New Turkic Alphabet (VTsK NTA) decided to form "five separate Latin alphabets for the five major dialects" of Shandong, Guangdong, Fujian, Jiangsu, and Hunan, out of which only the Shandong dialect alphabet was actually designed. As for the Korean Latin alphabet, VTsK NTA was said to have approved the plan for it but never materialized it; see Martin, *The Affirmative Action Empire*, 119, 200.

47. Estimates of the population of the Dungan people in the Soviet Union in the 1920s vary from 14,600 to 25,000. According to John DeFrancis, illiteracy among them amounted to almost 100 per cent; *Nationalism and Language Reform in China* (Princeton, N.J.: Princeton University Press, 1950), 88. For a more recent study on the new Dunganese alphabet in relation to the First All-Union Turcology Congress and Latinization across Eurasia, see Ulug Kuzuoglu, "Codes of Modernity: Infrastructures of Language and Chinese Scripts in an Age of Global Information Revolution" (PhD diss., Columbia University, 2018), chap. 6.

48. Qu mentions Kolokolov often in *Qu Qiubai wenji wenxue bian*, 1:103–5, 141, 166, 168. Aside from Kolokolov, other Soviet scholars such as A. A. Dragunov, B. M. Alexeiev, B. A. Vasil'ev, Y. K. Tschutskii, and A. G. Shirintsin also participated in researching, devising, and critiquing the Chinese Latinized alphabet. See DeFrancis, *Nationalism and Language Reform*, 97–98. After Stalin abandoned Marr's Japhetic theory, Kolokolov, like many other linguists who participated in Latinization, became implicated. For a critique of Kolokolov's involvement in the Chinese Latinization campaign, see A. O. Tamazishvili, "Incident na vostochnom otdeleni'i instituta krasnoi professuri istori'I," *Vostok*, no. 1 (1994): 160–66.

49. Qu Qiubai 瞿秋白, *Zhongguo Latinhuadi zemu* 中國拉丁化字母 (Moscow: KYTY Press, 1929), in *Qu Qiubai wenji wenxue bian*, 3:351–418; Qu Qiubai 瞿秋白, *Xin Zhongguowen cao'an* 新中國文草案, in *Qu Qiubai wenji wenxue bian*, 3:423–91.

50. Qu, *Zhonguo Latinhuadi zemu*, 355, 362.

51. Li Jinxi compiled a series of essays criticizing Sin Wenz and defending GR and asking the question, is it better to devise the national alphabet ourselves or have foreigners do it for us?; *Guoyu yundong shigang*, 291–96.

52. The version presented to the conference was a slight revision of Qu's *Zhongguo ladinghua de zimu*, titled *Ladinghua zhongguozi* 拉丁化中國字 (Latinized Chinese). Ni Haishu, *Zhongguo pinyin wenzi yundongshi jianbian*, 119.

53. DeFrancis, *Nationalism and Language Reform*, 93, 99.

54. Paul Pickowicz and Theodore Huters disagree over whether Qu Qiubai was well informed enough to understand and introduce the different schools of Marxist literary thought in the Soviet Union. While Pickowicz maintains a negative answer, Huters makes an important point in flagging Qu's knowledge of the issues related to the Proletkult. See Paul Pickowicz, *Marxist Literary Thought in China: The*

Influence of Ch'ü Ch'iu-pai (Berkeley: University of California Press, 1981); Theodore Huters, "The Difficult Guest: May Fourth Revisits," *Chinese Literature* 6, no. 1/2 (July 1984): 125–49.

55. The primer that Qu mentions was Li Jinxi's *Guoyu mofan duben shouce* (1928); Qu, *Qu Qiubai wenji wenxue bian*, 3:325–26.

56. Qu Qiubai 瞿秋白, "Guimenguan yi wai de zhanzheng" 鬼門關以外的戰爭 (War outside the gate of the demons) (May 30, 1931), in *Qu Qiubai wenji wenxue bian*, 3:169.

57. See Guo Moruo's essay taking Yu Dafu to task for his passive adoption of the Japanese term and his potential bourgeoise tastes, "Xinxing dazhong wenyi de renshi" 新興大眾文藝的認識 (Understanding new mass culture), *Dazhong wenyi* 大眾文藝 (Literature and art of the masses) 2, no. 3 (March 1930): 276–79. The journal hosted the first round of the discussions in 1930, when its chief editor, Tao Jingsun, who succeeded Yu Dafu, solicited suggestions to the journal, thus kicking off debates over the concept of *dazhong*, which paid little attention to the related question of the script revolution. For an excellent compilation of the massification problem, see Wen Zhenting 文振庭, ed., *Wenyi dazhonghua wenti taolun ziliao* 文艺大众化问题讨论资料 (Materials on the discussions of the massification of literature and art) (Shanghai: Shanghai wenyi chubanshe, 1987). Tao, Yu, and Guo were all members of the League of Left-Wing Writers in support of a class-theory-oriented discussion of *dazhong*. It is interesting to note that Yuen Ren Chao was said to have declined invitation to participate in the massification discussion; see Wen, *Wenyi dazhonghua*, 409. For a representative theorization of massification that does not embrace class theory, see Li Jinxi, *Guoyu yundong shigang*, 46–81.

58. Wen, *Wenyi dazhonghua*, 54–62, 109–38; for Lu Xun's essay, see 159–62.

59. Qu Qiubai 瞿秋白, "Dazhong wenyi de wenti" 大眾文藝的問題, "Puluo dazhong wenyi de xianshi wenti" 普羅大眾文藝的現實問題, "'Women' shi shei?" 我們是誰?), "Ouhua wenyi" 歐化文藝, and "Zailun dazhong wenyi da zhijing" 再論大眾文藝答止敬), in Wen, *Wenyi dazhonghua*, 54–62, 34–53, 100–103, 104–8, 119–38, respectively. I should note that according to Wen's compilation, "Puluo dazhong wenyi de xianshi wenti" 普羅大眾文藝的現實問題 was originally written in October 1931 and published under Qu's nom de plume Shi Tie'er 史鐵兒 on April 25, 1932. Qu also wrote an earlier essay titled "Dazhong wenyi he fandui diguozhuyi de douzheng" 大眾文藝和反對帝國主義的鬥爭 (Mass literature and art as well as anti-imperialist struggles), which was published in *Wenxue daobao* 文學導報 (The literature guide), September 28, 1931, 5–6. See Zhou Yongxiang, *Qu Qiubai nianpu*, 93. Also, the two shorter pieces—"'Women' shi shei?" and "Ouhua wenyi"—were sent to Lu Xun for safekeeping and not published.

60. Qu's language was most colorful and pointed in "Realistic Questions of Proletarian Mass Literature and Culture"; see Wen, *Wenyi dazhonghua*, 36, 38. For Mao Dun's 1932 response to Qu and his 1984 recollection of his differences with Qu Qiubai and the three rounds of the massification discussion, see Wen, *Wenyi dazhonghua*, 109–18, 413–32.

61. Qu, "More on Mass Literature and Art, a Reply to Zhijing," in Wen, *Wenyi dazhonghua*, 133.

62. Gayatri Chakravorty Spivak, "Can the Subaltern Speak?," in *Can the Subaltern Speak? Reflections on the History of an Idea*, ed. Rosalind C. Morris, 21–78 (New

York: Columbia University Press, 2010); Spivak distinguishes, by way of a reading of Karl Marx's *The Eighteenth Brumaire of Louis Bonaparte*, two senses of representation—"speaking for" (*Vertretung*) and "re-presentation," "as in art or philosophy" (*Darstellung*)—and advocates the latter (28–31).

63. A lively account of the Japanese occupation of Manchuria, Qu's poem diagnosed that the only reliable force of national resistance would come from the alliance of workers, soldiers, and peasants, though Qu did not give voice to or speak on behalf of them. See Shi Tie'er 史鐵兒, "Dongyang ren chubing" 東洋人出兵, *Wenxue daobao*, September 28, 1931, 6–12.

64. The Students Social Club was founded by the American missionary John Stewart Burgess in 1911. The journal *New Society* began publication in November 1919 and was banned in May 1920 for its overtly socialist inclination. Qu Qiubai, Xu Dishan, and Zheng Zhenduo, among others, were involved in the journal. See *Xin shehui* 新社會 (New society), nos. 1–19 (November 1, 1919–May 1, 1920). Both Qu and Xu wrote extensively about gender, labor, and other social issues. Qu's contributions included "Xiaoxiao yige wenti—funü jiefang de wenti" 小小一個問題—婦女解放的問題 (A small problem—the problem of women's liberation), "Laodong di fuyin" 勞動底福音 (The gospel of labor), "Shehui yu zui'e" 社會與罪惡 (Society and evil); Xu Dishan penned the following: "Shijiu shiji liangda shehui xuejia di nüziguan" 十九世紀兩大社會學家底女子觀 (Two nineteenth-century sociologists' views on women), "Laodong di yanjiu" 勞動底研究 (A study on labor), and "Shehui kexue de yanjiu fangfa" 社會科學的研究方法 (Research methods of social science), among others.

65. The twelve founding members were Zhou Zuoren, Mao Dun, Xu Dishan, Zheng Zhenduo, Ye Shengtao, Geng Jizhi, Wang Tongzhao, Guo Shaoyu, Sun Fuyuan, Qu Shiying, Zhu Xizu, and Jiang Baili.

66. Xu Dishan 許地山, *Yu Guan, Da feng* 大風 (Great wind), nos. 29–36 (1939).

67. Mrs. W. B. Hamilton, *The Chinese Bible Woman* (New York: Women's Board of Foreign Missions of the Presbyterian Church, n.d.), 5.

68. C. T. Hsia, *A History of Modern Chinese Fiction, 1917–1957* (New Haven, Conn.: Yale University Press, 1971), 85.

69. See Zheng Zhenduo's preface to Xu Dishan 許地山, *Xu Dishan xuanji* 許地山選集 (The selected works of Xu Dishan) (Beijing: Renmin wenxue chubanshe, 1958), 3.

70. Xu Dishan 許地山, "Lun 'fan xinshi fenghua xueyue' " 論"反新式風花雪月" (On "anti–new Romanticism"), *Ta kung pao* 大公報, November. 14, 1940.

71. These articles include "Zhongguo wenzi di mingyun" 中國文字底命運 (The fate of the Chinese script), "Qingnian jie dui qingnian jianghua" 青年節對青年講話 (A speech to the youths on May Fourth), "Guocui yu guoxue" 國粹與國學 (National essence and national learning), and "Zhongguo wenzi di jianglai" 中國文字底將來 (The future of the Chinese script). See Xu Dishan 許地山, *Xu Dishan yuyan lunwenji* 許地山語言論文集 (Collection of Xu Dishan's essays on language and writing) (Hong Kong: Xinwenzi xuehui, 1941).

72. My translation here is modeled on Cecile Chu-chin Sun's translation of *Yu Guan* in *Modern Chinese Stories and Novellas, 1919–1949*, ed. Joseph S. M. Lau, C. T. Hsia, and Leo Ou-fan Lee (New York: Columbia University Press, 1981), 53. For Xu's original prose, see Xu Dishan 許地山, *Yu Guan* 玉官, in *Wu you hua* 无忧花 (Flowers of no sorrow) (Nanjing: Jiangsu wenyi chubanshe, 2008), 238.

73. For accounts of Bible women's literacy classes, see pamphlets such as *Chinese Bible Women: How They Are Trained, What They Do* (publication information unclear) and Grace O. Smith, *Tien Da Niang: The Story of Our Chinese Bible Woman* (publication information unclear).

74. John A. Davis, *The Chinese Slave-Girl: A Story of Woman's Life in China* (Chicago: Student Missionary Campaign Library, 1880), and *Leng Tso, the Chinese Bible-Woman: A Sequel to "The Chinese Slave-Girl"* (Philadelphia: Presbyterian Board of Publication, 1886).

75. Davis, *Leng Tso*, 15, 16, 32.

76. Xu Dishan, *Yu Guan*, 236–78. For a recent study on Xu Dishan's relations with Nanyang, see Brian Bernards, *Writing the South Seas: Imagining the Nanyang in Chinese and Southeast Asian Postcolonial Literature* (Seattle: University of Washington Press, 2015), 29–53.

77. See Benjamin Elman, "The Rites Controversy and Its Legacy," in *On Their Own Terms: Science in China, 1550–1900* (Cambridge, Mass.: Harvard University Press, 2005), 160–67.

78. Xu Dishan, *Yu Guan*, 253; Lau, Hsia, and Lee, *Modern Chinese Stories and Novellas*, 66.

79. But even when Yu Guan decides to start her religious life anew, she still keeps with her "the ancestral tablets"; Lau, Hsia, and Lee, *Modern Chinese Stories and Novellas*, 84.

80. Yu Guan does enunciate "A, B, C" when first encountering the Bible and another character mumbles "my baby, my precious, my darling" when her son—a classmate of Yu Guan's grandson—dies, but such stand-alone quotes do not constitute substantial conversations and are not pronounced in Minnan. See Xu Dishan, *Yu Guan*, 238, 259; Lau, Hsia, and Lee, *Modern Chinese Stories and Novellas*, 53, 71.

81. Xu Dishan 許地山, "Chuangzuo di sanbao he jianshang di siyi" 創作底三寶和鑑賞底四依 (The three treasures of creation and the four fundamentals of appreciation), originally published in *Xiaoshuo yuebao* 小說月報 (Fiction monthly) 12, no. 7 (July 10, 1921), as quoted in Xu Dishan 許地山, *Xu Dishan sanwen* 許地山散文 (Essays of Xu Dishan) (Beijing: Zhongguo guangbo dianshi chubanshe, 1996), 214. The three treasures are wisdom, life, and beauty (*zhihui bao* 智慧寶, *rensheng bao* 人生寶, *meili bao* 美麗寶), while the four fundamentals are meaning, rule, intelligence, and feeling (*yiyi* 依義, *yifa* 依法, *yizhi* 依智, *yiliaoyi* 依了義).

82. Xu Dishan, *Yu Guan*, 274; Lau, Hsia, and Lee, *Modern Chinese Stories and Novellas*, 83.

83. Hsia, *History of Modern Chinese Fiction*, 90.

84. Marston Anderson, *The Limits of Realism: Chinese Fiction in the Revolutionary Period* (Berkeley: University of California Press, 1990), 24–25.

85. Anderson also points to how Chinese writers, in their search for social intervention, paid "little attention" to "the technical problems of fictional representation, a preoccupation of such Western realists as Flaubert and James" (Anderson, *The Limits of Realism*, 37). While Xu Dishan's attention to and struggle with narratology confirms the limits of phonocentric realism, it also contests Anderson's assertion that Chinese writers lack awareness of technical difficulties of representation.

3. CAN SUBALTERN WORKERS WRITE?

1. Xu Dishan's original quote reads, "Without reforming the Chinese script, progress of the Chinese nation will be hopeless. This much I can assert. I dare even say that to promote *zhuyin fuhao* will not do. We have to adopt the alphabetic script." See Xu Dishan 許地山, "Qingnian jie dui qingnian jianghua" 青年節對青年講話 (A speech to the youths on May Fourth), in *Xu Dishan yuyan lunwenji* 許地山語言論文集 (Collection of Xu Dishan's essays on language and writing) (Hong Kong: Xinwenzi xuehui, 1941), 10–16. For the quote on the Roman-Latin alphabet, see 10–11.

2. Qu Qiubai drew a distinction between the May Fourth new *baihua* and the late imperial old *baihua* but denounced both as dead words or the speech of demons. See Qu Qiubai 瞿秋白, "Guimenguan yi wai de zhanzheng" 鬼門關以外的戰爭 (War outside the gate of the demons) (May 30, 1931), in *Qu Qiubai wenji wenxue bian* 瞿秋白文集文學編 (The literary compilation of the Qu Qiubai collection) (Beijing: Renmin wenxue chubanshe, 1985–1989), 3:137–73.

3. Theodore Huters, "Legibility vs. the Fullness of Expression: Rethinking the Transformation of Modern Chinese Prose," *Journal of Modern Literature in Chinese* 10, no. 2 (December): 80–104.

4. James Yen was not the only YMCA volunteer who worked with the laborers in the literacy program. According to the *YMCA Chinese Labor Workers' Weekly*, Fu Ruoyu (Daniel Fu) and Lu Shiying (Z. Ying Loh) worked alongside him, but Yen remained the main architect behind the literacy program.

5. Chen Hansheng 陳翰笙, ed., *Huagong chuguo shiliao* 華工出國史料 (Historical materials of overseas Chinese laborers) (Beijing: Zhonghua shuju, 1980), vol. 10.

6. The number of one hundred fifty thousand Chinese laborers was Cai Yuanpei's estimate. See Cai Yuanpei 蔡元培, "Laogong shensheng" 勞工神聖 (Sacred, the laborers), *Xin qingnian* 新青年 (New youth) 5, no. 5 (November 15, 1918): 43–89.

7. Wellington Koo was the chief spokesman of the Chinese delegation at the Paris Peace Conference. He invoked the dagger metaphor in response to the conference's decision to hand Qingdao to Japan. See Margaret MacMillan, *Paris 1919: Six Months That Changed the World* (New York: Random House, 2002), 334.

8. Cai, "Laogong shensheng," 438.

9. Tse-Tsung Chow, *The May Fourth Movement: Intellectual Revolution in Modern China* (Cambridge, Mass.: Harvard University Press, 1960); Vera Schwarcz, *The Chinese Enlightenment: Intellectuals and the Legacy of the May Fourth Movement of 1919* (Berkeley: University of California Press, 1986).

10. Fabio Lanza, *Behind the Gate: Inventing Students in Beijing* (New York: Columbia University Press, 2010).

11. Paul J. Bailey, "'An Army of Workers': Chinese Indentured Labour in First World War France," in *Race, Empire and First World War Writing*, ed. Santanu Das (New York: Cambridge University Press, 2011), 37–38. The work-study program, sponsored by several Francophile Guomindang leaders, including Cai Yuanpei, Li Shizeng, and Wu Zhihui, attracted and cultivated numerous future political elites, such as Zhou Enlai, Xu Teli, and Deng Xiaoping, to name a few. Marilyn A. Levine has pointed out that the Chinese Labor Corps in World War I was in fact "an

important prelude to the Work-Study Movement" (*The Found Generation: Chinese Communists in Europe during the Twenties* [Seattle: University of Washington Press, 1993], 71). For a comprehensive collection of primary materials on the work-study program, see *Fufa qinggong jianxue yundong shiliao* 赴法勤工儉學運動史料 (Historical records of the work-study program in France) (Beijing: Beijing chubanshe, 1979), 1:227–74.

12. Recent years have seen a revival of the study of Chinese laborers in World War I. For important articles by historians such as Paul Bailey, Xu Guoqi, Sam Chiu, and Peter Cunich, among others, see the Chinese-English bilingual volume Zhang Jianguo 張建國, ed., *Zhongguo laogong yu diyici shijie dazhan* 中國勞工與第一次世界大戰 (Chinese labourers and the First World War) (Jinan: Shandong University Press, 2009). Journalist Mark O'Neill has produced two books on the Chinese laborers in Europe and Russia during World War I, *The Chinese Labour Corps: The Forgotten Chinese Labourers of the First World War* (London: Penguin, 2014), and *From the Tsar's Railway to the Red Army: The Experience of Chinese Labourers in Russia during the First World War and Bolshevik Revolution* (London: Penguin, 2014). Xu Guoqi alone has contributed two substantial English monographs on the Chinese Labor Corps in World War I: *China and the Great War: China's Pursuit of a New National Identity and Internationalization* (New York: Cambridge University Press, 2005), and *Strangers on the Western Front: Chinese Workers in the Great War* (Cambridge, Mass.: Harvard University Press, 2011).

13. Bailey, "'An Army of Workers,'" 48.

14. Xu Guoqi, *Strangers on the Western Front*, 243. For a critical review of Xu's work, see Rebecca Karl, "A World Gone Wrong," *London Review of Books* 33, no. 23 (December 2011): 23–24.

15. Xu Guoqi, *China and the Great War*, 13.

16. Xu Guoqi, *China and the Great War*, 15.

17. Xu Guoqi offers a patient account of China's stalled entry into the war in Xu Guoqi, *China and the Great War*, 90–91.

18. For details of the conception and initial stages of the Laborers as Soldiers program, including the Chinese negotiation for a written contract from the French and the British, the British and French competition in recruitment, and the colonial and racist treatment of the laborers, etc., see Chen Sanjing 陳三井, Lü Fangshang 呂芳上, and Yang Cuihua 楊翠華, eds., *Ouzhan huagong shiliao* 歐戰華工史料 (Historical records of Chinese laborers in the European war) (Taipei: Academia Sinica, 1997); Zhang Jianguo 張建國 and Zhang Junyong 張軍勇, eds., *Wan li fu rong ji* 萬里赴戎機 (Over there: The pictorial chronicle of Chinese laborer corps in the Great War) (Jinan: Shandong huabao chubanshe, 2009); Shirley Frey, "The Chinese Labor Corps of World War I: Forgotten Ally, Imperialist Pawn," in Zhang Jianguo, *Zhongguo laogong yu diyici shijie dazhan*, 30–45; Levine, *The Found Generation*, 65–71; Gloria Tseng, "Chinese Pieces of the French Mosaic: The Chinese Experience in France and the Making of a Revolutionary Tradition" (PhD diss., University of California, Berkeley, 2002); Xu Guoqi, *China and the Great War*, 114–26; Xu Guoqi, *Strangers on the Western Front*, 10–54; and Stephen G. Graft, "Angling for an Invitation to Paris: China's Entry into the First World War," *International Historical Review* 16, no. 1 (February 1994): 1–24.

19. Although the laborers were not indentured to engage in direct military conflict, there were accounts that the laborers fought German troops and some became prisoners of the Germans. See Xu Guoqi, *Strangers on the Western Front*, 89, 93.

20. The lower estimate of 140,000 counted 100,000 laborers under the British command and 40,000 under the French, from whom the American Expeditionary Forces borrowed 10,000 in 1917. The higher number added up to a total of 200,000 laborers serving in the Allies' camps all over France, Britain, Egypt, Mesopotamia, Palestine, and Africa, from 1916 to shortly after 1919. For the lower estimate, see Michael Summerskill, *China on the Western Front: Britain's Chinese Work Force in the First World War* (London: Michael Summerskill, 1982), 39, Nicholas John Griffin, "The Use of Chinese Labour by the British Army, 1916–1920: The 'Raw Importation,' Its Scope and Problems" (PhD diss., University of Oklahoma, 1973), 191, and Xu Guoqi, *China and the Great War*; for the higher number, see Chen Sanjing 陳三井, *Huagong yu ouzhan* 華工與歐戰 (Chinese laborers and the European war) (Taipei: Academia Sinica, 1986), 34–35, 189.

21. It is of course naive to assume both parties played by the rules, since there are reports of Chinese laborers being treated as less than free laborers, as their contracts specified, and more like colonized subjects or slaves; see Chen, Lü, and Yang, *Ouzhan huagong shiliao*. For the Chinese experience in the United States and Peru, see Adam McKeown, *Chinese Migrant Networks and Cultural Change: Peru, Chicago, Hawaii, 1900–1936* (Chicago: University of Chicago Press, 2001); Michael J. Gonzales, "Chinese Plantation Workers and Social Conflict in Peru in the Late Nineteenth Century," *Journal of Latin American Studies* 12, no. 3 (October 1989): 385–424.

22. The complete Chinese contract can be found in Chen Sanjing, *Huagong yu ouzhan*, 191–203; or in Chen, Lü, and Yang, *Ouzhan huagong shiliao*, 184–95.

23. Chen Sanjing, *Huagong yu ouzhan*, 192. The English translation and the emphasis are mine.

24. Chen Ta claimed to have synthesized the Chinese and French versions of the contract and offered an English translation of it in *Chinese Migrations with Special Reference to Labor Conditions*, which was quoted verbatim in Xu's *Strangers on the Western Front*. This synthesized version is not accurate. It cuts the contract articles from twenty-eight, in the Chinese original, to twenty-one, missing seven entire articles. The crucial two-part payment structure is also distorted. Xu, following Chen Ta's rendition, put it as follows: "At the request of the laborer, the employer shall arrange a convenient way for remitting his money to his family in China." See Xu Guoqi, *Strangers on the Western Front*, 246, and Chen Ta, *Chinese Migrations with Special Reference to Labor Conditions* (Taipei: Ch'eng Wen, 1967), 207.

25. For sections regarding letter writing in both contracts, see Chen Sanjing, *Huagong yu ouzhan*, 198, 208. While the British allowed a quota of two letters per laborer per month and required standard envelopes be used by the laborer and his family, there is no record indicating that the French practiced the same limitation and requirement. See Zhang and Zhang, *Wan li fu rong ji*, 107–8.

26. For a historical survey of the YMCA during the Social Gospel Movement, see Charles Howard Hopkins, *History of the Y.M.C.A. in North America* (New York: Association Press, 1951), 510–48; Gary Dorrien, *The Making of American Liberal*

Theology: Idealism, Realism, and Modernity, 1900–1950 (Louisville, Ky.: Westminster John Knox Press, 1989), 117–22. For detailed accounts of the YMCA's wartime contribution, see Peter Chen-main Wang, "Caring beyond National Borders: The YMCA and Chinese Laborers in World War I Europe," *Church History* 78, no. 2 (2009): 327–49.

27. This is a direct quote from James Yen's memoir "Jiu shi zi shu" 九十自述 (Memoir at the age of ninety), in *Yan Yangchu quanji* 晏陽初全集 (The complete works of James Yen), 2:492–555. See also Gu Xingqing 顧杏卿, *Ouzhan gongzuo huiyilu* 歐戰工作回憶錄 (Recollections of working in the European war) (Changsha: Commercial Press, 1937), 48.

28. Barry D. Karl and Stanley N. Katz explicate how the Progressive Era witnessed the change from traditional charity to modern philanthropy, which promoted scientific methods in social work and in turn transformed the study of sciences (including social sciences), American universities, and philanthropic foundations; "The American Private Philanthropic Foundations and the Public Sphere (1890–1930)," *Minerva* 19, no. 2 (1981): 236–70. Hopkins accounts for the YMCA's development toward scientific method in its service in *History of the Y.M.C.A*, 532–38. Stefan Huebner gives an excellent example of how the YMCA integrated scientific methods into its promotion of physical education throughout East Asia, in *Pan-Asian Sports and the Emergence of Modern Asia, 1913–1974* (Singapore: National University of Singapore Press, 2016), chap. 1.

29. Wu Xiangxiang 吳相湘, *Yan Yangchu zhuan: Wei quan qiu xiang cun gai zao fen dou liu shi nian* 晏陽初傳：為全球鄉村改造奮鬥六十年 (A biography of James Yen: Sixty years of struggle for global rural reconstruction) (Taipei: Shibao wenhua chuban, 1981), 5–7.

30. Yen was the only Chinese to receive the honor and accepted the award on May 24, 1943—the four-hundredth anniversary of Copernicus's death—in Carnegie Hall, New York City. See Wu Xiangxiang 吳相湘, "Yan Yangchu sao chu tian xia wen mang" 晏陽初掃除天下文盲 (Yan Yangchu sweeps clear illiteracy all over the world), in box 166, International Institute of Rural Reconstruction records, Rare Book and Manuscript Library, Columbia University, New York.

31. Yen, "Jiu shi zi shu," 542.

32. Yen, "Jiu shi zi shu," 533–34.

33. Yen, "Jiu shi zi shu," 536.

34. Yen's original English formulation is in James Yen, *The Mass Education Movement, Bulletin No. 1 of the National Association of the Mass Education Movement* (Peking: National Association of the Mass Education Movement, 1924), 3. Chen was a founding member of the Chinese National Association for the Advancement of Education, established in 1921. Yen started collaborating with the association in 1923. Chen Heqin later published his work in the book *Yutiwen yingyong zihui* 語體文應用字彙 (The vocabulary of applied *yutiwen*) (Shanghai: Commercial Press, 1933). Later editions of the one thousand characters are based on the character list put together by Chen Heqin. Yen took pride in the fact that his statistical hunch in 1918 did not stray too far from the later mathematical calculation.

35. Both journals were established by the Société franco-chinoise d'éducation. The *Magazine of Chinese in Europe*, with Cai Yuanpei as its chief editor, was in

circulation between August 1916 and March 1918, and then between August and December 1928. The *Chinese Laborers' Magazine* ran from January 1917 to December 1920.

36. Chow, *The May Fourth Movement*, 5–6.

37. Chow, *The May Fourth Movement*, 273.

38. Schwarcz, *The Chinese Enlightenment*, 80.

39. For the constructed genealogy of May Fourth *baihua*, see Xia Xiaohong夏曉虹, "Wusi baihua wenxue de lishi yuanyuan" 五四白話文學的歷史淵源 (The historical origin of the May Fourth *baihua* movement), *Zhongguo xiandai wenxue yanjiu congkan* 中國現代文學研究叢刊 (Modern Chinese literature studies), no. 3 (1985): 22–41; Wang Feng王風, *Shiyun tuiyi yu wenzhang xingti—zhongguo jindai wenxue lunji* 世運推移與文章興替—中國近代文學論集 (Shifting times and changing writing: Anthology of modern Chinese literature) (Beijing: Beijing daxue chubanshe, 2015), 210–30; Stephen Owen, "The End of the Past: Rewriting Chinese Literary History in the Early Republic," in *The Appropriation of Cultural Capital: China's May Fourth Project*, ed. Milena Doleželová-Velingerová, Oldřich Král, and Graham Martin Sanders (Cambridge, Mass.: Harvard University Press, 2001), 167–92; and Wang Hui 汪暉, *Xiandai zhongguo sixiang de xingqi* 現代中國思想的興起 (The rise of modern Chinese thought), vol. 2, part 2 (Beijing: Sanlian shudian, 2004), 1134–45.

40. See the introduction, n. 31.

41. Yen most likely meant "160,000,000" counts of characters, with repetition; see James Yen, *China's New Scholar-Farmer* (Peking: National Association of the Mass Education Movement, 1929), 1.

42. The *Weekly* proposed other prose competition topics, including "What is the Republic of China?" "The cause of the decline of China," and "If the Republic were to promote education, what do you think we should do?" See figure 3.1 and appendix 3.1 for the laborer Fu Xingsan's essay.

43. The Chinese original reads as follows: 論著有獎。本會因要鼓勵能著寫的弟兄。特獎第一名以二十佛郎。第二名十佛郎。著作以六百字為限。文字以普通話為合宜。交卷須在陽曆二月十五號以前。過期不收。著好之後，可交青年會幹事先生代寄巴力。以免誤延。茲將此次論題列后。華工在法與祖國的損益。*YMCA Chinese Labor Workers' Weekly*, no. 2 (January 29, 1919). I have added the punctuation.

44. The original microfilm is missing and this paragraph is quoted from Yen's memoir, "Jiu shi zi shu," 536.

45. Jerry Norman postulates the early formation of "Mandarin" in the eighth or ninth century; see "Some Thoughts on the Early Development of Mandarin," in *In Memory of Mantaro Hashimoto*, ed. Anne O. Yue and Mitsuaki Endo, 21–28 (Tokyo: Uchiyama Shoten, 1997); Chinese translation by Mei Tsu-lin, published in *Fangyan*, no. 4 (2004): 295–300. The concept of *guanhua* was an unstable one and changed over time and differed from place to place. For a historical and phonetic overview of *guanhua*, see Geng Zhensheng 耿振生, ed., *Jindai guanhua yuyin yanjiu* 近代官話語音研究 (Studies of the phonology of Mandarin in early modern China) (Beijing: Yuwen chubanshe, 2007); Ye Baokui 葉寶奎, *Mingqing guanhua yinxi* 明清官話音系 (The phonetic systems of Ming–Qing Mandarin) (Xiamen: Xiamen daxue chubanshe, 2001).

46. The *Weekly*, no. 7 (March 12, 1919).

47. Yen is referencing the late-Qing poet and scholar-official Huang Zunxian when he quotes "my hand writing my mouth." The Chinese original reads as follows: "這段文字，是當時的一種'官話'，既不是文言，也沒完全做到'我手寫我口'。標點符號，僅限於豆點'、'和圈'。'。" Yen, "Jiu shi zi shu," 536.

48. The speech was delivered in English as part of the Haskell Lectures at the University of Chicago in 1933 and published by the University of Chicago Press in 1934. See Hu Shi, "Chinese Renaissance," in *Hu Shi quanji* 胡適全集 (The complete works of Hu Shi) (Hefei: Anhui jiaoyu chubanshe, 2003), 37:84. The section where Hu Shi discusses the script revolution and the literary revolution is 80–100.

49. Hu Shi confirms that "China should have an alphabetic script in the future"; see Hu Shi 胡適, "Ba" 跋 (Postscript), in *Xin qingnian* 4, no. 4 (April 15, 1918): 356–57. For Hu's theorization on *baihua*, see Hu Shi 胡適, "Wenxue gailiang chuyi" 文學改良芻議 (Preliminary discussions of the literature reform), *Xin qingnian* 2, no. 5 (January 1, 1917): 1–11.

50. Hu, "Chinese Renaissance," 94.

51. For Hu Shi's more elaborate attempt to construct a *baihua* genealogy, delineating different shades of colloquialization in premodern *baihua* as a written language, thus contradicting his own program of pure orality, see Hu Shi 胡適, *Baihua wenxueshi* 白話文學史 (A history of *baihua*) (Tianjin: Baihua wenyi chubanshe, 2002). For a sharp observation of how Hu's convoluted but effective discourse of *baihua* dominated modern Chinese literary history, see Wang Feng, *Shiyun tuiyi yu wenzhang xingti*, 8–11. For an elucidation on the vernacular question in the Ming and Qing dynasties, see Shang Wei, "Writing and Speech: Rethinking the Issue of Vernaculars in Early Modern China," in *Rethinking East Asian Languages, Vernaculars, and Literacies, 1000–1919*, ed. Benjamin Elman (Leiden: Brill, 2014), 254–301.

52. In a parallel context, Steven G. Yao gives a revelatory analysis of poems written by Chinese workers at the Angel Island Immigration Station between 1910 and 1940 and categorizes their chosen language as the "classical style" of *wenyan*; see "Transplantation and Modernity: The Chinese/American Poems of Angel Island," in *Sinographies: Writing China*, ed. Eric Hayot, Haun Saussy, and Steven G. Yao (Minneapolis: University of Minnesota Press, 2008), 309.

53. There is no more biographical information on Fu Xingsan, except that he was from Pingdu, Shandong Province. There is also no way to determine if Fu was literate before coming to France or gained basic literacy in the literacy program. Fu Xingsan 傅省三, "Huagong zai fa yu zuguo de sunyi" 華工在法與祖國的損益 (The pros and cons of Chinese laborers' being in France), *YMCA Chinese Labor Workers' Weekly*, no. 7 (March 12, 1919). All punctuation and paragraph divisions in the English translation are mine.

54. Douglas Haig's remark is quoted in the English original in Gu, *Ouzhan gongzuo huiyilu*, 61–62.

55. *Far Eastern Review* 15, no. 4 (1918): 126–27, quoted in Xu Guoqi, *China and the Great War*, 147.

56. In a rich study surveying anticolonial and proindependence movements around the world in the wake of World War I, Erez Manela defines the "Wilsonian moment" as lasting from the autumn of 1918 to the spring of 1919 and offers an important account of how the moment helped shape the post–World War I geopolitical order;

The Wilsonian Moment: Self-Determination and the International Origins of Anticolonial Nationalism (New York: Oxford University Press, 2007), 6, 37; see also Pankaj Mishra's excellent review, "Ordained as a Nation," *London Review of Books* 30, no. 4 (February 2008): 3–8.

57. Manela, *The Wilsonian Moment*, 6, 193.

58. Michael Adas included figures such as Paul Valéry, Hermann Hesse, Georges Duhamel, Rabindranath Tagore, Mohandas Gandhi, Aurobindo Ghose, René Maran, and Léopold Senghor, among others, in his long list of international figures who contributed to the post–World War I discourse; "Contested Hegemony: The Great War and the Afro-Asian Assault on the Civilizing Mission Ideology," *Journal of World History* 15, no. 1 (March 2004): 61.

59. Zhang Taiyan challenged the universalizing tendency of the modern concept of equality and read it against Buddhist and Daoist traditions of equality; see Viren Murthy, *The Political Philosophy of Zhang Taiyan: The Resistance of Consciousness* (Leiden: Brill, 2011).

60. Rebecca Karl argues that late-Qing thinkers looked beyond the China-Japan-West triangle and understood China to be an integral part of the "uneven global modernity"; *Staging the World: Chinese Nationalism at the Turn of the Twentieth Century* (Durham, N.C.: Duke University Press, 2002).

61. Karl, *Staging the World*, 201.

62. A good example of late-Qing journalistic writing is Liang Qichao 梁啟超, *Yinbingshi wenji* 飲冰室文集 (Collected essays from the ice-drinker's studio) (Shanghai: Zhonghua shuju, 1926). The colloquialized written language covers a wide spectrum and I do not suggest that the level of colloquialization remained the same across late-Qing publications, the laborers' compositions, and the modern Chinese language as we know it today.

63. Fu's style attests to the influence of late-Qing writings on the May Fourth generation. David Der-wei Wang convincingly demonstrates such deep connections in his influential study of late-Qing fiction, *Fin-de-Siècle Splendor: Repressed Modernities of Late Qing Fiction, 1848–1911* (Stanford, Calif.: Stanford University Press, 1997).

64. Li Zhixue 李志學, "Diyici shijie dazhan zhong de fu e huagong" 第一次世界大戰中的赴俄華工 (Chinese laborers in Russia during World War I), in *Zhongguo laogong yu diyici shijie dazhan*, 109–18.

65. Albeit the laborers were required by the terms of their contracts to return to China after the war, many stayed in France and found employment in postwar reconstruction; see Yu-Sion Live, "The Contribution of Chinese Workers during the First World War in France: Memory of Facts and Occultation of Memory," in *Zhongguo laogong yu diyici shijie dazhan*, 49–50.

66. Ni Huiru and Zou Ningyuan provide a moving account of Chinese participation in the Spanish Civil War; see *Gan lan gui guan de zhao huan: Can jia xibanya nei zhan de zhongguo ren, 1936–1939* 橄欖桂冠的召喚：參加西班牙內戰的中國人 (The call of Spain: Chinese volunteers in the Spanish Civil War) (Taipei: Renjian chubanshe, 2001).

67. *Huagong juntuan* 華工軍團 (The army of Chinese laborers) (Beijing: China Central Television, 2009), documentary, 25 min., episode 5, "Xuese langman" 血色浪漫 (Romance in red).

68. For a collection on the interpretation of May Fourth, see Yu Yingshi 余英時 et al., *Wu si xin lun* 五四新論 (New commentaries on the May Fourth Movement) (Taipei: Lianjing chuban shiye gongsi, 1999).

69. Eric Hobsbawm, *The Age of Extremes: A History of the World, 1914–1991* (New York: Vintage Books, 1996), ix–xii.

70. John Fitzgerald discusses "awakening and dream fiction" in the late-Qing and early-Republican period in his important study on awakening China as a historical narrative; *Awakening China: Politics, Culture, and Class in the Nationalist Revolution* (Stanford, Calif.: Stanford University Press, 1996), 57–62.

71. Liang Qichao 梁啟超, *Ou you xin ying lu* 歐遊心影錄 (Reflections on a European journey) (Hong Kong: San da chubanshe, 1963), 5–6.

72. *The Weekly*, no. 7 (March 12, 1919).

73. Edgar Snow titled his article on James Yen and the Ting Hsien Experiment "Awakening the Masses in China," published in the *New York Herald Tribune*, December 17, 1933. Snow, in *Red Star Over China* (London: Gollancz, 1937), 183–84, compares Yen's mass-education program with CCP-led literacy initiatives, calling Yen's program "the Rockefeller-backed *de luxe* mass education experiment." The reference to Yen and Rockefeller was deleted in subsequent editions.

74. *The Weekly*, no. 1 (January 22, 1919), and no. 2 (January 29, 1919).

75. Schwarcz, *The Chinese Enlightenment*, 4.

76. James Yen, *New Citizens for China* (Peking: National Association of the Mass Education Movement, 1929), 2. Yen's benefactors included a wide array of major American philanthropists, including the Rockefeller family, the Carnegie family, the Ford Foundation, and the Milbank Memorial Fund to list a few. For the account books of Yen's fund-raising, see box 11, International Institute of Rural Reconstruction records. For an account of Yen's U.S. fund-raising trips, see Charles Hayford, *To the People: James Yen and Village China* (New York: Columbia University Press, 1990), 19–20.

77. The same story is quoted in "Jiu shi zi shu," *Yan Yangchu quanji*, and *Yan Yangchu wenji* 晏陽初文集 (The collected works of James Yen) (Chengdu: Sichuan daxue chubanshe, 1990) and in Pearl Buck, *Tell the People: Talks with James Yen About the Mass Education Movement* (New York: Day, 1945), to give a few examples.

78. Buck, *Tell the People*, 8.

79. Yen defined his philosophy as the "3Cs": "Confucius, Christ, and Coolies." See Wu Xiangxiang, *Yan Yangchu zhuan*, 24. He elucidated his reform vision in three serialized pamphlets (*New Citizens for China*; *China's New Scholar-Farmer*; *Ting Hsien Experiment 1930–1931*). For the connection between the literacy program and rural reconstruction, see Hayford, *To the People*, 39–59, and Kate Merkel-Hess, *The Rural Modern: Reconstructing the Self and State in Republican China* (Chicago: University of Chicago Press, 2016), 23–54.

4. REINVENTING CHILDREN

1. Both James Yen and Tao Xingzhi wrote about the founding of the association. See James Yen, *The Mass Education Movement, Bulletin No. 1 of the National Association of the Mass Education Movement* (Peking: National Association of the Mass

Education Movement, 1924); Tao Xingzhi, *Education in China 1924* (Beijing: Commercial Press, 1925). For Yen's role at the conference—introducing his World War I experience with the laborers, leading the conference participants in singing morale-boosting songs, and delivering a formal speech—see Wu Xiangxiang 吳相湘, *Yan Yangchu zhuan: Wei quan qiu xiang cun gai zao fen dou liu shi nian* 晏陽初傳：為全球鄉村改造奮鬥六十年 (A biography of James Yen: Sixty years of struggle for global rural reconstruction) (Taipei: Shibao wenhua chuban, 1981), 54–55.

2. Yen, *The Mass Education Movement*, 12.

3. James Yen, "Chinese Mass Education Movement Progresses Strongly," *News Bulletin*, October 16, 1926, 1, 8–12.

4. Tao's Romanizations for *pingmin jiaoyu* and *dazhong jiaoyu* are "ping ming giao yü" and "Dazhung Giao Yü"; see Tao Xingzhi, "The New Mass Education Movement" (March 15, 1936), in *Tao Xingzhi quanji* 陶行知全集 (The complete works of Tao Xingzhi), 12 vols. (Chengdu: Sichuan jiaoyu chubanshe, 1991), 6:151–52; for the Chinese version of the essay, see 364–66. Tao's more lengthy critique of the old mass-education movement appears in his article "Dazhong jiaoyu wenti" 大眾教育問題 (The problem of mass education), 4:49–59.

5. Tao, "New Mass Education Movement," 150–51, 153.

6. Tao Xingzhi 陶行知, *Xingzhi shuxinji* 行知書信集 (The collected correspondence of Tao Xingzhi) (Hefei: Anhui renmin chubanshe, 1981), 11. It remained unclear why the association was lukewarm at best to Yen's candidacy, especially when it had adopted in large part Yen's approach to the literacy campaign. However, it does explain to a certain degree why Yen was not involved in the initial conversion of his "foundation characters" to the *People's Thousand Character Lessons*.

7. The essay was originally published under the coauthorship of W. Tchishin Tao (Tao Xingzhi) and C. P. Chen, with the joint auspices of the National Federation of Provincial Educational Associations and the National Association for the Advancement of Education in 1925. "Mex." referred to Mexican silver dollars, the currency of the time. See Tao, *Tao Xingzhi quanji* (1991), 6:56.

8. Tao, *Tao Xingzhi quanji* (1991), 6:57.

9. Tao wrote to Cai Yuanpei, Jiang Menglin, and Mrs. Hu Shi urging them to convert their homes to People's Reading Circles and to ensure that all their family members and staff gain basic literacy with the help of the *People's Thousand Character Lessons*; see Tao, *Xingzhi shuxinji*, 13–14. People's Reading Circles and the "little teachers" were also seen in literary writings and theater productions—for example, Xia Yan 夏衍, *Shanghai wuyan xia: Sanmu huaju* 上海屋簷下：三幕話劇 (Under the roof of Shanghai: A three-act play) (Beijing: Zhongguo xiju chubanshe, 1957).

10. Tao, *Tao Xingzhi quanji* (1991), 6:57.

11. Yen, *The Mass Education Movement*, 15. Advocates of the Mass Education Movement often used the term "people's thousand characters" to refer to both the publication *People's Thousand Character Lessons* and the teaching method of one thousand characters.

12. Brian Bernards delineates how Lao She, instead of executing his epic plan, ended up creating a "transcolonial" and "postimperial" future of multiplicity and equality using his experiences from teaching Singaporean schoolchildren; *Writing the*

South Seas: Imagining the Nanyang in Chinese and Southeast Asian Postcolonial Literature (Seattle: University of Washington Press, 2015), 59–70.

13. Lao She 老舍, Laoniu poche *xinbian: Lao She chuangzuo zishu* 《老牛破車》新編—老舍創作自述 (New edition of the *Old Bull and the Broken Cart*: Autobiographical account of Lao She's writing) (Hong Kong: Sanlian shudian, 1986), 25.

14. Yan Yangchu [James Yen], "Pingmin jiaoyu xin yundong" 平民教育新運動 (The New Mass Education Movement), *Xin jiaoyu* 新教育 (New education) 5, no. 5 (December 1922): 1007–26. A less-detailed version of this article was translated into English, presumably by Yen himself, claiming the total number of characters to amount to "over one million characters"; Yen, *The Mass Education Movement*, 3. Tao Xingzhi quoted a total of ninety thousand characters in his preface to Chen Heqin's book *Yutiwen yingyong zihui* 語體文應用字彙 (The vocabulary of applied *yutiwen*) (Shanghai: Commercial Press, 1933), 2. While Chen himself gave the number of half a million, it remains unclear why Yen and Tao claimed such differing figures in their respective estimations.

15. These primers include but are not limited to *Peasants' Thousand Character Lessons, Urbanites' Thousand Character Lessons, Masses' Thousand Character Lessons, People's Religion Primer*, and *Elementary Peasants' Religion Primer* and can be found in box 131, International Institute of Rural Reconstruction records, Rare Book and Manuscript Library, Columbia University, New York.

16. Chen Heqin, *Yutiwen yingyong zihui*, 1.

17. Chen referenced in the introduction of the book the following scholars (listing only the last names) and their work: Ayres, Jones, Anderson, Thorndike, as well as Southhill and a certain Pastor P. Kronz; *Yutiwen yingyong zihui*, 4.

18. Tao Xingzhi's preface to Chen Heqin, *Yutiwen yingyong zihui*, 2.

19. The six categories with selected titles from each are (1) children's books: *Little Children All Over the World* and *Children's Novels*; (2) newspapers: *Xiamen Popular Education Newspaper* and the *National Alphabet Newspaper*; (3) journals: *Women's Magazine*; (4) extracurricular writings of primary-school students: *Student Newspaper of the Nanjing Affiliated Elementary School*; (5) old and new novels: *Dream of the Red Chamber, Miss Yansan from Beijing*, and *Saturday*; (6) miscellanies: *The Problem of Student Marriage, Speeches in Mandarin on National Shame*, and the Holy Bible; Chen Heqin, *Yutiwen yingyong zihui*, 7–10.

20. Chen Heqin, *Yutiwen yingyong zihui*, 1.

21. For the least (used only once) and most frequently used characters (the number of times they appear marked in parentheses) in the total 554,478 characters, see Chen Heqin, *Yutiwen yingyong zihui*, 77, 116, respectively.

22. Chen's philosophy in learning was, "Try to know something of everything and everything of something." He took a wide range of courses at Johns Hopkins, including geology, biology, economics, education, and psychology. He also took a public administration class with Frank Goodnow, then president of Johns Hopkins and adviser to the Beiyang Yuan Shikai government. Chen also spent two summers at Cornell University and Amherst College, studying ornithology, gardening, beekeeping, and automobile studies, etc. For Chen's vivid account of his years studying in the United States, see *Wo de bansheng* 我的半生 (Half my life) (Shanghai: Huahua shudian, 1946).

23. It was hardly a coincidence that James Yen, Tao Xingzhi, and Chen Heqin were all Christians, which testified to the strong connections between the Protestant missionary tradition, its Social Gospel Movement, progressive education in the United States, and its spread in China. For a discussion of the Social Gospel Movement and its impact on education in both the United States and China, see Ronald C. White Jr. and Howard Hopkins, *The Social Gospel: Religion and Reform in Changing America* (Philadelphia: Temple University Press, 1975); Philip West, *Yenching University and Sino-Western relations, 1916–1952* (Cambridge, Mass.: Harvard University Press, 1976); and James C. Thomson Jr., *While China Faced West: American Reformers in Nationalist China, 1928–1937* (Cambridge, Mass.: Harvard University Press, 1969).

24. There articles—"Hanzi ladinghua" 漢字拉丁化 (Latinizing Chinese characters), "Xin wenzi yu nanmin jiaoyu" 新文字與難民教育 (Sin Wenz and refugee education), "Xiaopengyou! Dajia qilai, saochu wenmang" 小朋友！大家起來，掃除文盲 (Little friends! Rise and eradicate illiteracy), and "Xin wenzi yu funü" 新文字與婦女 (Sin Wenz and women)—can be found in *Chen Heqin quanji* 陳鶴琴全集 (The complete works of Chen Heqin), 6 vols. (Nanjing: Jiangsu jiaoyu chubanshe, 1992), 6:160–86.

25. The 1872 novel *A Dog of Flanders* was written by the English novelist Marie Louise de la Ramée under the pseudonym Ouida. It was translated by Lou Shiyi from a Japanese edition into Chinese, which served as the basis for Chen's Sin Wenz translation. For a list of Chen's Sin Wenz primers, see *Chen Heqin quanji*, 6:187–230.

26. Chen gave a speech at a committee meeting of the Committee of Chinese Script Reform in 1955 called "Zai quanguo wenzi gaige huiyishang de fayan" 在全國文字改革會議上的發言 (A speech at the national meeting on script reform), in *Chen Heqin quanji*, 6:234–38. After 1958, Chen continued his interest in alphabetizing Chinese and was advocating Sin Wenz as late as 1979 in a report titled "Wenzi gaige shi kexue shijian he renmin qunzhong ziji jiefang ziji de shiye" 文字改革是科學實踐和人民群眾自己解放自己的事業 (Script reform is a scientific practice and the people's cause of self-liberation), in *Chen Heqin quanji*, 6:243–46.

27. Tao Xingzhi confused language and script as well in his English essay "China's New Language," which came out in the *Voice of China* 1, no. 4 (May 1, 1936), whose Chinese title was "Zhongguo xinwenzi" 中國新文字 (The new Chinese script). See both English and Chinese versions of the essay in *Tao Xingzhi quanji* (1991), 6:155–61, 368–72, respectively.

28. Chen Heqin, "Latinization of the Chinese Language," *China Quarterly* 3 (1938): 155–66; Chen Heqin 陳鶴琴, "Hanzi ladinghua" 漢字拉丁化 (Latinizing Chinese characters), trans. Wang Xialiang 王霞量, in *Chen Heqin quanji*, 6:160–73.

29. The Chinese subsections read as follows: 學習中國文字的困難, 中國字的羅馬化, 白話文運動, 注音符號運動, 國語羅馬字, 漢字拉丁化.

30. Chen Heqin, "Latinization of the Chinese Language," 159.

31. For a close-to-complete list of the 688 signatures to the letter, see Tao Xingzhi 陶行知, *Tao Xingzhi quanji* 陶行知全集 (The complete works of Tao Xingzhi), 8 vols. (Changsha: Hunan jiaoyu chubanshe, 1985), 3:50–55.

32. John King Fairbank, *The Great Chinese Revolution* (New York: Harper and Row, 1986), 200. John Dewey's other Chinese students and associates included Hu Shi,

Zhang Boling (president of Nankai University), Jiang Menglin (president of Peking University), and Guo Bingwen (president of Southeast University). For an overview of John Dewey's education theory in China, see Wang Ying 王穎, *Duwei jiaoyu xuepai yu zhongguo jiaoyu* 杜威教育學派與中國教育 (Dewey's philosophy of education and education in China) (Beijing: Beijing ligong daxue chubanshe, 2007). For Fairbank's recollection of Tao, see John King Fairbank, *Chinabound: A Fifty-Year Memoir* (New York: HarperCollins, 1983), 262–63.

33. Tao's other educational institutions included the Chinese Nonprofessional School in Hong Kong and the Society University in Chongqing, as well as a number of education societies, such as the Life Education Society and Shanhai Work Study Society.

34. Tao was a registered member of the China Democratic League.

35. Wu Xun founded his own schools through begging. Tao appreciated his devotion to grassroots literacy movements and his self-sacrificing spirit. In addition to his own writings about Wu Xun, Tao encouraged the film director Sun Yu 孫瑜 (1900–1990), another Columbia alumnus, to make a biographical film, resulting in *The Life of Wu Xun* (1950). Initially well received, it soon incurred severe criticism from CCP officials as high up as Mao Zedong, zooming in on Wu Xun's revisionist approach in collaboration with the antirevolutionaries. The Wu Xun campaign was the first case of party politics interfering with artistic production in the PRC (People's Republic of China). For a brief introduction to the film and its director, see Yingjin Zhang and Zhiwei Xiao, "Sun Yu," in *Encyclopedia of Chinese Film*, 324–25 (London: Routledge, 1998). For an overview of the campaign, see Yuan Xi 袁晞, *"Wu Xun zhuan" pipan jishi* 武訓傳批判紀事 (Historical account of the criticisms of *The Life of Wu Xun*) (Wuhan: Changjiang wenyi chubanshe, 2000). Criticism of Tao lasted well into the Cultural Revolution, and Tao's name was not rehabilitated until 1981.

36. Tao composed the following on the issue of Sin Wenz: "China's New Language" (in English); "Sin Wenz ge 1, 2, 3" 新文字歌 1，2，3 (Three songs of Sin Wenz); "Wenzi xinlun" 文字新論 (New theory on the script); "Dazhong jiaoyu wenti" 大眾教育問題 (The problem of mass education); "Xin wenzi wei tuijin dazhong wenhua zhi zui youxiao de gongju" 新文字為推進大眾文化之最有效的工具 (Sin Wenz as the most efficient instrument to promote mass culture); "Xin zhongguo yu xin jiaoyu" 新中國與新教育 (New China and new education); "Zai Guangdong sheng Sin Wenz yanjiu hui chengli dahui shang de yanci" 在廣東省新文字研究會成立大會上的演詞 (Speech at the inaugural meeting of the Guangdong Provincial Sin Wenz Research Society); "Zhongguo Sin Wenz" 中國新文字 (China's Sin Wenz), all in *Tao Xingzhi quanji* (1991), vols. 4, 6, and 7.

37. Tao Xingzhi 陶行知, "Dazhong jiaoyu wenti" 大眾教育問題 (The problem of mass education), dated May 1, 1936, in *Tao Xingzhi quanji* (1991), 4:58.

38. Tao Xingzhi 陶行知, "Sin Wenz he GR—dafu Li Jinxi xiansheng" 新文字和國語羅馬字—答覆黎錦熙先生 (Sin Wenz and GR—in response to Mr. Li Jinxi), first published in *Shenghuo jiaoyu* 生活教育 (Life education) 3, no. 4, cited from *Tao Xingzhi quanji* (1985), 3:41–42.

39. Tao, "Dazhong jiaoyu wenti"; "Dazhong jiaoyu yu minzu jiefang yundong" 大眾教育與民族解放運動 (Mass education and the national liberation movement) (May 10, 1936); "Minzu jiefang yu dazhong jiefang" 民族解放與大眾解放 (National

liberation and mass liberation) (May 17, 1936); "Puji minzu zijiu de jiaoyu" 普及民族自救的教育 (The popularization of education and national salvation) (June 1936); "Xin zhongguo yu xin jiaoyu" 新中國與新教育 (New China and new education) (July 16, 1936), all in *Tao Xingzhi quanji* (1985), vol. 3, and *Tao Xingzhi quanji* (1991), vol. 4.

40. Tao, "Minzu jiefang yu dazhong jiefang," in *Tao Xingzhi quanji* (1991), 4:96, 97.

41. Tao, "Dazhong jiaoyu yu minzhong jiefang yundong," cited from *Tao Xingzhi quanji* (1985), 3:63. The quotation here is the lyrics of the second of a total of three "Songs of Sin Wenz." For all three songs, see *Tao Xingzhi quanji* (1991), 7:432–34, 574.

42. The First United Front took place in the 1920s and disintegrated in 1927 after the GMD's purge of the CCP. The Second United Front was the anti-Japanese alliance formed after the Xi'an Incident in 1936 and that fell apart as soon as the Second Sino-Japanese War had ended. For a picture of Tao accompanying Mao Zedong, Chen Cheng, and Zhang Zhizhong after a round of GMD-CCP negotiations in Chongqing in 1945, see *Tao Xingzhi quanji* (1991), vol. 4, fig. 2.

43. Tao Xingzhi 陶行知, "Kuoda lianhe zhanxian shi dangqian jiuwang de weiyi zhengce" 擴大聯合戰線是當前救亡的唯一政策 (The extension of the United Front is the only solution to national salvation), in *Tao Xingzhi quanji* (1991), 4:119.

44. These include but are not limited to "Da xingzhou jibao jizhe wen" 答星洲日報記者問 (An interview with *Sin Chew Daily*) (July 1936); "Lianhe shi ke jiu zhongguo" 聯合始可救中國 (Only the United Front can save China) (July 1936); "Xin zhongguo yu xin jiaoyu" 新中國與新教育 (New China and new education) (July 1936); "Wo dui lianhe zhanxian de renshi" 我對於聯合戰線的認識 (My understanding of the United Front) (August 1936); "Guogong hezuo zhujian chengshu" 國共合作逐漸成熟 (Cooperation between the GMD and the CCP is maturing) (September 1936), all in *Tao Xingzhi quanji* (1991), 4:123–24, 134–48, 151–52, 162.

45. Tao Xingzhi 陶行知, "Tuanjie yuru de jige jiben tiaojian yu zuidi yaoqiu" 團結禦辱的幾個基本條件與最低要求, in *Tao Xingzhi quanji* (1991), 4:169–82. The article, drafted by Shen Junru, Zhang Naiqi, Zou Taofen, and Tao, first appeared in a Hong Kong journal called *Daily Life*, July 31, 1936, and then in *Life Education* on August 1, 1936, before its wide circulation as a pamphlet.

46. For Mao's response, dated August 10, 1936, see *Tao Xingzhi quanji* (1991), 4:183–92.

47. See Marshal Zhang Xueliang's firsthand account of the incident, in the Peter H. L. and Edith Chang Papers, Rare Book and Manuscript Library, Columbia University, New York.

48. Tao left two accounts of his two-year sojourn, "Haiwai de gushi" 海外的故事 (Overseas stories) and "Haiwai guilai tanhua yaodian" 海外歸來談話要點 (Talking points after the return from overseas), in *Tao Xingzhi quanji* (1991), 4:233–44. Aside from the two articles he wrote after the two-year trip, discussions of Tao's overseas activities are scarce. Tao's incomplete records of his daily activities between 1936 and 1938 can be found at the Tao Xingzhi Museum, She County, Anhui Province, China.

49. Tao Xingzhi, "John Dewey's Statement," in *Tao Xingzhi quanji* (1991), 6:471–72.

50. Tao Xingzhi 陶行知, "Shishi minzhu jiaoyu de tigang" 實施民主教育的提綱 (An outline to implement a democratic education), in *Tao Xingzhi quanji* (1985), 3:546.

51. The famous quote was in fact a paraphrase of Dewey's work, including and not limited to John Dewey and Evelyn Dewey, *Schools of Tomorrow* (New York: Dutton, 1915); John Dewey, *Democracy and Education: An Introduction to the Philosophy of Education* (New York: Macmillan, 1916); and *Experience and Education* (New York: Kappa Delta Pi, 1938). "Experience" was a key term that Dewey shared with his mentor, William James. The term functioned for both men as a linchpin connecting philosophy, psychology, and religion. See John M. Capps and Donald Capps, eds., *James and Dewey on Belief and Experience* (Urbana: University of Illinois Press, 2005), 1–40.

52. For Dewey's influence on Tao and comparisons between the two men's education philosophies, see Philip Kuhn, "T'ao Hsing-chih, 1891–1946: An Educational Reformer," *Papers on China* 13 (1959): 163–95; Wu Junsheng 吳俊升, "Tao Xingzhi yu duwei zai zhongguo de yingxiang" 陶行知與杜威在中國的影響 (The impact of Tao Xingzhi and John Dewey in China), in *Tao Xingzhi yanjiu zai haiwai* 陶行知研究在海外 (Overseas Tao Xingzhi studies), ed. Zhou Hongyu 周洪宇, 48–74, 399–400 (Beijing: Renmin jiaoyu chubanshe, 1991); Su Zhixin, "Teaching, Learning, and Reflective Acting: A Dewey Experiment in Chinese Teacher Education," *Teachers College Record* 98, no. 1 (Fall 1996): 126–52. Scholars debate the degree of Dewey's influence on Tao. For instance, Hubert Brown has argued that Tao did not have extensive contact with Dewey until 1919 during the latter's visit to Nanjing, and Tao remained heavily influenced by the Ming-dynasty philosopher Wang Yangming's theory on direct intuition and the unity of thought and action, changing his name from Tao Zhixing to Tao Xingzhi, from "knowing-doing" to "doing-knowing"; "Tao Xingzhi: Progressive Educator in Republican China," *Biography* 13, no. 1 (Winter 1990): 21–42.

53. Tao Xingzhi 陶行知, "Zhongguo shifan jiaoyu jianshelun" 中國師范教育建設論 (On building Chinese normal education) (December 1926), in *Tao Xingzhi quanji* (1991), 1:90–97. Xiaozhuang Normal College was founded in 1927, and Tao's fuller explication of the trinity of teaching, learning, and doing can be found in a collection titled *Jiaoxuezuo heyi taolunji* 教學做合一討論集 (Collection of discussions of teaching, learning, and doing all in one) (1929), in *Tao Xingzhi quanji* (1991), 2:3–34.

54. Tao Xingzhi 陶行知, "Jiaoyu taozou" 教育逃走, in *Tao Xingzhi quanji* (1991), 3:723.

55. Tao Xingzhi 陶行知, "Shaoye men qian" 少爺門前, in *Tao Xingzhi quanji* (1991), 5:777–82.

56. Yuen Ren Chao composed the melody for Tao's "Song of the Little Teacher"; in *Tao Xingzhi quanji* (1991), 5:810–11.

57. Tao Xingzhi 陶行知, "Zenyang xuanshu" 怎樣選書 (How to choose a book), in *Tao Xingzhi quanji* (1991), 5:757–59.

58. Tao Xingzhi 陶行知, "Xiaopengyou shi minzu weilai de juzi" 小朋友是民族未來的巨子 (Children are the future giants of the nation), in *Tao Xingzhi quanji* (1991), 4:258.

59. Andrew F. Jones discusses how the interwar period molded children into future "bourgeois consumers of culture"; *Developmental Fairy Tales: Evolutionary Thinking and Modern Chinese Culture* (Cambridge, Mass.: Harvard University Press, 2011), 112.

60. This appraisal came from the literary critic Qian Xingcun; see Qian Xingcun 錢杏邨, "Ye Shaojun de chuangzuo de kaocha" 葉紹鈞的創作的考察 (Examining the writings of Ye Shaojun), in *Xiandai zhongguo wenxue zuojia* 現代中國文學作家 (Contemporary Chinese literary writers) 2 (March 1930), cited from Liu Zengren 劉增人 and Feng Guanglian 馮光廉, eds., *Ye Shengtao yanjiu ziliao* 葉聖陶研究資料 (Research materials on Ye Shengtao) (Beijing: Shiyue wenyi chubanshe, 1988), 380.

61. Hsia went on to praise Ye that "in his quiet and methodical way" he "has maintained in over half a dozen collections a standard of competence which few of his contemporaries could rival"; *A History of Modern Chinese Fiction* (New Haven, Conn.: Yale University Press, 1971), 57–58.

62. Ye confessed that his first *Saturday* story, "Qiongchou" 窮愁 (Dearth and depression), was written in imitation of Washington Irving. Aside from a few *Saturday* essays written in classical Chinese, the rest of Ye's corpus was all in *yutiwen*; see "Zatan wo de xiezuo" 雜談我的寫作 (Miscellaneous comments on my writings), in Liu and Feng, *Ye Shengtao yanjiu ziliao*, 245–47.

63. See chapter 2, n. 65, for a list of the twelve founding members of the Literary Research Society.

64. Ye says that *Wenxin* "used the format of a novel to convey the knowledge and skills of learning Chinese"; Ye Shengtao, "Zatan wo de xiezuo," 246.

65. Ye's biographical information is taken from Shang Jinlin 商金林, *Ye Shengtao nianpu* 葉聖陶年譜 (A chronicle of Ye Shengtao) (Nanjing: Jiangsu jiaoyu chubanshe, 1986).

66. For instance, "Gemo" 隔膜 (Barriers), "Fan" 飯 (Rice), "Huozai" 火災 (The fire incident), "Pan xiansheng zai nan zhong" 潘先生在難中 (Mr. Pan in distress), and "Xiaozhang" 校長 (The principal); see Ye Shengtao 葉聖陶, *Ye Shengtao ji* 葉聖陶集 (The collected works of Ye Shengtao) (Nanjing: Jiangsu jiaoyu chubanshe, 1987), vols. 1 and 2.

67. Ye produced the novel in twelve installments running from January to November 15, 1928; Ye Shengtao 葉聖陶, "*Ni Huanzhi* zuozhe zixu" 倪煥之作者自序 (Preface by *Ni Huanzhi*'s author), in *Ye Shengtao ji*, 3:285.

68. Qian Xingcun 錢杏邨, "Guanyu *Ni Huanzhi* wenti" 關於《倪煥之》問題 (On the problem of *Ni Huanzhi*), in Liu and Feng, *Ye Shengtao yanjiu ziliao*, 397. Xia Mianzun 夏丏尊, "Guanyu *Ni Huanzhi*" 關於《倪煥之》 (Regarding *Ni Huanzhi*), and Mao Dun 茅盾, "Du *Ni Huanzhi*" 讀《倪煥之》 (Reading *Ni Huanzhi*), in *Ye Shengtao ji*, 3:281, 279.

69. The figure of the rural primary-school teacher runs through different periods of modern Chinese literature—critical realism, revolutionary literature, and socialist realism—and has important implications for the cultural, administrative, epistemological, and political turn in modern Chinese rural society. For an excellent study, see Sun Xiaozhong 孫曉忠, "Cunzhuang zhong de wenshu xingzheng" 村莊中的文書行政 (Administrating the village through documents and writing), *Zhongguo xiandai wenxue yanjiu congkan* 中国现代文学研究丛刊 (Modern Chinese literature studies), no. 6 (2017): 41–57; with a passing mention of *Ni Huanzhi*, 43.

70. Pan Maoyuan 潘懋元, "Cong zhongguo xiandai jiaoyu shi de jiaodu kan *Ni Huanzhi*" 從中國現代教育史的角度看《倪煥之》 (Reading *Ni Huanzhi* from the perspective of modern Chinese education history), *Xiamen daxue xuebao* 廈門大學學報

(Journal of Xiamen University) 1 (March 1963): 69–85; Xu Longnian 徐龍年, "Cong *Ni Huanzhi* kan Ye Shengtao de zaoqi jiaoyu zhuiqiu" 從《倪煥之》看葉聖陶的早期教育追求 (Understanding Ye Shengtao's early educational pursuit from *Ni Huanzhi*), *Zhongguo jiaoyu xuekan* 中國教育學刊 (Journal of the Chinese Society of Education), no. 8 (August 2003): 35–37.

71. Mao Dun was the first to define *Ni Huanzhi* as such; see Mao, "Du *Ni Huanzhi*." The other critics who valorized the revolution part over the education part include Xia Mianzun, Qian Xingcun, and Wolfgang Kubin. See Xia Mianzun, "Guanyu *Ni Huanzhi*"; Qian Xingcun, "Guanyu *Ni Huanzhi* wenti"; and Mao, "Du *Ni Huanzhi*"; also Wolfgang Kubin, "Deguo de youyu he zhongguo de panghuang" 德國的憂鬱和中國的傍徨 (German melancholy and Chinese wandering), trans. Xiao Ying and Shen Yong, *Qinghua daxue xuebao* 清華大學學報 (Journal of Tsinghua University) 17, no. 2 (2002): 75–78, 84. The original article is in German, "Der Schreckensmann: Deutsche Melancholie und chinesische Unrast: Ye Shengtaos Roman *Ni Huanzhi* (1928)," *minima sinica* 8, no. 1 (1996): 61–73.

72. Hsia, *History of Modern Chinese Fiction*, 64.

73. Marston Anderson gives a brilliant reading of the limits that Ye's literary production encounters, finding, in the case of *Ni Huanzhi*, instantiations in all three arenas of the protagonist's unsatisfactory life—"the pedagogic, the romantic, and the political"; *The Limits of Realism: Chinese Fiction in the Revolutionary Period* (Berkeley: University of California Press, 1990), 110, 116.

74. Ye Shengtao 葉聖陶, *Ni Huanzhi* 倪煥之, in *Ye Shengtao ji* 3:6.

75. The Chinese original reads, "煥之接稿子在手，是二十多張藍格紙，直行細字，塗改添加的地方確實不少，確還保存著清朗的行款。" Ye Shengtao, *Ni Huanzhi*, in *Ye Shengtao ji*, 3:30. My translation of quotes from *Ni Huanzhi* is modified from *Schoolmaster Ni Huan-chih*, trans. A. C. Barnes (Beijing: Foreign Languages Press, 1958); the quote is on 43–44.

76. Ye Shengtao, *Ni Huanzhi*, 60.

77. Ye Shengtao, *Ni Huanzhi*, 79.

78. Ye Shengtao, *Ni Huanzhi*, 197. Dewey's influence on Ye can be traced to as early as a 1919 article, "Xiaoxue jiaoyu de gaizao" 小學教育的改造 (Educational reform in primary schools), *Xinchao* 新潮 (New tide) 2, no. 2 (December 1919): 317–32.

79. Ye Shengtao, *Ni Huanzhi*, 279.

80. Ye Shengtao 葉聖陶, "*Ye Shengtao xuanji zixu*" 葉聖陶選集自序 (Author's preface to *The Selected Works of Ye Shengtao*), in *Ye Shengtao xuanji* 葉聖陶選集 (The selected works of Ye Shengtao) (Beijing: Kaiming shudian, 1951), 8. Anderson rightfully points out that Ye's early writings, including *Ni Huanzhi*, display "a high degree of self-reference and sentimentality"; *The Limits of Realism*, 94.

81. Jaroslev Průšek, *The Lyrical and the Epic: Studies of Modern Chinese Literature* (Bloomington: Indiana University Press, 1980), 178–94, and Marston Anderson, *The Limits of Realism*, trace Ye's literary influences to Chinese *biji* 筆記 (literary jotting) writing and works by Anton Chekhov, which, according to Anderson "exhibit a highly restrained use of narrative resources" (95).

82. Since the language is central to the discussion, I include the Chinese original for the Jin–Ni correspondence: "試用白話體寫信，這還是第一次。雖不見好，算不得文學，確覺說來很爽利，無異當面向你說；這也是文學改良運動會成功的一個證明。你該不會笑我喜新趣時吧？" Ye Shengtao, *Ni Huanzhi*, 140.

83. The Chinese reads, "白話體為文確勝，宜於達情，無模糊籠統之弊。惟效顰弗肖，轉形其醜，今故藏拙，猶用文言。先生得毋笑其篤舊而不知從善乎？" Ye Shengtao, *Ni Huanzhi*, 141.

84. The Chinese quote goes, "寫起信來，是簡捷的白話，決不會什麼什麼'也'地糾纏不清 . . ." Ye Shengtao, *Ni Huanzhi*, 218.

85. Anderson, *The Limits of Realism*, 96, 116–18.

86. Ye Shengtao, *Ni Huanzhi*, 213.

87. The first ellipsis is mine and the second is in the original; Ye Shengtao, *Ni Huanzhi*, 214.

88. Chen Wangdao 陳望道, preface to Ye Shengtao 葉聖陶 and Xia Mianzun 夏丏尊, *Wenxin* 文心 (The heart of literature) (Beijing: Zhongguo qingnian chubanshe, 1983), 1.

89. For Charles Laughlin's discussion of both *Wenxin* and the so-called White Horse Group of writers, which included Xia Mianzun, see "Wenzhang Zuofa: Essay Writing as Education in 1930s China," in *Tradition and Modernity: Comparative Perspectives*, ed. Kang-I Sun Chang and Hua Meng (Beijing: Beijing daxue chubanshe, 2007), 188–205; Charles A. Laughlin, *The Literature of Leisure and Chinese Modernity* (Honolulu: University of Hawai`i Press, 2008), 77–102. The two other works mentioned here are Liu Xie 劉勰, *Wenxin diaolong* 文心雕龍 (The literary mind and the carving of dragons) (Shanghai: Shanghai guji chubanshe, 2008); Edmondo De Amicis, *Cuore: The Heart of a Boy*, trans. Desmond Hartley (London: Owen, 1986).

90. The H city No.1 Middle School is most likely modeled on the Hangzhou No.1 Middle School (formally Zhejiang Secondary Normal School and Zhejiang Provincial No. 1 Normal School), where an exceptional group of faculty congregated in the 1920s and 1930s. Besides Xia Mianzun and Ye Shengtao, Lu Xun, Jiang Menglin, Li Shutong, Feng Zikai, Zhu Ziqing, Xu Shoushang, Jing Hengyi, Shen Junru, and Liu Dabai, among others, were associated with the school.

91. Chapters 13 and 19 invoke the differences between the two types of knowledge. Chapter 13 is organized around a letter from Lehua's father to Lehua, urging him and his classmates to read "books without characters," which is echoed by Lehua's manifestation upon leaving school to learn from "books that are not written in characters" in chapter 19; Ye and Xia, *Wenxin*, 89, 146.

92. Ye and Xia, *Wenxin*, 3–5.

93. 病院 is a loanword from the Japanese kanji formulation. The popular column Composition Hospital stirred at the time great controversy and faced censorship, as it published articles criticizing Chiang Kai-shek. Censorship of Ye Shengtao continued in Taiwan after 1949, since Ye remained in mainland China and served government positions in the PRC. The Taiwan Kaiming Bookstore published a 1977 edition of *Wenxin*, erasing Ye's name from the book, leaving only Xia Mianzun as the author. The whole chapter on "Composition Hospital" was also removed from the same edition. See Xia Mianzun 夏丏尊, *Wenxin* 文心 (Taipei: Kaiming shudian, 1977).

94. Ye and Xia, *Wenxin*, 59.

95. The journal also often published essays introducing leftist thought and revolutionary figures. For instance, no. 25 of the journal alone included Qu Qiubai's two

essays "Marx and Engels" and "Lenin," Ba Jin's "Kropotkin," and Mao Dun's "Gorky"; *Zhongxuesheng*, no. 25 (June 1932): 1–6, 56–61, 6–50, 61–73, respectively.

96. Ye and Xia, *Wenxin*, chaps. 6, 12, and 15.

97. Ye and Xia, *Wenxin*, chap. 6.

98. Zhou's father recommends two poems by Ilya Sadofiev and Pavel Kogan, collected and translated by Feng Xuefeng 馮雪峰 in *Liubing xin'e shixuan* 流冰新俄詩選 (Running ice: Poetry collection from the new Russia) (Shanghai: Shuimo shudian, 1929); Ye and Xia, *Wenxin*, chap. 8. I thank Chen Xi and Thomas Lahusen for helping me identify the poets and Feng's translated anthology.

99. Ye and Xia, *Wenxin*, 144, 146.

100. Ye and Xia, *Wenxin*, chaps. 21, 24, and 32.

101. Both Robert Culp and Peter Zarrow argue for and demonstrate the critical role textbooks played in imagining, planning, and cultivating a modern Chinese participatory citizenship. See Robert Culp, *Articulating Citizenship: Civic Education and Student Politics in Southeastern China, 1912–1940* (Cambridge, Mass.: Harvard University Press, 2007); Peter Zarrow, *Educating China: Knowledge, Society, and Textbooks in a Modernizing World, 1902–1937* (Cambridge: Cambridge University Press, 2015). Carl Kubler shows how the reinvention of children as "laboring contributors" of the state continued well into the early PRC years; "Imagining China's Children: Lower-Elementary Reading Primers and the Reconstruction of Chinese Childhood, 1945–1951," *Cross-Currents* 7, no. 1 (May 2018): 153–96.

102. Mao Zedong 毛澤東, "Zai Yan'an wenyi zuotanhui shang de jianghua" 在延安文藝座談會上的講話, in *Mao Zedong xuanji* 毛澤東選集 (The selected works of Mao Zedong), 5 vols. (Beijing: Renmin chubanshe, 1953), 3:869–900. For a translation of the document, see Kirk A. Denton, ed., *Modern Chinese Literary Thought: Writings on Literature, 1893–1945* (Stanford, Calif.: Stanford University Press, 1996), 458–84.

103. For a succinct definition of "proletarian novel," see M. H. Abrams and Geoffrey Galt Harpham, eds., *A Glossary of Literary Terms* (Stamford, Conn.: Cengage Learning, 2015), 256.

104. Evgeny Dobrenko delves into the making of proletarian writers, socialist realism, and literary utopia in *The Making of the State Writer: Social and Aesthetic Origins of Soviet Literary Culture*, trans. Jesse M. Savage (Stanford, Calif.: Stanford University Press, 2001). Katherine Clark charts the literary history of the Soviet Union in her classic *The Soviet Novel: History as Ritual* (Chicago: University of Chicago Press, 1981). Thomas Lahusen showcases how socialist state building bears on the writing and rewriting of socialist realist literature, which would see parallel developments in other socialist countries; *How Life Writes the Book: Real Socialism and Socialist Realism in Stalin's Russia* (Ithaca, N.Y.: Cornell University Press, 1997); see also Thomas Lahusen, "Cement," in *The Novel, Volume 2: Forms and Themes*, ed. Franco Moretti (Princeton, N.J.: Princeton University Press, 2006), 476–82.

105. For two important studies on Korean and Japanese literary making toward the end of Japanese rule in Korea, see Janet Poole, *When the Future Disappears: The Modernist Imagination in Late Colonial Korea* (New York: Columbia University Press, 2014); Samuel Perry, *Recasting Red Culture in Proletarian Japan: Childhood,*

Korea, and the Historical Avant-garde (Honolulu: University of Hawai`i Press, 2014).

106. For an expansive bibliographic compilation of international proletarian writing, see Bill Mullen, "Proletarian Literature," *Oxford Bibliographies*, DOI: 10.1093/OBO /9780199827251-0130.

107. Michael Denning identifies three major groups—the American working class, the left-wing modernists, and international antifascist émigrés—in the formation of the Popular Front; *The Cultural Front: The Laboring of American Culture in the Twentieth Century* (London: Verso, 2010).

108. Cai Xiang 蔡翔 carries out a series of illuminating investigations on the first seventeen years of PRC literary life in *Geming/xushu: Zhongguo shehui zhuyi wenxue— wenhua xiangxiang 1949–1966* 革命/叙述：中国社会主义文学—文化想象 (Revolution and its narratives: China's socialist literary and cultural imaginations, 1949–1966) (Beijing: Beijing daxue chubanshe, 2010).

5. TOWARD A CHINESE GRAMMATOLOGY

1. Ye became a member of the committee in 1949 in its initial form as the Association of the Chinese Script Reform. For a list of committee members, see *Renmin ribao* 人民日報 (People's daily), October. 11, 1949, as quoted in Wang Jun 王均, *Dangdai zhongguo de wenzi gaige* 當代中國的文字改革 (The script reform in contemporary China) (Beijing: Dangdai zhongguo chubanshe, 1995), 57. Ye's other titles after the founding of the PRC (People's Republic of China) included director of the General Administration of Press and Publication, member of the Standing Committee of the National People's Congress, and president of the Central Research Institute of Culture and History, among many others. See Shang Jinlin 商金林, *Ye Shengtao nianpu changbian* 葉聖陶年譜長編 (An extended chronicle of Ye Shengtao) (Beijing: Renmin jiaoyu chubanshe, 2004), vol. 3, "Table of Contents," 1–6; vol. 4, "Table of Contents," 4–5. For a list of other committee members, see Wang Jun, *Dangdai zhongguo de wenzi gaige*, 63.

2. Shang Jinlin, *Ye Shengtao nianpu changbian*, 3:592.

3. Zhou Enlai 周恩来, "Dangqian wenzi gaige de renwu" 當代文字改革的任務 (The current tasks of script reform), in Wang Jun, *Dangdai zhongguo de wenzi gaige*, 556.

4. The key source is Zhou Youguang's interview, cited by many. For instance, Peter Hessler, *Oracle Bones: A Journey Between China's Past and Present* (New York: HarperCollins, 2006), 416–17; Zhou Minglang, *Multilingualism in China: The Politics of Writing Reforms for Minority Languages, 1949–2002* (Berlin: Mouton de Gruyter, 2003), 165; Fei Jinchang 費錦昌, *Zhongguo yuwen xiandaihua bainian jishi* 中國語文現代化百年記事 (The hundred-year chronicle of Chinese language and script modernization) (Beijing: Yuwen chubanshe, 1997), 125. Zhou recapped the alleged interview in his autobiography, *Shi nian ru shui* 逝年如水 (Lost years like water) (Hangzhou: Zhejiang daxue chubanshe, 2015), 270–71.

5. For instance, Zhou Minglang, ed., *Language Policy in the People's Republic of China: Theory and Practice Since 1949* (Boston: Kluwer Academic, 2004); Zhou Minglang, *Multilingualism in China*. For the initial planning of the simplification of characters, see Wu Yuzhang 吳玉章, *Hanzi jianti wenti* 漢字簡體問題 (The

question of simplified characters) (Beijing: Zhonghua shuju, 1956); see also Wang Jun, *Dangdai zhongguo de wenzi gaige*, 139–85.

6. The committee changed its name eventually to the State Language Commission (Guojia Yuyan Wenzi Gongzuo Weiyuanhui 国家语言文字工作委员会) in 1985, belatedly acknowledging its shifted focus from script to language. It remained under the direct leadership of the State Council until 1998, when the Ministry of Education took over.

7. Wang Jun, *Dangdai zhongguo de wenzi gaige*, 57, 61.

8. Wu Yuzhang's speech on the first meeting of the renamed committee on December 23, 1954; *Hanzi jianti wenti*, 63.

9. Mao gave the order at the end of 1951, according to *Diyici quanguo wenzi gaige huiyi wenjian huibian* 第一次全国文字改革会议文件汇编 (Document compilation of the first national script reform conference) (Beijing: Wenzi gaige chubanshe, 1957), 5. In 1952, Guo Moruo delivered the mandate at the founding conference of the Research Committee for Chinese Script Reform; see Wang Jun, *Dangdai zhongguo de wenzi gaige*, 60. Hu Qiaomu also recalled Mao's instruction in his memoir, Hu Qiaomu 胡乔木, *Hu Qiaomu huiyi Mao Zedong* 胡乔木回憶毛澤東 (Hu Qiaomu remembering Mao Zedong) (Beijing: Renmin chubanshe, 1994), 23.

10. Zhou Minglang surveys the adoption of the Cyrillic alphabet for ethnic minority groups in *Multilingualism in China*, 169–71.

11. Wu's three other proposals were two IPA-based alphabets and one Latin-alphabet scheme. Wu Yuzhang also mentioned the following names and their respective proposals: Ding Xilin, Wei Que, Lin Handa, Lu Zhiwei, as well as comrades from the committee's secretariat. See Wu's internal report, "Caoni xialie sige zhongguo pinyin wenzi fang'an (cao'an) de jingguo" 草拟下列四个中国拼音文字方案（草案）的经过 (The process of drafting the following four Chinese alphabets), courtesy of the Library of the State Language Commission, Beijing.

12. Wang Jun cited 655 as the total number of proposals; see *Dangdai zhongguo de wenzi gaige*, 210. I follow the number tallied in "Note of Explanation" in volume 2. A handful of proposals were sent by people on the committee or related to it—for instance, Tang Lan, Du Dingyou, and Yin Binyong—while most names are unfamiliar. *Gedi renshi jilai hanyu pinyin wenzi fang'an huibian* 各地人士寄来汉语拼音文字方案汇编 (A compilation of plans for alphabetic Chinese mailed in from all over China), 2 vols. (Beijing: Zhongguo wenzi gaige weiyuanhui pinyin fang'an bu, 1954–1955).

13. *Gedi renshi jilai hanyu pinyin wenzi fang'an huibian*, 1:6, 102, 119.

14. Althusser's original formulation is, "There is no ideology except for concrete subjects, and this destination for ideology is only made possible by the subject: meaning, by the category of the subject and its functioning"; "Ideology and Ideological State Apparatus (Notes Towards an Investigation)," in *Lenin and Philosophy and Other Essays*, trans. Ben Brewster (London: New Left Books, 1971), 159, 160.

15. I do not suggest that there was no other state policy turned state ideology. For instance, Tang Lan invoked another salient example of the agricultural co-op in *Tang Lan quanji* 唐蘭全集 (The complete works of Tang Lan), 12 vols. (Shanghai: Shanghai guji chubanshe, 2015), 3:969.

16. Aside from Chen's own writing and that of his wife, Zhao Luorui 趙蘿蕤 (also known as Lucy Chao), Chen is best remembered in Ningkun Wu's autobiography,

A Single Tear: A Family's Persecution, Love, and Endurance in Communist China (New York: Atlantic Monthly Press, 1993). Peter Hessler's *Oracle Bones* has more recently revived Chen's life story, cultivating much online commemoration.

17. The first batch of simplified characters was announced on January 31, 1956; see Wang Jun, *Dangdai zhongguo de wenzi gaige*, 537.

18. For more on how the Luo Longji–Zhang Bojun alliance impacted the script reform, see *1957 nian wenzi gaige bianlun xuanji* 1957年文字改革辩论选辑 (Selected works of the 1957 debate on script reform) (Beijing: Xin zhishi chubanshe, 1958).

19. Though it was commonly acknowledged that Chen had committed suicide, it is not entirely ruled out that he might have been killed. Zhao Luorui phrased her husband's death as follows: "In early September of 1966, Mengjia, suffering from severe persecution inflicted by Lin Biao's and the Gang of Four's antirevolutionary revisionist route, passed away at the age of fifty-five." The Institute of Archaeology at the Chinese Academy of Social Sciences—formerly known as the Chinese Academy of Sciences, its name changing in 1977—held his memorial service in 1978, which was followed by his rehabilitation in 1980. See Zhao Luorui, "Yi Mengjia" 憶夢家 (Remembering Mengjia), in *Dushu shenghuo sanzha* 讀書生活散札 (Scribbles on my reading life) (Nanjing: Nanjing shifan daxue chubanshe, 2009), 221.

20. See Zhou Youguang's account of Li Rong's position on the script reform in *Shi nian ru shui*, 287; see also Li Ling's moving recollection of his father-in-law, Fu Maoji, in "Li Ling tebie zhuanji" 李零特別專輯 (Special issue on Li Ling), *Jintian* 今天 (Today literary magazine), no. 106 (2014): 13–20.

21. Chen's poetry career began around 1927 when he met Wen Yiduo and Xu Zhimo, and it ended in 1934 when he published his anthology *Tie ma ji* 鐵馬集 (Iron horse collection) (Shanghai: Kaiming shudian, 1934).

22. For how members and critics of the Crescent Moon Society contested its literary identity, see Lawrence Wang-chi Wong, "Lions and Tigers in the Groups: The Crescent Moon School in Modern Chinese Literary History," in *Literary Societies of Republican China*, ed. Kirk A. Denton and Michel Hockx (Lanham, Md.: Lexington Books, 2008), 279–312.

23. Fellow poet Yu Dawang was one of the first critics to praise Chen's Chinese temperament; see Yu's preface to *Tie ma ji*, 2. Chen came from a Christian family and married into another. For more information on the Chen family, see Chen's essay "Qing de yiduan" 青的一段 (A passage of green) in Chen Mengjia 陳夢家, *Mengjiashi cun wen* 夢甲室存文 (An essay collection of the Mengjia studio) (Beijing: Zhonghua shuju, 2006), 89–113, as well as Chen's brother Chen Mengxiong's autobiography, Chen Mengxiong 陳夢熊, *Wo de shuiwen dizhi zhi lu* 我的水文地質之路 (My life in hydrogeology) (Changsha: Hunan jiaoyu chubanshe, 2013).

24. Selected poems include "Wo wang zhe ni lai" 我望著你來 (I watch you come), "Tie ma de ge" 鐵馬的歌 (Song of the iron horse), "Shengdan ge" 聖誕歌 (A Christmas song), and "Jiu long bi" 九龍壁 (The wall of nine dragons), in *Tie ma ji*, 9–11, 26–28, 30–32, 81–82.

25. Chen Mengjia 陳夢家, *Xinyue shixuan* 新月詩選 (Selected poems of the Crescent Moon) (Shanghai: Xinyue shudian, 1931), 21–24; Chen Mengjia 陳夢家, "Qiutian tanshi" 秋天談詩 (Words on poetry on an autumn day), *Beiping chenbao* 北平晨報 (Peking morning post), November 7 and 8, 1932.

26. Hessler, *Oracle Bones*, 244, states that critics compared Chen to "A. E. Housman and Thomas Hardy." However, it was made explicit by Fang Weide in the "Afterword" to Chen's *Iron Horse Collection* that Chen had not read the two authors. Fang Weide, together with Yu Dawang, were the two critics who compared Chen to Wordsworth, Tennyson, and Wang Bo. See Chen Mengjia, *Tie ma ji*, 5.

27. Chen edited *Xinyue shixuan* at the age of twenty and, a few years later, his own *Iron Horse Collection*; Chen Mengjia, *Tie ma ji*, 10, 41.

28. Both Timothy Ting-fang Lew and T. C. Chao were teaching at Yenching at the time. Lew was a pioneer in Chinese linguistics and psychology. See Timothy Ting-fang Lew, "The Psychology of Learning Chinese: A Preliminary Analysis by Means of Experimental Psychology of Some of the Factors Involved in the Process of Learning Chinese Characters" (PhD diss., Columbia University, 1920). It is alleged that as much as T. C. Chao recognized Chen's talent, he opposed the marriage between his daughter Zhao Luorui and Chen at first, saying, "If you want to marry Lucy, show me real scholarship." See Yan Wen 言文, "Caixue rensheng" 才學人生 (A life of talent and scholarship), in Zhao Luorui, *Dushu shenghuo sanzha*, 284.

29. The three targets of objection were corruption, waste, and bureaucracy.

30. In an early poem, "Who Am I" (Wo shi shei 我是誰), Chen's concluding stanza reads, "Aren't you the one who wanted to hear my story / I am flustered and flushed / Gently I turn over twenty blank pages / And sometimes, I want to write only one line: I'm a minister's good son"; in *Tie ma ji*, 6–8. Chen would become, in fact, "a good son" of "two ministers": Chen's own father, Chen Jinyong 陳金鏞 (1868–1939), was a prominent Presbyterian minister, and Chen's father-in-law, T. C. Chao 趙紫宸 (1888–1979), was a onetime Anglican minister and one of the key figures of the Chinese Christian Indigenization Movement. For more on the Chao family, see Peter Tze Ming Ng, *Chinese Christianity: An Interplay between Global and Local Perspectives* (Leiden: Brill, 2012), 167–78; Zhao Luorui 赵萝蕤, *Wo de dushu shengya* 我的讀書生涯 (My life of books) (Beijing: Beijing daxue chubanshe, 1998), 1–6.

31. Chen had published widely before 1957 on issues of language, script, and pedagogy, and it was not until 1957 that he started articulating his objections to the script reform. His earlier essays, such as "Shu yu" 書語 (Written language) and "Jieshao Wang Liaoyi xiansheng hanzi gaige" 介紹王了一先生漢字改革 (Introduction to Wang Liaoyi [Wang Li]'s script reform), are included in *Mengjiashi cun wen*, 220–25, 226–31.

32. Chen Mengjia 陳夢家, "Lue lun wenzixue" 略論文字學, *Guangming ribao* 光明日報 (Guangming daily), February 4, 1957, quoted from *Mengjiashi cun wen*, 235–39.

33. Chen Mengjia, *Mengjiashi cun wen*, 239.

34. Chen Mengjia, *Mengjiashi cun wen*, 237.

35. Chen Mengjia, *Mengjiashi cun wen*, 238.

36. Chen Mengjia 陳夢家, "Guanyu hanzi de qiantu—1957 nian 3 yue 22 ri zai zhongguo wenzi gaige weiyuanhui de jiangyan" 關於漢字的前途—1957年3月22日在中國文字改革委員會的演講 (Regarding the future of Chinese characters: A speech delivered to the script reform committee on March 22, 1957), *Guangming ribao*, May 19, 1957, quoted from *Mengjiashi cun wen*, 244–51.

37. *Mengjiashi cun wen*, 244, 250. Between February and March of 1957, Chen received a letter by a certain Mr. Guan Xi. Chen wrote that despite Guan's specific

instructions not to hand the letter to the committee and its institutional journal *Zhongguo yuwen* 中國語文 (Chinese language and writing), he took it upon himself to recommend the letter to the journal to emphasize the importance of mutual understanding between official script reformers and regular enthusiasts. Both the letter and his recommendation appeared in *Chinese Language and Writing* in its June issue and were criticized two months later. See *Zhongguo yuwen*, no. 6 (1957): 48–49, no. 8 (1957): 12–13, 47.

38. Chen composed a series of short essays for *Guowen zhoukan* 國文週刊 (The national language weekly), some of which are included in *Mengjiashi cun wen*.

39. Chen Mengjia, *Mengjiashi cun wen*, 251.

40. For an account of the composition, negotiation, and promotion of the simplified characters, see Wang Jun, *Dangdai zhongguo de wenzi gaige*, 139–54. In spite of the many sources that the committee consulted and absorbed, Yuen Ren Chao maintained that a solid 80 percent of the 1956 batch of simplified characters came from historical precedents; in Yuen Ren Chao 趙元任, *Zhao Yuanren quanji* 趙元任全集 (The complete works of Yuen Ren Chao) (Beijing: Commercial Press, 2007), 16:245.

41. Chen Mengjia 陳夢家, "Shenzhong yidian 'gaige' hanzi" 慎重一點『改革』漢字, *Wenhui bao* 文匯報 (Wenhui daily), May 17, 1957, quoted from *Mengjiashi cun wen*, 240–43.

42. Chen Mengjia, *Mengjiashi cun wen*, 242.

43. Chen cited both Guan Xi's letter and an interview published in the *Guangming Daily*, where an anonymous biologist questioned whether an overhaul of writing would not upset scientific research; *Mengjiashi cun wen*, 242. It was later revealed by Chen that the biologist was Bing Zhi 秉志, a founding member of the Research Institute of Biology, Chinese Science Society, as well as of the Chinese Association of Animal Studies; see *Pinyin* 拼音, no. 12 (July 1957): 7.

44. The transcript in *Pinyin* is most likely an abridged version; see *Pinyin*, no. 12:1–35. This was the last issue of *Pinyin* before it changed its name to *Wenzi gaige* 文字改革 (Script reform) in August 1957.

45. For the incomplete guest lists of the three meetings, see *Pinyin*, no. 12:1, 10, 18.

46. *Pinyin*, no. 12:21.

47. Tang studied at Jiaxing County No. 2 Business School, Jiaxing Academy of Traditional Chinese Medicine, and later worked at the Jingliang Clinic. During his Shanghai sojourn, he learned poetry composition at Chen Diexian's Xuyuan Translation Society and wished to join the revolution under Sun-Yat-sen's leadership. For a short English introduction of Tang, see *Tang Lan quanji*, 1:1–39; the Chinese version can be found at 1:1–24.

48. Tang served as editor in chief at the *Shangbao wenxue zhoukan* 商報文學週刊 (The literary weekly of *Shangbao*) in Tianjin, as well as of the *Jianglai yuekan* 將來月刊 (The future weekly). Tang held various lectureships at Peking, Tsinghua, Yenching, and Northeastern Universities. Tang's groundbreaking early work, *Gu wenzi xue daolun* 古文字學導論 (An introduction to paleography, 1934), and *Yinxu wenzi ji* 殷墟文字記 (Notes on the inscriptions from Yinxu, 1934) were compiled from his lecture notes. Tang was said to have admired only four scholars: Sun Yirang, Wang Guowei, Guo Moruo, and Chen Yinque. Wang praised Tang as one of the four most notable young philologists of the time. Guo asked Tang to write a preface for his magnum opus on bronze inscriptions; see *Tang Lan quanji*, 1:6–7, 12, 39.

49. For an excellent collection on the question of the "national form," see Xu Naixiang 徐迺翔, ed., *Wenxuede "minzuxingshi" taolun ziliao* 文學的「民族形式」討論資料 (Materials on the literary question of the "national form") (Beijing: Zhishi chanquan chubanshe, 2010); for Wang Hui's discussion of the national form during the Second Sino-Japanese War, see *Xiandai zhongguo sixiang de xingqi* 現代中國思想的興起 (The rise of modern Chinese thought), 4 vols. (Beijing: Sanlian shudian, 2004), vol. 2, part 2:1493–1526.

50. *Pinyin*, no. 12:3.

51. Tang adopted the Chinese term *xingsheng* but did not invoke the English terms "ideo-phonograph" or "ideo-phonogram." I use the concept in the context of Rousseau's use of it when describing the second of the three stages of human writing; see Rousseau, *Essay on the Origin of Languages*, as quoted in Jacques Derrida, *Of Grammatology*, trans. Gayatri Chakravorty Spivak (Baltimore: Johns Hopkins University Press, 2016), 318–21.

52. One of the best-known debates on ideographs in the English language might be the debate between Peter Boodberg and Herrlee Creel. While Creel was on the side of identifying Chinese characters as ideographs, Boodberg was on the side of criticizing the ideographic myth. David Lurie examines "the Boodberg-Creel controversy" in "Language, Writing, and Disciplinarity in the Critique of the 'Ideographic Myth': Some Proleptical Remarks," *Language and Communication* 26 (2006): 250–69.

53. Gao Mingkai sent in written comments. Whereas Gao did not agree with Tang's proposal completely, he did object to the "encircling attack" on Tang; see *Pinyin*, no. 12:29–35.

54. The journal was created in 1952 by the committee as well as by the Institute of Linguistics, CAS; see Wang Jun, *Dangdai zhongguo de wenzi gaige*, 535.

55. Tang Lan 唐蘭, "Lun makesi zhuyi lilun yu zhongguo wenzi gaige jiben wenti" 論馬克思主義理論與中國文字改革基本問題, *CLW*, no. 1 (1956): 28–39, 12; also available in *Tang Lan quanji*, 3:916–40.

56. The cluster of essays includes Wei Que, "Critique of Tang Lan's View on the Script Reform"; Wang Li, "On the Thoughts and Logic of Tang Lan's Essay"; Cao Bohan, "On the Transitioning Period of the Chinese Script Reform"; Hu Mingyang, "Several Thoughts Regarding 'On Marxism and the Basic Question of the Chinese Script Reform'"; Liang Donghan, "Several Questions Regarding 'On Marxism and the Basic Question of the Chinese Script Reform'"; see *CLW*, no. 1 (1956): 10–27.

57. Zheng Linxi, Wei Jiangong, Li Jinxi, and Liu Youxin wrote individual reviews in *CLW*, no. 2 (1956): 6–19. One more coauthored essay and a roundtable discussion critiquing Tang appeared in *CLW*, no. 3 (1956): 27–38.

58. Tang seemed to be on amicable terms with Chen Mengjia before he turned against Chen; see Tang Lan 唐蘭, "Youpai fenzi Chen Mengjia shi 'xuezhe' ma?" 右派分子陳夢家是'學者'嗎？ (Is the rightist Chen Mengjia a "scholar"?), *CLW*, no. 10 (1957): 13–16.

59. Tang Lan 唐蘭, "Zailun zhongguo wenzi gaige jiben wenti" 再論中國文字改革基本問題, *CLW*, no. 3 (1957): 7–11. Wei Que wrote a second review, *CLW*, no. 3 (1957): 11; so did Cao Hanbo, *CLW*, no. 5 (1957): 47–48.

60. The two accusations were from Wang Li and Wei Que, *CLW*, no. 1 (1956): 15, 12, respectively.

61. Tang, "Lun makesi zhuyi lilun," 28.

62. Tang, "Lun makesi zhuyi lilun," 31.

63. Tang, "Lun makesi zhuyi lilun," 30. Tang's critics argued that the conflation of language and script was not warranted according to Marxist theory, so that while the Chinese language could not be subject to explosive changes, its script could; see the reviews by Wei, Wang, and Cao, *CLW*, no. 1 (1956): 10–21.

64. Tang, "Lun makesi zhuyi lilun," 31.

65. Tang, "Lun makesi zhuyi lilun," 32.

66. Tang, "Lun makesi zhuyi lilun," 36.

67. Tang, "Lun makesi zhuyi lilun," 36.

68. Tang, "Lun makesi zhuyi lilun," 38.

69. Tang, "Lun makesi zhuyi lilun," 39.

70. *Gedi renshi jilai hanyu pinyin*, 1:1.

71. *Gedi renshi jilai hanyu pinyin*, 1:1.

72. Tang, *Tang Lan quanji*, 11:1439–51. The editor dated the heretofore unpublished proposal to October 1949.

73. *Gedi renshi jilai hanyu pinyin*, 1:1. Tang's proposal, like most of the proposals in the two volumes, did not concern itself with tonal representation.

74. Tang, *Tang Lan quanji*, 3:971.

75. Tang, *Tang Lan quanji*, 3:969.

76. Tang, *Tang Lan quanji*, 3:971.

77. Tang, *Tang Lan quanji*, 3:970.

78. Tang, *Tang Lan quanji*, 3:972.

79. Tang, *Tang Lan quanji*, 3:973.

80. Tang, *Tang Lan quanji*, 3:972–73.

81. Tang's *An Introduction to Paleography* constitutes all of volume 5 of *Tang Lan quanji*, and Tang's *Zhongguo wenzixue* 中國文字學 (A study of Chinese writing) (Shanghai: Shanghai guji chubanshe, 2001) is also available in volume 6 of *Tang Lan quanji*; see *Tang Lan quanji*, vol. 5; vol. 6:389–521. There have been altogether four editions of *An Introduction to Paleography*: 1934 lecture edition, 1957 amended and mimeographed edition, 1963 Party School edition (*dangxiao* 党校), and 1981 Qilu Press edition. The edition that *Tang Lan quanji* adopted is the fourth edition with further amendments; see editor's note, 5:466. Tang's *A Study of Chinese Writing* is reprinted less frequently, for according to Tang, "This book was published by the Kaiming Bookstore in 1948. Because it disagreed with the government's policies of Romanization of the Chinese writing system, it was not reprinted and is now very hard to find in China" (1:19–20).

82. The quote is from Qiu Xigui 裘錫圭, among many others who praised Tang's 1934 masterpiece; see *Tang Lan quanji*, 1:6, 13.

83. Tang was certainly not the first to raise questions about the six principles of the *Shuowen* throughout the philological history. Others who have critically engaged with the six principles include but are not limited to Zheng Qiao 鄭樵, Yan Kejun 嚴可均, Wu Dacheng 吳大澂, and Lin Xiguang 林義光. See Tang, *An Introduction to Paleography*, in *Tang Lan quanji*, 5:275–76.

84. *Tang Lan quanji*, 5:292; Tang, *Zhongguo wenzixue*, 66–69.

85. Tang, *Zhongguo wenzixue*, 89.

86. Tang announced, "From a historical point of view, a radically progressive alphabet is not viable. The path in front of the Chinese script should be how to reform these phonetic ideo-phonographs"; *Zhongguo wenzixue*, 98. Mistaking ideo-phonographs with either ideographs or pictographs is a historical problem: from Fang Yizhi to Qian Xuantong.
87. *Zhongguo wenzixue*, 96–97.
88. See Tang's unpublished proposal "Zhongguo wenzi gaige de lilun he fang'an" 中國文字改革的理論和方案 (A theory and plan for the Chinese script reform), in *Tang Lan quanji*, 11:1433.
89. Tang includes principles and examples of the new ideo-phonographs in *Tang Lan quanji*, 5:295–310.
90. The main points of the ten principles include five hundred basic characters, forty or so phonographs, tonal representation around all four sides of the vowel, and the left-right character formation as the only combinational method for the new ideo-phonographs; see *Tang Lan quanji*, 5:302–4.
91. *Tang Lan quanji*, 5:306–8.
92. *Tang Lan quanji*, 5:308.
93. Tang, *Zhongguo wenzixue*, 6–7.
94. Derrida, *Of Grammatology*, 3.
95. Derrida, *Of Grammatology*, 3–4.
96. Plato, *Phaedrus*; Heidegger's concept of *Urwort* in *Das Wesen der Sprache* and *Das Wort* in *Unterwegs zur Sprache* (1959), as quoted in Derrida, *Of Grammatology*, part 1, chap. 1, n. 11, 380. Derrida devotes part 2, chap. 1, 109–52, to an associative and comparative reading of Claude Lévi-Strauss's *Tristes tropiques* and Jean-Jacques Rousseau's *Essay on the Origin of Languages*.
97. Derrida, *Of Grammatology*, 3, 13.
98. Tang, *Tang Lan quanji*, 3:970.
99. Tang, *Tang Lan quanji*, 3:970.
100. As Derrida puts it, the epoch of logocentrism is enabled by first a separation between speech and writing and then a concealment of this separation: "The traditional and fundamental ethnocentrism which, inspired by the model of phonetic writing, separates writing from speech with an ax, is thus handled and thought of as anti-ethnocentrism." This separation gives rise to a particular "concept of writing in a world where the phoneticization of writing must dissimulate its own history as it is produced" (*Of Grammatology*, 3, 131).
101. Within the tradition of the six principles of character formation, philologists agree that pictographs were invented first. Some pictograph fundamentalists would argue that all other five principles were corruptions of the pictographs, such as the thirteenth-century philologist Dai Tong; see *Liu shu tong shi*, as cited in Bruce Rusk, "Old Scripts, New Actors: European Encounters with Chinese Writing, 1550–1700," *East Asian Science, Technology, and Medicine*, no. 26 (2007): 88. Rusk lists examples of the Chinese use of paleography, valorizing the pictographic form over the phonetic elements, but it is important to note that any case of preference indicates the coexistence of the pictographic and phonetic (85, 87).
102. Rusk, "Old Scripts, New Actors," 104. In addition to a comparison between the Egyptian hieroglyph and Chinese ideogram, Rusk also points to the irony that

Jean-François Champollion, who coined the term "ideogram," also proved that "the Egyptian hieroglyphs were used phonetically" (108).

103. Tang, *Tang Lan quanji*, 3:996.

104. I use the term "inversion" in the same way Kojin Karatani uses the term *tentō* 転倒. See Brett de Bary's introduction to Kojin Karatani, *Origins of Modern Japanese Literature*, trans. Brett de Bary et al. (Durham, N.C.: Duke University Press, 1993), 1–10.

105. Derrida, *Of Grammatology*, 34, 37.

106. Derrida, *Of Grammatology*, 343.

107. This is Derrida's language summarizing Rousseau's idea; *Of Grammatology*, 319.

108. Derrida, *Of Grammatology*, 317.

109. The quotations are Derrida's language in discussing Rousseau's idea of the alphabet; see the section "The Alphabet and Absolute Representation" in *Of Grammatology*, 321–29.

110. Derrida, *Of Grammatology*, 319.

111. Rousseau's—by extension Derrida's—fascination with the ideo-phonogram extends itself from the previous section on "The History and System of Scripts" to the next one on "The Alphabet and Absolute Representation." The full quote reads, "Direct—or hieroglyphic—pictography represents the thing—or the signified. The ideo-phonogram already represents a mixture of signifier and signified. It already paints language [*langue*]. It is the moment located by all historians of writing as the birth of phoneticization, for example, through the procedure of the picture puzzle [*rébus à transfert*]; a sign representing a thing named in its concept ceases to refer to the concept and keeps only the value of a phonic signifier. Its signified is no longer anything but a phoneme deprived by itself of all sense. But before this decomposition and in spite of the 'double convention,' representation is reproduction; it repeats the signifying and signified masses en bloc, without analysis. This synthetic character of representation is the pictographic residue of the ideo-phonogram that 'paints voices'" (Derrida, *Of Grammatology*, 325).

112. Derrida, *Of Grammatology*, 326.

113. Derrida, *Of Grammatology*, 327.

114. Derrida, *Of Grammatology*, 325.

115. Derrida, *Of Grammatology*, 37, 40. Derrida devotes the entire second chapter in part 1 to illustrating the traditional exclusion of writing from the field of linguistics by linguists, Saussure being the most prominent example.

116. Derrida, *Of Grammatology*, 176.

117. Spivak amends her translation in the new edition, Derrida, *Of Grammatology*, 25.

118. Derrida, *Of Grammatology*, 20.

119. Derrida, *Of Grammatology*, 25.

120. Derrida, *Of Grammatology*, 350.

121. Derrida, *Of Grammatology*, 3–4.

122. At the time of the official decree of the first batch of simplified characters, the committee also announced another 285 simplified characters and 54 simplified radicals for experimentation. Although the use of simplified characters was mandatory, there were exceptions, such as reprints of classic works. See Wang Jun, *Dangdai zhongguo de wenzi gaige*, 73–74, 106.

123. Liu Xie 劉勰, *Wenxin diaolong* 文心雕龍 (The literary mind and the carving of dragons) (Shanghai: Shanghai guji chubanshe, 2008), 1–2.
124. This article was published by the *People's Daily* on October 6, 1956, in the middle of his engagement in the public debate; see Tang, *Tang Lan quanji*, 3:953–55.
125. Tang, *Tang Lan quanji*, 3:955. Tang's call for the independence of grammatology is particularly poignant if read in contrast with Ku-ming Kevin Chang's brilliant study on the split between linguistics and philology in favor of linguistics in the naming of the Institute of History and Philology at Academia Sinica, "Philology or Linguistics?," in *World Philology*, ed. Sheldon Pollock, Benjamin A. Elman, and Ku-ming Kevin Chang (Cambridge, Mass.: Harvard University Press, 2015), 311–31. I thank Meng Yue for urging me to piece together the parallel developments that weakened the study of writing in favor of the study of language across the strait.

EPILOGUE

1. Although the Committee for Chinese Script Reform changed its name to the State Language Commission in 1985, its address at No. 51 Chaoyangmennei nanxiaojie remained the same.
2. See Benjamin A. Elman, *Classicism, Politics, and Kinship: The Ch'ang-chou School of New Text Confucianism in Late Imperial China* (Berkeley: University of California Press, 1990).
3. The 1925 May Thirtieth Movement was the landmark event leading to the founding of Guanghua University—later renamed East China Normal University—by a group of Chinese students and faculty from St. John's in protest of the proimperialist and antilabor movement stance of St. John's. The key figure who led the "breakup" was another Changzhou local, Meng Xiancheng, who also played a big role in attracting Zhou to mass education upon graduation. See Zhou Youguang 周有光, *Shi nian ru shui* 逝年如水 (Lost years like water) (Hangzhou: Zhejiang daxue chubanshe, 2015), 27–34, 40–49.
4. Zhou documented his discussions of Sin Wenz with the CCP Latinization veteran Xu Teli in Changsha during the Civil War (1947–1949); Zhou Youguang, *Shi nian ru shui*, 87, 155.
5. Zhou Youguang 周有光, *Zhongguo pinyin wenzi yanjiu* 中國拼音文字研究 (Shanghai: Shanghai dongfang shudian, 1953).
6. For a series of commemorative essays on the official recognition of pinyin, see *Hanyu pinyin fang'an de zhiding he yingyong* 漢語拼音方案的制定和應用 (The design and application of the Chinese pinyin plan) (Beijing: Wenzi gaige chubanshe, 1983). Zhou's essay on the three principles—Latinized, phonemicized, and colloquialized—of pinyin is included in Zhou Youguang, *Zhongguo pinyin wenzi yanjiu*, 53–59.
7. For Zhou's account of the ISO conference, see *Shi nian ru shui*, 394–98.
8. For a few samples of Zhou's essays on *yuwen* modernization, see "Xin yuwen de jianshe" 新语文的建设 (Constructing a new language and writing), in Zhou Youguang 周有光, *Zhou Youguang wenji* 周有光文集 (The collected works of Zhou Youguang), 15 vols. (Beijing: Zhongyang bianyi chubanshe, 2013), 5:13–53; "Xin

yuwen he xin jishu" 新语文和新技术 (New *yuwen*, new technology), *Zhou Youguang wenji*, 5:317–58; "Wo he yuwen xiandaihua" 我和语文现代化 (*Yuwen* modernization and I), *Zhou Youguang wenji*, 14:468.

9. Zhou's *Hanzi gaige gailun* 漢字改革概論 was a compilation of lecture notes for a course he taught at Peking University between 1958 and 1959 at the invitation of fellow linguist and committee member Wang Li. The book was first published in 1961 and was revised and collected in *Zhou Youguang wenji*, 1:9–420; the quote is on 405.

10. Zhou explains how both the so-called simplified and traditional characters have violated the six principles of character formation and could be unified based on the two lists of simplification; see *Zhou Youguang wenji*, 10:138. Employing the two concepts, Zhou proposes a new *genbun itchi* of Chinese language and writing (5:671–79).

SELECTED BIBLIOGRAPHY

ARCHIVES

American Bible Society, New York.
International Institute of Rural Reconstruction records, Rare Book and Manuscript Library, Columbia University, New York.
Qu Qiubai Museum, Changzhou, Jiangsu Province.
Rulan Chao Pian Music Collection, Chung Chi College Elisabeth Luce Moore Library, Chinese University of Hong Kong, Hong Kong.
Tao Xingzhi Archive, Tao Xingzhi Museum, She County, Anhui Province.
Yuen Ren Chao papers, Bancroft Library, University of California, Berkeley.

NEWSPAPERS AND PERIODICALS

Guoyu yuekan 國語月刊 (National language monthly).
Guoyu zhoukan 國語週刊 (National language weekly).
Jidujiao qingnianhui zhufa huagong zhoubao 基督教青年會駐法華工週報 (YMCA Chinese labor workers' weekly).
Pinyin 拼音 (renamed *Wenzi gaige* in August 1957).
Wenzi gaige 文字改革 (Script reform).
Xin jiaoyu 新教育 (New education).
Xin qingnian 新青年 (New youth).
Xin shehui 新社會 (New society).
Zhongguo yuwen 中國語文 (Chinese language and writing)

OTHER SOURCES

Anderson, Benedict. *Imagined Communities: Reflections on the Origin and Spread of Nationalism*. London: Verso, 2006.

——. *Language and Power: Exploring Political Cultures in Indonesia*. Ithaca, N.Y.: Cornell University Press, 1990.

——. "Western Nationalism and Eastern Nationalism." *New Left Review* 9 (May–June 2001): 31–42.

Anderson, Marston. *The Limits of Realism: Chinese Fiction in the Revolutionary Period*. Berkeley: University of California Press, 1990.

Bachner, Andrea. *Beyond Sinology: Chinese Writing and the Scripts of Culture*. New York: Columbia University Press, 2014.

Bell, Alexander Melville. *Visible Speech: The Science of Universal Alphabetics*. London: Simpkin, Marshall, 1867.

Bernards, Brian. *Writing the South Seas: Imagining the Nanyang in Chinese and Southeast Asian Postcolonial Literature*. Seattle: University of Washington Press, 2015.

Bloomfield, Leonard. *An Introduction to the Study of Language*. New York: Holt, 1914.

Boase, Paul, ed. *The Rhetoric of Christian Socialism*. New York: Random House, 1969.

Broomhall, Marshall. *The Bible in China*. London: China Inland Mission, 1934.

Buck, Pearl. *Tell the People: Talks with James Yen About the Mass Education Movement*. New York: Day, 1945.

Bush, Christopher. *Ideographic Modernism: China, Writing, Media*. Oxford: Oxford University Press, 2010.

Capps, John M., and Donald Capps, eds. *James and Dewey on Belief and Experience*. Urbana: University of Illinois Press, 2005.

Chan, Gerald. "China and the Esperanto Movement." *Australian Journal of Chinese Affairs*, no. 15 (January 1986): 1–18.

Chao, Yuen Ren 趙元任. "Guanyu su'e de ladinghua zhongguoyu" 关于苏俄的拉丁化中国语 (Regarding the Latinization of Chinese in the Soviet Union). *Guoyu zhoukan* 國語週刊 (National language weekly) 6, no. 139 (May 26, 1934).

——. *Language and Symbolic Systems*. Cambridge: Cambridge University Press, 1968.

——. *Mandarin Primer: An Intensive Course in Spoken Chinese*. Cambridge, Mass.: Harvard University Press, 1948.

——. "The Problem of the Chinese Language: Scientific Study of Chinese Philology." *Chinese Students' Monthly* 11, no. 6 (1916): 437–43; no. 7 (1916): 500–509; no. 8 (1916): 572–93.

——. *Tzueyhow wuu-fen jong* 最後五分鐘 (The last five minutes). Shanghai: Zhonghua shuju, 1929.

——. *Xiandai wuyu de yanjiu* 現代吳語的研究 (Studies of the modern Wu dialects). 1928. Reprint, Beijing: Commercial Press, 2011.

——. *Zhao Yuanren quanji* 趙元任全集 (The complete works of Yuen Ren Chao). Vols. 1, 3, 11, 14–16. Beijing: Commercial Press, 2002–2007.

——. *Zhao Yuanren yuyanxue lunwenji* 趙元任語言學論文集 (Collection of Yuen Ren Chao's linguistic essays). Beijing: Commercial Press, 2002.

Chen Feng 陳奮, ed. *Liang Shiyi shi liao ji* 梁士詒史料集 (Historical materials of Liang Shiyi). Beijing: Zhongguo wenshi chubanshe, 1991.

Chen Hansheng 陳翰笙, ed. *Huagong chuguo shiliao* 華工出國史料 (Historical materials of overseas Chinese laborers). 10 vols. Beijing: Zhonghua shuju, 1980.

Chen Heqin 陳鶴琴. *Chen Heqin quanji* 陳鶴琴全集 (The complete works of Chen Heqin). 6 vols. Nanjing: Jiangsu jiaoyu chubanshe, 1992.

———. "Latinization of the Chinese Language." *China Quarterly* 3 (1938): 155–66.

———. *Wo de bansheng* 我的半生 (Half my life). Shanghai: Huahua shudian, 1946.

———. *Yutiwen yingyong zihui* 語體文應用字彙 (The vocabulary of applied *yutiwen*). Shanghai: Commercial Press, 1933.

Chen Mengjia 陳夢家. *Mengjiashi cun wen* 夢甲室存文 (An essay collection of the Mengjia studio). Beijing: Zhonghua shuju, 2006.

———. *Tie ma ji* 鐵馬集 (Iron horse collection). Shanghai: Kaiming shudian, 1934.

Chen Sanjing 陳三井. *Huagong yu ouzhan* 華工與歐戰 (Chinese laborers and the European war). Taipei: Academia Sinica, 1986.

Chen Sanjing 陳三井, Lü Fangshang 呂芳上, and Yang Cuihua 楊翠華, eds. *Ouzhan huagong shiliao* 歐戰華工史料 (Historical records of Chinese laborers in the European war). Taipei: Academia Sinica, 1997.

Chow, Tse-tsung. *The May Fourth Movement: Intellectual Revolution in Modern China.* Cambridge, Mass.: Harvard University Press, 1960.

Clark, Katherine. *The Soviet Novel: History as Ritual.* Chicago: University of Chicago Press, 1981.

Coulmas, Florian. *The Writing Systems of the World.* Oxford: Blackwell, 1989.

Crespi, John. *Voices in Revolution: Poetry and the Auditory Imagination in Modern China.* Honolulu: University of Hawai'i Press, 2009.

Culp, Robert. *Articulating Citizenship: Civic Education and Student Politics in Southeastern China, 1912–1940.* Cambridge, Mass.: Harvard University Press, 2007.

Darwin, Charles. *The Descent of Man, and Selection in Relation to Sex.* 1871. Reprint, Cambridge: Cambridge University Press, 2009.

Davis, John A. *The Chinese Slave-Girl: A Story of Woman's Life in China.* Chicago: Student Missionary Campaign Library, 1880.

———. *Leng Tso, the Chinese Bible-Woman: A Sequel to "The Chinese Slave-Girl."* Philadelphia: Presbyterian Board of Publication, 1886.

DeFrancis, John. *The Chinese Language: Fact and Fantasy.* Honolulu: University of Hawai'i Press, 1984.

———. *Colonialism and Language Policy in Vietnam.* The Hague: Mouton, 1977.

———. *Nationalism and Language Reform in China.* Princeton, N.J.: Princeton University Press, 1950.

Denning, Michael. *The Cultural Front: The Laboring of American Culture in the Twentieth Century.* London: Verso, 2010.

Denton, Kirk A., ed. *Modern Chinese Literary Thought: Writings on Literature, 1893–1945.* Stanford, Calif.: Stanford University Press, 1996.

Derrida, Jacques. *Monolingualism of the Other; or, The Prosthesis of Origin.* Translated by Patrick Mensah. Stanford, Calif.: Stanford University Press, 1998.

———. *Of Grammatology.* Translated by Gayatri Chakravorty Spivak. Baltimore: Johns Hopkins University Press, 2016.

Ding Wenjiang 丁文江. *Liang Qichao nian pu chang bian* 梁啟超年譜長編 (The long genealogy of Liang Qichao). Shanghai: Shanghai renmin chubanshe, 1983.

Dirlik, Arif. "The Ideological Foundations of the New Life Movement: A Study in Counterrevolution." *Journal of Asian Studies* 34, no. 4 (August 1975): 945–80.

Driver, Godfrey Rolles. *Semitic Writing: From Pictograph to Alphabet*. London: Oxford University Press, 1976.

Du Zijing 杜子劲, ed. *1949 nian zhongguo wenzi gaige lunwenji* 一九四九年中國文字改革論文集 (Papers on Chinese language reform in 1949). Beijing: Dazhong shudian, 1950.

Eco, Umberto. *The Search for the Perfect Language*. Oxford: Blackwell, 1997.

Elman, Benjamin A. *Classicism, Politics, and Kinship: The Ch'ang-chou School of New Text Confucianism in Late Imperial China*. Berkeley: University of California Press, 1990.

——. *From Philosophy to Philology: Intellectual and Social Aspects of Change in Late Imperial China*. 2nd ed. Los Angeles: University of California Press, 2001.

——. *On Their Own Terms: Science in China, 1550–1900*. Cambridge, Mass.: Harvard University Press, 2005.

Ertürk, Nergis. *Grammatology and Literary Modernity in Turkey*. Oxford: Oxford University Press, 2011.

Fabian, Johannes. *Time and the Other: How Anthropology Makes Its Object*. New York: Columbia University Press, 2002.

Fairbank, John King. *Chinabound: A Fifty-Year Memoir*. New York: HarperCollins, 1983.

——. *The Great Chinese Revolution*. New York: Harper and Row, 1986.

Feng Gang 鳳岡 et al., eds. *Minguo Liang Yansun xiansheng shiyi nianpu* 民國梁燕孫先生士詒年譜 (The life chronology of Liang Shiyi). Taipei: Commercial Press, 1978.

Fitzgerald, John. *Awakening China: Politics, Culture, and Class in the Nationalist Revolution*. Stanford, Calif.: Stanford University Press, 1996.

Fitzpatrick, Sheila. *The Commissariat of Enlightenment: Soviet Organization of Education and the Arts under Lunacharsky, October 1917–1921*. Cambridge: Cambridge University Press, 1970.

Fufa qinggong jianxue yundong shiliao 赴法勤工儉學運動史料 (Historical records of the work-study program in France). 3 vols. Beijing: Beijing chubanshe, 1979–1981.

Gedi renshi jilai hanyu pinyin wenzi fang'an huibian 各地人士寄来汉语拼音文字方案汇编 (A compilation of plans for alphabetic Chinese mailed in from all over China). 2 vols. Beijing: Zhongguo wenzi gaige weiyuanhui pinyin fang'an bu, 1954–1955.

Gelb, I. J. *A Study of Writing*. Chicago: University of Chicago Press, 1952.

Geng Zhensheng 耿振生, ed. *Jindai guanhua yuyin yanjiu* 近代官話語音研究 (Studies of the phonology of Mandarin in early modern China). Beijing: Yuwen chubanshe, 2007.

Gitelman, Lisa. *Scripts, Grooves, and Writing Machines: Representing Technology in the Edison Era*. Stanford, Calif.: Stanford University Press, 1999.

Graft, Stephen G. "Angling for an Invitation to Paris: China's Entry into the First World War." *International Historical Review* 16, no. 1 (February 1994): 1–24.

Grenoble, Lenore A. *Language Policy in the Soviet Union*. Dordrecht: Kluwer Academic, 2003.

Griffin, Nicholas John. "The Use of Chinese Labour by the British Army, 1916–1920: The 'Raw Importation,' Its Scope and Problems." PhD diss., University of Oklahoma, 1973.

Gu Xingqing 顧杏卿. *Ouzhan gongzuo huiyilu* 歐戰工作回憶錄 (Recollections of working in the European war). Changsha: Commercial Press, 1937.

Gunn, Edward. *Rendering the Regional: Local Language in Contemporary Chinese Media*. Honolulu: University of Hawai`i Press, 2006.

Hamilton, W. B., Mrs. *The Chinese Bible Woman*. New York: Women's Board of Foreign Missions of the Presbyterian Church, n.d.

Harootunian, Harry. *Overcome by Modernity: History, Culture, and Community in Interwar Japan*. Princeton, N.J.: Princeton University Press, 2000.

Harris, Roy. *Language, Saussure and Wittgenstein: How to Play Games with Words*. New York: Routledge, 1990.

Harris, Roy, and Talbot Taylor, eds. *Landmarks in Linguistic Thought I: The Western Tradition from Socrates to Saussure*. New York: Routledge, 1997.

Haugen, Einar. "Dialect, Language, Nation." *American Anthropologist* 68, no. 4 (August 1966): 922–35.

Havelock, Eric. *Origins of Western Literacy*. Toronto: Ontario Institute for Studies in Education, 1976.

Hayford, Charles. *To the People: James Yen and Village China*. New York: Columbia University Press, 1990.

Hayles, N. Katherine. *How We Became Posthuman: Virtual Bodies in Cybernetics, Literature, and Informatics*. Chicago: University of Chicago Press, 1999.

Hayot, Eric, Haun Saussy, and Steven G. Yao, eds. *Sinographies: Writing China*. Minneapolis: University of Minnesota Press, 2008.

Heidegger, Martin. *The Question Concerning Technology and Other Essays*. Translated by William Lovitt. New York: Harper Torchbooks, 1977.

Hessler, Peter. *Oracle Bones: A Journey Between China's Past and Present*. New York: HarperCollins, 2006.

Hill, Michael G. "New Script and a New 'Madman's Diary.'" *Modern Chinese Literature and Culture* 27, no. 1 (Spring 2015): 75–104.

Hobsbawm, Eric. *The Age of Extremes: A History of the World, 1914–1991*. New York: Vintage Books, 1996.

Hsia, C. T. *A History of Modern Chinese Fiction, 1917–1957*. New Haven, Conn.: Yale University Press, 1971.

Hu Shi 胡適. *Hu Shi quanji* 胡適全集 (The complete works of Hu Shi). 37 vols. Hefei: Anhui jiaoyu chubanshe, 2003.

——. *Hu Shi wenji* 胡適文集 (The collected works of Hu Shi). 12 vols. Beijing: Beijing daxue chubanshe, 1998.

Huang Dekuan 黃德寬 and Chen Bingxin 陳秉新. *Han yu wen zi xue shi* 漢語文字學史 (History of Chinese philology). Hefei: Anhui jiaoyu chubanshe, 1990.

Hung, Chang-tai. *Going to the People: Chinese Intellectuals and Folk Literature, 1918–1937*. Cambridge, Mass.: Harvard University Press, 1985.

Huters, Theodore. "The Difficult Guest: May Fourth Revisits." *Chinese Literature* 6, no. 1/2 (July 1984): 125–49.

——. "Legibility vs. the Fullness of Expression: Rethinking the Transformation of Modern Chinese Prose." *Journal of Modern Literature in Chinese* 10, no. 2 (December): 80–104.

Ivy, Marilyn. *Discourses of the Vanishing: Modernity, Phantasm, Japan*. Chicago: University of Chicago Press, 1995.

Jameson, Fredric. *The Antinomies of Realism*. London: Verso, 2013.

——. *The Prison-House of Language: A Critical Account of Structuralism and Russian Formalism*. Princeton, N.J.: Princeton University Press, 1972.

Ji Jianqing 季劍青. "'Sheng' zhi tanqiu: Lu Xun baihua xiezuo de qiyuan" 聲之探求：魯迅白話寫作的起源 (In search of "sheng": The origin of Lu Xun's *baihua* writing). *Wenxue pinglun* 文學評論 (Literary review), no. 3 (2018): 104–14.

Jones, Andrew F. *Developmental Fairy Tales: Evolutionary Thinking and Modern Chinese Culture*. Cambridge, Mass.: Harvard University Press, 2011.

Joseph, John E. *Saussure*. Oxford: Oxford University Press, 2012.

Kalfus, Ken. *The Commissariat of Enlightenment*. New York: Ecco, 2003.

Karatani, Kojin. "Nationalism and *Écriture*." *Surfaces* 5, no. 201.1 (1995): 1–25.

——. *Origins of Modern Japanese Literature*. Translated by Brett de Bary et al. Durham, N.C.: Duke University Press, 1993.

Karl, Rebecca. *Staging the World: Chinese Nationalism at the Turn of the Twentieth Century*. Durham, N.C.: Duke University Press, 2002.

——. "A World Gone Wrong." *London Review of Books* 33, no. 23 (December 2011): 23–24.

Karlgren, Bernhard. *Études sur la phonologie chinoise*. Leiden: Brill, 1915–1926.

——. *Philology and Ancient China*. Oslo: Aschehoug; Cambridge, Mass.: Harvard University Press, 1926.

——. *The Romanization of Chinese: A Paper Read Before the China Society on January 19, 1928*. London: China Society, 1928.

——. *Zhongguo yinyunxue yanjiu* 中國音韻學研究 (A study on Chinese philology). Translated by Yuen Ren Chao and Fang-Kuei Li. Taipei: Taiwan Commercial Press, 1962.

Kaske, Elizabeth. *The Politics of Language in Chinese Education, 1895–1919*. Leiden: Brill, 2008.

Kemp-Welch, A. *Stalin and the Literary Intelligentsia, 1928–39*. New York: Palgrave Macmillan, 1991.

Kittler, Friedrich. *Gramophone, Film, Typewriter*. Stanford, Calif.: Stanford University Press, 1999.

Kiyama Hideo 木山英雄. *Wenxue fugu yu wenxue geming* 文学复古与文学革命 (Literary restoration and literary revolution). Translated by Zhao Jinghua. Beijing: Beijing daxue chubanshe, 2004.

Koeneke, Rodney. *Empires of the Mind: I. A. Richards and Basic English in China, 1929–1979*. Stanford, Calif.: Stanford University Press, 2004.

Lahusen, Thomas. "*Cement*." In *The Novel, Volume 2: Forms and Themes*, edited by Franco Moretti, 476–82. Princeton, N.J.: Princeton University Press, 2006.

——. *How Life Writes the Book: Real Socialism and Socialist Realism in Stalin's Russia*. Ithaca, N.Y.: Cornell University Press, 1997.

Lanza, Fabio. *Behind the Gate: Inventing Students in Beijing*. New York: Columbia University Press, 2010.

Lao She 老舍. *Laoniu poche xinbian: Lao She chuangzuo zishu* 《老牛破車》新編—老舍創作自述 (New edition of the *Old Bull and the Broken Cart*: Autobiographical account of Lao She's writing). Hong Kong: Sanlian shudian, 1986.

Lau, Joseph S. M., C. T. Hsia, Leo Ou-fan Lee, eds. *Modern Chinese Stories and Novellas, 1919–1949*. New York: Columbia University Press, 1981.

Lee, Yeounsuk. *The Ideology of* Kokugo: *Nationalizing Language in Modern Japan.* Translated by Maki Hirano Hubbard. Honolulu: University of Hawai`i Press, 2010.

Lehmann, Winfred P. *Historical Linguistics: An Introduction.* New York: Routledge, 1993.

Levin, Thomas Y. "'Tones from out of Nowhere': Rudolph Pfenninger and the Archaeology of Synthetic Sound." *Grey Room*, no. 12 (Summer 2003): 32–79.

Lew, Timothy Ting-fang. "The Psychology of Learning Chinese: A Preliminary Analysis by Means of Experimental Psychology of Some of the Factors Involved in the Process of Learning Chinese Characters." PhD diss., Columbia University, 1920.

Li, Fang-Kuei 李方桂. "Languages and Dialects of China." *Chinese Year Book*, 1936–1937, 121–28. Reprinted in *Journal of Chinese Linguistics* 1, no. 1 (1973): 1–13.

Li Jinxi 黎錦熙. *Guoyu mofan duben shouce* 國語模範讀本首冊 (First volume of the model reader of the national language). Shanghai: Zhonghua shuju, 1928.

——. *Guoyu si qian nian lai bianhua chaoliu tu* 國語四千年來變化潮流圖 (Diagram showing the evolution of Chinese over the past four millenniums). Beiping: Wenhua xue she, 1929.

——. *Guoyu yundong shigang* 國語運動史綱 (The historical *Grundrisse* of the national language movement). 1935. Reprint, Beijing: Commercial Press, 2011.

Liang Qichao 梁啟超. *Ou you xin ying lu* 歐遊心影錄 (Reflections on a European journey). Hong Kong: San da chubanshe, 1963.

Lin Tao 林燾 and Geng Zhensheng 耿振生. *Yinyunxue gaiyao* 音韵学概要 (An outline of phonology). Beijing: Commercial Press, 2004.

Lin, Yü-sheng [林毓生]. *Crisis of Chinese Consciousness: Radical Antitraditionalism in the May Fourth Era.* Madison: University of Wisconsin Press, 1979.

Liu Jincai 劉進才. *Yuyan yundong yu zhongguo xiandai wenxue* 語言運動與中國現代文學 (The language movement and modern Chinese literature). Beijing: Zhonghua shuju, 2007.

Liu, Lydia H. *The Clash of Empires: The Invention of China in Modern World Making.* Cambridge, Mass.: Harvard University Press, 2004.

——. *The Freudian Robot: Digital Media and the Future of the Unconscious.* Chicago: University of Chicago Press, 2010.

——. "Translingual Folklore and Folklorics in China." In *A Companion to Folklore*, edited by Regina F. Bendix and Galit Hasan-Rokem, 190–210. Malden, Mass.: Wiley-Blackwell, 2012.

——. *Translingual Practice: Literature, National Culture, and Translated Modernity—China, 1900–1937.* Stanford, Calif.: Stanford University Press, 1995.

Liu Xie 劉勰. *Wenxin diaolong* 文心雕龍 (The literary mind and the carving of dragons). Shanghai: Shanghai guji chubanshe, 2008.

Liu Zengren 劉增人 and Feng Guanglian 馮光廉, eds. *Ye Shengtao yanjiu ziliao* 葉聖陶研究資料 (Research materials on Ye Shengtao). Beijing: Shiyue wenyi chubanshe, 1988.

Lu Fayan 陸法言. *Qieyun* 切韻 (Rhyme phoneticization). Nanjing: Jiangsu guangling guji keyinshe, 1987.

Lu Xun 魯迅. *Lu Xun quanji* 魯迅全集 (The complete works of Lu Xun). 18 vols. Beijing: Renmin wenxue chubanshe, 2005.

Lu Zhuangzhang 盧戇章. *Yimu liaoran chujie* 一目了然初階 (A primer at a glance). 1892. Reprint, Beijing: Wenzi gaige chubanshe, 1956.

Luo Changpei 羅常培. "Yesuhuishi zai yinyunxue shang de gongxian" 耶穌會士在音韻學上的貢獻 (The Jesuits' contributions in philology). *Bulletin of the Institute of History and Philology, Academia Sinica* 1, no. 3 (1930): 267–338.

Luo Jialun 羅家倫. *Jiantizi yundong* 簡體字運動 (The movement for simplified characters). Taipei: Zhongyang wenwu gongyingshe, 1954.

Lurie, David. "Language, Writing, and Disciplinarity in the Critique of the 'Ideographic Myth': Some Proleptical Remarks." *Language and Communication* 26 (2006): 250–69.

——. *Realms of Literacy: Early Japan and the History of Writing.* Cambridge, Mass.: Harvard University Press, 2011.

MacMillan, Margaret. *Paris 1919: Six Months That Changed the World.* New York: Random House, 2002.

Mair, Victor H. "Advocates of Script Reform." In *Sources of Chinese Tradition*, edited by Wm. Theodore de Bary and Richard Lufrano, 2:302–7. New York: Columbia University Press, 2000.

——. "Language and Script." In *The Columbia History of Chinese Literature*, edited by Victor H. Mair, 19–57. New York: Columbia University Press, 2001.

Malmqvist, N. G. D. *Bernhard Karlgren: Portrait of a Scholar.* Bethlehem, Penn.: Lehigh University Press, 2010.

Manela, Erez. *The Wilsonian Moment: Self-Determination and the International Origins of Anticolonial Nationalism.* Oxford: Oxford University Press, 2007.

——. *Zhongguo gongchandang zai minzu zhanzheng zhong de diwei* 中國共產黨在民族戰爭中的地位 (The Chinese Communist Party's status in the national war). Beijing: Waiwen chubanshe, 1958.

Martin, Terry. *The Affirmative Action Empire: Nations and Nationalism in the Soviet Union, 1923–1939.* Ithaca, N.Y.: Cornell University Press, 2001.

McLuhan, Marshall. *Understanding Media: The Extensions of Man.* Corte Madera, Calif.: Gingko Press, 2003.

Mei Tsu-lin 梅祖麟. "Bijiao fangfa zai zhongguo, 1926–1998" 比較方法在中國, 1926–1998 (The comparative method in China, 1926–1998). *Yuyan yanjiu* 語言研究 (Studies in language and linguistics) 23, no. 1 (March 2003): 16–27.

Meng, Yue. *Shanghai and the Edges of Empires.* Minneapolis: University of Minnesota Press, 2006.

Milne, A. A. *Second Plays.* London: Chatto and Windus, 1928.

Mishra, Pankaj. "Ordained as a Nation." *London Review of Books* 30, no. 4 (February 2008): 3–8.

Mitchell, Timothy. *Colonizing Egypt.* Berkeley: University of California Press, 1991.

Moser, David. *A Billion Voices: China's Search for a Common Language.* Sydney: Penguin Books Australia, 2016.

Mullaney, Thomas. *The Chinese Typewriter: A History.* Cambridge, Mass.: MIT Press, 2017.

Murthy, Viren. *The Political Philosophy of Zhang Taiyan: The Resistance of Consciousness.* Leiden: Brill, 2011.

Ni Haishu 倪海曙. *"Latinxua Sin Wenz yndong" de shi-mo he biannian jishi* 拉丁化新文字運動的始末和編年紀事 (The beginning and end of the Chinese Latinization movement and its chronology). Shanghai: Zhishi chubanshe, 1987.

——. *Qingmo hanyu pinyin wenzi yundong biannianshi* 清末漢語拼音文字運動編年史 (Chronology of the late-Qing Chinese alphabetization movement). Shanghai: Shanghai renmin chubanshe, 1959.

——. *Zhongguo pinyin wenzi yundongshi jianbian* 中國拼音文字運動史簡編 (A concise chronology of the Chinese alphabetization movement). Shanghai: Shidai shubao chubanshe, 1948.

——. *Zhungguo pinjin wenz gailun* 中國拼音文字概論 (An introduction to the Chinese alphabetic script). Shanghai: Shidai chubanshe, 1948.

——. *Zhungguo yunwen de xinsheng: Latinxua zhungguoz yndung 20 nian lunwenzi* 中國語文的新生：拉丁化中國字運動二十年論文集 (The new life of Chinese: Anthology of the Chinese Latinization movement on its twentieth anniversary). Shanghai: Shidai chubanshe, 1949.

Ni Huiru 倪慧如 and Zou Ningyuan 鄒寧遠. *Gan lan gui guan de zhao huan: Can jia Xibanya nei zhan de zhongguo ren, 1936–1939* 橄欖桂冠的召喚：參加西班牙內戰的中國人 (The call of Spain: Chinese volunteers in the Spanish Civil War). Taipei: Renjian chubanshe, 2001.

Nie Hongyin 聶鴻音. *Zhongguo wenzi gailue* 中國文字概略 (A concise introduction to Chinese writing). Beijing: Yuwen chubanshe, 1998.

Norman, Jerry. *Chinese.* Cambridge: Cambridge University Press, 1988.

O'Conner, Timothy Edward. *The Politics of Soviet Culture: Anatolii Lunacharskii.* Ann Arbor, Mich.: UMI Research Press, 1983.

Ogden, C. K. *C. K. Ogden and Linguistics.* London: Routledge/Thoemmes Press, 1994.

——. *Debabelization: With a Survey of Contemporary Opinion on the Problem of a Universal Language.* London: K. Paul, Trench, Trubner, 1931.

Ong, Walter. *Orality and Literacy: The Technologizing of the Word.* London: Routledge, 1991.

Phan, John. "Lacquered Words: The Evolution of Vietnamese under Sinitic Influences from the 1st Century BCE through the 17th Century." PhD diss., Cornell University, 2013.

Pickowicz, Paul. *Marxist Literary Thought in China: The Influence of Ch'ü Ch'iu-pai.* Berkeley: University of California Press, 1981.

Pollock, Sheldon, Benjamin A. Elman, and Ku-ming Kevin Chang, eds. *World Philology.* Cambridge, Mass.: Harvard University Press, 2015.

Poole, Janet. *When the Future Disappears: The Modernist Imagination in Late Colonial Korea.* New York: Columbia University Press, 2014.

Porter, David. *Ideographia: The Chinese Cipher in Early Modern Europe.* Stanford, Calif.: Stanford University Press, 2001.

Potter, Ralph K., George A. Kopp, and Harriet C. Green. *Visible Speech.* New York: Van Nostrand, 1947.

Průšek, Jaroslav. *The Lyrical and the Epic: Studies of Modern Chinese Literature.* Bloomington: Indiana University Press, 1980.

Pusey, James Reeve. *China and Charles Darwin.* Cambridge, Mass.: Harvard University Asia Center, 1983.

Qian Xuantong 錢玄同. *Qian Xuantong wenji* 錢玄同文集 (The collected works of Qian Xuantong). 6 vols. Beijing: Renmin daxue chubanshe, 1999.

Qu Qiubai 瞿秋白. *Qu Qiubai wenji wenxue bian* 瞿秋白文集文學編 (The literary compilation of the Qu Qiubai collection). 6 vols. Beijing: Renmin wenxue chubanshe, 1985–1989.

Ramsey, S. Robert. *The Languages of China.* Princeton, N.J.: Princeton University Press, 1987.

Rusk, Bruce. "Old Scripts, New Actors: European Encounters with Chinese Writing, 1550–1700." *East Asian Science, Technology, and Medicine,* no. 26 (2007): 68–116.

Saussure, Ferdinand de. *Course in General Linguistics.* Translated by Wade Baskin. Edited by Perry Meisel and Haun Saussy. New York: Columbia University Press, 2011.

Saussy, Haun. *The Ethnography of Rhythm: Orality and Its Technologies.* New York: Fordham University Press, 2016.

Schwarcz, Vera. *The Chinese Enlightenment: Intellectuals and the Legacy of the May Fourth Movement of 1919.* Berkeley: University of California Press, 1986.

Shang Jinlin 商金林. *Ye Shengtao nianpu* 葉聖陶年譜 (A chronicle of Ye Shengtao). Nanjing: Jiangsu jiaoyu chubanshe, 1986.

——. *Ye Shengtao nianpu changbian* 葉聖陶年譜長編 (An extended chronicle of Ye Shengtao). Beijing: Renmin jiaoyu chubanshe, 2004.

Shang, Wei. "Writing and Speech: Rethinking the Issue of Vernaculars in Early Modern China." In *Rethinking East Asian Languages, Vernaculars, and Literacies, 1000–1919,* edited by Benjamin A. Elman, 254–302. Leiden: Brill, 2015.

Shih, Shu-mei. *Visuality and Identity: Sinophone Articulations across the Pacific.* Berkeley: University of California Press, 2007.

Shih, Shu-mei, Tsai Chien-hsin, and Brian Bernards, eds. *Sinophone Studies: A Critical Reader.* New York: Columbia University Press, 2013.

Smith, Michael G. *Language and Power in the Creation of the USSR, 1917–1953.* Berlin: Mouton de Gruyter, 1998.

Snow, Edgar. "Awakening the Masses in China." *New York Herald Tribune,* December 17, 1933.

——. *Red Star Over China.* London: Gollancz, 1937.

Spivak, Gayatri Chakravorty. "Can the Subaltern Speak?" In *Can the Subaltern Speak? Reflections on the History of an Idea,* edited by Rosalind C. Morris, 21–78. New York: Columbia University Press, 2010.

Steinberg, Mark D. *Proletarian Imagination: Self, Modernity, and the Sacred in Russia, 1910–1925.* Ithaca, N.Y.: Cornell University Press, 2002.

Sterne, Jonathan. *The Audible Past: Cultural Origins of Sound Reproduction.* Durham, N.C.: Duke University Press, 2003.

Summerskill, Michael. *China on the Western Front: Britain's Chinese Work Force in the First World War.* London: Michael Summerskill, 1982.

Sun Xiaozhong 孙晓忠. "Cunzhuang zhong de wenshu xingzheng" 村莊中的文書行政 (Administrating the village through documents and writing). *Zhongguo xiandai wenxue yanjiu congkan* 中国现代文学研究丛刊 (Modern Chinese literature studies), no. 6 (2017): 41–57.

Tang Lan 唐蘭. *Tang Lan quanji* 唐蘭全集 (The complete works of Tang Lan). 12 vols. Shanghai: Shanghai guji chubanshe, 2015.

Tao, Xingzhi [陶行知]. *Education in China 1924.* Beijing: Commercial Press, 1925.

——. *Tao Xingzhi quanji* 陶行知全集 (The complete works of Tao Xingzhi). 8 vols. Changsha: Hunan jiaoyu chubanshe, 1984–1985.

——. *Tao Xingzhi quanji* 陶行知全集 (The complete works of Tao Xingzhi). 12 vols. Chengdu: Sichuan jiaoyu chubanshe, 1991.

——. *Xingzhi shuxinji* 行知書信集 (The collected correspondence of Tao Xingzhi). Hefei: Anhui renmin chubanshe, 1981.

Thomas, Lawrence L. *The Linguistic Theories of N. Ja. Marr*. University of California Publications in Linguistics, vol. vol. 14:85–116. Berkeley: University of California Press, 1957.

Thomson, James C., Jr. *While China Faced West: American Reformers in Nationalist China, 1928–1937*. Cambridge, Mass.: Harvard University Press, 1969.

Tseng, Gloria. "Chinese Pieces of the French Mosaic: The Chinese Experience in France and the Making of a Revolutionary Tradition." PhD diss., University of California, Berkeley, 2002.

Tsu, Jing. *Sound and Script in Chinese Diaspora*. Cambridge, Mass.: Harvard University Press, 2010.

Tsui, Brian. *China's Conservative Revolution: The Quest for a New Order, 1927–1949*. New York: Cambridge University Press, 2017.

Wang, David Der-wei. *Fin-de-Siècle Splendor: Repressed Modernities of Late Qing Fiction, 1848–1911*. Stanford, Calif.: Stanford University Press, 1997.

Wang Feng 王風. *Shiyun tuiyi yu wenzhang xingti—zhongguo jindai wenxue lunji* 世運推移與文章興替—中國近代文學論集 (Shifting times and changing writing: Anthology of modern Chinese literature). Beijing: Beijing daxue chubanshe, 2015.

Wang Hui 汪暉. *Xiandai zhongguo sixiang de xingqi* 現代中國思想的興起 (The rise of modern Chinese thought). 4 vols. Beijing: Sanlian shudian, 2004.

——. "The Voices of Good and Evil: What Is Enlightenment? Rereading Lu Xun's 'Toward a Refutation of Malevolent Voices.'" Translated by Ted Huters and Zong Yangyang. *Boundary 2* 38, no. 2 (2011): 67–124.

Wang Jun 王均. *Dangdai zhongguo de wenzi gaige* 當代中國的文字改革 (The script reform in contemporary China). Beijing: Dangdai zhongguo chubanshe, 1995.

Wang Li 王力. *Lun hanyu guifanhua* 論漢語規範化 (On the standardization of the Chinese language). Beijing: Xiandai hanyu guifanhua wenti xueshu huiyi wenjian huibian, 1955.

Wang, Pu. "Poetics, Politics, and *Ursprung/Yuan*: On Lu Xun's Conception of 'Mara Poetry.'" *Modern Chinese Literature and Culture* 23, no. 2 (Fall 2011): 34–63.

Wang Wenshen 王文參. *Wusi xinwenxue de minzuminjian wenxue ziyuan* 五四新文學的民族民間文學資源 (Folk literary sources of May Fourth literature). Beijing: Minzu chubanshe, 2006.

Wang Zhongchen 王中忱. *Zuowei shijiande wenxue yu lishi xushu* 作為事件的文學與歷史敘述 (Literature and historical narrative as events). Taipei: Renjian chubanshe, 2016.

Wen Zhenting 文振庭, ed. *Wenyi dazhonghua wenti taolun ziliao* 文艺大众化问题讨论资料 (Materials on the discussions of the massification of literature and art). Shanghai: Shanghai wenyi chubanshe, 1987.

West, Philip. *Yenching University and Sino-Western Relations, 1916–1952*. Cambridge, Mass.: Harvard University Press, 1976.

White, Ronald C., Jr., and Howard Hopkins. *The Social Gospel: Religion and Reform in Changing America*. Philadelphia: Temple University Press, 1975.

Wo Dan 渥丹. *Zhungguo wenz latinxua wenxian* 中国文字拉丁化文献 (Documents on the Latinization of the Chinese script). Shanghai: Latinxua chubanshe, 1940.

Wu, Shengqing. *Modern Archaics: Continuity and Innovation in the Chinese Lyric Tradition, 1900–1937*. Cambridge, Mass.: Harvard University Asia Center, 2013.

Wu Xiangxiang 吳相湘. *Yan Yangchu zhuan: Wei quan qiu xiang cun gai zao fen dou liu shi nian* 晏陽初傳：為全球鄉村改造奮鬥六十年 (A biography of James Yen: Sixty years of struggle for global rural reconstruction). Taipei: Shibao wenhua chuban, 1981.

Wu Xiaofeng 吳曉峰. *Guoyu yundong yu wenxue geming* 國語運動與文學革命 (National language movement and literary revolution). Beijing: Zhongyang bianyi chubanshe, 2008.

Xia Mianzun 夏丏尊. *Wenxin* 文心 (The heart of literature). Taipei: Kaiming shudian, 1977.

Xia Yan 夏衍. *Shanghai wuyan xia: Sanmu huaju* 上海屋簷下：三幕話劇 (Under the roof of Shanghai: A three-act play). Beijing: Zhongguo xiju chubanshe, 1957.

Xu Dishan 許地山. "Lun 'fan xinshi fenghua xueyue'" 論"反新式風花雪月" (On "anti-new Romanticism"). *Ta Kung Pao* 大公報, November. 14, 1940.

——. *Xu Dishan sanwen* 許地山散文 (Essays of Xu Dishan). Beijing: Zhongguo guangbo dianshi chubanshe, 1996.

——. *Xu Dishan xuanji* 許地山選集 (The selected works of Xu Dishan). Beijing: Renmin wenxue chubanshe, 1958.

——. *Xu Dishan yuyan lunwenji* 許地山語言論文集 (Collection of Xu Dishan's essays on language and writing). Hong Kong: Xinwenzi xuehui, 1941.

——. *Yu Guan* 玉官. In *Wu you hua* 无忧花 (Flowers of no sorrow). Nanjing: Jiangsu wenyi chubanshe, 2008.

Xu Guoqi. *China and the Great War: China's Pursuit of a New National Identity and Internationalization*. Cambridge: Cambridge University Press, 2009.

——. *Strangers on the Western Front: Chinese Workers in the Great War*. Cambridge, Mass.: Harvard University Press, 2011.

——. *Wen ming de jiao rong: Diyici shijie dazhan qijian de zaifa huagong* 文明的交融：第一次世界大戰期間的在法華工 (Convergence of civilizations: Chinese laborers in World War I France). Beijing: Wuzhou chuanbo chubanshe, 2007.

Yasar, Kerim. *Electrified Voices: How the Telephone, Phonograph, and Radio Shaped Modern Japan, 1868–1945*. New York: Columbia University Press, 2018.

Ye Baokui 葉寶奎. *Mingqing guanhua yinxi* 明清官話音系 (The phonetic systems of Ming–Qing Mandarin). Xiamen: Xiamen daxue chubanshe, 2001.

Ye Shengtao 葉聖陶. *Schoolmaster Ni Huan-chih*. Translated by A. C. Barnes. Beijing: Foreign Languages Press, 1958.

——. *Ye Shengtao ji* 葉聖陶集 (The collected works of Ye Shengtao). 26 vols. Nanjing: Jiangsu jiaoyu chubanshe, 1987.

——. *Ye Shengtao xuanji* 葉聖陶選集 (The selected works of Ye Shengtao). Beijing: Kaiming shudian, 1951.

Ye Shengtao 葉聖陶 and Xia Mianzun 夏丏尊. *Wenxin* 文心 (The heart of literature). Beijing: Zhongguo qingnian chubanshe, 1983.

Yeang, Chen-Pang. "From Modernizing the Chinese Language to Information Science: Chao Yuen Ren's Route to Cybernetics." *Isis* 108, no. 3 (September 2017): 553–80.

Yen, James [Yan Yangchu 晏陽初]. "Pingmin jiaoyu xin yundong" 平民教育新運動 (The New Mass Education movement). *Xin jiaoyu* 新教育 (New education) 5, no. 5 (December 1922): 1007–26.

——. *The Mass Education Movement, Bulletin No. 1 of the National Association of the Mass Education Movement*. Peking: National Association of the Mass Education Movement, 1924.

——. *New Citizens for China*. Peking: National Association of the Mass Education Movement, 1929.

——. *China's New Scholar-Farmer*. Peking: National Association of the Mass Education Movement, 1929.

——. *Ting Hsien Experiment 1930–1931*. Peking: National Association of the Mass Education Movement, 1931.

——. *Yan Yangchu quanji* 晏陽初全集 (The complete works of James Yen). 3 vols. Changsha: Hunan jiaoyu chubanshe, 1992.

——. *Yan Yangchu wenji* 晏陽初文集 (The collected works of James Yen). Chengdu: Sichuan daxue chubanshe, 1990.

Yu Yingshi 余英時 et al. *Wu si xin lun* 五四新論 (New commentaries on the May Fourth Movement). Taipei: Lianjing chuban shiye gongsi, 1999.

Yuan Jiahua 袁家驊. *Hanyu fangyan gaiyao* 漢語方言概要 (An introduction to Chinese dialects). Beijing: Wenzi gaige chubanshe, 1960.

Zarrow, Peter. *Educating China: Knowledge, Society, and Textbooks in a Modernizing World, 1902–1937*. Cambridge: Cambridge University Press, 2015.

Zhai Shiyu 翟時雨. *Hanyu fangyan yu fangyan diaocha* 漢語方言與方言調查 (Chinese dialects and dialect surveys). Chongqing: Xinan shifan daxue chubanshe, 1986.

Zhang Jianguo 張建國, ed. *Zhongguo laogong yu diyici shijie dazhan* 中國勞工與第一次世界大戰 (Chinese labourers and the First World War). Jinan: Shandong daxue chubanshe, 2009.

Zhang Jianguo 張建國 and Zhang Junyong 張軍勇, eds. *Wan li fu rong ji* 萬里赴戎機 (Over there: The pictorial chronicle of Chinese laborer corps in the Great War). Jinan: Shandong huabao chubanshe, 2009.

Zhang Taiyan 章太炎. *Zhang Taiyan quanji* 章太炎全集 (The complete works of Zhang Taiyan). Vol. 4. Shanghai: Shanghai renmin chubanshe, 1985.

Zhang, Yingjin, and Zhiwei Xiao. "Sun Yu." In *Encyclopedia of Chinese Film*, 324–25. London: Routledge, 1998.

Zhao Luorui 赵萝蕤. *Dushu shenghuo sanzha* 讀書生活散札 (Scribbles on my reading life). Nanjing: Nanjing shifan daxue chubanshe, 2009.

Zhao Xinna 趙新那. *Zhao Yuanren nianpu* 趙元任年譜 (A chronicle of Yuen Ren Chao). Beijing: Commercial Press, 2001.

Zhao Yintang 趙蔭棠. *Dengyun yuanliu* 等韻源流 (The origins of *Dengyun*). Beijing: Commercial Press, 2011.

Zhou Enlai 周恩来. "Dangqian wenzi gaige de renwu" 当前文字改革的任务 (The current tasks of script reform). In *Dangdai zhongguo de wenzi gaige* 当代中国的文字改革 (The script reform in contemporary China), edited by Wang Jun, 556–69. Beijing: Dangdai zhongguo chubanshe, 1995.

Zhou, Gang. *Placing the Modern Chinese Vernacular in Transnational Literature*. New York: Palgrave Macmillan, 2011.

Zhou Guangqing 周光慶. *Hanyu yu zhongguo zaoqi xiandaihua sichao* 漢語與中國早期現代化思潮 (The Chinese language and early thoughts on modernization in China). Harbin: Heilongjiang chubanshe, 2001.

Zhou, Minglang, ed. *Language Policy in the People's Republic of China: Theory and Practice Since 1949*. Boston: Kluwer Academic, 2004.

——. *Multilingualism in China: The Politics of Writing Reforms for Minority Languages, 1949–2002*. Berlin: Mouton de Gruyter, 2003.

Zhou Youguang 周有光. *Hanzi gaige gailun* 漢字改革概論 (Brief discussions on Chinese script reform). Beijing: Wenzi gaige chubanshe, 1961.

——. *Pinyinhua wenti* 拼音化問題 (The problem of alphabetization). Beijing: Wenzi gaige chubanshe, 1980.

——. *Shi nian ru shui* 逝年如水 (Lost years like water). Hangzhou: Zhejiang daxue chubanshe, 2015.

Zhou, Youming. *Historicizing Online Politics: Telegraphy, the Internet, and Political Participation in China*. Stanford, Calif.: Stanford University Press, 2005.

Zhou Zhenhe 周振鶴 and You Rujie 游汝杰. *Fangyan yu zhongguo wenhua* 方言與中國文化 (Dialects and Chinese culture). Shanghai: Shanghai renmin chubanshe, 2006.

Zhu Jingnong 朱經農 and Tao Xingzhi 陶行知, eds. *Pingmin qianzi ke* 平民千字課 (People's thousand-character lessons). Shanghai: Commercial Press, 1923.

Zhu Lingong 朱麟公, ed. *Guoyu wenti taolun ji* 國語問題討論集 (An anthology of discussions on the national language). Shanghai: Zhongguo shuju, 1921.

INDEX

Academia Sinica, 43, 77, 208n60
Adas, Michael, 118, 119, 226n58
Afro-Asian People's Solidarity
    Conference (1957), 7
Afro-Asian Writers' Conference (1958), 7
Agamali-Ogly, Samed, 81, 215n38
Ai de jiaoyu (De Amicis; trans. Xia
    Mianzun), 149
Alexeiev, B. M., 216n48
alphabetic universalism: defined, 28;
    Gwoyeu Romatzyh as the Chinese
    bid for, 21, 42, 72; limits of, 54, 69;
    and phonocentrism, 28, 31, 52, 60–61;
    and the Roman-Latin alphabet, 45,
    181; as a scholarly pursuit, 75; as a
    socialist, internationalist enterprise,
    83. *See also* phonocentrism; Roman-
    Latin alphabet
Althusser, Louis, 162, 239n14
American Bible Society, 77, 91
Amherst College, 229n22
Amoy dialect, 10, 11, 73, 76–77
analytical phonography, 184
Anderson, Benedict, 100
Anderson, Marston, 98, 143, 147, 200n43,
    219n85, 235nn73, 81

Anglo-Japanese Treaty of Alliance, 104
Anhui dialect, 77, 79
anti-imperialism, 7–8, 15, 22, 117–20, 180
Anti-Rightist Campaign, 162, 164, 166
The Antinomies of Realism (Jameson), 68
Arab-Persian script, 6, 208n56
Arabic script, 6, 161
Armenian script, 82
Art of Signs (*Ars signorum;* Dalgarno),
    44
Assyrian people, 82
Azerbaijan, 81

Ba Jin, 30, 75, 141, 236–37n95
Bacon, Francis, 2
baihua: defined, 100–101, 113; and dialect
    representation, 69, 97; and the
    Laborers as Soldiers program, 102,
    110–13, 114; and the limits of
    phonocentrism, 97, 98; May Fourth
    discourse of, 97, 100–101, 102, 108–10,
    112–13, 119, 132; and the modern
    Chinese language, 108–9; new
    literature in, 129; opposed to *wenyan,*
    101, 109, 111, 145–46, 150; orality of,
    109, 113–14, 133; premodern literature

Mass Education Movement (*continued*)
Fourth Movement, 128–29; Old and
New, 126–27; primers used in, 128–29,
229n15; and the reinvention of
children, 139–40, 149. *See also*
literacy; *yutiwen*
massification of literature and art: as a
global phenomenon, 153; Lu Xun and,
16, 19–20, 87, 201n50; and Proletkult,
69, 154; Qu Qiubai and, 68–69, 85–87;
three rounds of discussion on, 85–86,
152, 217n57; Xu Dishan and, 68–69,
88, 90
May Fourth movement: as alliance
between laborers and intellectuals,
119; *baihua* discourse, 97, 100–101,
102, 108–10, 112–13, 119, 132; children
as central to, 140; as the "Chinese
enlightenment," 103, 114–23, 140, 148;
conventional scholarship on, 103;
depicted in fictional works, 142–43,
145, 146, 147, 148; influence of
late-Qing writings on, 226n63; and
mass education, 130; and the modern
Chinese language, 108; new literature
of, 101, 109, 128–29, 142; Qu Qiubai's
attack on literary revolution of, 85,
86, 90; and World War I, 101; Xu
Dishan and, 88, 100. See also *baihua*
The May Fourth Movement (Chow), 103
May Thirtieth Movement, 142–43, 145,
147, 247n3
Medhurst, Walter Henry, 10, 76
Mei Tsu-lin, 79
Meng Xiancheng, 247n3
Mesopotamia, 222n20
Mexico, 106
Meyer, Paul, 203n13
Miao people, 80
Midnight (Mao Dun), 86
Millbank Memorial Fund, 227n76
Milne, A. A., 48, 51, 52
Min dialects, 71
Ming dynasty, 13, 29, 109, 172, 182
Minnan dialect: alphabetic Bibles in, 10,
11, 76–77, 91; in literary narrative,
96–97; phoneticization in Sin Wenz,

73, 212n15; in reconstruction of Old
and Middle Chinese, 79, 214n33. *See
also* Chinese dialects; Xu Dishan
The Miracle of Western Letters (Ricci), 10
Mongol people, 81
Mongolia, 81
Monroe, Paul, 131
Morrison, Robert, 10, 76
Mountain Jews, 81
Müller, Max, 41

Nanjing Normal University, 132
National Alphabet (*zhuyin fuhao*):
among proposed pinyin schemes, 161;
establishment, 204n17; failure to
replace characters, 28–29, 100, 220n1;
and Gwoyeu Romatzyh, 41, 206n35;
late-Qing origins, 11; and the Second
United Front, 138; Wu Zhihui and,
191; Zhang Taiyan and, 12, 34, 199n36,
204n17
national language: and *baihua*, 109, 113;
and dialectal variation, 21, 36–37, 70,
72, 77–78, 80; and Gwoyeu Romatzyh,
41–43; and Japanese *kokugo*, 204n19;
proposal of Esperanto as, 30; and
putonghua, 72–73; teleological view
of, 13–14; two versions of, 28, 36–41
National Language Monthly (journal), 38
National Language Records, 37, 38
National Language Weekly (journal), 67,
242n38
National Treasure (television series), 1
Nehru, Jawaharlal, 138
New Century (journal), 30
New Culture movement, 85, 88, 108, 109,
113, 132, 145
*New National Dictionary (Guoyin
zidian)*, 37, 38
New National Language Records, 41
New Society (journal), 88, 218n64
New Tide (journal), 141
Ni Haishu, 9, 73, 167, 198n10, 199n33,
212nn15–16
Nietzsche, Friedrich, 186
Ningbo dialect, 76
Ningxia Province, 68

most advanced script, 5, 28, 45, 57, 192, 197n15; as a techne for phoneticization, 180; and telecommunications technologies, 35, 192; universality of, 31; and Western ethnocentrism, 5, 180–81, 187. *See also* alphabetic universalism; phonocentrism

Romanization movement: and bid for alphabetic universalism, 54, 61; and dialectology, 77–78; Guomindang's support for, 4, 29, 67; and the "national language," 36, 43, 72; opposition to and by Latinization movement, 67, 75–76, 83, 84; phonocentrism of, 29, 48; and Roman-Latin alphabet, 170; Yuen Ren Chao and, 31–32, 42, 205n26. *See also* Chao, Yuen Ren; Gwoyeu Romatzyh (GR); Latinization movement

Rousseau, Jean-Jacques: *Essay on the Origin of Languages,* 185; on ideo-phonography, 184, 188, 243n51, 246n111; and the metaphysics of phonetic writing, 180, 183, 196n12; theory on writing and civilizational hierarchy, 184, 197n16, 243n51

Ruggieri, Michele, 10

Russell, Bertrand, 138

Russian, 6, 82

Sadofiev, Ilya, 237n98

Sanskrit, 9, 13, 78, 89, 196n13

Saturday (journal), 141

Saussure, Ferdinand de: alternative terms for synchronic and diachronic linguistics, 214n28; and comparative, historical linguistics, 5; *Course in General Linguistics,* 4, 31–32, 188, 196nn9, 13; privileging of speech over writing, 185, 246n115; and the rise of linguistics as a discipline, 4, 31–32; on writing, 4, 100, 185; Yuen Ren Chao and, 203n13. *See also* linguistics; phonocentrism

Schwarcz, Vera, 103, 109, 119, 122

Scientific Research Institute of China, 82

Second Sino-Japanese War, 134, 135, 136, 149, 232n42

Second United Front, 137

Serdyuchenko, G. P., 160

Shaanxi dialect, 77, 79

Shaanxi Province, 68

Shandong dialect, 216n46

Shandong Province, 101, 102, 120, 126, 220n7

Shang dynasty, 176

Shanghai Chinese Latinization Research Society, 75

Shanghainese, 74–75, 76

Shaw, George Bernard, 50, 208n55

Shen Junru, 236n90

Shen Xue, 11, 199n33

Shirintsin, A. G., 216n48

Shou Wen, 9–10

Shuowen jiezi (Explaining Graphs and Analyzing Characters; Xu Shen), 33, 178, 181, 244n83

Sin Wenz: in campaign for mass education, 127; created by the Chinese Latinization movement, 67–68; as forerunner of *hanyu pinyin,* 195n2; Guomindang's ban on, 68, 69, 75; Li Jinxi's critiques of, 216n51; and literary revolution, 85, 87–88; public letter in support of, 75, 134, 212n20; publications using, 73–74, 212n16; representation of dialects in, 70–75, 212n15; and the Second United Front, 138; V. S. Kolokolov's contribution to, 83; and *yutiwen,* 132–34; Zhou Youguang's work on, 191. *See also* Latinization movement; literacy; Mass Education Movement; massification of literature and art

Singapore, 129

Sino-Soviet Treaty of Friendship, Alliance and Mutual Assistance, 160

Social Gospel Movement, 106

Society of a Few Men (Shuren Hui), 41, 206n34

Song dynasty, 9, 109, 178, 195n1

sound spectrograph, 21, 28, 54–61, 208n60, 209n67

Zamenhof, Ludwig Lazarus, 30, 58
Zhang Boling, 230–31n32
Zhang Changsong, 119
Zhang Shiyi, 205n24
Zhang Taiyan: dialect studies, 77; and
  National Alphabet, 12, 34, 199n36,
  204n17; objection to abolishing
  characters, 202n3; objection to
  Esperanto, 30, 202n58; in the
  post- World War I milieu, 118; views
  on equality, 226n59
Zhao Luorui, 240n19, 241n28
Zhao Yuanren. *See* Chao, Yuen Ren
Zhao Zichen, 164
Zhejiang Province, 70, 101, 126
Zheng Qiao, 178, 244n83
Zheng Zhenduo, 89, 141, 218nn64–65
Zhong Wen'ao, 27, 32

Zhongguo Baihua Newspaper, 109
Zhongguo yuwen (*CLW;* journal), 171–72,
  241–42n37, 243n54
Zhongxuesheng (journal), 149, 150,
  151–52, 236–37n95
Zhou Enlai, 2, 7, 157, 188, 192, 220n11
Zhou Youguang, 157, 167, 190–93, 211n9,
  247nn3, 4, 248nn9, 10
Zhou Yutong, 142
Zhou Zuoren, 30, 37, 202n6, 218n65
Zhouli (*Rites of Zhou*), 182
Zhu De, 211n3
Zhu Jingnong, 128
Zhu Qihui, 126, 127
Zhu Xiang, 163
Zhu Xizu, 218n65
Zhu Ziqing, 236n90
Zhuang Cunyu, 191